Brief Table of Contents

Table of Contents

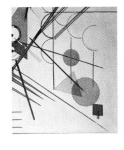

Preface

Welcome to *Digital Media Primer*, a book for introductory students from all disciplines interested in learning the foundational scientific concepts and basic techniques in digital media production. This book is written for introductory courses in digital media. There are no specific prerequisites. The courses that will find this textbook useful include:

- non-major introductory computer science courses that adopt a digital media theme; it integrates both scientific concepts and hands-on production of digital images, video, and audio, and gives students exposure to basic computer programming through animation and programming games
- introductory digital art courses that would like to help students harness digital media tools; it teaches the underlying scientific concepts, thereby achieving intended artistic results and improving confidence to experiment with creative uses of the tools
- introductory media production in introducing students a solid technical foundation of digital video and audio

After completing this book, students will understand the underlying concepts of computer terms common to digital media and should be able to make connection of these concepts with the tools and techniques of digital media application programs.

The connection between scientific concepts and applications will help students make educated decisions, rather than relying on defaults or recipes, in using tools and techniques in application programs. In addition, the approach of this book intends to instill in students the ability to explore and teach themselves new application programs. By completing Chapters 1–7, students will be able to create and edit digital images, audio, and video. Students will also learn basic computer programming concepts through programming games with Flash ActionScript in the multimedia authoring chapters (Chapters 8–11).

Text Organization

The digital media curriculum of this book is organized around a core concept of digital media: the digitization process—sampling and quantization. For example, the **sampling** process gives rise to the image resolution in digital images and sampling rate in digital audio. The **quantization** process gives rise to the color depth in digital images and bit depth in digital audio. Digital video also deals with frame size which relates to image resolution. This way, students learn the image resolution, audio sampling rate, color depth, audio bit depth, and video frame size from the same conceptual framework applied in different context, rather than as separate bits and pieces of factual information of different media.

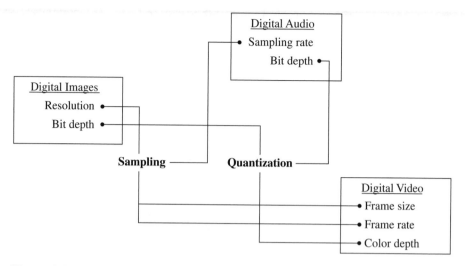

Figure 1 Sampling and quantization serve as the central concepts to unify the topics for different media.

One Chapter on Concepts and One on Applications

Each of the image, audio, and video topics consist of two chapters: one on **concepts** and the second one on **applications**.

Chapter 1: Background

Chapter 2: Digital Image (concepts)

Chapter 3: Digital Image (applications)

Chapter 4: Digital audio (concepts)

Chapter 5: Digital audio (applications)

Chapter 6: Digital video (concepts)

Chapter 7: Digital video (applications)

Chapters 8–11: Multimedia Authoring

The scientific concepts are discussed in the concepts chapters (Chapters 2, 4, 6). The applications of the concepts and the general tools and techniques of application programs are discussed in the application chapters (Chapters 3, 5, and 7). For example, Chapter 2 explains the concept of resolution of images. Correspondingly, Chapter 3 discusses how to estimate the scanning resolution and printing resolution. The determination of the scanning or printing resolution is an application of the concept of resolution.

For the multimedia authoring chapters, Chapter 8 introduces the animation basics and working with Adobe Flash. Chapter 9 provides an overview on programming fundamentals that are common to most programming languages. Chapter 10 discusses some specific aspects in programming with Flash ActionScript. Chapter 11 explains how to add interactivity. The lab exercises are designed around programming computer games.

Approach to Teaching Software Tools

Media creation and production is an important component in digital media education. I recognize the importance of fluency in software application tools for the student's performance in digital media. However, one of the challenges in teaching digital media is rapidly evolving technology and software application tools.

This book introduces students to the software tools by focusing on the underlying tasks and scientific concepts. The concepts chapters provide the scientific foundations to understand the tools. The applications chapters discuss the tools from a task-based perspective first, followed by a demonstration of the corresponding commands in a software program. The goal is to instill in the students the ability to teach themselves new software.

Features in the Textbook

There are several elements used in the book.

- **Key terms:** Key terms are printed in boldface italic where its definition is given.
- **Learning aids:** There are several types of learning aids accompanying this text (see the subsequent subsection). They are integral to the text and noted in the text in blue boxes. A title and a brief description are given for each learning aid. The learning aids can be found on the accompanying Web site of this text.
- **Boxed materials:** Boxed materials provide more in-depth discussion and explanation of the concept or terminology relevant to the current part of the text. The materials may be branched off from the main flow of the text. Thus, they are separated from the main text to avoid diversion from the flow of thoughts.
- **Side notes:** They are generally used for a quick reminder of terminology, or for referring to the chapter that covers the basics that are needed for the current part of the text.
- **Self-test questions:** These questions are found in the text of some chapters. The answers are provided at the bottom of the page. These questions, unlike the end-of-chapter review questions, intend to provide the students an instant review of the topics. These topics are a little too involved to wait for the end-of-chapter review questions.
- **Summary:** Each chapter concludes with a summary of central concepts.
- **End-of-chapter review questions:** These are multiple-choice and short-answer questions to reinforce the retrieval of the learned foundational knowledge. They are to ensure that the student reaches the same level of competence of foundational knowledge.
- **Exploring the applications:** At the end of an application chapter, there is a list of suggested commonly-used features and functionalities for the students to look up and explore in the application programs. Our goal is to help students to learn how to explore application programs in terms of tasks and then apply the basic concepts they have learned in the textbook. By taking this approach, the student is not tied to learning a particular software package or version.

activeBook and Online Learning Aids

This textbook is delivered as *integrated learning system*. Students can learn from the printed text and/or by using the *first-time free* access code to access the **activeBook** and associated **online learning aids resources.** The interactive multimedia resources and activeBook can be accessed at www.prenhall.com/digitalmedia.

The activeBook and online learning aids provide a more exciting learning experience—The activeBook touches students on multiple levels. It is embedded with numerous active examples, programming exercises, problem-solving and concept-testing worksheets, interactive tutorials, mathematical modeling exercises, and video tutorials. The online text stimulates student learning by making them active participants in the learning process. Because activeBook marries print content with dynamic online resources, content is brought to life and available anytime, from anywhere.

The activeBook experience is customizable by faculty and students. Students can annotate their activeBook and customize their view of the book's dynamic resources. The diagnostic tools within activeBook can create custom study plans tailored to the student's or the class's weaknesses and strengths in the subject matter. An activeBook can contain course management tools, exist only as a linked resource from an external course management system, or it can be used as a help link with no navigation between online pages.

There are several types of online learning aids accompanying this text. They appear in blue boxes with a small icon (a computer mouse or a film strip) followed by a title and a brief description. The computer mouse icon indicates that the learning aid is interactive or has a hands-on component. These include interactive tutorials and demonstrations, labs, and worksheets. The film strip icon means that the learning aid is a movie, for example, the screen-captured movies that show how to use a tool in an application program, or video files that demonstrate the effect of different compression settings.

- **Tutorials**

   The tutorials are used for various purposes:

   - Conceptual: To explain concepts, such as sampling and quantizing
   - Software tool how-to's: Short screen-captured movies showing how-to's of application programs
   - Example files: Files that you can download to open and see how they work
   - Visualization: To help visualize difficult concepts
   - Explanation of terminology
   - Step-by-step guide to solve a problem: such as Chapter 1's binary-decimal conversion

   All the tutorials can be used as outside class review by students. Some of the tutorials can be used by the instructor as interactive animated presentations during lectures. For example: Chapter 1's *Converting Analog to Digital—Sampling and Quantizing,* Chapter 2's *Sampling and Quantizing in Digital Images,* Chapter 3's *Understanding and Applying Histograms,* Chapter 4's *Sound as a Pressure Wave* and *Sampling and Quantizing in Digital Audio.*

- **Demonstrations:** Audio files let you hear how different sampling rates and bit depths affect the audio quality; video files let you see how different compression settings affect visual quality.

- **Worksheets:** Worksheets are question-based PDF files that can be downloaded and printed out. They require more thinking than the end-of-chapter review questions. Some may require exploration or experimentation to discover answers.

- **Labs:** These are lab manuals, with instructions to edit or create digital media files. They are designed to provide hands-on opportunities to process and manipulate digital images, sound, and video. The labs for the multimedia authoring include creating animation in Adobe Flash and programming games in ActionScript. In developing the labs, I tried to emphasize the tasks rather than giving step-by-step recipe type of instructions.

Worksheets and labs are different. Worksheets are question-based homework intended to help student review a topic at a time. Labs are hands-on instruction-based activities that create or modify media files. Labs provide opportunities for students to apply various learned concepts and techniques into practice.

Some online resources require Shockwave plug-in, some require Flash player, some require QuickTime player, and some require JavaScript enabled. The file format and requirements of each of these learning aids are noted with its link on the Web site.

Digital Media Community Forum

The ability to exchange ideas and experiences make every learning experience more meaningful. Access to the Digital Media Community site is free with the activeBook subscription. Students and instructors can share ideas and learning materials, make contributions, participate in discussion forums, and connect with other students and faculty teaching digital media.

I encourage you to share your digital media project, lab, and assignment ideas with me and other instructors. I also encourage you to showcase your students' projects and assignments. You may use email or the publisher's community forum for this book to share your ideas and students' work.

Please visit the course Web site often to find new project and assignment ideas, or to share your ideas with other instructors.

Instructor Resources

Protected instructors resources are available on the Prentice Hall Instructor Resource Center (IRC). Please contact your local Prentice Hall Sales Representative to gain access to this site. Instructors will find the following support material on the IRC:

- Answers to the end-of-chapter questions

- Answers to the worksheets

- Completed lab files

Software Tools for Practice and Labs

Although this book's approach to teaching media application tools emphasizes identifying tasks, it is inevitable that certain application programs are required to demonstrate the tools and techniques in the text. Table 1 lists the different application programs used in this book. The application programs that appear the most in the text, tutorials, labs, and worksheets are in boldface.

TABLE I	
Media Topic	Application Programs Used as Examples in the Text (The main programs used the most in the text, tutorials, labs, and worksheets are in boldface.)
Digital Image	**Adobe Photoshop,** Adobe Illustrator
Digital Audio	**Adobe Audition, Audacity,** Apple Garage Band, Sony Sound Forge, SONAR, Sony ACID Pro, RealProducer Basic
Digital Video	**Adobe Premiere Pro, Apple Final Cut Pro,** Sony Vegas, Adobe Encore DVD, Apple DVD Studio Pro, Sony DVD Architect
Multimedia Authoring	**Adobe Flash**

This Book is a Part of a Three Book Digital Media Series

This book is the **Primer** in a three book digital media series. The purpose of this series is to connect the digital media tools and techniques with the underlying scientific concepts. This book introduces the foundational scientific concepts of digital media for students who are taking digital media courses. These include digital art, media production, and computer science courses that adopt a digital media theme.

Digital media encompasses a broad range of academic disciplines—from art to computer science. This three book series intends to pull interdisciplinary elements together in a coherent and organized manner. The three books (sometimes referred to as modules in the text) include a primer and two advanced modules—one on art and the other on computer science.

- **Primer:** *Digital Media Primer* (this book) ISBN: 0-13-223944-2
- **Art Module:** *Digital Art: Its Art and Science*[1] ISBN: 0-13-175703-2
- **Computer Science Module:** *The Science of Digital Media*[2] ISBN: 0-13-243580-2

All three books cover the following digital media topics:

- **Digital images**
- **Digital audio**
- **Digital video**
- **Multimedia authoring** (Primer and Computer Science Module) and **Web authoring** (Art Module)

Primer (This Book):

Despite the different disciplinary perspectives of digital media, there is a common ground for all perspectives—resolution, bit depth, and file size optimization. This common ground is grouped into the Primer. It presents the central concepts of digital media necessary for all students, regardless of their later area of specialization. The Primer is designed to serve as the **core module for all students** interested in digital media.

---

[1]Another text of this series; also by this author.
[2]Another text of this series; by Jennifer J. Burg.

The Primer also explains concepts using analogies from everyday life and everyday reasoning. For example, in Chapter 1, eye signals are used to illustrate the concept of bits in the binary system.

Advanced Modules

The two **advanced modules** (Art and Computer Science) allow further specialization at the advanced, discipline-specific level.

- **Art Module:** *Digital Art: Its Art and Science*
  The Art Module follows the topics of the Primer, but elaborates further from the perspective of art making.
- **CS Module:** *The Science of Digital Media*
  The CS Module includes more in-depth explanations of the underlying mathematical principles, computer algorithms, and elementary physics and electronics.

Parallel Chapters Across the Three Books

All three books maintain the same number of parallel chapters—one on background, two on each of the image, audio, and video, and one (or more) on multimedia/Web authoring. Parallel chapters allow students to easily look up relevant information across perspectives.

Coordinating Coursework with This Text

The three book series allows flexibility for different courses with respect to the breadth (the number of media) and depth (depth in the direction of art or computer science perspective) of the course content.

You can pick and choose to add the computer science or digital art components, depending on the depth of the art or computer science components you want to incorporate into the course. The three books' parallel chapters help students look up information across different perspectives.

For computer science courses that incorporate a digital media theme:

- **Introductory courses for non-CS majors** can use all the chapters of this book. Either the Art or CS book can be an accompanying text depending on the focus of the course. The Art module expands the focus to aesthetics. It emphasizes the production of digital media work. It has more activities and projects that require creativity and thought about the intention of the work. The CS module, on the other hand, goes deeper into the underlying scientific concepts and algorithms. It has programming assignments that reinforce the concepts.
- **Upper-level courses for CS-majors** can use this book as outside class background reading, and use *The Science of Digital Media* as the main textbook. For more suggestions, please see the Preface of *The Science of Digital Media*.

For **digital art courses**, it seems to work best if you start using the Art Module chapters before assigning the Primer chapters. Although the Primer contains the foundational scientific concepts that are needed to understand the terminology and how and why a tool works that way, students tend to learn better after they have hands-on experience with the creation and production of the media first. The foundational concepts and terminology in the Primer text will then make more sense to the students.

Table 2 lists several suggested treatments employing this book and the series of three books.

TABLE 2	
	Suggested Chapter Coverage
A course that covers the breadth of all three media: images, audio, and video	Chapters 1–7 (this book)
A course that covers only one medium	• Chapter 1 (this book) • Two chapters of the medium (this book) • Chapter 1 (either the Art or CS book) • Two chapters of the medium (either the Art or CS book) For example, for a course that focuses on digital images from the art perspective, you could cover Primer Chapters 1, 2, 3, and Art Module Chapters 1, 2, 3.
A course that covers multimedia authoring or basic programming through animation and games	• Chapters 1–3 (this book) • Chapters 8–11 (this book)
A course focuses on concepts with minimal hands-on: the concept chapters	• Chapters 1, 2, 4, 6 (this book) • Chapters 1, 2, 4, 6 (either the Art or CS book)
A course focuses on hands-on practice	• Chapters 1, 3, 5, 7 (this book) • Chapters 1, 3, 5, 7 (either the Art or CS book) • The concepts chapters (Chapters 2, 4, and 6) are highly recommended. If it is not possible to go over the concepts in class, refer students to self-study these concepts chapters. You may want to assign the end-of-chapter review questions to ensure they understand the concepts.

Acknowledgments

The material has been class-tested and I would like to thank the students who provided us feedback; their comments have helped us improve the text and its organization.

My thanks also go to the professors who participated in pilot-testing of these modules: Julie Carrington of Rollins College, Kristian Damkjer of the University of Florida, Ian Douglas of Florida State University, Edward A. Fox of Virginia Polytechnic Institute and State University, Martha Garrett of Bishop McGuinness High School (North Carolina), Kim Nelson of the University of Windsor (Ontario, Canada), Naomi Spellman of the University of California San Diego and San Diego State University, Christopher Stein of Borough of Manhattan Community College, and Mark Watanabe of Keaau High School (Hawaii).

I would also like to thank my student assistants, who helped develop the materials and suggested some of the learning aids, and my students who let me include their work as demonstrations in the book: Kevin Crace, Gretchen Edwards, Lindsay Ryerse, Caldwell Tanner, and Daniel Verwholt.

I would also like to thank the reviewers of this book for their comments and suggestions: Panagiotis T. Metaxas of Wellesley College, Jody Culkin of Borough of Manhattan Community College, Hsin-liang Chen of the University of Missouri, Daniel Bogaard of Rochester Institute of Technology, Diana Hill of Chesapeake College, Sandra K. Williams of Palm Beach Community College, and Mark Grabe of the University of North Dakota.

Support

This material is based on work supported by the National Science Foundation under Grant No. DUE-0127280 and DUE-0340969. Any opinions, findings and conclusions or recommendations expressed in this material are those of the author(s) and do not necessarily reflect the views of the National Science Foundation. The PI and co-PI of the two grants are Yue-Ling Wong and Jennifer J. Burg, respectively. Professor Leah McCoy is the assessment expert in the second grant.

Photo Credits

Chapter 1 opening: M.C. Escher (1898–1972) "Day and Night" © 1999 Cordon Art B.V.-Baarn, Holland. All rights reserved.

Chapter 2 opening: Georges Pierre Seurat, (1859–1891) French, Sunday On The Isle of La Grande Jatte, Metropolitan Museum of Art, New York City/Superstock, Inc.

Chapter 3 opening: Hans Hofmann (1880–1966) © ARS, NY. Pompeii. 1959. Oil on canvas, 214.0 × 132.7 cm. Tate Gallery, London, Great Britain. Photo credit: Tate Gallery, London/Art Resource, NY.

Chapter 4 opening: Pablo Picasso (1881–1973), "Violin". 1912. Charcoal and papier colles on paper. Musee National d'Art Moderne, Centre Georges Pompidou, Paris, France. Musee National d'Art Moderne. Centre National d'Art et de Culture. Georges Pompidou. CNAC/MNAM/Reunion des Musees Nationaux/Art Resource, NY. © 2008 Estate of Pablo Picasso/Artists Rights Society (ARS), New York

Chapter 5 opening: Pablo Picasso "Three Musicians", Fontainebleau, summer 1921, oil on canvas, 6 ft. 7 in. × 7 ft. 3 3/4 in. (200.7 × 222.9 cm). The Museum of Modern Art/Licensed by Scala-Art Resource, NY. Mrs. Simon Guggenheim Fund. Photograph © 1997 The Museum of Modern Art, New York. © 2008 Estate of Pablo Picasso/Artists Rights Society (ARS), New York

Chapter 6 opening: Thomas Eakins, "The Pole Vaulter". 1884. Pennsylvania Academy of the Fine Arts PAFA

Chapter 7 opening: The Bridgeman Art Library International

Chapter 8 opening: Wassily Kandinsky (Russian, 1866–1944), "Composition #8." © Summit Labs/Superstock. © 1998 Artists Rights Society (ARS), New York/ADAGP, Paris.

Chapter 9 opening: Wassily Kandinsky (Russian, 1866–1944), "Composition #8." © Summit Labs/Superstock. © 1998 Artists Rights Society (ARS), New York/ADAGP, Paris.

Chapter 10 opening: Wassily Kandinsky (Russian, 1866–1944), "Composition #8." © Summit Labs/Superstock. © 1998 Artists Rights Society (ARS), New York/ADAGP, Paris.

Chapter 11 opening: Wassily Kandinsky (Russian, 1866–1944), "Composition #8." © Summit Labs/Superstock. © 1998 Artists Rights Society (ARS), New York/ADAGP, Paris.

Cover images 1–7: IKO\Shutterstock, Shutterstock

Trademarks

Adobe Flash, Adobe Photoshop, Adobe Illustrator, Adobe Premier Pro, Adobe Encore DVD are trademarks of Adobe Systems, Incorporated.

Audacity is a trademark of Dominic Mazzoni.

Apple Garage Band and Apple DVD Studio Pro are trademarks of Apple, Inc.

Sony Sound Forge, Sony ACID Pro, Sony Vegas, and Sony DVD Architect are trademarks of Sony Electronics, Inc.

SONAR is a trademark of Twelve Tone Systems, Inc.

Prentice Hall's
Digital Media
Series
AN INTEGRATED LEARNING SYSTEM

Textbook, *activeBook*, dynamic multimedia learning aids, collaborative online community portal

At the section level, the textbook contains margin icons that indicate the availability of online learning aids.

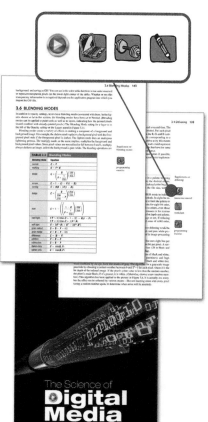

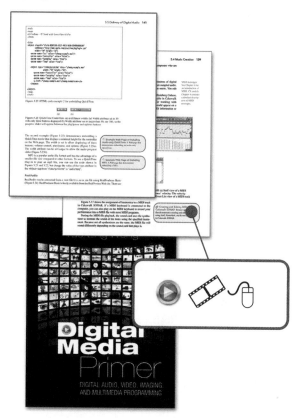

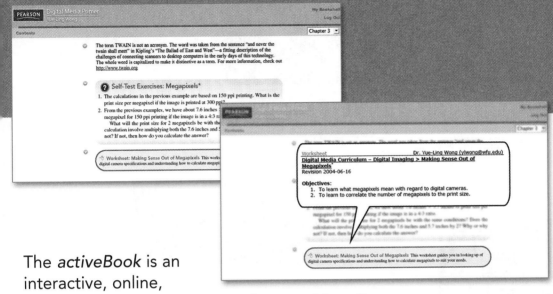

The *activeBook* is an interactive, online, digital book that integrates robust multimedia resources with the textbook to enhance the learning experience. *activeBooks* are embedded with:

- active examples
- programming exercises
- problem-solving and concept-testing worksheets
- interactive tutorials and demos
- mathematical modeling exercises
- video tutorials

The authors and Prentice Hall have worked together to integrate the textbook, the *activeBook* and the dynamic multimedia learning aids to make teaching and learning easier!

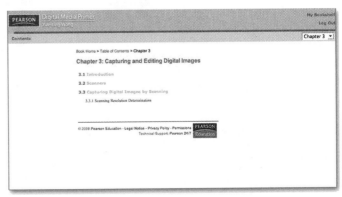

Everything works together for a unified teaching and learning experience!

STUDENTS BECOME PARTICIPANTS
IN THE LEARNING PROCESS!

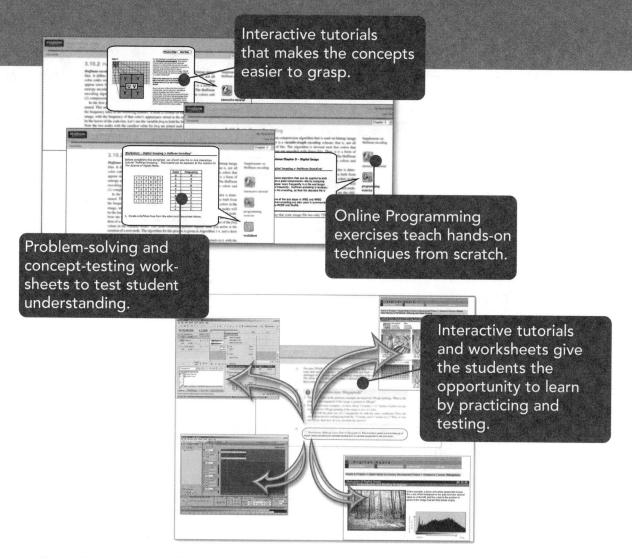

Interactive tutorials that makes the concepts easier to grasp.

Online Programming exercises teach hands-on techniques from scratch.

Problem-solving and concept-testing worksheets to test student understanding.

Interactive tutorials and worksheets give the students the opportunity to learn by practicing and testing.

To gain access to the *activeBook*, the community portal and the dynamic and interactive media that accompanies this product, visit www.prenhall.com/digitalmedia and enter the access code printed on the card in the front of this book. If your book does not include an access card, you can purchase access at www.prenhall.com/digitalmedia.

Digital Media Series

We heard the cry! In response to the need for new interdisciplinary curriculum material, Prentice Hall is publishing a three-book set of interactive digital media products:

- *Digital Media Primer*, by Yue-Ling Wong, fundamentals of digital media that are relevant to both artists and scientists

- *The Science of Digital Media*, by Jennifer Burg, the mathematics, science, and algorithms that underlie digital media applications

- *Digital Arts: Its Arts and Science*, by Yue-Ling Wong, digital media from the perspective of making art

Background

TABLE OF CONTENTS

KEY CONCEPTS
- Analog information versus digital data
- Converting analog to digital data: sampling and quantizing
- Bits and bytes
- Base-10 versus base-2
- File size calculation
- File compression

GENERAL LEARNING OBJECTIVES
At the end of this chapter, you should be able to demonstrate that you understand
- The meaning of fundamental computer terms common to digital media.
- The difference between analog information and digital data.
- The binary system.
- The basic steps of digitization: sampling and quantization.
- General strategies for reducing digital media file sizes.
- The need for file compression and types of file compression.

1.1 INTRODUCTION

Digital media studies rely on both conceptual and creative knowledge. While knowing how to use digital media application programs, such as Adobe Photoshop and Corel Paint Shop Pro for digital imaging, Adobe Premiere Pro and Apple Final Cut for digital video, and Adobe Audition and Sony Sound Forge for digital audio, is required, understanding the underlying principles and concepts helps to realize a creative idea with predictable results. Simply learning a particular version of a particular program restricts your creativity to what that version of that program can do. If you generalize by associating the task you want to accomplish with the basic concept behind the tool, then when you have to switch to another program or a new version, you can easily look up the information associated with the task in the program's Help menu.

Many application programs have default settings to create digital media products, allowing you to create a file without any knowledge of digital media fundamentals. For example, it is possible to apply a special effect with a filter without considering how its many settings affect the image. No error message will prevent you from applying the effect and saving the file, but achieving a desired effect often requires some trial-and-error. Understanding the concepts behind the tools helps you to make rational, educated decisions in using these tools to produce predictable and effective results.

1.1.1 Relevance of Binary Notation, Bits, and Bytes to Digital Media Studies

The chapter intends to provide the foundational knowledge that is required to understand the digital media concepts introduced in the later chapters. Because computers handle data in the units of bits and bytes, it is inevitable that you will encounter these terms in studying digital media. This chapter will explain the meaning of bits and bytes. It also will explain the conversion between decimal and binary notations. The direct relevance of these concepts to digital media may not be obvious within this chapter alone, but these fundamentals will help you comprehend the terminology you encounter in studying digital media. For example:

- *File size* and *prefixes*. Digital files—image, sound, and especially video files—can be very large. The file size is often an important consideration that affects your decisions in the creation and export steps. You often will need to monitor your file's size, which is reported in bits and bytes using prefixes (such as kilo, mega, and giga). In addition, later chapters have examples on file size calculations in bits, which then are converted to mega bytes or giga bytes. Thus, you will need to know how to read a file's size and understand these units.

  Understanding the conversion of decimal to binary notations helps you understand why a number, representing a piece of information, requires a certain number of bits to store.
- By learning binary notation and decimal to binary conversion, you will see how information actually can be stored and handled on a computer as bits.
- *Bit depth*. You may have encountered the term bit depth or color depth (Chapters 2 and 3) if you have worked with digital images. Understanding binary systems helps you comprehend the connection between the bit depth or color depth of an image and the number of colors; for example, 8-bit refers to 256 colors and 24-bit refers to millions of colors.

  With an understanding of bits, you will understand why an image with more colors or higher bit depth has a larger file size.
- *Bit rate*. In working with digital video, you will often encounter the term bit rate (Chapters 6 and 7). The bit rate of a video affects the smoothness of its playback. Understanding bits helps you comprehend what bit rate is, its significance, and how you can calculate your video's average bit rate to predict its playback.
- In Web page creation, you use hexadecimal notation to designate a color for text color and background color. For example, #FF0000 represents red. The conversion from decimal to binary and decimal to hexamdecimal notations are similar. What you learn in the conversion of decimal to binary notations also will help you learn how the hexadecimal notation of a color is obtained.

1.2 ANALOG VERSUS DIGITAL REPRESENTATIONS

It is often said that we live in a digital age. However, the natural world we live in is an analog world. For example, the sounds and music we hear are ***analog*** signals of sound waves. Computers store and transmit information using ***digital*** data. To connect our analog world with computers, analog and digital information must be converted from one form to the other and back again. Unfortunately, the conversion process may sacrifice the exactness of the original information. We will discuss the conversion process—sampling and quantization—in more detail later in this chapter. In order to understand the process, we must first understand the nature of analog and digital representations of information.

1.2.1 Analog Information

Most information that we perceive in the natural world is in analog form. To illustrate, let's try to measure the length of a pencil (Figure 1.1). The ruler shows that the pencil is between 7¼ and 7½ inches long, but the point is a little less than halfway between 7¼ and 7½ inches. Would you round it down to 7.25? You cannot reproduce the exact length of this pencil with 7.25 inches. But wait—the pencil tip is about midway between 7¼ and 7½. So should we say it is 7⅜ or 7.375? This measurement is a little closer to the pencil length than 7.25, but the pencil is shorter than 7⅜ inches. So, is it 7.374, 7.373, 7.3735, 7.37355, . . .? An infinite number of divisions exist between two points. How small should the divisions of a ruler be to allow us to make an exact measurement? Infinitely small, because there is always another value between two values!

(a)   (b)

Figure 1.1 (a) Measuring the length of a pencil with a ruler (b) Close-up view of the pencil tip

Examples of continuous information are time, weight, temperature, lines, waves (such as sound waves), and planes (such as photographs). Analog clocks, thermometers (Figure 1.2a), and weighing scales are examples of analog devices.

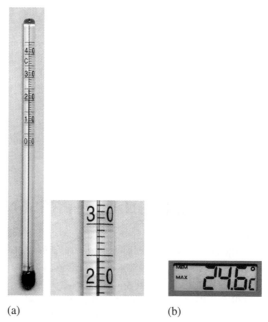

(a)   (b)

Figure 1.2 (a) Analog thermometer and its close-up view (b) Digital thermometer

1.2.2 Digital Data

Computers are built from electronic devices that have only two possible states because they are only stable at one of two voltages. Thus, they operate on a binary system, also called base-2. Regardless of the actual voltages of these two states, we might denote them as *off* and *on* or *false* and *true*. In computer science, we denote this pair of states numerically as 0 and 1, respectively.

Most people associate the binary system exclusively with computers. It is true that computers use it, while in our daily lives, we use many other numbers. For this reason, many people think it's difficult to understand the binary concept.

However, the binary system is not that difficult. For example, imagine using eye signals to communicate with your friends. Each eye has closed and open positions (Figure 1.3). When you want to signal your friend, you first will have to assign meaning to the various combinations of open and closed eyes. You will **encode** the message. Of course, your friend would have to know how to **decode** your signal—that is, interpret the meaning associated with each signal. For example, you may assign "yes" to "closed left eye, open right eye" and "no" to "both eyes closed." There are four open and closed combinations for two eyes. Therefore, you can send four different messages using eye signals. If we assign a numeric value to each of the open and closed eyes—say, open eye as 1 and closed eye as 0—then the four combinations can be represented as 00, 01, 10, and 11.

Figure 1.3 The four combinations of open and closed eyes

Suppose you want to use eye signals to send your friend a message about a color—one out of 16 different choices. You would need another friend to help because you would need four eyes—a 4-bit system, as in Figure 1.4. Using two eyes lets you signal your friend a color out of only four different choices.

Let's look at another example using hand signals. Suppose we consider only two possible positions for each finger: raised up or bent down. The number of different combinations with five fingers is $2^5 = 32$. How about with both hands using ten fingers? $2^{10} = 1024$. Wow! This means that you can send your friend 1024 different messages using the hand signals with each finger either up or down. Of course, some combinations of the raised and bent fingers are quite challenging to make, if not impossible.

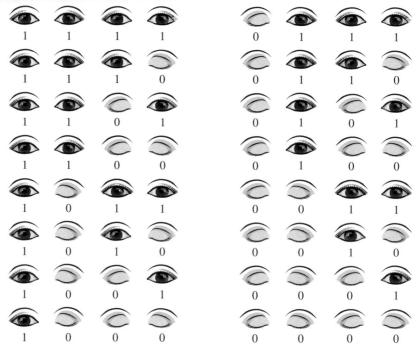

Figure 1.4 Sixteen different open and closed eye patterns created using four eyes

1.3 BITS

In computer systems, data is stored and represented in *binary digits*, called ***bits***. A bit has two possible values, 0 or 1. In the eye signal example, each eye can be considered a bit, since it can denote two possible states: open or closed. Although the two possible values of a bit are denoted numerically as 0 and 1, they can be used for much more than arithmetic.

One bit is not very useful in representing information, but a combination of bits forming larger sequences can represent content information, such as text characters, color information for digital images, and audio amplitudes.

In the eye signal analogy, each eye is like a bit—it has two states: closed and open, or 0 and 1. Using two eyes, we would call your system a 2-bit system. In the hand signal analogy, if you are using one hand, your system is 5-bit. As you see, the number of possible values corresponds to 2^{bit}.

1.3.1 Prefixes

Computer file sizes are reported in bits and bytes. Eight bits make a ***byte***. Digital files—image, sound, and especially video files—can be very large, and the file size is often an important consideration that affects your decisions in the file creation and export steps. You often will need to look up your files' size and monitor the available disk space on your computer's hard drive to make sure you have enough space for new files during the production.

TABLE 1.1	The Relationship between Sizes and Prefixes under the Base-2 Definition	
Prefix Name	**Abbreviation**	**Size**
Kilo	K	$2^{10} = 1,024$
Mega	M	$2^{20} = 1,048,576$
Giga	G	$2^{30} = 1,073,741,824$
Tera	T	$2^{40} = 1,099,511,627,776$
Peta	P	$2^{50} = 1,125,899,906,842,624$
Exa	E	$2^{60} = 1,152,921,504,606,846,976$
Zetta	Z	$2^{70} = 1,180,591,620,717,411,303,424$
Yotta	Y	$2^{80} = 1,208,925,819,614,629,174,706,176$

Because a file contains lots of bits and bytes, we use prefixes, such as *kilo* (K), *mega* (M), *giga* (G), and *tera* (T) to better conceive the size. In order for you to correcly interpret the size of your digital media file, you will need to have a clear idea of what these prefixes mean. Table 1.1 lists the prefixes, abbreviations, and sizes.

DOES A KILO EQUAL 1000 OR 1024?

Although in common parlance one kilo equals 1000 (e.g., one kilogram equals 1000 grams), notice that under this base-2 definition, a kilobyte (KB) is 1024 bytes, a megabyte (MB) is 1,048,576 bytes, and so forth (Table 1.1). Most people know that one kilo equals exactly 1000, and the other prefixes imply a number based on 10 to the power of an integer. This discrepancy has caused confusion among manufacturers of computer storage devices, telecommunication engineers, and the general public. Not everyone knows that one kilobyte means 1,024 bytes.

To avoid such confusion, in December 1998, the International Electrotechnical Commission (IEC) approved the prefixes for binary multiples for use in the fields of data processing and data transmission (Table 1.2).* However, at the time of this writing, these new standard names are not widely used by or known to the public.

TABLE 1.2	IEC Prefixes for Binary Multiples		
Original	**Prefix Name**	**Symbol**	**Size**
Kilo	Kibi	Ki	$2^{10} = 1,024$
Mega	Mebi	Mi	$2^{20} = 1,048,576$
Giga	Gibi	Gi	$2^{30} = 1,073,741,824$
Tera	Tebi	Ti	$2^{40} = 1,099,511,627,776$
Peta	Pebi	Pi	$2^{50} = 1,125,899,906,842,624$
Exa	Exbi	Ei	$2^{60} = 1,152,921,504,606,846,976$

*http://physics.nist.gov/cuu/Units/binary.html

With these new standard names and symbols, we have the following:

1 kilobyte = 1,000 bytes
1 kibibyte = 2^{10} bytes = 1,024 bytes
1 megabit = 1,000,000 bits
1 mebibit = 2^{20} bits = 1,048,576 bits

YOUR COMPUTER HARD-DRIVE SPACE

The following exercise shows you how to look up your hard-drive space, both in bytes and gigabytes (GB).

- If you are using Windows, you can right-click on the C: drive in My Computer and select Properties. Under the General tab, look up the Used Space and Free Space in bytes and GB. Verify that the numbers match the conversion, according to Tables 1.1 and 1.2.
- If you are using Mac OS, select the hard drive, and press Command-I.

For example, say that your computer lists 120,031,539,200 bytes for 111 GB. To convert 120,031,539,200 bytes into GB, you divide 120,031,539,200 by 2^{30} or 1,073,741,824:

$$\frac{120,031,539,200 \text{ bytes}}{1,073,741,824 \text{ bytes/GB}} = 111.8 \text{ GB}$$

The calculation shows you how the number of GB reported is obtained.

1.4 USING BITS TO REPRESENT NUMERIC VALUES

The mathematics we commonly use is based on the *decimal system*, a *base-10* notation. However, computer systems use *base-2* (the *binary system*), which relates to their basic storage units (bits and bytes) and measures file sizes. By learning what base-2 is and how it works, you will understand how binary notation is used to represent decimal numbers.

1.4.1 Base-10

The base-10 system uses ten numerals: 0, 1, 2, 3, 4, 5, 6, 7, 8, and 9. The position of the digits in a number has significance. See the following interpretation of the decimal number 3872.

$$3872$$
$$3 \times 10^3 + 8 \times 10^2 + 7 \times 10^1 + 2 \times 10^0$$
$$= 3 \times 1000 + 8 \times 100 + 7 \times 10 + 2 \times 1$$
$$= 3000 + 800 + 70 + 2$$
$$= 3872$$

The position of each digit represents a power of 10.

1.4.2 Base-2

In the binary system, there are only two possible numerals: 0 and 1. In binary notation, the position of each digit represents a power of 2. For example, the binary notation of 1011 can be interpreted as shown here.

$$10 \ 1$$
$$1 \times 2^3 + 0 \times 2^2 + \ \times 2^1 + 1 \times 2^0$$
$$= 1 \times 8 + 0 \times 4 + \ \times 2 + 1 \times 1$$
$$= 11 \text{ (in decimal notation)}$$

This example shows you how to convert binary notation to decimal notation by breaking it down into products of the power of 2.

Decimal Notation to Binary Notation

Decimal notation can be converted to binary notation through two methods. Either one will give you the same binary representation. We will introduce you one method here.

In this method, you repeatedly divide the decimal number by 2 until it becomes 0, noting the remainder of each division. The *reverse* order of the sequence of the remainders is the binary representation of the decimal number. For example, to convert 19 to binary notation:

> ⌐ **Base-10 and Base-2** An interactive tutorial explaining base-10 and base-2.

> ⌐ **Decimal to Binary Guided Practice** An interactive exercise guides you step-by-step to convert decimal to binary notation. You can practice with a decimal number of your choice or let the program randomly generate one for you.

Division of Number	Remainder
$19/2 = 9$	**1**
$9/2 = 4$	1
$4/2 = 2$	()
$2/2 = 1$	**0**
$1/2 = 0$	1

The sequence of the remainders you get in the repeated divisions is **11 01.** The *reverse* order of this sequence **10 11** is the binary notation of the decimal number 19.

A "DIGITAL" CLOCK GADGET

A binary coded decimal (BCD) clock (Figure 1.5) is built with six columns of LEDs. The first two read the hours; the middle two the minutes; and the last two the seconds. An off LED represents 0, and on represents 1.

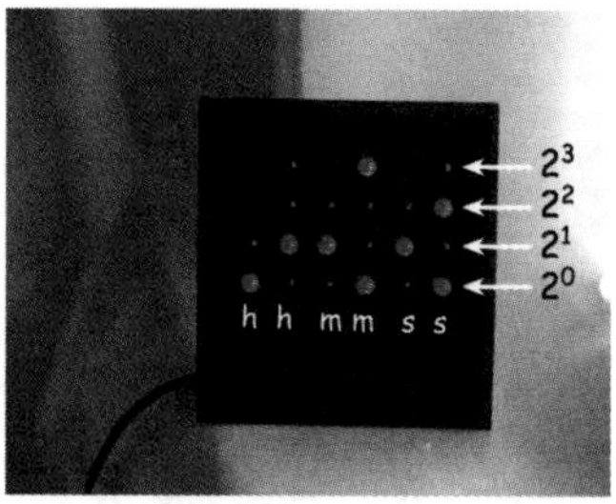

Figure 1.5 A binary coded decimal (BCD) clock

The binary notation for the LED pattern shown in Figure 1.5 is

> 🖱 **Binary Coded Decimal (BCD) Clock**
> This shows a BCD clock in action. It could be fun to race to decode the time, since the LED patterns change by the second.

	0		1		0
	0	0	0	0	1
0	1	1	0	1	0
1	0	0	1	0	1
h	**h**	**m**	**m**	**s**	**s**

The bottom row represents 2^0 (=1), the next row up 2^1 (=2), then 2^2 (=4), and then 2^3 (=8).

Each decimal notation for the hour, minute, and second uses two digits. Let's see how the LED pattern representing the hour shown in Figure 1.5 represents 12.

- The leftmost digit: The pattern shows that the bit pattern for the leftmost digit of the hour is 01. It is converted to 1 in the decimal system because

$$0 \times 2^1 + 1 \times 2^0 = 1$$

- The rightmost digit: The bit pattern for the rightmost digit of the hour is 0010. It is converted to 2 in the decimal system because

$$0 \times 2^3 + 0 \times 2^2 + 1 \times 2^1 + 0 \times 2^0 = 2$$

Questions
1. Verify that the time shown in Figure 1.5 is 12:29:25.
2. Explain the number of LEDs available in each column. That is, why are two LEDs sufficient for the first, four needed for the second, and so forth?

1.5 USING BITS TO REPRESENT NON-NUMERIC VALUES

Although computers use bits to deal with numbers, a sequence of bits can be used to represent almost anything. Recall that you can associate eye signals with "yes" and "no", colors, or even more complicated messages.

TABLE 1.3		The Lower 128 ASCII Codes													
0	NUL	16	DLE	32		48	0	64	@	80	P	96	`	112	p
1	SOH	17	DC1	33	!	49	1	65	A	81	Q	97	a	113	q
2	STX	18	DC2	34	"	50	2	66	B	82	R	98	b	114	r
3	ETX	19	DC3	35	#	51	3	67	C	83	S	99	c	115	s
4	EOT	20	DC4	36	$	52	4	68	D	84	T	100	d	116	t
5	ENQ	21	NAK	37	%	53	5	69	E	85	U	101	e	117	u
6	ACK	22	SYN	38	&	54	6	70	F	86	V	102	f	118	v
7	BEL	23	ETB	39	'	55	7	71	G	87	W	103	g	119	w
8	BS	24	CAN	40	(	56	8	72	H	88	X	104	h	120	x
9	TAB	25	EM	41	)	57	9	73	I	89	Y	105	i	121	y
10	LF	26	SUB	42	*	58	:	74	J	90	Z	106	j	122	z
11	VT	27	ESC	43	+	59	;	75	K	91	[	107	k	123	{
12	FF	28	FS	44	,	60	<	76	L	92	\	108	l	124		
13	CR	29	GS	45	-	61	=	77	M	93	]	109	m	125	}
14	SO	30	RS	46	.	62	>	78	N	94	^	110	n	126	~
15	SI	31	US	47	/	63	?	79	O	95	_	111	o	127	DEL

The binary system can be used to represent non-numeric information. For example, each letter of the alphabet or other text characters can be represented by a different combination of bits. In the ASCII character set, each character is represented using 8 bits, which permits $2^8 = 256$ different characters. Table 1.3 shows the lower 128 ASCII codes. The upper 128 values can be used to handle special characters, such as accented characters in foreign languages.

ASCII stands for American Standard Code for Information Interchange. It is an encoding standard for text characters, including the 26-letter English alphabet and symbols in computer programs.

Another standard is called Unicode, which is not introduced in this chapter. It can represent a large repertoire of multilingual characters.

1.6 THE FINITE AND DISCRETE NATURE OF COMPUTERS

Information in analog media is **continuous** and made up of an *infinite* number of data points. Computers can only handle data that are **discrete** and *finite*. This section will discuss the limitations and advantages of these two properties.

1.6.1 Limitations

1. As you can see from the eye-signal analogy, the more eyes you use, the more information the signal can represent. With a 2-bit system, we can represent four possible values. If we are representing shades of gray using a 2-bit system, we can only represent four different shades. We can represent 16 different shades with a 4-bit system. The more shades of gray we want to represent, the more bits we need.

    To represent colors that change from one point to the next in a natural image would require an infinite number of points, because there are always more points between any two points in the analog world. However, computers have a limit on the number of bits that are allowed for each piece of data. A sequence of bits in a computer cannot be infinite. Only a finite set of data can be represented digitally.

2. No matter what the bit limit, each value can only represent one discrete shade of gray. There are always shades of gray in between two consecutive gray values that cannot be captured in digital form.

Thus, the discrete and finite nature of computers restricts the exactness with which analog media—natural sights and sounds—can be captured and reproduced in digital form.

1.6.2 Advantages

Although digital representation sacrifices exactness in reproducing analog information, its discrete nature offers an advantage in precision, and its finite nature offers an advantage in compactness for media.

INTEGERS AND DECIMAL NUMBERS

Integers are an example of a discrete number system. There is no other integer between any two consecutive integers. Computers can represent integers exactly, because they encode them in the discrete values of 0 and 1. Integers are inherently discrete; they are not inherently finite. A list of integers goes on forever. Although computers can only deal with a finite number of things, handling integers is not a problem, because they set a limit on the number of bits used to represent them.

Numbers with decimal points, such as 0.123, 1.30, and 1.7608 are an example of a continuous number system. Between any two numbers are other numbers. Although these numbers are inherently continuous, computers can handle them by limiting their precision by setting a limit on the number of bits used to represent them. Thus, some such numbers cannot be represented exactly, but only approximately, on computers.

1.7 CONVERTING ANALOG TO DIGITAL

The conversion of analog information to digital is a two-step process: *sampling* and *quantizing*. Measuring the length of a pencil (Figure 1.1) illustrates a sampling and quantizing process. For this example, we only sample once; that is, we measure the length of the pencil once. In digital media, you often have to sample more than once, because color value changes over an image's 2-D plane or the amplitude of a sound wave changes over time, for example. In these cases, you must sample multiple times to collect enough information to represent the whole piece. The *sampling rate*—how frequently you take measurements—determines the level of detail at which the collected data can represent the original analog media.

To illustrate the sampling and quantizing steps, let's monitor a puppy's first year of growth by measuring its weight. Use an analog scale that uses a spring-loaded mechanism to sample the puppy's weight. The more the puppy weighs, the more compressed the spring will be. The spring responds to the extent of compression and rotates the pointer on the scale. This scale is an analog scale, because the spring can be compressed continuously. The weight, correspondingly, is analog information.

When you record the weight, you note down a discrete number. You have to decide how to round up the data, for example to 0.1, 0.2, or 0.5. The process of assigning a discrete value to something is called *quantizing*.

What number would you record for the puppy's weight (Figure 1.6)? You may choose to round off the reading to the nearest hash mark or estimate the reading between the hash

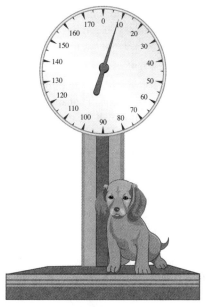

Figure 1.6 Sampling a puppy's weight on an analog scale

marks. Either way, you may not be recording an exact weight. You sacrifice the accuracy of the measurement when you convert analog information into a discrete number but gain the advantage of reporting the puppy's weight as a precise value—although not necessarily an accurate one. Distinct and unambiguous, discrete values easily can be processed mathematically, compared, or plotted on a chart. On the other hand, if you record the weight as "somewhere between 5 and 10 pounds," it will not be distinct and precise, and you probably will be asked to round it off to a discrete number.

⏚ **Converting Analog to Digital— Sampling and Quantizing** An interactive tutorial illustrating the process of sampling and quantizing using a task to monitor a puppy's first year of growth in weight.

In recording a number, you must decide the number of decimal places to use. This will determine the precision of the measurement. Generally, increasing the number of decimal places increases the precision. However, recording the puppy's weight using more decimal places will require more paper and paperwork.

In digitizing analog media, the precision of the data is determined by the number of discrete values to which the data can be assigned. Increasing the decimal places is one way to increase the discrete values. For example, allowing one decimal place gives you 10 discrete levels of precision between two consecutive integers; between 2 and 3, there are 2.0, 2.1, 2.2, 2.3, 2.4, 2.5, 2.6, 2.7, 2.8, and 2.9. In digital media, the number of possible levels is called *bit depth*.

BIT DEPTH DOES NOT MEAN NUMBER OF DECIMAL PLACES

The number of decimal places is used in the simple example of weighing the puppy to illustrate the concept of bit depth. However, increasing the bit depth does not necessarily mean increasing the number of decimal places.

Increasing bit depth means having more discrete levels to which the captured data can be assigned. For 10 discrete levels, you can have the 10 allowable values as

(1) 2.0, 2.1, 2.2, 2.3, 2.4, 2.5, 2.6, 2.7, 2.8, and 2.9

(2) 0, 5, 10, 15, 20, 25, 30, 35, 40, 45

Using the first 10-level scale for recording the puppy's weight, you get a precision of one decimal place within 2 to 3 pounds. That means that if the puppy's weight is between 2 and 3 pounds, you can distinguish the difference to one decimal place. However, any weight lower than 2.0 will be recorded as 2.0, and any weight higher than 2.9 will be capped at 2.9. The weight obtained from Figure 1.6 would be recorded as 2.9. If it this scale is used, it certainly would not be very useful for tracking the puppy's progress.

Using the second 10-level scale, a weight of 2 pounds would be rounded to 0 and a weight of 3 pounds to 5. The difference between 2 and 3 pounds is altered after they are mapped to the allowable value on this 10-level scale. The difference becomes 5 pounds not 1 pound. However, because this scale has a wider range, a weight of, say, 45 pounds can be distinguished from 5 pounds. The weight obtained from Figure 1.6 would have been recorded as 10 pounds if this scale were used. This scale is a better choice than the first for weighing the puppy.

Increasing the number of allowable levels—increasing the bit depth—in digital media can

- Increase the precision of the captured data
- Increase the overall range of the scale
- Increase the file size

To monitor the puppy's first year growth by weight, you will have to decide how frequently you want to weigh it. This is the *sampling rate*. Do you want to weigh it annually, monthly, weekly, daily, or hourly? What factors do you take into consideration when you make this decision?

Based on how fast a puppy normally grows in the first year, weighing it monthly or weekly is reasonable. However, if you do not know how fast a puppy should normally grow, you probably feel a little lost when you are asked to choose how frequently to weigh it. If you sample too infrequently, you will miss critical details that show how the weight changes over time. In that case, how frequently do you sample so that you do not miss any information at all?

As mentioned earlier, when converting analog to digital data, no matter how high the sampling rate is, some analog information will be missed. If you sample too frequently, you will be busy weighing the puppy, need more paper to keep the record, more shelf space to store the record, and more time to read through the records later (besides annoying the puppy).

By analogy, if you increase the sampling rate, you increase the accuracy in digitally representing the original analog media. The computer has to sample faster, and the resulting file will have more samples or data. Files will be larger and require more time to process, which may cause noticeable delay in opening or editing the file.

What sampling rate should we use, then? There is no one strictly right or wrong sampling rate. The optimal sampling rate for your purpose will depend on the source content, its intended use, and technical limitations (for example, the rate of change of the original analog source and limitations on the file size and processing time). In weighing the puppy, either monthly or weekly seems a reasonable sampling rate. Weekly data may represent the first few months' rapid growth rate more accurately but may yield redundant information in later months. In real life, you can choose to sample the first month's weight more frequently than the other months if you anticipate more dramatic changes. You can change the sampling rate in a task. However, in digital media, one sampling rate is normally set for a session.

How is this analogy related to digital media, such as images and sound? In general, the sampling rate for digital images is related to the image resolution (or amount of detail). Quantization is related to the image's bit depth or color depth, which affects the number of colors allowed in the image. For digital audio, quantization also is related to the bit depth, which determines how well the differences in sound amplitude can be represented, and the sampling rate relates to how frequently the amplitude is sampled.

Detailed discussions of sampling and quantizing digital images and audio are covered in the chapters devoted to these media.

1.7.1 Problems in Representing Analog Media on Computers

Sound and pictures are by nature continuous phenomena. Each piece of sound or picture is made up of an infinite amount of information. Due to the finite and discrete way that computers handle data, two inevitable problems arise when we want to represent sound and pictures on a computer

1. Since computers operate on discrete values, the sampling step is required to choose some discrete samples of the information. Computers have only finite capacity, so the sampling rate has to be finite.
2. A computer cannot represent numbers with infinite precision. The precision with which we represent colors or sounds is limited. Quantization maps the values of the samples to a discrete scale; that is, rounded up to an allowable discrete value on the scale.

1.8 FILE SIZES

In a text document that uses ASCII code to represent text characters, each byte stores an ASCII code that corresponds to a character. The more characters in a text document, the more bytes are required to store the file.

ACTIVITY/EXERCISE

Using Windows 95, 98, 2000, or XP: Open a new text file in Notepad and type the sentence, "Eight bits make a byte." Save the file as file-size-exercise.txt. Then to look at its file size right-click on the file-size-exercise.txt file and select Properties. You should find that the file size is 23 bytes because there are 23 characters in this sentence— 1 byte for each character (including spaces, which are characters, too). What is the ASCII code for a space? Look it up in the Table 1.3.

Using Mac OSX: Open a new text file in TextEdit and type the sentence, "Eight bits make a byte." Select Format > Make Plain Text. Then save the file as file-size-exercise.txt. In the Save dialog box, choose Western for the Plain Text Encoding. Verify that the file size is 23 bytes.

Questions

In the file-size-exercise.txt file you created, add a blank line at the end of the sentence by hitting the Enter (Windows) or Return (Mac) key on your keyboard. Save the file. Then look at its file size again. What is the file size now? By how many byte(s) has it increased?

Creating a blank line in Notepad actually involves both a carriage return (CR) and a line feed (LF). Are they characters? Look them up in Table 1.3.

If you create a Microsoft Word document with the same sentence, "Eight bits make a byte.", will the file size also be 23 bytes? No. It is larger because other information (such as text formatting) is saved with the file.

Pixels and pixel dimensions will be discussed in more detail in the digital imaging chapters.

You will learn more about bit depth of digital images in the chapter on digital imaging.

A byte is not just for storing a character in a text document. A byte is 8 bits, with 256 possible values. It can be used for many purposes. If you use a byte to store the color information of each pixel in an image, then 256 colors can be used for each pixel. Color images can use more than one byte per pixel to represent color information. Whether one or more bytes are used for each pixel, the file size increases with the number of pixels in an image. The more pixels an image has, the more bytes are needed to store the image and the larger the file size.

Multimedia files—image, sound, and especially video files—can be very large and require tremendous amounts of storage space. In addition, the larger the file, the longer the transmission time to send it over the Internet and the longer the processing time. Longer processing time means that it may take longer for your audience to open your files and slow down your productivity when you are editing the file.

Generally, there are three strategies to reduce the size of a digital media file:

- Reduce the sampling rate
- Reduce the bit depth
- Apply file compression

When you reduce the sampling rate and bit depth, the resulting digital image will resemble the original subject less, and digital audio quality may be noticeably degraded. In working with digital media files, you often have to weigh quality against file size.

1.9 COMPRESSION

You will learn more about different codecs (compression/decompression methods) and corresponding data rates in the digital video chapter.

File compression lets you reduce the total number of bits and bytes in a file, so it can be transmitted faster over a network and take up less storage space on a disk. Nowadays, storage space is inexpensive, and many people have access to a high-speed network, but you still have to consider the playback performance of video files. Uncompressed videos require a very high data rate. Video playback will become jerky and skip frames if the computer cannot process the video data fast enough.

In later chapters, you will learn some of the most common data compression methods applied to multimedia files. Some are not specific to multimedia files. Others are available only for a certain category of media files. For example, Sorenson is available for creating QuickTime movies but not for sound compression.

By learning the concepts behind these compression methods, you will understand the strengths and weaknesses of each. Some allow you to control certain parameters when saving a file in a multimedia application. Understanding what these parameters mean and how they affect your files will help you make decisions that are best for your multimedia work.

✎ **Video Examples of Different Levels of Compression: Uncompressed, Low Compression, and High Compression** These sample videos are 60-frame computer animations, rendered frame-by-frame (720 × 480 pixels) as an image sequence, imported in Adobe Premiere Pro, and exported as QuickTime and MPEG-2 movies. Each exported movie uses a different compressor.

- QuickTime, uncompressed (*Note:* This file takes longest to download and has the least smooth playback.)
- QuickTime, using Animation Codec
- QuickTime, using Cinepak Codec
- QuickTime, using Sorenson Codec
- MPEG-2

Note the following properties of each movie:

1. Image quality for different codecs
2. File sizes
3. Smoothness of playback

Why are the image quality, file size, and playback different with different compressors? You will understand better when you learn more about digital video compression in the later chapters on digital video.

1.9.1 Lossy and Lossless Compression

Compression methods can be categorized as either lossy or lossless. With *lossy compression*, some information in the original file will be lost and cannot be recovered. You should avoid using this type of compression for any file that you want to keep as the start file for further editing. JPEG, a popular image file format for Web images, is an example of lossy compression. MP3, a popular file format for digital audio, is another example of lossy compression. Many video codecs are also lossy, although a few use lossless algorithms.

For details on the compression algorithms, see the CS Module.

1.10 SUMMARY

The analog information we perceive through our senses is continuous and infinite. However, computers store and transmit information using discrete, finite data, which presents some limitations but also advantages in capturing and reproducing analog media.

Converting from analog to digital data involves a two-step process—sampling and quantizing. How frequently an analog media is sampled during the sampling step is called the sample rate. For example, the sample rate in digital imaging determines the resolution of a digital image. In the quantization step, the number of discrete levels used to map the samples' values is called the bit depth. For example, the bit depth of a digital image specifies the number of colors available in the image. The discrete and finite nature of computers restricts the precision with which analog media—natural sights and sounds—can be reproduced in digital form. In converting from analog to digital, we sacrifice exactness.

Because of the current electronic technology that computer systems are built on, they operate on the binary system, which uses base-2 notation. Only two numerals are available in base-2, denoted as 0 and 1 in the language of computers. Base-10 can be converted to base-2 notation and vice versa. For example, the binary notation for the decimal number 19 is 10011.

Multimedia files—image, sound, and especially video files—can be very large. Such large file sizes can require tremendous amounts of storage space. In addition, the larger the file, the longer it takes to send the file over the Internet.

Generally, there are three strategies to reduce the size of a digital media file:

- Reduce the sampling rate
- Reduce the bit depth
- Apply file compression

Reducing the sampling rate or bit depth sacrifices the quality of your resulting digital media. When working with digital media files, you often have to weigh the quality against the file size. Compression methods can be categorized as either lossy or lossless. With lossy compressions, like JPEG and MP3, some information in the original file will be lost and cannot be recovered. Whenever possible, you should not use this type of compression for any file that you want to reproduce the exact original or to keep as the start file for further editing.

TERMS

analog, 5	decimal system, 10	kilo (K), 9
base-10, 10	decode, 7	lossy compression, 19
base-2, 10	digital, 5	mega (M), 9
binary system, 10	discrete, 13	quantizing, 14
bit depth, 15	encode, 7	sampling, 14
bits, 8	file compression, 18	sampling rate, 14
byte, 8	finite, 13	tera (T), 9
continuous, 13	giga (G), 9	

LEARNING AIDS

The following learning aids can be found at the book's companion Web site.

🖰 **Base-10 and Base-2**
An interactive tutorial explaining base-10 and base-2.

🖰 **Decimal to Binary Guided Practice**
An interactive exercise guides you step-by-step to convert decimal to binary notation. You can practice with a decimal number of your choice or let the program randomly generate one for you.

🖰 **Binary Coded Decimal (BCD) Clock**
This shows a BCD clock in action. It could be fun to race to decode the time since the LED patterns change by the second.

↻ Converting Analog to Digital—Sampling and Quantizing

An interactive tutorial illustrating the process of sampling and quantizing using a task to monitor a puppy's first year of growth in weight.

✎ Video Examples of Different Levels of Compression: Uncompressed, Low Compression, and High Compression

These sample videos are 60-frame computer animations, rendered frame-by-frame (720 × 480 pixels) as an image sequence, imported in Adobe Premiere Pro, and exported as QuickTime and MPEG-2 movies. Each exported movie uses a different compressor.

- QuickTime, uncompressed (*Note:* This file takes longest to download and has the least smooth playback.)
- QuickTime, using Animation Codec
- QuickTime, using Cinepak Codec
- QuickTime, using Sorenson Codec
- MPEG-2

Note the following properties of each movie:

1. Image quality for different codecs
2. File sizes
3. Smoothness of playback

Why are the image quality, file size, and playback different with different compressors? You will understand better when you learn more about digital video compression in the later chapters on digital video.

REVIEW QUESTIONS

When applicable, please select all correct answers.

1. Our everyday decimal numbering system is base-_____. Computers use base-_____, which is also known as the _____ numbering system.

2. The smallest unit in a binary system is a _____,
   A. bit
   B. byte

   which refers to a binary digit (i.e., a _____ or a _____ .) (Enter a digit or number.)

3. Fill in the blanks with "bit(s)" or "byte(s)": Eight _____ equals one _____.

4. The word bit comes from the shortening of the words _____ _____.

5. If you want to use hand signals to communicate only two possibilities—yes or no—to your friend, what is the minimum number of finger(s) you need? _____ We can call this hand-signal system _____-bit.

6. A pixel that can have only one of two possible color values requires _____ bit(s) to store the color information.

7. If you use a byte to store the grayscale information of each pixel in a grayscale image, how many gray levels are possible for each pixel?

8. Which of the following sizes is the largest?

A. 24 GB

B. 24 MB

C. 240 MB

D. 2400 KB

9. Fill in the names and abbreviations for the followings:

Name	Abbr.	Size in bytes
Kilo bytes	KB	$2^{10} = 1{,}024$
		$2^{20} = 1{,}048{,}576$
		$2^{30} = 1{,}073{,}741{,}824$
		$2^{40} = 1{,}099{,}511{,}627{,}776$

10. How many bits is each of the following binary numbers? Also, convert each to a decimal number.

(i)   00000000

(ii)   0000

(iii) 01101000

(iv)   0110100

(v)   11

(vi)   111

(vii) 0000000000000010

11. Convert the following decimal numbers into binary.

(i)   0

(ii)   1

(iii) 2

(iv)   3

(v)   12

(vi)   123

(vii) 11

(viii) 111

(ix)   128

(x)   255

12. Converting from analog to digital involves a two-step process: _____ and _____ .

13. When analog information is converted to digital data, we must consider two properties that affect the exactness of the digital representation, one from sampling and one from quantizing. Which of the following is from sampling?

A. sampling rate

B. bit depth

14. When analog is converted to digital data, two properties affect the exactness of the digital representation, one from sampling and one from quantizing. Which of the following is a result of quantization?

A. sampling rate
B. bit depth

15. (i) Name three general strategies to reduce the size of a digital media file.
    (ii) Which of these strategies does not necessarily sacrifice the quality of the media file? How?

16. You should avoid using lossy compression for any file that you want to keep as the start file for further editing because _____.

Fundamentals of Digital Imaging

TABLE OF CONTENTS

KEY CONCEPTS
- Sampling and quantizing in digitizing images
- Pixels and image resolution
- Image bit depth
- How pixels, image resolution, and bit depth are related to sampling and quantizing
- Color representation in digital images
- Bit-mapped images versus vector graphics

GENERAL LEARNING OBJECTIVES

At the end of this chapter, you should be able to demonstrate that you
- Know the meaning of the common terms in digital imaging.
- Know the commonly used color models in digital imaging.
- Know the common file types for digital images.
- Understand the basic steps of digitization: sampling and quantization in digital imaging.
- Understand resolution and color depth.
- Comprehend the effects of resolution and color depth on image file size.
- Comprehend the difference between bit-mapped image and vector graphics.
- Comprehend color representation in digital imaging.
- Can apply the basic steps of digitization in digital imaging.
- Can apply the general strategies for reducing digital image file sizes.

2.1 INTRODUCTION

In Chapter 1, you learned that digitization of analog information involves a two-step process: sampling and quantizing. Digitization of any digital medium—images, sound, or videos—always involves these two steps. However, if you have worked with digital image processing programs, you may have noticed that you never encounter the terms "sampling" and "quantizing" explicitly in the program. So, how are these concepts applied to digital images? If you never encounter these terms in digital image processing programs, why do we need to talk about them here?

In digital imaging, you may have already heard about pixels, resolution, and bit depth. What do sampling and quantizing have to do with pixels, resolution, and bit depth? In this chapter, we are going to show the relationships among these fundamental concepts and their applications in digital imaging.

To understand pixels, resolution, and bit depth, we need to start with the concepts of sampling and quantizing. In fact, it is only by means of the two-step process of digitization that we ever arrive at pixels, resolution, and bit depth in digital imaging. Although you may not encounter the terms when you use digital imaging applications to work with pixels or manipulate the resolution or bit depth of digital images, you are applying the concepts of sampling and quantizing. Understanding these fundamental concepts and how they are applied to digital images will help you take full advantage of digital media tools and produce predictable results effectively in your creative process.

2.2 DIGITIZING IMAGES

Look up and let your eyes fall on the scene in front of you. Draw an imaginary rectangle around what you see. This is your "viewfinder." Imagine that you are going to capture this view on a pegboard. Why a pegboard, you may ask? A pegboard is a good analogy for a digitized image because each peg hole represents a *discrete sample*. In the following sections we will use the pegboard analogy to discuss sampling and quantization in detail.

> ✎ **Sampling and Quantizing in Digital Images** An interactive tutorial, complementary to the materials covered in Sections 2.2.1 and 2.2.2 explains sampling and quantizing in digitizing an image.

2.2.1 Step 1: Sampling

The natural scenes you see in the world around you are colored in continuous tones. There is no sharp division between one point of color and the next. Each point blends continuously into the next. In this respect, color is an analog phenomenon in human perception. In order to put it into a language that computers can understand, color must be digitized.

The first step of the digitization process is **sampling**, a process by which you record or sample the color in a natural image at discrete, evenly spaced points. Let's say that Figure 2.1a represents the natural image that you want to capture as a digital image with a digital camera.

Say this image is going to be sampled into a grid of 25×20 discrete samples (Figure 2.1b). Using the pegboard analogy, we could say that this image is going to be recreated on a pegboard with 25×20 peg holes. The color of each of these discrete samples is averaged to a single uniform value to represent the corresponding area in the image (Figure 2.1c). This 25×20 sampled image looks blocky. Details are lost because the grid is too coarse for this image.

In digital imaging, each of these discrete sample points is called a *picture element*, or *pixel* for short. Each pixel stores the color information of the corresponding position on the image. The position is defined by its horizontal and vertical coordinates. *Pixel dimension* refers to the image's width and height in pixels. In the pegboard analogy, the dimension of your resulting digitized image in pixels will be 25 pixels $\times$ 20 pixels. Note that 25 pixels $\times$ 20 pixels is by no means a realistic pixel dimension in digital photography; it is only for illustration purposes here. Most digital cameras can capture images of over a thousand pixels in each dimension—for example, 3000 pixels $\times$ 2000 pixels.

Why discrete points? See discussion of analog versus digital in Chapter 1.

Capturing Digital Images. There are two methods of capturing digital images—scanning and digital photography. The concept of sampling and quantizing applies to both methods, not just digital photography. Topics in capturing digital images are discussed in the Chapter 3.

The relationship between pixel dimension and the image's physical dimension (in inches) is discussed in Chapter 3.

MEGAPIXEL

Often, the word *megapixel* is associated with digital cameras. One megapixel is equal to 1,000,000 pixels. The total number of pixels in a 3000 $\times$ 2000-pixel digital image is

$$3000 \text{ pixels} \times 2000 \text{ pixels} = 6{,}000{,}000 \text{ pixels}$$

This is sometimes referred to as six megapixels.

The implication of the megapixel is discussed and explored with a worksheet exercise in the Chapter 3.

Figure 2.1 (a) A natural image (b) A grid of 25 × 20 discrete samples on an image (c) The color averaging of each of the 25 × 20 discrete samples (d) A grid of 100 × 80 discrete samples (e) The color averaging of each of the 100 × 80 discrete samples

How frequently you take a sample is defined by the sampling rate. The words "frequent" and "rate" are often associated with time. However, for an image, *frequency* refers to how close neighboring samples are in a 2-D image plane. If you sample the image with a finer grid than in the previous example, say 100 × 80 (Figures 2.1d and 2.1e), you are increasing the sampling rate because you are sampling more frequently within the same spatial distance. In digital imaging, increasing the sampling rate is equivalent to increasing the image **resolution**. With higher resolution, you have more samples (pixels) to represent the same scene. The pixel dimensions of the captured image are increased, and so is the file size of the digitized image. You gain more detail from the original scene (Figure 2.2).

(a)   (b)

Figure 2.2 The relative sizes of a 25 pixels × 20 pixels image (left) and a 100 pixels × 80 pixels image (right) captured from the same scene

A PIXEL IS A PIXEL IS A POINT SAMPLE—NOT A LITTLE SQUARE BLOCK

When you zoom in on a digital image in an image editing program, you often see the pixels represented as little square blocks. However, keep in mind that a pixel is a sample at a single point; it is a point sample that does not really have a *physical* dimension associated with it.

2.2.2 Step 2: Quantizing

A natural image is colored in continuous tones, and thus it theoretically has an infinite number of colors. The discrete and finite language of the computer restricts the reproduction of an infinite number of colors and shades. The process of encoding an infinite number of possibilities—that is, an infinite number of colors and shades in the case of digital imaging—with a finite list of numbers—that is, a finite number of color codes in the case of digital imaging—is called **quantization**.

Quantizing the sampled image involves mapping the color of each pixel to a discrete and precise value. Before you do that, you need to consider how many possible colors you want to use in the image. To illustrate this process, let's use the example of the sampled image in Figure 2.1 and continue onto the quantization step.

The color of each sample in the 100×80-pixels image (Figure 2.1e) is quantized into one of four discrete colors (Figure 2.3a) by mapping it to the closest color. Figure 2.4a shows the resulting quantized image. This 4-color palette obviously does not give sufficient color levels for this scene.

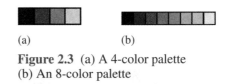

(a)   (b)

Figure 2.3 (a) A 4-color palette
(b) An 8-color palette

(a)   (b)

Figure 2.4 The sampled image is quantized into (a) 4 colors (b) 8 colors

The image fidelity and details are lost because different colors from the original are now mapped to the same color on the palette. For example, the area outlined in red in Figure 2.5b is made up of many different green colors. The same area in the 4-color image (Figure 2.5a) now has only one color. The details that rely on the subtle color differences are lost during quantization.

YOU MAY ASK: WHY THE CHOICE OF THOSE FOUR OR EIGHT PARTICULAR COLORS?

Good question! The palette do not have to be restricted to those exact four or eight colors. The 4-color and 8-color palettes in this example all contain shades of green because the original scene is mainly green. However, you do not have to use only green colors for a scene like this. For any images, no matter what colors you choose, the bit depth for four colors is still 2 bits, and the bit depth for eight colors is still 3 bits.

(a)   (b)

Figure 2.5 (a) The colors in the original image (b) are quantized into four colors using the palette shown in Figure 2.3a. Some of the similar green colors, such as those pointed out in the red box, are now mapped to a single color

The number of colors used for quantization is related to the color depth or ***bit depth*** of the digital image. A bit depth of n allows 2^n different colors. Therefore, a 2-bit digital image allows 2^2 (i.e., 4) colors in the image.

USING BINARY BITS TO REPRESENT COLORS ON COMPUTERS

Internally, a computer uses the binary system to represent colors. For example, for 2-bit color, the binary bits for the four colors are 00, 01, 10, and 11.

Bit 1	Bit 2
0	0
0	1
1	0
1	1

Then, will increasing the number of colors in the palette improve the image fidelity? The answer is: it depends, and in most cases, can be yes. The number of colors or the bit depth is not the only determining factor for image fidelity in quantizing an image; the choice of colors for the quantization also plays an important role in the reproduction of an image.

To illustrate the importance of the choice of colors in the palette, let's increase the bit depth to 3 ($2^3 = 8$ colors). An 8-color palette (Figure 2.6a) that is drastically different from the overall colors of the original natural image will be used. The resulting quantized image with this new palette is shown in Figure 2.6b.

The 8-color image (Figure 2.6b) that is quantized using a drastic 8-color palette does not look any closer to the original scene than the 4-color one (Figure 2.4a) that is quantized

(a) (b)

Figure 2.6 (a) Using a different 8-color palette (b) the sampled image is quantized

using a 4-color palette made up of green shades. Although the larger palette increases the image detail a little in certain areas—for example, in the sky and the water areas—because it allows more levels of color distinction, the colors are not faithful to the original image.

24-BIT, 32-BIT, AND 48-BIT COLOR DEPTH

A single 8-bit byte can be used to represent one of 256 different possible values. The values range from 0 to 255. An RGB (red, green, blue) color can be represented in three 8-bit bytes, one byte for each component of the R, G, and B. Thus, in this case, the color depth is *24 bits* which means it allows $2^{24} = 16,777,216$ colors. Each of the R, G, and B components allows 2^8 levels—that is 256 levels (from 0 to 255).

Although 24-bit color is often sufficient for human vision to represent colors, as computer processors get faster and storage media get cheaper, higher color depth (such as 48-bit color) is increasingly supported by scanners and image editing programs. 48-bit RGB color is represented using 16 bits per component of R, G, and B.

Questions*
1. How many possible colors can be represented with 48-bit color depth?
2. How many possible levels of red can be represented with 48-bit RGB color?
3. How many times would a file size increase by going from 24-bit to 48-bit?

A 32-bit image is basically 24-bit RGB with an additional 8-bit alpha channel. The alpha channel is used to specify the level of transparency. Unlike 24-bit images that are fully opaque, 32-bit images can be smoothly blended with other images.

Question
4. How many levels of transparency does an 8-bit alpha channel allow?

---
*Answers to Questions: (1) 2^{48}; (2) 2^{16}; (3) double; (4) 2^8, i.e., 256

2.3 BITMAPPED IMAGES

Each pixel contains the color information composed of numeric values, which can be represented by a sequence of bits—1s and 0s. A 1-bit image allows two (2^1) colors, which can be represented by 1 and 0. The digit 1 can be used to designate a particular color and 0 another color. A simple purple diagonal line on a yellow background can be represented in 1s and 0s, as shown in Figure 2.7.

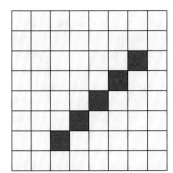

1	1	1	1	1	1	1	1
1	1	1	1	1	1	1	1
1	1	1	1	1	1	0	1
1	1	1	1	1	0	1	1
1	1	1	1	0	1	1	1
1	1	1	0	1	1	1	1
1	1	0	1	1	1	1	1
1	1	1	1	1	1	1	1

Figure 2.7 For each pixel in an 1-bit (i.e., 2-color) bitmap image, its color value can be represented by 0s and 1s

Digital images described by pixel values such as the one shown in Figure 2.7 are called **bitmapped** images. The term "bitmapping" refers to how these bits representing the image are stored in computer memory. Bitmapped images also are called **raster graphics** because "rastering" refers to the way most video displays translate the images into a series of horizontal lines on the screen.

Bitmapped images commonly are used in image-editing applications. Because they are composed of pixels, the image content can be edited pixel by pixel easily. However, their size and appearance depend on their output resolution to the device, for example, dots per inch for a monitor and pixels per inch for a printer. Bitmapped images can appear jagged and lose detail when they're scaled onscreen or printed at a low resolution.

2.4 VECTOR GRAPHICS

Besides using pixels to describe digital images, there is another way to create imagery—it is to describe the graphic mathematically. This type of digital image is called **vector graphics**. For example, to describe a line like the one in Figure 2.8, you can use a simple equation. Using equations to represent graphics is more concise than bitmapping. Consider this analogy in the context of getting directions for a trip: Bitmapped images are like a triptik map. Vector graphics, on the other hand, are analogous to written directions. Instead of tracing out a route on a triptik, someone could give you written directions that say, for example, "Go 3.2 miles. When you come to the stoplight, turn right. Go past the mall and turn at the first entrance to the restaurant." It may take you more time to translate the written directions into a mental image of where you're going, as compared to understanding a triptik map that is already in visual form. One advantage of the written directions, however, is that they might actually be more concise and require less space than a full printed map.

Similarly, vector graphics are generally more concise descriptions of digital images than bitmaps are. But the most distinct advantage of vector graphics is that they are resolution independent. Let's explain what resolution independence means and what characteristic of vector graphics makes them resolution independent.

In contrast to bitmapped images that already have the number of pixels or resolution specified when they are stored, vector graphics do not use pixels but equations. The images of vector graphics are produced for output or display by calculating the points, according to the equations that make up the graphics. The coordinate system for the equations is arbitrary. That is, its scale can be set to any level. So, the shapes can be coarse or fine, and the resolution of the output can be low or high. Vector graphics are resolution independent because they can be scaled to any size and printed on any output device at any resolution, without losing detail or clarity in the picture. To illustrate resolution independence, let's return to the analogy of driving directions versus a triptik map. You can produce a map from written directions at any size you want simply by following the description. However, to make a triptik map into the size you want, you may need to rescale it on a photocopier. This will produce a fuzzy reproduction of the map, no matter whether you are blowing it up or shrinking it down.

Examples of vector graphic application programs are Adobe Illustrator, Adobe Flash, and CorelDraw.

Consider a simple example of vector graphics, a line. A line can be described mathematically with an equation. In vector graphic programs, the line is defined by two end points (Figure 2.8a). The line can be stroked at a certain width, but it is still a vector graphic. When you zoom in on the line on a monitor display, the line is still clear (Figure 2.8b). When the line is rasterized to a bitmapped image at a low resolution, as shown in Figure 2.8c, zooming in on the line will show that it is jagged. If the same vector graphic line is rasterized to a bitmapped image at a higher resolution setting (Figure 2.8d), the rasterized line appears smoother than the one from the lower resolution although it still appears jagged.

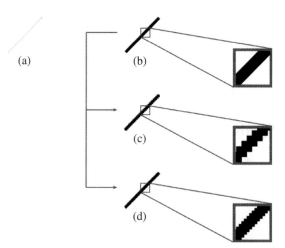

Figure 2.8 Vector graphics and rasterized bitmapped images (a) A line defined by two end points (b) The line stroked at a certain width (c) The line rasterized at a low resolution (d) The line rasterized at a higher resolution

RASTERIZING VECTOR GRAPHICS

Most vector graphics programs let you **rasterize** or convert vector graphics into pixel-based bitmapped images. Because you are making a resolution-independent vector graphic into a resolution dependent image, you need to specify a resolution for rasterizing, that is, how coarse or how fine the sampling.

The rasterized image will appear jagged. This jagged effect is a form of **aliasing** caused by undersampling or insufficient sampling rate. In addition, as you see in Figure 2.9b, the high contrast between black and white pixels makes the effect very noticeable. To soften the jaggedness, we can color the pixels with intermediary shades in the areas where the sharp color changes occur (Figure 2.9c). This technique is called **anti-aliasing**. With the same raster resolution setting, you can make the rasterized graphics appear smoother with anti-aliasing than without.

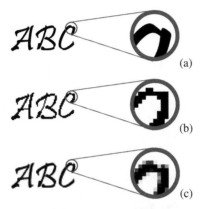

Figure 2.9 Vector graphics versus rasterized graphics (a) edges still appear smooth at higher magnification (b) rasterized vector graphic without anti-aliasing (c) rasterized vector graphic with anti-aliasing

2.5 FILE TYPES OF DIGITAL IMAGES

The file types you will most commonly see and use are given in the Tables 2.1 and 2.2.

2.6 DIGITAL IMAGE FILE SIZE AND OPTIMIZATION

Resolution and bit depth directly affect the file size of an image. The higher the resolution or the higher the bit depth, the larger the image file. Without compression, image files would take up an unreasonable amount of disk space and would be too large for network transfer.

TABLE 2.1	Common File Types of Bitmapped or Pixel-Based Images			
File Type	**File Suffix**	**Standard Color Modes**	**Use**	**Compression**
JPEG (Joint Photographic Experts Group)	.jpg or .jpeg	RGB, CMYK	Best for continuous tone images such as photographs; can be used for Web images	Lossy compression method called JPEG compression that works well with photographs
GIF (Graphics Interchange Format)	.gif	Indexed color, grayscale	• Supports up to 8-bit color, best for illustration graphics or cartoon-like pictures with large blocks of solid color and clear divisions between color areas • a proprietary format of CompuServe • can be used for Web images	Lossless compression method called LZW compression
PNG (Portable Network Graphics)	.png	RGB, indexed, grayscale, black and white	Supports 8-bit and 24-bit color; can be used for Web images	Lossless compression
PICT (Macintosh Picture Format)	.pict	RGB, indexed, grayscale, black and white	Used on Macintosh computers	Allows jpeg compression
BMP (Bitmapped Picture)	.bmp	RGB, indexed, grayscale, black and white	For Windows; good for black and white pictures and also as an intermediary form for color pictures moving from a scanner to a photographic processing program	Allows run-length encoding compression (lossless)
TIFF (Tag Image File Format)	.tif or .tiff	RGB, CMYK, CIE-Lab, indexed, grayscale, black and white	• Supported on both Windows and Mac • common file format • supports alpha channel	Allows uncompressed, LZW compression (lossless), ZIP (lossless), and JPEG (lossy)
PSD (Photoshop Digital Image)	.psd	RGB, CMYK, CIE-Lab, indexed, grayscale, black and white	• Proprietary format of Adobe Photoshop • good for any types of digital images that Photoshop supports • stores layers • supports alpha channel	Lossless compression

TABLE 2.2	Common File Types of Vector Graphics	
File Type	**File Suffix**	**Information and Use**
Encapsulated PostScript	.eps	Standard file format for storing and exchanging files in professional printing
Adobe Illustrator file	.ai	
Adobe Flash file	.fla, .swf	
Windows Metafile format	.wmf	Many cliparts from Microsoft Office are in this format
Enhanced Metafile format	.emf	Developed by Microsoft as a successor to .wmf

Let's look at the size of a typical high resolution image file without compression. A 6-megapixel digital camera can produce digital images of 3000 × 2000 pixels in 24-bit color depth. The uncompressed file size can be computed as follows:

Total pixels: 3000 × 2000 pixels = 6,000,000 pixels

File size in bits: 6,000,000 pixels × 24 bits/pixel = 144,000,000 bits

File size in bytes: 144,000,000 bits/(8 bits/byte) = 18,000,000 bytes

An uncompressed 6-megapixel image would require 144,000,000 bits, which is 18,000,000 bytes of disk space. There are three ways to reduce the file size of a digital image—reduce the pixel dimension, lower the bit depth, and compress the file.

- **Reducing the pixel dimension.**
  This can be achieved by either of the following:
  (a) Capture the image at a lower resolution in the first place.
    - If you are capturing the image by scanning, use a lower scanning dpi. The scanned image will have a smaller pixel dimension.
    - If you are capturing the image by digital photography, lower the image size—the pixel dimension of the digital photo.
  (b) Resample, or scale, the existing digital image to a lower pixel dimension.
      As you see in the file size calculation, the file size is directly proportional to the number of pixels in an image. This means that reducing the pixel dimension in half will lower the file size to half of the original.
      Exercise: The pixel dimension of the image used in this example of file size calculation is 3000 × 2000 pixels. If you scale both the width and height of this image to half (i.e., 1500 × 1000 pixels), how much will the file size be reduced?
      The destined pixel dimension you choose depends on the amount of detail you need in your image and your intended use of the image—that is, whether you intend to print out the picture or display it on a computer monitor. Lowering the pixel dimension sacrifices the image detail, which affects the image quality. Therefore, in reducing the pixel dimension to reduce file size, you need to weigh the image detail against the file size.
- **Lowering the bit depth.**
  The bit depth determines the number of distinct colors available in your image. The available options of bit depth given to you during capturing depend on your scanner

or digital camera. At the time of writing this chapter, the most common bit depth for color digital images is 24-bit.

As shown in the file size calculation for a 6-megapixel, 24-bit image, the bit depth is multiplied by the total number of pixels. This means that the file size is directly proportional to the bit depth. For example, reducing the bit depth from 24-bit to 8-bit will reduce the file size to one-third of the original. Depending on the content of your image, reducing bit depth may produce a very noticeable degradation of the image's aesthetics.

WEIGHING BIT DEPTH AGAINST FILE SIZE

A color depth of 24-bits allows 2^{24} (i.e., 16,777,216) colors—about 16 million colors. 8-bit allows 2^8 (i.e., 256) colors. In reducing 24-bit to 8-bit, you can reduce the file size to one-third. However, you reduce the number of colors from 16,777,216 to 256. That is, you lose about 16 million allowable colors in the image—this is about a factor of 65,000 decrease—to trade for a factor of 3 decrease in file size.

On the other hand, not all images need more than 256 colors. You do not have to keep a higher bit depth than the image needs.

- Grayscale images, such as scanned images of black-and-white photos and handwritten notes in pen or pencil, can have a bit depth of 8-bits without much noticeable degradation in image quality.
- Some handwritten notes even may be reduced to 2-bit or 1 bit.
- An illustration graphic, such as a poster or logo, contains only a few colors as large areas of solid colors and can benefit from a lower bit depth. If you capture these graphics, whether by scanning or digital photography, solid colors (such as Figure 2.10) will become continuous tones. In this case, if you consolidate all these slightly different colors into the one single color it is supposed to be, you may be able to reduce the bit depth, thus reducing the file size. The additional advantage of doing so is that the resulting digital image actually will be more faithful to the ideas of the original analog source in the solid color areas.

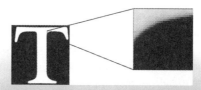

Figure 2.10 A 24-bit scanned image from a book cover has a supposedly solid blue background. The zoomed-in view would show that this square is now made up of many slightly different colors

FILE SIZES OF DIGITAL IMAGES

In a 24-bit color image, you use 8 bits for each of the red, green, and blue components. In principle (using the same pixel dimensions), how many times is a 24-bit image file larger than a file for a grayscale image? The following exercises will help you confirm your answer.

Activity/Exercise

If you have access to Adobe Photoshop, create a new file of 12 × 10 pixels. Convert the image to Grayscale by selecting Image > Mode > Grayscale. Save the image as a RAW file format by selecting File > Save As . . . In the Save dialog box, choose RAW (*.RAW) for the File Format, and name the file grayscale.raw. What do you think the file size of this grayscale.raw is?

Check out the file size.
(For Windows: Right-click on the file and choose Properties.)
(For Mac: Select the file and hit Command-I.)
Answer: The file size of grayscale.raw is 120 bytes (12 × 10 pixels, and each pixel uses one byte (8 bits) to hold its gray value).

Now convert the original image to 24-bit color by selecting Image > Mode > RGB Color. Save the image as rgb.raw. What do you think the file size of this rgb.raw is?

Check out the file size.
Answer: The file size of rgb.raw is 360 bytes (12 × 10 pixels × 3 bytes per pixel; one byte for red color information, one for green, and one for blue.)

As you see, in raw files, 1 byte is used for each pixel in a grayscale picture, and 3 bytes are used for each pixel in a 24-bit image. What if you save the image as another format, such as .PSD, .BMP, or .TIF? Why does the file size change for these file formats? The other file formats may embed additional image information in the file, such as dimensions. (Try opening in Adobe Photoshop the .raw file you have created. Notice that it prompts you for the pixel dimensions of the image and other information. But it does not prompt you for such information if you are opening a .PSD or a .BMP file.) In addition, some file formats are compressed using different compression algorithms. Therefore, the file sizes for the image files in these different formats are difficult to predict by doing simple math. However, it is generally true that the following factors will increase the file size of a digital image:

- Larger pixel dimensions of the image
- Higher bit depth

- **Compress the file.**
  Compression is a method for reducing the size of a file by squeezing the same information into fewer bits. In a lossless compression algorithm, no information is lost. In a lossy compression algorithm, some information is lost. Lossy algorithms, however, are usually designed so that the information to be left out is the information that the human sensory system is not sensitive to anyway.

  When you choose a format in which to save a digital image, you are implicitly choosing whether and how to compress the file. When you scan in a picture, you might be given the option of opening it with an image editing program or saving it as a bitmapped picture, a JPEG file, or a GIF file. The file type is identified by a suffix on the file name: .bmp for a bitmapped picture, .jpg for a JPEG file, or .gif for a Graphics Interchange Format.

  Generally, when working with digital images, it is best to keep the image in an un-compressed format. If you want to compress the image when you are still in the editing stage, you should use only a lossless compression method. For example, you can scan a color picture in as a TIFF file and open it in an image editing program to work on tonal adjustment, contrast, color enhancement, refinements, and compositing. After you have made the desired changes, you should save a copy of this final image either uncompressed or with lossless compression. When you are ready to save the image for distribution, you can choose a different file type with compression, even lossy, as is suitable for the intended use of the image. The file format depends on the type and use of the picture. For the Web, you can save the image as a JPEG, GIF, or PNG file. In the case of JPEG files, you also can choose the extent to which you want the file compressed, trading off image quality for file size that is suitable for your needs.

AN EXAMPLE OF LOSSLESS COMPRESSION

More extensive coverage of RLE algorithm and other compression algorithms can be found in the CS module of this book series.

Run-length encoding (RLE) is an example of a simple lossless compression algorithm. In this method, a sequence of the same repeated value is replaced by one instance of the value followed by the number of times it is repeated. For example, imagine that the color blue is represented in 8 bits as 00001010. If there is a section of sky in a digital image where blue is repeated for 100 pixels, then with no compression this section would require 800 bits. With run-length encoding, we could encode this section as one instance of blue—00001010—followed by the number 100 in binary (01100100). Instead of 800 bits, we've now used 16 bits.

This type of compression is used in .bmp files. For example, the file size of an uncompressed .bmp file of 100×100 pixels is 11,080 bytes. If the image contains only one single color, the file size can be reduced to 1,480 bytes with RLE compression. If the image contains two color blocks (Figure 2.11), the file size is 1,680 bytes with RLE compression.

Figure 2.11 A bitmapped image containing two color blocks

2.7 COLOR REPRESENTATION

Color models are used to describe colors numerically, usually in terms of varying amounts of primary colors. Each model use a different method and a set of primaries to describe colors. The most common color models are RGB, CMYK, HSB, and CIE and their variants.

2.7.1 RGB Color Model

In the RGB color model, the three primary colors are red, green, and blue, and the combination of the three at their maximum intensity yields white (Figure 2.12). This model is appropriate to the physiology of the human eye, which has receptors for the three components. Red light added with green light gives yellow; green and blue given cyan; blue and red gives magenta. Adding full intensity of all red, green, and blue light gives white.

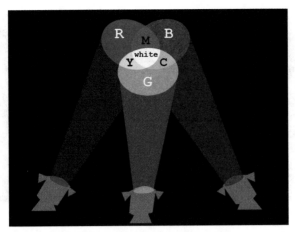

Figure 2.12 RGB: an additive color system

THE HUMAN EYE'S RESPONSE TO COLOR

The wavelengths of visible light range from about 380 to 700 nm (nanometers)—creating a continuous spectrum of rainbow color, from the violet end (380 nm) to the red end (700 nm). A particular wavelength in this spectrum corresponds to a particular color.

The retina of the human eye has two categories of light receptors: rods and cones. Rods are active in dim light but have no color sensitivity. Cones are active in bright light and have color sensitivity. There are three types of cones. Roughly speaking, one type is sensitive to red, one to green, and one to blue. They are designated by Greek letters *rho* (ρ), *gamma* (γ), and *beta* (β), respectively. The curves representing the relative sensitivity of these three receptors for the normal human eye are shown in Figure 2.13. The γ and β cone types correspond quite closely to green and blue regions.

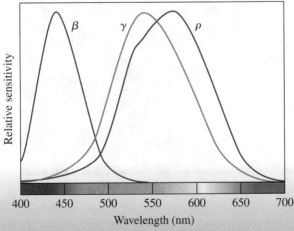

Figure 2.13 Human spectral sensitivity to color

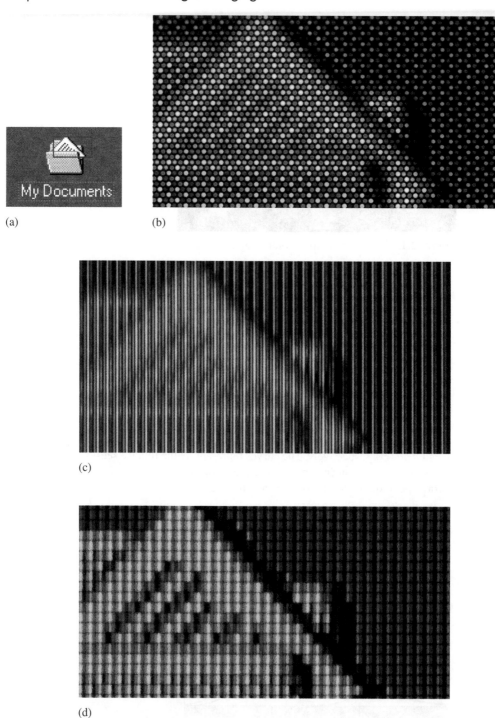

Figure 2.14 Computer monitors (a) An image displayed with a red square where the close-up photographs (b) through (d) were taken (b) Close-up of a standard monitor screen (c) Close-up view a SONY Trinitron monitor screen (d) A close-up view of a LCD display

For computer monitors, colors are represented by points of light. Computers are therefore based on an *additive color system*, where the more colored light is blended in, the higher the overall light intensity.

Computer monitors can be designed so that each pixel's color results from combined beams of red, green, and blue light. The close-up views of two CRT monitors and a LCD display shown in Figure 2.14 show the dots or bands of red, green, and blue light. Despite the different shapes and patterns of the light spots used in the different monitors, each pixel's color of the image is displayed by a combined beam of red, green, and blue light of various intensity.

The RGB color model can be depicted graphically as a cube defined by three axes in 3-D space, as illustrated in Figure 2.15. The x-axis represents the red values, the y-axis the green values, and the z-axis the blue values. The origin $(0,0,0)$ of the RGB color cube corresponds to black. The corners of the cube correspond to red, green, blue, and their complementary colors—cyan, magenta, and yellow— respectively. The corresponding RGB color mode in digital image editing programs usually has values ranging between 0 and 255 for each of the three components, since each component is captured in 8 bits. In this case, white has an RGB value of $(255, 255, 255)$. A light orange can be described as $(255, 166, 38)$.

> 🖱 **RGB Color Cube** An interactive tutorial lets you select a color and display its location in the 3-D space of the RGB color cube. You can drag to rotate the color cube to examine the color location.

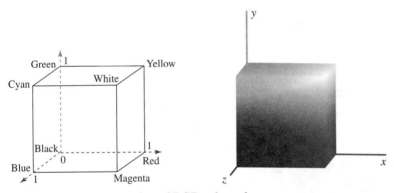

Figure 2.15 An illustration of RGB color cube

CORRELATING RGB COLOR CUBE WITH COLOR PICKERS

If you have worked with digital image editing programs such as Adobe Photoshop, you should have worked with color pickers like the one shown in Figure 2.16.

The color picker is often represented as a 2-D plane made up with gradients of colors. If you choose one of the R, G, or B components in the color picker, the color slider displays the range of color for that component (0 is at the bottom of the slider and 255 is at the top). The 2-D plane next to the slider is a color field that uses the other two color components as the x- and y-axes. For example, if you click the red component (R), the color slider displays the range of color for red. A circle on the color field corresponds to the current selected color.

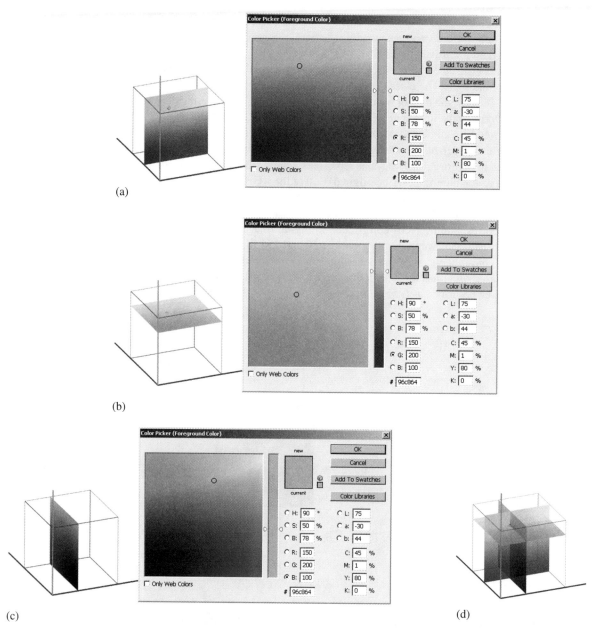

Figure 2.16 Relationship between an RGB color cube and the color picker used in digital image applications

The RGB value is a 3-D coordinate of that color within the 3-D space of the cube. The color field is only a rectangular slice from the RGB color cube. For example, with a color of an RGB value of (150, 200, 100), if you can click on the R component, the color field is a 2-D slice from the RGB color cube at R = 150 (Figure 2.16a) with the green axis as the *y*-axis and the blue axis as the *x*-axis. This is analogous for the selection of G and B components (Figures 2.16b and 2.16c).

As you see in Figure 2.16, the same color can be found on three different color fields or slices. You see one color field at a time in Photoshop's color picker. The choice of the color axis determines which color field is displayed in the color picker. If you imagine that all three slices are showing in the color cube, they will intersect at a single point in space (Figure 2.16d). The 3-D coordinates of this intersection point is the RGB value of the selected color.

2.7.2 CMYK Color Model

At some point in your art education, you may have been told that you could create nearly any color by mixing red, yellow, and blue painting media—crayons, watercolor, oil paint, or acrylics. These three colors are the primary colors in a *subtractive color model*. The model is subtractive in that the more color pigment you layer on top or mix together, the more light you subtract out. Therefore, theoretically speaking, layering or mixing equal amounts of all three primaries gives you black.

> **Color Value Appraisal** Be a "color value appraiser" and see how accurate you can estimate a color's "color value" in RGB.

In the CMYK color model, the three primaries are magenta, yellow, and cyan (Figure 2.17) instead of red, yellow, and blue. *CMYK* stands for cyan, magenta, yellow, and black. Mixing cyan with magenta gives blue; magenta with yellow gives red; and yellow with cyan gives green. In theory, mixing all cyan, magenta and yellow gives black. The CMY are the colors that are complementary to red, green, and blue, respectively. This means that mixing cyan with red gives black. This is same for mixing magenta with green or yellow with blue.

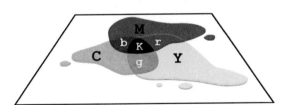

Figure 2.17 CMYK: a subtractive color system, in theory, mixing all cyan, magenta, and yellow gives black

The printing process is essentially a subtractive process, and CMYK is a subtractive color model. When one ink is added on top of another, it can effectively cause its complementary color not to be reflected. In that sense, the color is being subtracted out. Each of these components is specified in percentages.

In theory, (100%, 100%, 100%) gives black. In practice, due to the imperfections in the inks, (100%, 100%, 100%) actually gives a rather muddy brownish kind of black, not a deep black. The last component, K (black), is added to overcome this problem. In addition, using black ink in place of equal amounts of the three color inks is also a cost-effective choice.

2.7.3 HSB Color Model

Although RGB corresponds well to the technology of computer monitors and the physiology of the human eye, it is not necessarily the most natural way for us to think about color. When you have a color in mind, you would probably describe it in terms of its hue first, such as a color found in a rainbow. Then, you describe its brightness. However, it is not intuitive to think in terms of how much of each of the red, green, and blue components to make up the color.

An alternative to RGB is to specify a color by its hue, saturation, and brightness.

- *Hue* is the basic color. It is expressed as a degree between 0° and 360° to indicate its location on a color wheel, in the order of the colors in a rainbow.
- *Saturation* is the intensity or purity of the color—essentially how far away from the neutral gray of the same brightness, that is, how far away from the center point of the color wheel. As a color's saturation value decreases, it looks more washed out until eventually it becomes the neutral gray of the corresponding brightness.
- *Brightness* defines the lightness or darkness of the color. The lower the brightness value of a color is, the more it moves toward black.

This model matches well with the way humans intuitively think about colors. HSB (or HSV) and HSL (or HLS) are this type of color model. There are some differences between the mathematical representations of HSL and HSB, but they are built upon the same concepts of hue, saturation, and brightness.

As shown in Figure 2.18a, the HSB or HSV model looks like an inverted pyramid or cone with six sides—a hexacone. Arranged on a color wheel (Figure 2.18c) is a spectrum of color from red, yellow, green, cyan, blue, to purple and back to red.

- The color or the hue (H) is expressed as a degree between 0° (starting from red) and 360° (back to red again).
- The saturation (S) is expressed in the percentage of distance from the center of the color wheel. The color at the center of the color wheel is a neutral gray of the corresponding brightness.

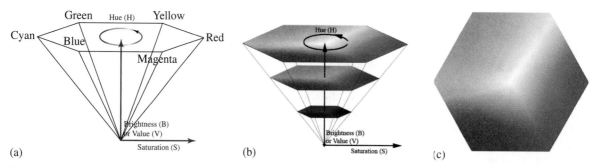

Figure 2.18 (a) Hexacone of the HSB or HSV color model (b) Hexacone with selected slices at different levels of brightness or value (c) A slice of the color wheel from the HSB or HSV color model

- The vertical axis is the brightness (B) or value (V). The higher the brightness or value is, the lighter the color. For example, at B = 0%, the color is black no matter what the values for saturation and hue are. At B = 100%, all colors are at their brightest. White is located at the center of the color wheel at B = 100%.

> ◇ **RGB Color Cube to HSV** A Quick-Time movie illustrating the relationship between the RGB color cube and the HSV hexacone.

HSB VERSUS HSL

HSL stands for hue, saturation, and luminance. The HSL color model is similar to the HSB model. In HSL, the most saturated colors can be found at L = 50%, which is compared to B = 100% in the HSB color model (Figure 2.19). At L = 0%, the color is black no matter what the hue and saturation are. Unlike the HSB color model, when L = 100% in HSL, the color is white no matter what the hue and saturation are.

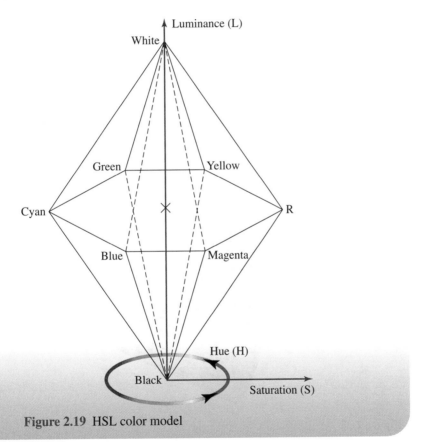

Figure 2.19 HSL color model

2.7.4 CIE XYZ

In 1931, the Commission Internationale d'Eclairage (CIE) worked out a color system to encompass all of the colors that are visible to average humans. It uses three "virtual primaries" designated as X, Y, and Z. These primaries are not any physical colors. With these primaries as the base, it is possible to graphically depict a space to encompoass all visible colors.

The CIE color model has evolved into new variants, but it is still the standard to which all other color models are compared, because its color space encompasses all of the colors humans can see.

COLOR GAMUTS: VISIBLE COLORS, RGB, AND CMYK

Color gamut refers to the range of colors of a specific system can produce or capture. The chromaticity diagram, like the one shown in Figure 2.20, often is used to define, compare, and explain color gamuts.

The given diagram is constructed based on the CIE XYZ color space. The colors encompassed in the horseshoe shape include all the colors visible to human. The boundary line of this horseshoe shape follows the visible color spectrum. Because no printing device can output all of the visible colors, the colors you see in this figure only give you a rough idea the distribution of colors within this color space.

Figure 2.20 is used here to show you a comparison of RGB and CMYK color gamuts. As you see, the combination of the R, G, and B light sources cannot duplicate the full gamut of human vision.

CMYK printers normally have smaller gamuts (Figure 2.20c) than RGB monitors (Figure 2.20b). This means that some colors in your digital images may look bright and saturated on your monitors but may appear a little duller when printed on an inkjet printer or an offset printer in a professional print shop. Printers with more than four colors (such as 6-color printers with additional light cyan and light magenta) can have larger gamuts.

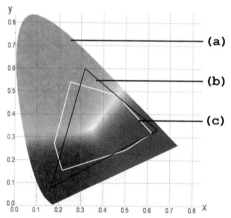

Figure 2.20 An illustration for color gamut comparison: (a) A CIE chromaticity diagram (b) RGB color gamut of typical CRT monitors. The exact shape of the device's color space depends on the monitor's red, green, and blue phosphors. Note that does not include all the colors human can see (c) CMYK color gamut of typical inkjet printers. The exact shape of the color space depends on the colorants of the printer's ink. Note that the three corners of the RGB color gamut that contain the most saturated colors are outside of the CMYK gamut. Also, although the CMYK gamut is smaller than RGB, some CMYK colors are outside of the RGB gamut

2.7.5 Other Color Models

When working with digital images, you also may see a reference to the L*a*b*, YUV, or YIQ color models. These color models divide color into one luminance (brightness) component and two chrominance (color) components.

You are not likely to need the YUV or YIQ models in image editing, although you may read about them with regard to JPEG image compression, video standard, and television transmission. Originally, both the YUV and YIQ models were found to be useful in television transmission (when color TV was invented), because these models separate out the information needed for black and white transmission (all contained in the Y component) from that needed for color. The same signal could then be used for both types of television. YUV was originally the color model for video transmission in Europe under their PAL standard. YIQ is the model adopted by the National Television System Committee (NTSC) in the United States.

The advantages of the YIQ and YUV models in data compression have to do with the way the human eye perceives color. Human vision is more sensitive to differences in luminance than differences in chrominance. Thus, it is possible to reduce the amount of detail in the chrominance information by using a smaller data size for these components. This makes the image data more compact in size.

You may encounter the L*a*b* color model in your work with digital images. Like YUV and YIQ, this model has one luminance component (L*) and two chrominance components (a* ranging from green to red, and b* ranging from blue to yellow). Based on the original CIE model, L*a*b* has the advantage of allowing you to create device-independent colors. That is, with L*a*b* and proper calibration of the display devices involved, you can ensure that the color you see on your own monitor will be faithfully reproduced on another monitor or printer—assuming that you choose colors that are in-gamut for the display or output device.

2.8 COLOR MODES

When you work in an image editing program, there are choices of color modes. For examples, the color modes available in Photoshop includes RGB color, CMYK color, Lab color, grayscale, bitmap, Duotone, indexed color, and Multichannel. You use one color mode at a time for your image file, although you can switch between different color modes during the image editing process.

Some color modes in digital image processing programs are adapted from the color models, but color modes differ from color models. Color modes specify which color method is used to display and print the image you're working on. They also determine the number of colors and the number of channels for the image you are working on.

For example, there are three channels in the RGB color mode—one for red, one for green, and one for blue. In most situations, each channel's default color depth is 8-bits, making the RGB mode 24-bit ($2^{24} = 16,777,216$ colors) in this case. In the grayscale color mode, there is only one channel. By default, the channel's color depth is 8-bits ($2^8 = 256$ colors).

The choice of color mode depends on the nature and intent of the digital image you are working on. Generally, you work and save your original images files in RGB mode. However, CMYK generally is used for images that are to be printed. If you are preparing a digital image for full-color offset printing, it is best to use the CMYK color mode. However, some inkjet printer models recommend RGB color mode. If your image is intended for the Web, then you should stay in RGB mode.

You can switch between different color modes during the image editing process. However, switching from one color mode to another may cause loss of original color information, because each mode has different color gamuts. The out-of-gamut colors will be altered to fit within the new gamut.

COLOR GAMUTS BETWEEN RGB AND CMYK COLOR MODES

Activities/Exercises

The objectives of these activities are to demonstrate: (1) the most saturated colors within RGB color gamut are outside of the CMYK gamut (as illustrated in Figure 2.20) and (2) switching between color modes may lose original color information of the image.

Acitivity #1: Switching from RGB Color Mode to CMYK Color Mode

1. Create a new Photoshop image in RGB color mode.
2. Create three solid blocks of most saturated red, green, and blue with RGB values of (255,0,0), (0,255,0), and (0,0,255), respectively.
3. Switch to CMYK color mode.

You will see these three colors become a little washed out.

If you switch back to RGB color mode, the colors will not be reverted to the original. If you check the color information of these colors using the eyedropper tool, you will see that the RGB values of these three colors are altered. They are not (255,0,0), (0,255,0), and (0,0,255) anymore.

Acitivity #2: Switching from CMYK Color Mode to RGB Color Mode

1. Create a new Photoshop image in CMYK color mode.
2. Create three solid blocks of most saturated cyan, magenta, and yellow with CMYK values of (100%,0,0,0), (0,100%,0,0), and (0,0,100%,0), respectively.
3. Switch to RGB color mode, then switch back to CMYK color mode.

If you check the color information of these colors using the eyedropper tool, you will see that the CMYK values of these three colors are altered. Note that the cyan color has the most significant change. Referring to Figure 2.20, the cyan area of the CMYK color gamut is outside of the RGB gamut.

INDEXED COLOR

An additional color mode available in digital image processing programs is indexed color. It is a technique for limiting the number of representable colors to no more than 256 (8-bit) based on those actually used in the image. The colors used in the image are stored as a palette called a *color lookup table (CLUT)*. Each color in the table is assigned a number or an index. The index number starts with zero. The color information of each pixel in the image is stored as a color number from the palette. This is analogous to paint-by-number art kits.

If the color of a particular index number in the palette is altered, all of the pixels in the image using the color of that index will be changed to that new color. The color is

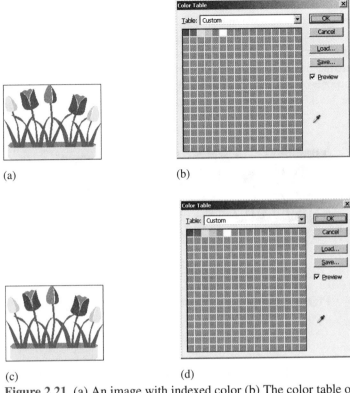

Figure 2.21 (a) An image with indexed color (b) The color table or palette for the indexed colors (c) The image with changes made to the indexed colors (d) The color table reflecting changes in (c)

changed, but the index number remains the same. As you see in Figure 2.21, you can change the color in an indexed color image just by changing the color on the color table or applying a different color table to the same image.

The color table in Figure 2.21b consists of six colors. The color number 0, which is the first color on the table, is the red color. The index for the sixth color, which is white, is 5. In Figure 2.21c the red and orange tulips now become blue by altering the color 0 from a red to a blue and color 4 from an orange to a light blue. The base of the tulip changes from orange to the new light blue, too, because the pixels in that area have the color index of 4. The color numbers assigned to the pixels in the image remain the same. The color table shown in Figure 2.21d shows the changes of color of indexes 0 and 4.

ALTERING COLORS IN CLUT

Activity/Exercise

The objectives of this activity are to demonstrate: (1) how to check out the CLUT of an indexed-color image in Photoshop and (2) how changing the color in the CLUT can alter the color in the image.

1. Open a color image in Photoshop. An image with big blocks of distinct solid colors, such as the one shown in Figure 2.21, will work best for the purpose of this activity. You also can download the sample file (Figure 2.21a) from the Web site of this book or create a new file and add several blocks of colors.
2. Convert the image to indexed color mode: Image > Mode > Indexed Color . . . For the purpose of this activity, any settings for Palette and Forced should work (Figure 2.22).

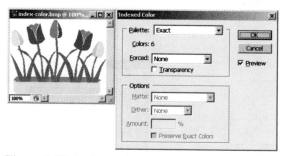

Figure 2.22 An image is converted to indexed-color mode

If your image has more than 256 colors, you will see the option Dither. Make sure to set the Dither option to None. This will help you see the changes you are going to make in the next steps.

3. Check out the color table for this indexed-color image: Image > Color Table . . . You should see a color table similar to Figure 2.21b. Depending on your image, there may be different colors and different number of colors in your table.
4. Try click on a color square in the color table and change it to a different color. You will see all the areas in the image that use this color change to the new color, as in Figure 2.23.

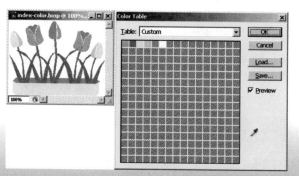

Figure 2.23 The first color (index 0) on the color table is changed to a light blue

2.9 DIFFICULTIES IN REPRODUCING COLORS IN DIGITAL IMAGES

There are at least two common problems in reproducing colors in digital images.

(1) **Digital devices cannot produce all of the colors visible to human.**

Human vision has a larger gamut than the current existing digital devices can produce. The term gamut refers to the range of colors of a specific system can produce or capture. The combination of R, G, and B phosphors of a computer monitor cannot create all the colors human can see. Printers use the CMYK system, which has even smaller gamuts than the RGB system used for monitors (Figure 2.20).

(2) **Difficulties exist in reproducing color across devices.**

The CMYK system used in printing is a subtractive color system, while the RGB system used in monitor displays is an additive color system. The colors in digital images may not be reproduced exactly, whether from monitors to printers or even from one monitor to another monitor. Although monitors and other RGB devices use RGB color models, not all of them can produce the exact same range of colors. Different devices have different color gamuts and color spaces.

COLOR SPACES

Color spaces differ from color models. A color model is a theoretical system that describes colors numerically in terms of primary colors or components. The primary components defined in a color model are used as the model's dimensional coordinates. For example, the RGB color model describes colors in terms of red, green, and blue values. A color space refers to a collection of colors that can be produced based on a color model.

When you work with colors of a digital image in an image editing program, you are adjusting numerical values in the file. These numerical values are not associated with absolute colors. For example, a red color with an RGB value of (255, 0, 0) may appear as different shades of red on different monitors and on prints from different printers. What specific color the numeric value means depends on the color space of the device that produces that color. The numeric value is interpreted by the color space of the device that is reproducing that color. The CIE XYZ color space usually is used as the reference color space for those colors, because it encompass all of the colors visible to human.

Example color spaces are Adobe RGB and sRGB. Both are based on the RGB model and have a triangular shape like the RGB one shown in Figure 2.20. Adobe RGB has a larger color space than sRGB. sRGB is recommended for Web images for on-screen viewing because sRGB defines color space of the standard monitor.

IDENTIFYING OUT-OF-GAMUT COLORS

Out-of-gamut colors are not reproduced correctly. In digital image editing programs such as Adobe Photoshop, you can tell whether a color is out of gamut based on your CMYK setting. In the Photoshop color picker and the color palette, you will see a warning symbol (Figure 2.24).

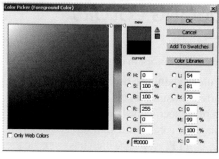 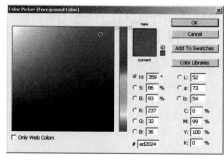

(a)   (b)

Figure 2.24 Adobe Photoshop color picker showing an example of the out-of-gamut colors (a) red color has the saturation S = 100% and RGB = (255, 0, 0). Note the exclamation mark icon ⚠ next to the color chip. It is a warning of out-of-gamut for printing. Clicking on the ⚠ icon gives the closest color in gamut for printing (b) Note the new RGB and HSB values of this new color

The difficulties in reproducing colors across devices and the concepts of color management are discussed in more details in the Art module's digital imaging chapter, Chapter 2.

A *color management system (CMS)* is a software solution intended to help reproduce colors across different devices—digital cameras, scanners, computer monitors, and printers—in a predictable and reproducible way by reading and translating colors between color gamuts of these different devices.

2.10 SUMMARY

Our vision of the world around us is inherently an analog phenomenon. Theoretically, an infinite number of color shades and tones are possible, and points of color in space are infinite because between every two points there is another. Because of the discrete and finite nature of computers, the analog information of natural images needs to be digitized. Digitization involves a two-step process—sampling and quantizing.

The sampling step is to record discrete point samples on an image plane. The point sample is called a picture element, or pixel for short. Each pixel stores the color information of the corresponding position on the image. The position is defined by its horizontal and vertical coordinates.

The sampling rate defines how frequently you take a sample. The higher the sampling rate, the more pixels you will have in the digital image—that is, the higher the image resolution.

The quantizing step is to represent an infinite number of colors and shades with a set of finite number of colors. The number of colors possible is defined by the bit depth.

The sampling rate and the bit depth affect the file size of the image. For an uncompressed file, doubling the sampling rate or the bit depth can double the file size.

Sampling and quantization errors are unavoidable results of the discrete, finite nature of digital media. It is not possible to create a digital version of a photograph or a real-world scene that has absolute fidelity to the original image. However, the human eye is not infinitely sensitive to differences in colors and color gradations across space, so it turns out that digital representations of pictures are often more than adequate for recreations of what we see in the world.

Color models are used to describe colors numerically, usually in terms of varying amounts of primary colors. Each model uses a different method and a set of primaries to describe colors. The most common color models are RGB, CMYK, HSB, and CIE and their variants.

Color modes in digital image processing programs generally are adapted directly from the color models. The color mode you use in an image processing program depends on the nature and intent of a digital image. In general, you work and save your original source files in RGB mode. If you are working for print output, you can always convert the file to CMYK as needed. Keep in mind that CMYK has a smaller gamut, and thus switching from RGB to CMYK may cause some loss of colors. Some inkjet printers, though using CMYK inks, recommend that you keep the images in RGB mode. If your image is intended for the Web, then you should stay in RGB mode.

TERMS

24 bit, 32
additive color system, 43
aliasing, 35
anti-aliasing, 35
bit depth, 31
bitmapped, 33
brightness, 46
CMYK color model, 45
color lookup table
  (CLUT), 50

color management system
  (CMS), 54
color space, 53
HSB color model, 46
hue, 46
indexed color, 50
megapixel, 27
picture element, 27
pixel, 27
pixel dimensions, 27

quantization, 29
raster graphics, 33
rasterize, 35
resolution, 29
RGB color model, 40
saturation, 46
subtractive color
  model, 45
vector graphics, 33

LEARNING AIDS

The following learning aids can be found at the book's companion Web site.

⌁ **Sampling and Quantizing in Digital Images**
An interactive tutorial, complementary to the materials covered in Sections 2.2.1 and 2.2.2 explaining sampling and quantizing in digitizing an image.

⌁ **RGB Color Cube**
An interactive tutorial that lets you select a color and display its location in the 3-D space of the RGB color cube. You can drag to rotate the color cube to examine the color location.

⌁ **Color Value Appraisal**
Be a "color value appraiser" and see how accurate you can estimate a color's "color value" in RGB.

✎ **RGB Color Cube to HSV**
A QuickTime movie illustrating the relationship between the RGB color cube and the HSV hexacone.

REVIEW QUESTIONS

When applicable, please select all correct answers.

I. The process of converting from analog to digital information is a 2-step process— sampling and quantizing. In capturing an analog image to a digital image, the sampling rate affects _____ .

A. the bit depth of the resulting digital image
B. the pixel dimensions of the resulting digital image

2. The process of converting from analog to digital information is a 2-step process—sampling and quantizing. In the quantization step, to capture an analog image to a digital image, _____.

   A. a 2-dimensional grid is applied on the image and each tiny cell on the grid is converted into a pixel
   B. a 2-dimensional grid is applied on the image to apply dithering to the image
   C. an infinite number of color shades and tones in an analog image is mapped to a set of discrete color values
   D. the resulting digital image file is compressed to have a smaller file size

3. Which of the following factors will increase the file size of a digital image?

   A. larger pixel dimensions of the image
   B. higher color depth

4. A digital image captured at a higher resolution _____.

   A. has more details than the same image stored at a lower resolution
   B. represents more colors than the same image stored at a lower resolution
   C. has greater bit depth than the same image stored at a lower resolution
   D. has a larger file size than the same image stored at a lower resolution
   E. has larger pixel dimension than the same image stored at a lower resolution

5. Bitmapped images are composed of _____.

   A. individual pixels which represent spatial samples of the image or scene
   B. mathematical descriptions of image elements which include points, lines, curves, and figures

6. Vector graphics are composed of _____.

   A. individual pixels which represent spatial samples of the image or scene
   B. mathematical descriptions of image elements which include points, lines, curves, and figures

7. The main advantage(s) of bitmapped images over vector graphics is (are) _____.

   A. scalability or resolution independence of images
   B. ease of editing the image content pixel by pixel
   C. more compact file size compared to vector graphics

8. The main advantage(s) of vector graphics over bitmapped images is (are) _____.

   A. scalability or resolution independence of images
   B. ease of editing the image content pixel by pixel
   C. more compact files compared to bitmapped images

9. Generally speaking, how does the file size change if the total number of pixels of an image is doubled?

10. Generally speaking, how does the file size change if the bit depth of an image is increased from 8-bit to 16-bit?

11. Generally speaking, how does the file size change if the bit depth of an image is increased from 8-bit to 24-bit?

12. Sometimes when you magnify a picture on your computer screen, lines that should be straight lines appear to be jagged. This effect is called _____.

    A. anti-aliasing
    B. aliasing
    C. dithering
    D. indexing

13. Give one example of the image file type that supports lossy compression and one that supports lossless compression.

14. The term "pixel" is contracted from the words _____ _____ .

15. **True/False**: A pixel is a point sample, not a little square.

16. **True/False**: An 1-bit color depth allows only black and white colors.

17. An 1-bit color depth allows _____ colors.

18. An 8-bit color depth allows _____ colors.

19. A 24-bit color depth allows _____ colors.

20. Which file extensions indicate graphics/image files?

    BMP   DOC   JPEG   TXT   PNG   GIF
    JPG   PSD   TIFF   EPS   WMF

21. What are the RGB values for (i) white, (ii) black, (iii) red, (iv) green, (v) blue, (vi) cyan, (vii) magenta, and (viii) yellow?
    (You can use the color picker in your image editing program to confirm your answers.)

22. What are the theoretical CMY values for (i) white, (ii) black, (iii) red, (iv) green, (v) blue, (vi) cyan, (vii) magenta, and (viii) yellow?

23. What is the HSB value for (i) white, (ii) black, (iii) red, (iv) green, (v) blue, (vi) cyan, (vii) magenta, and (viii) yellow?
    (You can use the color picker in your image editing program to confirm your answers.)

24. Does RGB model use an additive or a subtractive color mixing method?

25. Does CMYK model use an additive or a subtractive color mixing method?

26. What is the primary use of the CMYK color model?

Capturing and Editing Digital Images

3

KEY CONCEPTS

- Working with scanners and scanning
- Digital photography
- Common tools in digital image editing programs—selection, layer, color and tonal adjustment, fine-tuning specific parts, sharpening
- Working with vector graphics programs
- Image PPI versus Printer DPI
- Printing
- Images for Web

GENERAL LEARNING OBJECTIVES

At the end of this chapter, you should be able to demonstrate that you understand

- Common types of scanners.
- Common tools of image editing and vector graphics programs.
- Common file types for Web images.
- Scanning and printing resolution.
- Image editing processes and tools.
- Scanning and printing resolution.
- File types for Web images.

3.1 INTRODUCTION

The two commonly used methods for capturing digital images are scanning and digital photography. In this chapter, we will discuss types of scanners, common scanning options, and how to determine the optimal scanning resolution. This knowledge will help you capture optimal digital images to suit your expectations.

We will also have a brief discussion of digital cameras. Later in this chapter, we will cover topics on general digital image editing tools, how to determine the resolution for images that are to be printed, and how to optimize images created for the Web.

3.2 SCANNERS

Generally, there are four common types of scanners classified in terms of their mechanisms:

- **Flatbed scanners:** This versatile scanner is the one most commonly used for digital media labs, offices, and personal use. Flatbeds usually can scan documents of letter size (8.5 × 11 inches), legal size (8 × 14 inches), or even 11 × 14 inches on its flat glass plate. The motorized scan head, which consists of a light source and arrays of sensors, is underneath the glass. The scan head moves from one end to the other to capture the image.

Here is a general procedure for scanning a document with a flatbed scanner:

1. Put the document face down on the glass plate.
2. Align the document to the corner indicated on the scanner.
3. Close the flap cover.
4. Start the scanner software and preview the scanning. The scanner will scan the whole scanning area.
5. Select the region that you want if your document is smaller than the available scanning area.
6. Choose the scanning options—if available—such as color mode, resolution, sharpening level, histogram, and brightness/contrast adjustments. We will discuss these options in detail later in this chapter.
7. Finalize the scanning and save the file. You may have many different file formats available.

Digital artists also use flatbed scanners to scan 3-D objects, such as fabrics, keys, dried plants, and hands. In these cases, the flatbed scanner is used like a focus-free camera. When an object is scanned without the flatbed cover, the background appears black, allowing easy extraction of the object to compose with others in a project.

- **Sheet-fed scanners:** Many smaller portable scanners are sheet-fed scanners in which the document moves through a fixed scan head. Because of the feeding mechanism, this type of scanner is not able to scan thick objects, such as a page in a book. Sheet-bed scanners are generally designed to scan no larger than letter-size paper.
- **Handheld scanners:** These scanners are also portable. The basic mechanism of handheld scanners is very similar to that of flatbeds, except that handhelds rely on the user to move the scan head. The scanning width of each pass is limited by the width of the device, which usually is less than the width of letter-size paper. For some models of handheld scanners, the image quality may rely on the user's steady hand movement. In general, handheld scanners do not provide very good image quality, but they offer the most convenient and fastest way of capturing documents. They are most useful for capturing textual documents.
- **Drum scanners:** Drum scanners are capable of very high resolutions and can handle larger documents. They often are used in the publishing industry, where high-resolution images are required, or for scanning large documents, such as blueprints.

Scanners can handle not only paper documents but also film negatives and slides. For certain models of flatbed scanners, you can scan negatives or slides with a negative/slide adaptor.

TWAIN

TWAIN is a standard or specification for the interface between image software and image-capturing devices, such as scanners and digital cameras. Technically, TWAIN refers to an image capture API (Application Programming Interface) for Microsoft Windows and Apple Macintosh operating systems. It is not a driver of any image capturing devices.

The term TWAIN is not an acronym. The word was taken from the sentence "and never the twain shall meet" in Kipling's "The Ballad of East and West"—a fitting description of the challenges of connecting scanners to desktop computers in the early days of this technology. The whole word is capitalized to make it distinctive as a term. For more information, check out http://www.twain.org

3.3 CAPTURING DIGITAL IMAGES BY SCANNING

One factor affecting the amount of detail in a scanned image is scanning resolution. Generally, the higher the resolution at which you scan the image, the more detail you can get. Advertisements for scanners often cite the high resolutions they offer. However, you should beware of these claims, since the term "resolution" can be used in two different ways with regard to scanners. In the scanner specification, you may find two numbers for resolution: one for the optical resolution and one for the enhanced or interpolated resolution.

The ***optical resolution*** is the hardware resolution, which is dependent on the number of sensors the scanner has to capture the image information. On the other hand, the ***enhanced resolution*** interpolates the image using software. The interpolation process increases the resolution by adding extra pixels to the ones that are actually captured by the sensors. Interpolated pixels are not truly or directly captured by the sensors. The color information of these extra pixels is based on the adjacent pixels. Many scanners now have unlimited software-enhanced resolution.

Scanner resolution is usually reported in ***dpi*** (dots per inch). To understand what dpi is and what the practical meaning of this number is, let's consider the general mechanism of a scanner. A flatbed scanner has a moving scan head which contains an array of light sensors. The scan head moves across the scanner bed during scanning. Its movement is controlled by a stepper motor.

So, how is a picture—analog information—captured with only a row of light sensors? To answer this question, we return to the concept of sampling and sampling rate that are explained in Chapter 2. The number of sensors available in this single row corresponds to the sampling rate in the x-direction. The discrete stepwise movement of the scan head is related to the sampling rate in the y-direction. The sensor corresponds to the *dot* in the unit dpi. Each sample results in a pixel of the scanned image. For example, many flatbed scanners now have an optical resolution of at least 2400 dpi on each direction. If you scan a 1-inch-by-1-inch picture at this scanning resolution, you will get an image of 2400×2400 pixels. A detailed discussion of how to determine optimal scanning resolution is in the following section.

3.3.1 Scanning Resolution Determination

You should scan at a high enough resolution (in dpi) to generate sufficient pixels in each dimension in order to produce an image at the expected print size. If you are not sure about the exact final print size at the time of scanning but have only a rough estimate of the print size, then you calculate the dpi based on the largest size. If you scan at a higher resolution than you need, you can always resize the image to a make a smaller print. However, if the scan resolution is not set high enough to produce the required pixel dimensions, enlarging the image later will only add pixels by interpolation. Using interpolation, you do not get additional true color information. The more the enlargement, the more blurry the resize image will appear.

Before making a scan, you need to decide the scanning resolution. How the scanned image will be used determines the scanning resolution.

- Is the scanned image intended for print or Web?
- If it is intended for printing, then what are the physical dimensions of the print going to be and what are the requirements of the printing device?
- If the final image is for the Web, then what are the required pixel dimensions of the image?

Intended for Web or On-Screen Display

If the final image is for Web or on-screen display, then its pixel dimension is estimated relative to the resolution of the intended display device (e.g., monitor).

Suppose the monitor resolution of your target audience is 1280 × 960 pixels and you want your image to appear about half the width and height of the screen (i.e., size of a quarter screen). This means that the resolution of your final image is about 640 × 480 pixels.

Intended for Print

If you plan to print out the scan, you will need to know the resolution requirements of the printing device in addition to the print size (in inches). You should always think of the scan in terms of the pixel dimensions not the ppi or the physical print size (inches). Just like any digital images, scanned images do not possess any inherent physical dimensions. The physical dimensions materialize when the image is printed out, defined by both the image's pixel dimensions and the printing ppi.

The inch in the pixel per inch (ppi) and dots per inch (dpi) is in linear inches, not square inches.

The following equation shows the relationships among pixel dimensions, print dimensions, and print resolution.

$$\text{Pixel Dimensions (\textit{in pixels})} = \text{Print Dimensions (\textit{in inches})} \times \text{Print Resolution (\textit{in ppi})}$$

or,

$$\textit{Print Dimensions (in inches)} = \textit{Pixel Dimensions (in pixels)} / \textit{Print Resolution (in ppi)}$$

Let's see an example of determining the *print size* for a 3600 × 2400-pixel image using the equations.

If this image is printed out on a printer at 600 ppi, then the print size will be 4 × 5

$$2400 \text{ pixels}/600 \text{ ppi} = 4 \text{ inches}$$
$$3600 \text{ pixels}/600 \text{ ppi} = 5 \text{ inches}$$

If this same scan is printed out at 300 ppi, then the print will become 8 × 12.

$$2400 \text{ pixels}/300 \text{ ppi} = 8 \text{ inches}$$
$$3600 \text{ pixels}/300 \text{ ppi} = 12 \text{ inches}$$

If this same scan is printed out at 200 ppi, then the print will become 12 × 18.

$$2400 \text{ pixels}/200 \text{ ppi} = 12 \text{ inches}$$
$$3600 \text{ pixels}/200 \text{ ppi} = 18 \text{ inches}$$

These resulted are tabulated in Table 3.1. This demonstrates that different sizes of prints can be made from the same scanned image by varying the print resolution.

In most situations when you scan a picture, you usually know the size you want for the final print of the scanned image. Now let's reverse the previous calculation process.

Suppose you want to scan a 1 inch × 1.5 inches area of a picture to make a 10 × 13-inch print (on 11 × 14-inch paper) on an inkjet printer. To determine the scan resolution, you will first need to find out the pixel dimensions of the image you need. To find out the pixel dimensions, you need to know the print size and the print resolution.

TABLE 3.1	Various Physical Dimensions, or Print Sizes, from an Image of Same Pixel Dimensions	

| | | Pixel Dimensions | |
Print Resolution		2400 pixels	3600 pixels
	200 ppi	12 inches	18 inches
	300 ppi	8 inches	12 inches
	600 ppi	4 inches	6 inches

Let's step through the math for determining the scan resolution.

Step 1   **Determine the total pixels, or the pixel dimension of final image**
Recall that:

$$Pixel\ Dimensions\ (in\ pixels) = Print\ Dimensions\ (in\ inches)$$
$$\times Print\ Resolution\ (in\ ppi)$$

A print resolution of 150–300 ppi on an inkjet printer will give a good quality print. Let's say you decide to print the image at 150 ppi. The pixel dimensions of a 10-inch × 13-inch image need to be 1500 × 1950 pixels.

$$10\ inches \times 150\ ppi = 1500\ pixels$$
$$13\ inches \times 150\ ppi = 1950\ pixels$$

Step 2   **Calculate the scan resolution (dpi)**
To calculate the scan resolution, you use a similar equation:

$$Scan\ resolution\ (in\ dpi) = Pixel\ Dimensions\ (in\ pixels)/$$
$$Scan\ Source\ Dimensions\ (in\ inches)$$

The scan source in this example is 1 inch × 1.5 inches. Therefore, the scan resolution can be calculated as

1500 pixels/1 inch = 1500 ppi, or dpi (because each dot translates to a pixel in scanning)
1950 pixels/1.5 inch = 1300 ppi, or dpi

The discrepancy between the scan resolution calculations arises from the fact that the source picture and the target print have different width-to-height ratios, which is not an uncommon situation. But which calculated dpi should you use? In this example, no matter what resolution you choose, you will need to crop part of the image if you want the print to be exactly 10 inches × 13 inches.

If you are not sure whether you will crop the image to fit the exact size of 10 × 13, you should scan at the highest ppi calculated—in this case 1500 dpi. Scanning at 1500 dpi will give you an image of pixel dimensions of 2250 × 1500 pixels, which will be 10 inches × 15 inches if printed at 150 ppi. On the other hand, scanning at 1300 dpi will give you an image of pixel dimensions of 1300 × 1950 pixels, giving you an 8.7-inch × 13-inch print at 150 ppi print resolution.

Exercise: Verify that an image of 1300 × 1950 pixels will give you an 8.7-inch × 13-inch print when it is printed at 150 ppi.

Not all inkjet printers can print edge to edge or borderless. Depending on the printer, there are certain minimal margin requirements. In this example, although the image is intended to print on an 11-inch × 14-inch paper, we leave half an inch of margin on all four sides of the paper. Therefore, the dimensions of the image to be printed out are actually only 10 inches × 13 inches.

3.3.2 Tonal Adjustments

Although you can perform color correction and editing after the scanning process, it is best to optimize the tonal range and correct any significant color problems during the scanning process. Why? Because once you have scanned the picture, any image editing you make to the image will be based on the color information you got from the scan. Editing the image later in an image-editing program is not going to create any extra true color information. You will be stuck with a limited amount of information with which to work if you do not get enough color information or sufficient tonal range for the image during the scanning process.

> 🖱 **Tonal Adjustments During Scanning**
> An interactive tutorial that explains and demonstrates why tonal optimization is necessary during scanning.

Let's look at an example. Figure 3.1 shows some examples of scanned images without optimizing the tonal range during the scan. Figure 3.1d shows a comparative scan of the same picture with the tonal range maximized *during* scanning.

The image scanned with a narrow tonal range (Figure 3.1a) looks dull and low in contrast. Although its tonal range may be adjusted later in an image-editing program by stretching its histogram (Figure 3.1b), the result will not be as good as capturing the optimal tonal range during scanning.

Figure 3.1c shows a scanned image with the highlights (i.e., the brightness) clipped off. The pixels whose highlight information is lost all become white. Those highlights that have been cropped off during scanning cannot be recovered by tonal adjustment later in an image editing program.

A histogram is a graph showing the relative number of pixels at each color intensity level. Histogram-stretching concepts and techniques are discussed later in this chapter.

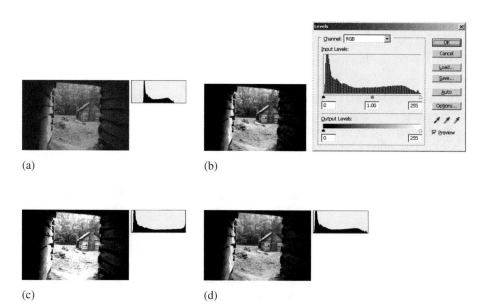

(a)   (b)

(c)   (d)

Figure 3.1 Scanned images with their histograms (a) Scanned using a narrow tonal range (b) The tonal range of the scanned image (a) is adjusted by stretching the histogram (c) Scanned with highlights cropped off (d) Scanned with a maximized tonal range

3.4 CAPTURING DIGITAL IMAGES BY DIGITAL PHOTOGRAPHY

In traditional film photography, the image on a negative is made up of microscopic silver grains. The larger the negative, the more information about the scene is imprinted on the negative, and therefore the more information can be printed on paper. A larger negative takes less magnification to make a big print than a smaller one. This means that for prints of the same size, you get a sharper print from a larger negative than from a smaller one.

Some may consider the storage media used in the digital camera as the "digital film."

Digital cameras, on the other hand, use light sensors as the digital equivalent of film. The light hits the sensor and triggers electrical signals based on the light intensity. Such electrical signals are then converted into digital data and stored on the camera's storing device. Nowadays the sensor that a digital camera uses is either a *CCD* (charge coupled device) or a *CMOS* (complementary metal-oxide semiconductor). The size of the sensor and the number of light-sensing sites determine the maximum resolution of the digital camera.

In traditional film photography, generally, the smaller the grain size, the higher the definition and detail of the image you can obtain. In digital images, a pixel is the basic unit that makes up the image. Therefore, when you look at the specifications of digital cameras, you often see them specified in number of pixels. Digital cameras are often advertised by the number of megapixels. Generally, the higher the number of megapixels, the more expensive the cameras. But what is the practical meaning of the number of megapixels aside from being an indicator of the cost? If you are going to pay more for more megapixels, you should know why and what impact megapixels have on the image quality of your creative photography work.

3.4.1 Megapixels

The total number of pixels in a digital image can be calculated by multiplying the pixel dimension of the width by the pixel dimension of the height. For example, an image of 1600×1200 pixels has a total number of pixels of:

$$1600 \times 1200 \text{ pixels} = 1,920,000 \text{ pixels}$$

One *megapixel* equals 1,000,000 pixels. In this example, the camera can be said to have 1.92 megapixels. The number tends to be rounded up in advertisements, so this camera would be advertised as offering 2 megapixels. The higher the total number of pixels, the higher the resolution of the image. But how exactly does the total number of pixels (reported in megapixels or not) affect an image?

Does a digital camera with more megapixels necessarily offer better image quality?

For the same CCD size, more mega-pixels means smaller sensor sites on the CCD. This in turn means that the sensor is less sensitve to light and may have more noise in the image.

As discussed in the Chapter 2, the resolution of the captured image corresponds to the amount of detail. An image can capture more details from the original scene at a higher resolution. However, higher resolution alone does not necessarily mean higher image quality. For film cameras, with all other conditions being equal, the image quality depends on the quality of the lens optics, the size and quality of the film, and the film grain size. Similarly, the image quality for digital cameras depends on the optics, the size and quality of the CCD, and the camera electronics. It also depends on the camera's image processing software—how it processes the electronic data captured from the CCD into an RGB value for each pixel of the resulting image file.

Does a digital camera with a higher megapixel rating give bigger prints?

The answer to this question either can be "yes" or "it depends." As discussed in Chapter 2, a pixel is a point sample; it does not possess any physical dimensions. The pixel dimensions of a digital image alone do not provide any information about physical dimensions. Recall the equations in the previous section on scanning:

$$\textit{Pixels Dimensions (in pixels)} = \textit{Print Dimensions (in inches)} \\ \times \textit{Print Resolution (in ppi)}$$

That is,

$$\textit{Print Dimensions (in inches)} = \textit{Pixel Dimensions (in pixels)}/\textit{Print resolution (in ppi)}$$

The print size of a digital image depends on both the total number of pixels and the print resolution in ppi. A higher megapixel rating only tells you that the image has larger pixel dimensions—only one of the two variables. *If* the ppi is kept the same, then, yes, the image with more pixels will be printed bigger in size.

PRINT SIZE PER MEGAPIXEL

"Megapixel" is one of those loaded terms in digital imaging. The number of megapixels has been used to label the feature of a digital camera. However, what exactly are the implications of the term "megapixel"? Many consumers are concerned more about the actual print size of an image rather than the number of pixels. Is it possible to correlate the print size with megapixels?

The calculation of print size based on megapixels requires a deeper understanding of how the number of megapixels is calculated. There are many ways to approach the answer. So, let's spend some time analyzing the question and finding a solution.

As discussed previously, the physical size of the printed digital image depends on both its pixel dimensions and the ppi setting. However, given a ppi setting, it is possible to estimate the print size per megapixel.

Complicating the relationship between print size and megapixels is the fact that megapixels represent an "area"—that is, the product of the width (in pixels) by the height (in pixels). If you want to know the print size in width-by-height, you need to know the pixel dimensions of both the width and the height. Just the number of megapixels does not give you this information, because the same area size can be made up with many possible combinations of width and height. For 1 megapixel, the dimensions can be 1000×1000 pixels, 500×2000 pixels, or approximately 1155×866 pixels, and so on. Therefore, to correlate the print size to megapixels, you should think in area (square inches) first.

Approach #1

You first make up a combination of width and height (in pixels) that will come to 1 megapixel—say, 1000 pixels $\times$ 1000 pixels.

If printing at 150 ppi, then for both width and height you set:

$$1000 \text{ pixels}/150 \text{ ppi} = 6.67 \text{ inches}$$

That means 6.67 inches $\times$ 6.67 inches which is **approximately 45 square inches per megapixel**.

Approach #2

Find an actual example of image size of a digital camera. Say, a Nikon D100 can produce images of 3008 × 2000 pixels, i.e. 6 megapixels.

Printing at 150 ppi, you get:

20 inches × 13.3 inches = 266 square inches per 6 megapixels

that is still **approximately 45 square inches per megapixel**.

In the first approach, we assume the width and height are the same. However, in the second approach, we start from 3008 × 2000 pixels and still come to the same number of square inches per megapixel. As you see, no matter what combination of width and height you use—even if you use 500 pixels × 2000 pixels—you will still come up with **about 45 square inches per megapixel** *if* **the image is printed at the same 150 ppi**.

Most digital cameras produce digital images with the width-to-height ratio of 4:3, not 1:1. If you want to take the 45 square inches apart to get a sense of width and height in a print size of **4:3** instead of thinking in area, then you will get a print size of **about 7.6 inches** × **5.7 inches**. (Well, roughly 8 inches × 6 inches if you round it up.)

If the image is in **3:2** ratio, then it will be **about 8.2 inches** × **5.4 inches**. (Note that these numbers are based on printing at 150 ppi.)

Let's emphasize again that the number of megapixels is a *product* of the pixel dimensions of width and height. But the same number of megapixels can be made up of many possible combinations of width and height. For example, both 7.6 inches × 5.7 inches and 8.2 inches × 5.4 inches can be from a 1-megapixel image, depending on the image's width to height ratio. If you are looking for a digital camera that can produce images that can be printed 8.2 inches × 5.4 inches at 150 ppi, you are looking for a 1-megapixel camera. However, this is based on a 3:2 ratio, and a 1-megapixel camera that only can produce images in 4:3 ratio will not meet your requirement.

? Self-Test Exercises: Megapixels*

1. The calculations in the previous example are based on 150 ppi printing. What is the print size per megapixel if the image is printed at 300 ppi?

2. From the previous examples, we have about 7.6 inches × 5.7 inches of print size per megapixel for 150 ppi printing if the image is in a 4:3 ratio.

   What will the print size for 2 megapixels be with the same conditions? Does the calculation involve multiplying both the 7.6 inches and 5.7 inches by 2? Why or why not? If not, then how do you calculate the answer?

⌐ **Worksheet: Making Sense Out of Megapixels** This worksheet guides you in looking up of digital camera specifications and understanding how to calculate megapixels to suit your needs.

---

*Answers to Questions:

1. About 11.1 square inches per megapixels if printed at 300 ppi.
   Explanation: Repeat either of the approaches shown in the example for 150 ppi. Let's follow approach #1. 1000 pixels/300 ppi = 3.33 inches for both width and height. Thus, the area = 3.33 inches × 3.33 inches = 11.1 square inches.

2. Not simply multiplying both dimensions by 2, but by the square root of 2.
   Explanation: For 150 ppi, we have 45 square inches per megapixels. Thus, for 2 megapixels, we have 90 square inches. 90 square inches translate to about 11 inches × 8.2 inches.

3.4.2 Digital Cameras

There are several types of digital cameras. Like traditional film cameras, digital cameras can be point-and-shoot or *single-lens reflex (D-SLR)*. Most D-SLR cameras have interchangeable-lenses. There are now digital camera backs available for selected models of medium-format cameras. Changing from film to digital with one of these medium-format cameras is just a matter of changing the camera back; you do not need to replace the whole camera body. Although this sounds like an economical solution, the digital back is very expensive, generally over $10,000. But the digital back supports higher resolution, for example, 39 megapixels at the time of writing.

3.5 DIGITAL IMAGE EDITING

When you take pictures with a film camera, you can drop the film at a photo store to develop and get prints of the pictures. And that is it. Unless you have access to a darkroom and have experience with darkroom techniques, you do not have much control over the picture's color or brightness or how it is cropped. In digital photography, most of the traditional darkroom techniques have been translated into digital imaging techniques by means of computer graphics programming. Digital image-editing programs are built on concepts and algorithms of computer graphics. But you don't need to be a computer graphics programmer to use image-editing software. At the user level, these application programs employ the language of photography and darkroom techniques, such as dodging, burning, filtering, and cropping.

When you take film to a photo store for processing, you probably do not know too much about how or why the machine produces the pictures in that particular brightness and color. Digital imaging programs allow you to have more control over the image tonal range, color, and even composition, without having to work in a darkroom using photographic chemicals. Now, with the power and availability of digital imaging programs, it is your responsibility to learn how to use the tools *effectively* and professionally to produce *predictable* results. Creating a good digital image still relies on traditional imaging basics, not just the "how-to" of using the digital imaging program.

What can digital imaging tools do? Most of these tools are based on traditional darkroom techniques. If you have experience in darkroom techniques, you already may be familiar with the tasks for which these tools are intended. The common tools available in most digital image editing programs allow you to perform image retouching (such as tonal adjustment, color correction and enhancement) and sharpening. Many programs also have layers that allow you to composite and blend images in more creative ways beyond basic retouching.

You can retouch digital images in many different ways. The general steps are similar to those for traditional darkroom printing. Generally, you need to color correct the images, especially in the case of scanned images. You can correct the color and tonal range problems during the scanning process and/or after the scanning. Many image editing programs, such as Adobe Photoshop, provide a comprehensive set of tools for color correction and image editing.

The general steps and tools for image retouching are explained as follows. Not all of the steps are necessary for all images. For example, dust and scratch clean-up is not necessary for digital photographs directly captured from a digital camera. Cropping and straightening often are not necessary for digital photographs. However, you still may want to straighten crooked pictures or selectively crop pictures to create a better composition.

Single-lens reflex (SLR) An SLR camera reflects the image optically onto the focusing screen or viewfinder by using the light coming through the lens. This means SLR cameras allow you to see the image area accurately from the viewfinder. However, many non-SLR digital cameras now have an LCD for previewing. An interchangeable lens is a lens that can be detached from the camera body and replaced with a different one. Cameras with interchangeable lenses allow you to use a wide variety of lenses, from telephoto and wide-angle to close-up lenses. Lenses generally are sold separately.

Step 1 **Cropping and straightening the image.**
If you scan a picture, the picture may be placed tilted on the scanner glass. Also, you may have included nonpicture areas in the scan. This is OK. You can straighten and crop the scanned image in the image editing program. For example, in Photoshop, you can use the *Crop tool* on the tool palette to achieve the cropping and straightening in one step.

Step 2 **Repairing imperfections.**
Dirt and dust are common imperfections in images acquired by scanning. You will need to inspect for and remove dust, scratches, and blemishes resulting from the scanning process.

One of the common tools for cleaning up these random small imperfections is a clone tool with which you can clone from one area of the image to cover the blemish. This is a direct copying from one part of the image to the other. Therefore, the part that you are using as the source should have the same color and texture as the area of the blemish to cover. Adobe Photoshop also has a tool called the **Healing Brush** that can match the shading and texture of the source with the area to be repaired.

Step 3 **Adjusting the overall contrast or tonal range of the image.**
Many image editing programs let you control the tonal range of the image by adjusting the *highlights*, *midtones*, and *shadows* of the histogram. For example, in Photoshop, you can choose Image > Adjustments > Levels . . . and you can stretch the histogram in the Level dialog box (Figure 3.2). Figure 3.3a shows that the contrast of the resulting image is higher. As seen in Figure 3.3b, the histogram now shows a full tonal range from white to black. But the relative differences in color values among these four colors are maintained after the adjustment.

Figure 3.2 (a) An image of medium contrast consisting of four different colors. Three of the colors have the same number of pixels. The other has three times the number of pixels. No white or black color is in this image. *Note*: Labels in red are not part of the image but are to show you the relationship between the color in the image and its corresponding "bar" in the histogram (b) The histogram of this image (c) Stretching the histogram by moving the highlight and shadow sliders to the edges

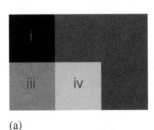

(a)

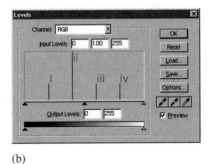

(b)

(c)

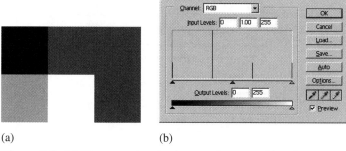

(a) (b)

Figure 3.3 (a) The same 4-color image after stretching the histogram (b) The histogram of this adjusted image

Although there is a ***Brightness/Contrast*** . . . command for image adjustments, stretching the histogram is the recommended tool over the simple brightness/contrast adjustment. This is because the *relative* color information of each pixel in the image remains the same when you stretch a histogram. However, the brightness/contrast adjustments will alter these relationships. (Compare Figure 3.4b to Figure 3.3b.)

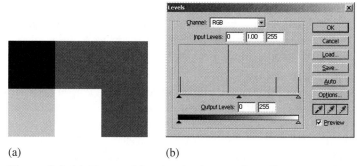

(a) (b)

Figure 3.4 (a) The resulting 4-color image after adjustment using the Brightness/Contrast command (b) The histogram of this adjusted image

Step 4 **Removing color casts.**

An image sometimes contains *color casts*—the image appears tinted. Color casts may be introduced during scanning or may have existed in the original source picture. Many digital cameras have a built-in color correction function. However, sometimes it may not color-correct the way you want, or there still may be a slight unwanted color cast. Image editing programs provide color correction tools. For example, in Photoshop (version 7 and up), a feature called **Auto Color** can automatically detect the imbalanced colors and correct them. You will find it under Image > Adjustments.

Another way to offset the color cast without using the auto function is to adjust the *color balance*. To use this tool, you need to determine the imbalanced colors and

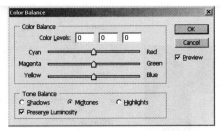

Figure 3.5 A Color Balance dialog box

then balance them by offsetting the color casts. In Photoshop, there are three sliders in the Color Balance dialog box (Figure 3.5), each labeled with a color at either end. The color pairs are complementary colors: cyan–red, magenta–green, and yellow–blue. If your image has a red cast, you should drag the slider away from the red towards the cyan end to offset the red cast. The color correction you make can be applied to the highlights, midtones, or shadows of the image.

Step 5 **Fine-tuning specific parts of the image.**

Note that the editing steps above are applied to the whole image. However, certain parts of the image may need specific enhancements. You can select those parts using selection tools and apply the adjustment. There are also other tools for fine-tuning specific parts of the image without having to make a selection first. Tools such as the dodge tool to bring out highlights, the burn tool to bring out shadows, and the sponge tool to saturate or desaturate colors work like a paint brush (except that you paint to apply the adjustment instead of a color).

Step 6 **Sharpening the image.**

Scanned images usually look a little soft-focused. Scaling an image also can make the image soft-focused. Even if your image is a straight digital photograph from a digital camera, it is a good idea to experiment with sharpening at the end of the image retouching to see if it improves the image's overall clarity. In any case, you should wait to do the sharpening until the final step in the editing process. Why? To understand why the sharpening step should be the last step in the retouching process, you need to understand how sharpening in digital imaging works.

In general, the sharpening algorithm finds edges which are defined by significant color changes. Sharpening creates the illusion of sharpness by lightening the pixels on one side of the edge and darkening on the other side. Thus, applying sharpening will alter the colors in the image, especially where there are color changes, that is, at the edges. Because the edges are detected by the extent of color changes, all the color and tonal corrections or adjustments have to be made prior to the sharpening.

Image resizing has to be done before the sharpening because resizing often softens the image focus. Sharpening should be the very last step of your image-editing project. One exception is when you need to add elements with crisp clean edges, such as a border, to the image, you should do so after the sharpening. The edge of the border may not remain clean and sharp in the final image if you apply sharpening to a border.

The sharpening tool in Photoshop is under Filters > Sharpen. There are four sharpening tools under Sharpen: Sharpen, Sharpen Edges, Sharpen More, and Unsharp Mask . . .

Generally, for professional image editing, ***Unsharp Mask*** is the recommended sharpening tool because it gives you more control on the sharpening settings. Using Unsharp Mask. . ., you can specify:

- Amount: the amount of the contrast increase around the edges
- Radius: the radius of the surrounding area where the color comparison and the sharpening take place
- Threshold: how much the pixels differ from surrounding pixels in order to be identified as "edges" to be sharpened

There are no magic numbers for these settings. It depends on the resolution of the image. For high resolution images, experiment with the Amount setting between 100% and 200%, a Radius setting between 1 and 2, and a Threshold between 0 and 20; lower these numbers for low resolution images. Setting the Amount too high will exaggerate the intensity of the lighter and darker lines around edges creating unnatural halos around edges. The halos will be spread out and become even more noticeable if the Radius setting is too high. If you notice increased graininess and unnatural halos in the image after sharpening, you have probably oversharpened the image.

If you want to limit the sharpening to the more pronounced edges, raise the threshold value. The softer edges will be left unsharpened. The graininess resulting from sharpening is especially an undesired side effect for skin texture. Thus, raising the threshold can be an effective way in sharpening portraits—sharpen the image while leaving the soft skin texture soft. What would be the best threshold setting for portraits then? It depends on your image—its content and resolution. But a threshold setting between 5 and 10 would be a good starting point for you to experiment with.

Try to keep the order of the steps listed here. Performing these steps out of order or jumping back and forth among steps may cause unwanted effects on the image. To understand why the order is important in the image retouching, let's think about the following questions.[†]

1. As mentioned in the scanning process, it is recommended to turn off the sharpening during scanning unless no further image retouching will be performed on the image. Now, in the image retouching process, the sharpening is saved until the last step. Why should the sharpening be one of the final steps in the process?
2. Why should cropping be the first step before you do anything to the image in the image editing program?
3. What happens if you do the dodging and burning *before* removing the color casts?

The word "unsharp" in the unsharp mask sounds counterintuitive to the sharpening function of the tool. However, unsharp mask is a traditional, film technique for sharpening an image by using a slightly out-of-focus (thus unsharp) duplicate negative as a mask. The original negative is sandwiched with this duplicate (an unsharp mask) during printing. This will make the lighter side of the edges lighter and the darker side of the edge darker, thereby making the image look sharper. Heightening the contrast between the lighter and darker lines around edges is basically the same technique of unsharp mask in digital imaging used to create a sharper look in an image.

> ⟲ **Image Retouching (Lab)** Use the example image available from the book's Web site and practice the retouching steps discussed.

[†]Answers to Questions:

1. The sharpening increases the contrast of the edges. This contrast increase may be exaggerated in the problem areas before they are fixed. This may create undesirable effects.
2. If you stretch the histogram before the cropping, you will be including a lot of unwanted color in the histogram that you do not need to take into consideration.
3. Color casts usually appears evenly in an image. The color cast at the dodged or burnt areas will be exaggerated or lessen. Either way, the color cast becomes uneven throughout the image. This will make it difficult to remove the color cast simply by applying one setting of color balance.

3.6 COLOR AND TONAL ADJUSTMENTS

Histograms and their application to color and tonal adjustment are discussed in the following sections.

Use of color curves for color and tonal adjustment are discussed in the Art module, Chapter 3.

There are a variety of color and tonal adjustment tools available in image editing programs. Depending on the program, the controls available in the tools and the interface may vary. However, generally the tools work by mapping the existing color or tonal values of the pixels to new ones. The common tools include adjusting the histogram, color balance, color curves, and hue/saturation. Different tools use different graphical representations to map color or tonal values of the pixels in the image and thus offer different types of control. Adjusting the histogram lets you define and map the shadows, midtones, and highlights using sliders. The **Color Balance** tool lets you offset one color by moving the corresponding slider towards its complementary color. This is useful for removing color casts of images. This tool is discussed in the previous section on removing color casts. The **Curve** tool lets you remap the color and tonal range by altering a curve. The horizontal axis of the graph used in the Curve tool represents the original color values of the pixels (input levels). Its vertical axis represents the new color values after adjustment (output levels). The **Hue/Saturation** tool has three basic controls—hue, saturation, and lightness.

3.6.1 Understanding and Reading Histograms

Sections of 3.6.1 and 3.6.2 are available as a standalone online interactive tutorial at the book's web site. You can read through the text while experimenting interactively in the tutorial. There are two practice exercise sections at the end of the tutorial to test your knowledge of applying histograms to image editing.

What does a histogram of an image represent? A **histogram** is a bar chart that shows the relative number of pixels plotted against the color value. Figure 3.6 shows an example of a grayscale image and its histogram. In this example, the x-axis of the histogram is the gray level (with the darkest value on the left), and the y-axis is the relative number of pixels in the image that have the corresponding shade of gray. The histogram in Figure 3.6b does not look like the kind of bar chart you may have seen in business presentations. This is because this picture has a full range of gray levels and the bars are packed next to each other, making the histogram look like a mountain range rather than a statistical bar chart.

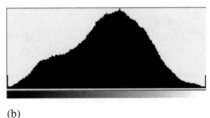

(a)   (b)

Figure 3.6 (a) A grayscale image (b) The histogram of the image

To learn how to read a histogram, let's first look at a very simple image that has only five different gray colors. The image shown in Figure 3.7a has five main different gray colors. Each gray takes up a different amount of space in the image. The background color is the lightest gray in this image. It is represented by the rightmost line (line (v)) in the histogram (Figure 3.7b). Notice that it is also the longest line in the histogram because this background color occupies the largest area in the image. In fact, the line is so long compared to other lines that it is truncated.

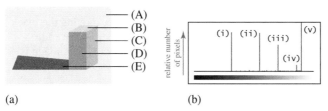
3.6.2 Applying Histograms to Adjustment of Brightness and Contrast

Many image editing programs let you adjust image ***brightness*** and ***contrast*** with the image's histogram. For example, this tool is called **Adjust Levels** in Adobe Photoshop. When you choose to adjust levels, a dialog box will appear showing the histogram of the image (Figure 3.8). There are usually three sliders on the *x*-axis of the histogram:

- A black slider on the left end defines the darkest color (shadow)
- A white slider on the right end defines the brightest color (highlight)
- A gray slider in the middle defines the 50% intensity of the color (midtone)

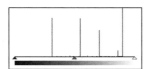

Figure 3.8 A histogram showing three sliders: black (shadow), gray (midtone), and white (highlight)

You can move these triangles to modify the image's *brightness* and *contrast*. You can map the pixels to the darkest by repositioning the black slider. For example, if you drag the black slider to the peak that corresponds to the second darkest gray color (Figure 3.9b), you set this gray color as the darkest color (i.e., black, in the image). Any color that is originally darker than this gray will become black after this adjustment of the black slider. The colors of the shadow and the front of the block were originally different tones of gray. But after

---

‡Answers to the self-test exercises:
  1. (B)
  2. (A)–(v), (B)–(iv), (C)–(iii), (D)–(ii), (E)–(i)

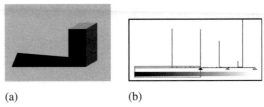

(a)   (b)

Figure 3.9 (a) The grayscale image after moving the black slider toward the right (b) The black slider is moved to where the bar for the second darkest color of the image is

the adjustment, they become totally black and indistinguishable (Figure 3.9a). Therefore, if you move the black slider past the left end of the original histogram, shadow details that were once made up of this area of gray will be lost.

The position of the white slider defines the brightness color—white. Similarly, if you move the white slider to the left, past the right end of the original histogram, the highlights that were once in this area of gray will be lost.

HISTOGRAM

Activity/Exercise

Experiment by dragging the sliders and observe how the position of the sliders affects the brightness and contrast in the image in the interactive tutorial or in Photoshop.

- Drag the white slider to the second peak on the right in the histogram. Note which colors in the image turn white.
- Drag the white slider to the rightmost peak and the black slider to the leftmost peak in the histogram. Note how the contrast of the image changes.

By defining the new positions of the black and the white sliders, you remap the whole spectrum of color values of the pixels. By repositioning the black slider to the leftmost peak and the white slider to the rightmost peak, you *stretch* the histogram (Figure 3.10a). That means you make the darkest color in the image to be black, and the brightest color in the

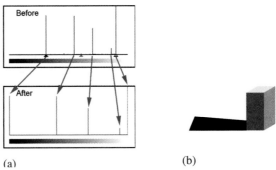

(a)   (b)

Figure 3.10 (a) The histograms before and after stretching (b) The image after stretching the histogram

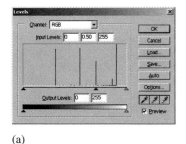 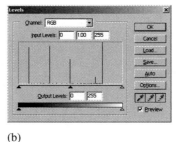 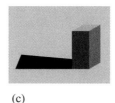

(a)   (b)   (c)

Figure 3.11 (a) The original histogram of Figure 3.7 with the midtone slider moved to the higher value (brighter side) (b) The histogram of the resulting image after the adjustment (c) The resulting image after the adjustment

image to be white, as in Figure 3.10b. All other colors will be mapped in between in the same relationship of their original gray tones. By stretching the histogram, you maximize the use of the full spectrum of the gray tones. The overall contrast of the image is increased by increasing the difference of the color values between colors.

You also can move the gray slider in the middle to set the midtone. For example, if you move the gray slider to a new position, as shown in Figure 3.11a, you set the gray color which is originally a lighter gray to a middle gray (value of 128 for an 8-bit color). If you click OK to accept the change and then look at the histogram again, you will see the bar that the gray slider was repositioned to is now in the middle (Figure 3.11b). That is, the color is changed to middle gray. All other colors are remapped accordingly. As a result, any color darker than it is mapped to between 0 and 128. Any color brighter than it is mapped to between 128 and 255.

Because you shift the midtone to the lighter gray of the original image, the resulted image becomes overall darker.

However, if you shift the midtone to the gray color which is originally a darker gray (Figure 3.12a), the resulted image becomes lighter overall (Figure 3.12c). If you look at the histogram of the resulted image, you will see the bar that the gray slider was repositioned to is now in the middle (Figure 3.12b). That is, the color is changed to middle gray. Again, all other colors are remapped accordingly.

In Figure 3.12, no color is darker than the midtone. Thus, all the bars in the histogram are positioned on the right side of the histogram. The image appears washedout.

In summary, a histogram is a bar chart showing the relative number of pixels versus color values. The color values of the x-axis are usually from 0 to 255. For a grayscale image (like the example shown here), the x-axis has 256 levels of possible gray tones, from 0 to 255—with 0 being black and 255 being white. The middle gray has a value of 128. For a color image, you can choose to adjust the levels for each of the red, green, and blue channels. You also can choose to adjust all three channels together to adjust the image's tonal range.

To illustrate the concept of histograms, the examples here adjusted the levels by moving the three triangular sliders in the histogram. However, many imaging-editing programs, such as Adobe Photoshop, let you adjust the shadows, highlights, and midtones by directly entering numbers in addition to moving the sliders—they also offer more controls and options for tonal adjustment.

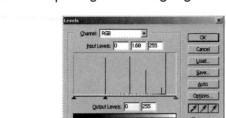 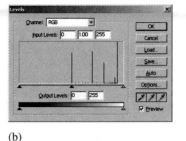 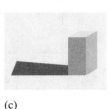

(a)   (b)   (c)

Figure 3.12 (a) The histogram of Figure 3.7 with the midtone slider moved to the lower value (darker side) (b) The histogram of the resulting image after the adjustment (c) The resulting image after the adjustment

It is not only in image-editing programs that you encounter histograms; many digital cameras and scanners show you the histogram of the captured image. This helps you see if you are getting the optimal tonal range of the captured image right away. By seeing the histogram instantaneously, you can decide immediately if you need to take the photograph again while you are on location.

An interactive simulation of photography metering with a histogram is available in the Art module of this book series. This simulation illustrates the relationship between spot metering and the image's midtone.

In Photoshop, you can add a new selection to the existing selection by holding down the Shift key while selecting. Hold down the ALT (Windows) or Option (Mac OS) key for subtracting.

> **Understanding and Applying Histograms** There are two parts of this learning aid: an interactive tutorial and practice exercises. The tutorial explains how to interpret an image's histogram and make tonal adjustments using histograms.
>   To test your knowledge of histograms, check out the two interactive exercises in the tutorial:
>   **Exercise I: Reading Histograms.** Practice relating the appearance of a histogram to the image characteristics.
>   **Exercise II: Improving Image Contrast and Brightness.** Identify the problem of the image by examining the histogram and improve it.

3.7 SELECTION TOOLS IN IMAGE-EDITING PROGRAMS

The ability to select a specific region of an image is crucial in image editing. Often, it is necessary to fine-tune specific parts of the image. If you apply any tonal or color changes on a selection, the changes only affect the selected area; the nonselected area is then protected from the alteration. Compositing or collaging several images together, also require the ability to extract only specific parts of the image, defining the specific parts in the selection process.

There are a variety of selection tools available in image-editing programs. However, instead of trying to list and explain these tools one by one, we will categorize these tools in terms of the way they are designed to work.

- **Predefined shapes:** The *Marquee* tools provide predefined shapes, such as rectangular and elliptical.
- **Lasso:** The *Lasso* tool and **Polygonal** tool let you create a freehand outline around an area you want to select. The **Magnetic Lasso** tool is useful for selecting an area that has well defined edges, because it traces edges.

- **By color:** With the **Magic Wand** tool, you can specify the tolerance or the similarity of the color in the surrounding pixels to be included in the selection. You also can use the **Eyedropper** tool to pick out a color in the foreground color chip, and then choose Select > Color Range...
- **By painting with a brush to select or deselect a specific area:** Editing in *Quick Mask* mode allows you to use the paintbrush to paint in black to deselect, white to select, and grays to create semitransparent areas, as well as feathering and anti-aliasing.
- **By drawing an outline around the area to be selected:** The *Pen* tool lets you draw a vector shape outline around an area that you want to select.

You can combine the uses of the selection techniques to add, subtract, or intersect selections. After you have made a selection, you can manipulate the selection. You can use the **Move** tool to move the pixels in the selected area. You can soften the hard edges of the selection by applying feathering (in Photoshop, choose Select > Feather...). You also can save the selection (Select > Save Selection...) and load the selection (Select > Load Selection...) later. This is particularly useful if the selection you have made requires a lot of steps, time, and labor. It is a good idea to save the selection after each step in case you accidentally lose the selection, and of course, save the final selection so you can load the selection any time later.

> 🖱 **Image Alteration (Lab)** Use the example images (available from the book's Web site) to practice selectively altering areas.

If you move the selection by using any of the selection tools instead of the **Move** tool, you will move the floating selection only. This may be useful if you want to use the shape of that selection for another area in the image.

Screen capture movie introducing the basics of the selection tools in Photoshop is available in the Art module, Chapter 3.

3.8 LAYER BASICS AND ADVANCED LAYER TECHNIQUES

Layers in Photoshop are like a stack of transparencies; the top layer can block out the bottom layer. However, layers are more than that, because you can set the opacity and blending mode of each layer. You can rearrange the stacking order by dragging a layer in the *Layers* palette up or down. Many image-editing programs support layers. The following discussion is based on Adobe Photoshop but should be applicable to other image-editing programs that support those features discussed here.

In Photoshop, there is a special layer called Background which is listed in italics in the Layers palette. This *Background* is not a transparent layer. When you use the **Eraser** tool to erase the image content on this layer, you reveal the color of the current color in the background color chip; a regular layer will reveal transparency. This Background layer cannot be rearranged; it only stays at the bottom of the stack. You can convert the Background layer to a regular standard layer, for example, by double-clicking on the Background layer.

You can create new layers, delete layers, rename layers, control the visibility of each layer, and copy layers from one file to another. You also can apply a layer style (Layer > Layer Style), such as a drop shadow or bevel, to a layer. You can link multiple layers together, so that you can move or scale multiple layers simultaneously.

Adjustment layers are for applying image adjustments, such as levels and color balance, to a layer without altering the pixel content on that layer. Instead, an image adjustment layer is a separate layer by itself. It applies the adjustments to all the layers below it—

Screen capture movie introducing the basics of the **Layers** palette in Photoshop is available in the Art module, Chapter 3.

unless you create a clipping group. The advantage of using an adjustment layer instead of applying the adjustment on an individual layer is that it allows you to change the adjustment settings. In addition, you can delete the adjustment layer to remove the adjustment later, or hide the adjustment effect temporarily by turning off the visibility just like any other layers.

A *layer mask* associated with a layer lets you *obscure*—just block, not delete—part of the image on that layer. This nondestructive method of editing offers the advantage of preserving the original image. Later, if you change your mind in how you want the image on that layer to show, you can edit the mask or remove the whole mask. See Figure 3.13 for an example of a layer mask. The black color of the mask hides the image while the white lets the content of the image show through.

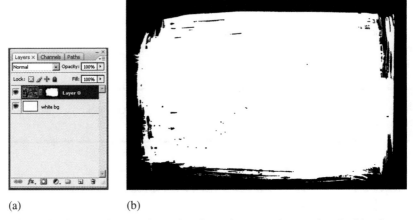

(a)   (b)

Figure 3.13 (a) A layer palette showing a layer mask associated with a layer (b) The layer mask

Clipping groups work very similarly to layer masks (Figure 3.14). While a layer mask is associated with one layer and only masks that one layer, the clipping group works like a cookie cutter cutting through multiple layers that are in the same group. In this example the clipping group is made up of two layers—the base layer (Figure 3.14c) that acts as a mask for the entire group, and a layer with the image (Figure 3.14d).

3.9 PRINTING THE FINAL IMAGE

In real life situations, if you want to change the size of an object, you would think of scaling it up or down. However, the intuitive sense of size that you have learned from the physical world is not always applicable to the concept of size in digital images. Image-editing programs let you resize or scale images by changing the pixel dimensions of the image. There are also options for scaling the physical print size (in inches) in addition to the pixel dimensions. And you can change the print size with or without changing the pixel dimensions.

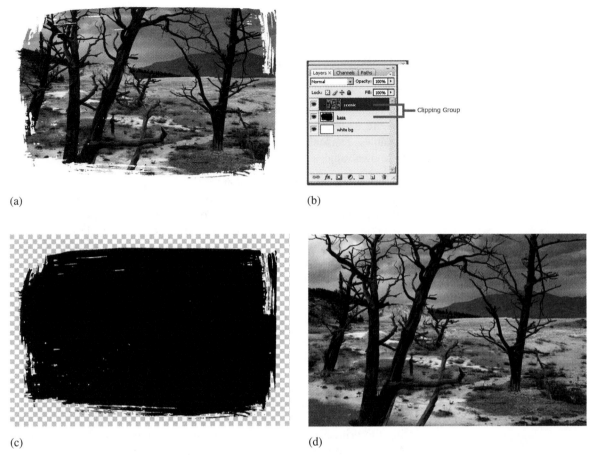

(a)   (b)

(c)   (d)

Figure 3.14 (a) The resulting image using a clipping group (b) The layer palette of the image showing the arrangement of the layers (c) The base layer of the clipping group (d) The image in the non-base layer of the clipping group.

As you have learned from the discussion of sampling and quantizing in digital images, the amount of detail in an image is related to its original pixel dimensions, which, in turn, are determined by the sampling rate. When you increase the pixel dimensions of an image by resizing, pixels are added. But what color information is contained in these new pixels? The color information of these new pixels is generated by interpolating the color information of the existing pixels. Therefore, although the pixel dimensions of the image increase, such resizing does not increase the detail of the image because it is not adding new pixel information. In fact, the resulting image often appears blurry. When you shrink an image by reducing its pixel dimensions, some pixels have to be removed—you lose information. Thus, to produce high-quality images, it is best not to scale the pixel dimensions of the image.

It is important to understand that both the pixel dimensions of an image and the image resolution (ppi) affect the image's print size. This relationship is discussed in the previous section on digital photography. It applies to all digital images, not only images that are obtained by digital photography. Let's revisit the equation.

Print Dimensions (in inches) = Pixel Dimensions (in pixels)/Print Resolution (in ppi)

Note that this equation involves three variables: print dimensions, pixel dimensions, and print resolution. To understand the implication of this equation and the relationships among these variables, let's look at three different scenarios—one variable in each scenario being fixed at a known value.

Scenario 1 **Maintaining the print dimensions**

In order to maintain the print dimensions, increasing the print resolution (ppi) requires higher pixel dimensions. For example, an image of 600 × 600 pixels printed at 100 ppi will give a print of 6 inches × 6 inches. If you want to print at 200 ppi and still have a 6-inch-by-6-inch print, then the pixel dimensions of the image need to be increased from 600 × 600 pixels to 1200 × 1200 pixels.

*Pixel Dimensions/Print Resolution (in ppi) = **Print Dimensions** (in inches)*

600 pixels/100 ppi = **6 inches**

1200 pixels/200 ppi = **6 inches**

1800 pixels/300 ppi = **6 inches**

and so forth.

Scenario 2 **Maintaining the pixel dimensions**

With fixed pixel dimensions, increasing the print dimensions requires lowering the print resolution (ppi). Using the previous example, an image of 600 × 600 pixels printed at 100 ppi will give a print of 6 inches × 6 inches.

***Pixel Dimensions**/Print Resolution (in ppi) = Print Dimensions (in inches)*

600 pixels/100 ppi = 6 inches

600 pixels/200 ppi = 3 inches

600 pixels/300 ppi = 2 inches

and so forth.

Scenario 3 **Maintaining the print resolution (ppi)**

Printing at the same ppi, an image with higher pixel dimensions will give larger print dimensions. Using the previous examples, you will see:

*Pixel Dimensions/**Print Resolution** (in ppi) = Print Dimensions (in inches)*

600 pixels/**100 ppi** = 6 inches

1200 pixels/**100 ppi** = 12 inches

1800 pixels/**100 ppi** = 18 inches

and so forth.

So, how are these scenarios translated into the settings used in an image-editing program? To adjust the output resolution or print size of an image, look in the image size setting. In Photoshop, for example, it is under Image > Image Size...

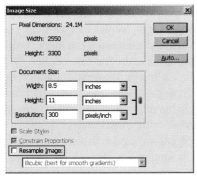
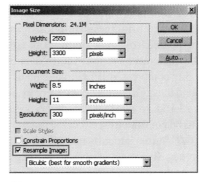

(a)   (b)

Figure 3.15 Adobe Photoshop's Image Size dialog box (a) Uncheck Resample Image option to change settings while maintaining the pixel dimensions (Scenario 2) (b) Check Resample Image option to change settings while maintaining the print dimensions (Scenario 1) or print resolution (Scenario 3)

The setting of the Resample Image option (Figure 3.15) separates Scenario 2 from the other two scenarios. For Scenario 2, in order to maintain the pixel dimensions of the image, you will need to uncheck Resample Image (Figure 3.15a). Then, when you alter the print size, the print resolution (ppi) will be updated automatically and vice versa if you change the print resolution.

If you check the **Resample Image** option (Figure 3.15b), then both Scenarios 1 and 3 apply. With the **Resample Image** option on, the pixel dimensions can be varied. That is, the pixel dimensions can be varied with the print resolution (ppi) while maintaining the print size. They also can be varied with the print size while maintaining the print resolution (ppi).

Printer resolution is measured in dots per inch (dpi)—the number of ink dots per inch. Color inkjet printers produce a microscopic spray of ink which appears to be very tiny dots of ink. These ink dots of different colors—but a limited number of colors—produce the required color by optical mixing. The color of a single pixel of an image is represented by a group of printer dots. Do not confuse the image print resolution (ppi) with the printer resolution (dpi). As you see in the Scenario 2, the print resolution (ppi) affects the print size of an image. However, the printer resolution (dpi) does not affect the print size of the image, but it affects the quality of the print. Generally, the higher the dpi, the smoother the colors appear on the print. However, higher dpi uses more ink and requires longer time to complete the print job.

Turning the **Resample Image** option on means that scaling of the image is allowed. Scaling the pixel dimensions of an image is referred to as resampling because the number of samples (pixels) is changed.

🖱 **Optical Color Mixing in Pointillism, Dithering, and Inkjet Printing** An interactive demonstration on optical color mixing.

🖱 **Worksheet: Image PPI versus Printer DPI** Learn the difference between the printer DPI and image PPI by:

1. Experimenting with how the image PPI affects the output dimensions of the image.
2. Experimenting with how the printer DPI affects the printing quality of the image.

3.10 OPTIMIZING THE FINAL IMAGE FOR WEB

The three image file formats currently supported by Web browsers are JPEG, GIF and PNG. Each employs different compression algorithms to compress the file size. Because of this, each format has its characteristics that work best for different types of images.

To learn more about how JPEG compression affects image quality and have hands-on experimentation on JPEG images, see the JPEG Compression Artifact worksheet in the Art module, Chapter 3.

The *JPEG* format works best with continuous-tone images with a broad color range and subtle color and brightness variations, such as photographs and images with gradients. JPEG supports 24-bit color (millions of colors). JPEG compression is a lossy compression method, which means it loses image data in order to make the file size smaller.

A highly compressed JPEG image tends to blur the image detail and shows a visible artifact around the high contrast edges. For example, note the noises around the dark brown edge in Figure 3.16d. Notice that the solid color areas in the original uncompressed image do not appear to be continuous solid color blocks any more in the JPEG images.

The *GIF* format supports up to 8-bit color (256 colors), and it also supports background transparency. It is most effective for images with solid colors such as illustrations, logos, and line art. It uses a palette of up to 256 colors to represent the image. If the original image has more than 256 colors, then you will need to reduce the colors.

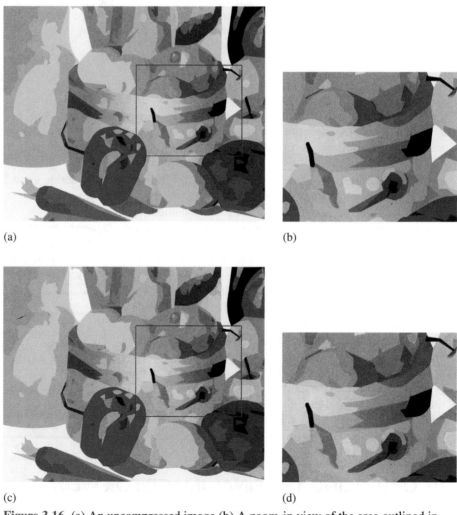

(a)

(b)

(c)

(d)

Figure 3.16 (a) An uncompressed image (b) A zoom-in view of the area outlined in the red box in image (a) (c) A highly compressed JPEG image of (a) (d) A zoom-in view of the area outlined in red in the JPEG image (b) showing the JPEG artifact

There are several color reduction options available, such as dithering options. ***Dithering*** is a technique to simulate colors that are outside of the palette by using a pattern of like-colored pixels. The GIF version on the lower left in Figure 3.17a is applied with dithering. The two versions in the second row in Figure 3.17c are also applied with dithering. The one

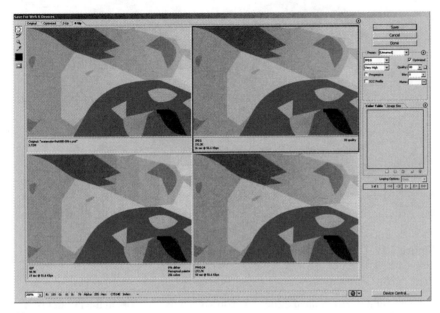

(a)

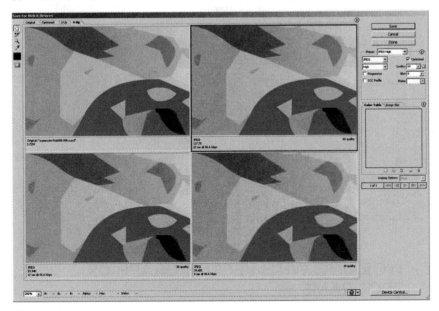

(b)

Figure 3.17 Adobe Photoshop CS3's Save for Web & Devices dialog box, displaying four versions of the image side by side (a) The original uncompressed image, JPEG, GIF, and PNG (b) The original uncompressed image and three different JEPG settings (*continued*)

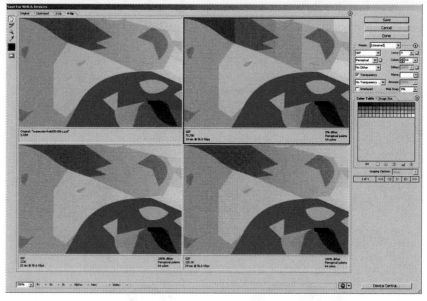

(c)

Figure 3.17 (*continued*) **(c)** The original uncompressed image and three different GIF settings

in the upper-right does not have dithering. You see bands of colors in the gradients. You can also customize the colors to be included in the palette. GIF images can be created as animated sequences and saved as animated GIF files.

The **PNG-8** format uses up to 256 colors to represent the image—similar to GIF. The **PNG-24** format supports 24-bit color and also transparencies. Unlike the JPEG format, PNG uses a lossless compression. Depending on the image and the level of JPEG compression, an image saved in PNG-24 format may result in a larger file than if it is saved and compressed in JPEG format.

Adobe Photoshop CS3's Save For Web & Devices dialog box (Figure 3.17) lets you preview different optimization settings before you save your images into a JPEG, GIF, or PNG. It also shows the estimated file size and download time for a specified network connection speed. Figure 3.17a shows a comparison of JPEG, GIF, and PNG. Figure 3.17b shows three sets of different JPEG settings with the original uncompressed image. Figure 3.17c shows three sets of different GIF settings.

> ⌦ **Worksheet: JPEG versus GIF versus PNG**
>
> 1. Learn to optimize files in JPEG, GIF, and PNG formats and to adjust the compression settings to achieve the balance between the file size and overall image quality.
> 2. Learn the type of images that each of these file formats is most effective at compressing.

3.11 WORKING WITH VECTOR GRAPHICS PROGRAMS

Vector graphic programs work differently from image editing or photographic editing programs because the basic units which they are dealing with are different. Image-editing programs such as Adobe Photoshop are pixel based. Images are represented with pixels. The amount of image detail depends on the pixel dimensions of the image. A bitmap image can be edited pixel by pixel. The physical dimensions of the print size of a bitmap image depend on its pixel dimensions and its image resolution in ppi. On the other hand, a vector graphic is not made up of pixels. Vector graphic programs, such as Adobe Illustrator and Flash, deal with objects or shapes made up with paths, points, strokes and fills.

3.11.1 Paths and Points

A *path* is a mathematical description of an abstract line or curve. It is defined by a set of points, called *anchor points* (Figure 3.18). A path can be open (Figure 3.18a) or closed (Figure 3.18b). Each point has *direction handles* or *tangent handles*. The curviness and the tangent at each point are controlled by its handle's length and angle, respectively (Figure 3.19).

(a)   (b)

Figure 3.18 (a) An open path, point, and handle (b) A closed path

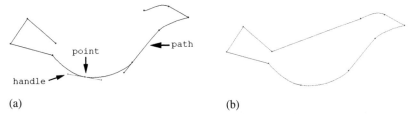

(a)   (b)   (c)

Figure 3.19 (a) and (b) The length of the handles controls the curviness of the path **(c)** The direction of the handle controls the tangent at the point

There are corner points and smooth points. A *corner point* appears sharp and angular. Its handles have zero length. In vector graphic programs, a corner point does not have handles. Corner points (shown in red in Figure 3.20) are used for creating straight segments. A *smooth point* has direction handles to let you adjust the tangent and curviness at the point.

Figure 3.20 A path with corner points

In most vector graphic programs, one of the tools for creating paths is called the **Pen** tool. You use the Pen tool to define points for the path. In Adobe Illustrator, simply clicking with a Pen tool places corner points, but if you hold the mouse and drag, you can extend the handles and change the direction of the new point. A handle has two sides, each of which can be adjusted separately. For example, in Adobe Illustrator, you can ALT-drag (Windows) or Option-drag (Mac OS) on one of the handles to break their dependency, like the middle anchor point shown in Figure 3.21. In addition, corner points can be converted to smooth points at any time and vice versa, by using the **Convert Anchor Point** tool.

Figure 3.21 The direction handles of the middle anchor point are broken out and can be adjust independently

DRAWING PATHS WITH PEN TOOL

The shape of a path is defined by:
- The position of each point
- The length of the handles of each point
- The direction of the handles of each point

The Pen tool lets you hold the mouse and drag to create and adjust the handles while you are creating new points. Many people who are new to the Pen tool often find it difficult to draw a path this way because the shape of a path is made up of multiple points and, on top of this, each point has the three variables you need to worry about.

Don't forget that the Pen tool also lets you simply click (instead of click-drag) to create corner points. You can convert corner points to smooth points later and adjust their handles at any time. This means that you can break up the complex task into multiple, simple stepwise tasks.

The following instructions intend to help you get started with Pen tool by dealing with one variable at a time.

Before you draw a path on computer, do some planning first:

1. Once you have the shape in mind, sketch it out on paper. Suppose you want to draw a path like Figure 3.22.

Figure 3.22 An example path going to be drawn

2. Decide where to put the anchor points and figure out the minimum number of anchor points for the job. If the path is an open path, then each of the two ends of the path needs to have an anchor point.

   To decide where the anchor points are, look for the sharp change of direction. Keep in mind that a C-shaped segment can be created using only two points (Figure 3.23).

Figure 3.23 A C-shaped curve can be created using only two smooth points

   The path shown in Figure 3.22 is an open path. Thus, each of the two ends of the paths will have an anchor point. There is a sharp change of direction in the middle. Thus, we can add one more anchor point there, like in Figure 3.24. Note that the whole path is basically made up of two C-shaped segments.

Figure 3.24 Decide the positions of the anchor points

3. Eyeball the tangent of each anchor point on the curve and sketch it on paper. It will serve as a guide for you to adjust the direction of the anchor points' tangent handles.

   Returning to the example, the tangent for each point can be sketched out, like in Figure 3.25.

Figure 3.25 Eyeball the tangent for each anchor point

   Once you have a sketch, drawing it in your vector graphic application program will be easy.

Activity/Exercise

1. Use the Pen tool to create all corner points, like Figure 3.26, based on your sketch. Only worry about the position of each anchor point for now. Do not worry about the curvature at each point.

Figure 3.26 Create a path with corner points first

2. After you have finished creating a path with all corner points, convert those points that need to be smooth points. Then, adjust each handle based on your sketch.

As you are getting more familiar with Pen tool and using it more often, you may prefer the click-drag method because it saves the step of converting corner points to smooth points.

3.11.2 Strokes and Fills

A line style does not have to be a standard solid line. It can have an appearance of natural media, such as a dry paint brush like the one shown in Figure 3.27c. It can also be a custom defined style, like the fish in Figure 3.27d.

A path does not have a physical appearance—line width or color—until the path is stroked and with a specified line style, width, and color in the vector graphic program (Figures 3.27a and 3.27b). The vector graphic program may be set up to stroke the path by default. If so, whenever you create a path, it will be stroked with a line style. If you set the *stroke* to none, the path will still be there, but you do not see it unless it is being selected and it will not be printed out.

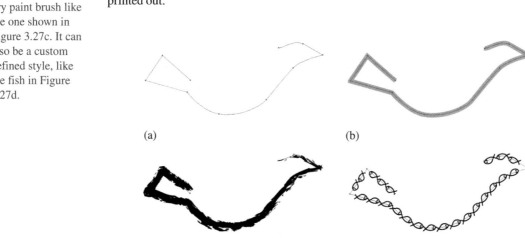

Figure 3.27 (a) A path without stroke (b) The path stroked with a yellow solid line (c) The path stroked with a line of charcoal brush style (d) The path stroked with a line of custom brush style of a small fish

A *fill* is a color, pattern, or gradient inside a shape defined by a path. Usually, fills also can be applied to open paths (Figure 3.28a) in addition to closed paths (Figure 3.28b).

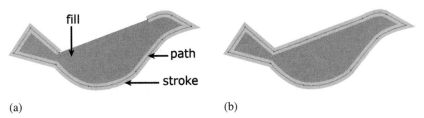

(a)   (b)

Figure 3.28 Path, stroke, and fill (a) An open path (b) A closed path

3.11.3 Preset Shapes and Free-Form Drawing

There are tools to create common shapes such as ellipses, rectangles, polygon, stars, and spirals. Some programs also have a free-form drawing tool with which you can draw a free-form path with a continuous stroke without manually defining the points. However, a freeform path is still made up of points.

3.11.4 Selection Tool

There are two basic selection tools in a vector graphic program: (1) *Selection* tool in Adobe Illustrator and Flash: it lets you select the whole object; (2) *Subselection* tool in Flash or *Direct Selection* tool in Illustrator: it lets you select the points and their handles. Using the Selection tool, you can select the whole object, move, rotate, or scale it as a whole. With the Subselection or Direct Selection tool, you can alter the shape of an object by moving the points or their handles.

3.11.5 Layers, Effects, and Filters

Like many image-editing programs, many vector graphic programs support layers which help you organize and manage the content. For example, you can toggle the visibility and the locking of a layer.

In addition, effects and filters are available in vector graphic programs. Some effects soften the vector graphic to make them look more like bitmap images.

3.12 SUMMARY

In general, there are two ways to acquire digital images: scanning a picture and digital photography.

To determine the scanning resolution (dpi), you need to first determine the final image's pixel dimensions. How you determine the final image's pixel dimensions depends on what the final image is intended for—the Web or print. If it is intended for print, then the pixel dimension of the image can be calculated by multiplying the image's intended physical dimension and its intended printing resolution. If the final image is for the Web, then its pixel dimension is estimated relative to the resolution of the intended display device, such as a monitor.

The equation used for estimating scanning resolution is:

$$\textit{Scan Resolution (in dpi)} = \textit{Pixel Dimensions (in pixels)} / \textit{Scan Source Dimensions (in inches)}$$

If you are scanning a picture, make sure the scan resolution and color mode are appropriate for the way you will use the image. Unless you are not going to do any retouching of the scan at all, you should turn off auto sharpening, which is often enabled by default in many scanner programs. If the scanning software lets you look at the histogram of the scan preview, make sure you are assigning the appropriate tonal range to the scan. It is best to optimize the tonal range and correct any significant color problems during the scanning process. This is because once you have scanned the picture, the color information got clipped off during scanning will not be able to be recovered with image editing afterwards. The quality of your final image depends on the quality of the scan.

There are several steps in image retouching in general. Although not all the steps are necessary, the order of these steps is important.

1. Crop and straighten the image.
2. Remove dirt and dust.
3. Adjust the overall contrast or tonal range of the image.
4. Remove color cast.
5. Fine-tune specific parts of the image.
6. Sharpen the image.

Megapixel is commonly used to describe the resolution capability of a digital camera. A megapixel refers to one million pixels. With the same printing resolution, an image with more megapixels can be printed at a larger size compared to the one with fewer megapixels. Digital cameras that support more megapixels do not necessarily offer a higher image quality; other factors, such as the optics of the camera and how the image data from the CCD is processed also determine the quality of digital photographs. This chapter shows you that for printing at 150 ppi, the print dimensions are about 45 square inches per megapixel. These numbers can be interpreted like these:

- 150 ppi, about 7.6 inches $\times$ 5.7 inches per megapixel for a print of 4:3 width: height ratio
- 150 ppi, about 8.2 inches $\times$ 5.4 inches per megapixel for a print of 3:2 width: height ratio

The physical print size of an image depends on two factors: its pixel dimension and the print resolution. The following equation shows the relationships among these three variables.

$$\textit{Print Dimensions (in inches)} = \textit{Pixel Dimensions (in pixels)} / \textit{Print Resolution (in ppi)}$$

You can adjust the print resolution to suit the print dimension. Be careful not to unknowingly resize the image's pixel dimensions. The Resample Image option in the Image Size dialog box lets you specify if you want to alter the image's pixel dimensions in changing the image size settings.

The two basic and essential tools in digital image editing are selection and layers. Selection tools allow you to limit the editing to the selected area. A variety of selection tools are available for different selection tasks. Layers allow you to organize components of an image, rearrange their stacking order, set opacity, and use blending options.

If the image is intended for the Web, then the image needs to be saved in JPEG, GIF, or PNG format. JPEG works best with continuous-tone images with a broad color range and subtle color and brightness variations, such as photographs and images with gradients. GIF is most effective for images with solid colors, such as illustrations, logos, and line art. PNG has two formats: (1) PNG-24 works well with continuous-tone and (2) PNG-8 (like GIF) works well with solid colors. An image saved in PNG-24 format may result in a larger file than if it is saved and compressed in JPEG format.

TERMS

anchor points, 87
background layer, 79
brightness, 75
CCD (Charge Coupled
  Device), 66
clipping groups, 80
CMOS (Complementary
  Metal-Oxide
  Semiconductor), 66
color balance, 71
color casts, 71
contrast, 75
Convert Anchor Point
  tool, 88
corner point, 87
Crop tool, 70
curve, 74
Direct Selection tool, 91

direction handles or tangent
  handles, 87
dithering, 85
dpi (dots per inch), 62
drum scanners, 61
enhanced resolution, 62
fill, 91
flatbed scanners, 60
GIF, 84
handheld scanners, 61
highlights, midtones, and
  shadows, 70
histogram, 74
Hue/Saturation tool, 74
JPEG, 84
Lasso tool, 78
layer mask, 80
Layers palette, 79

Marquee tool, 78
megapixel, 66
optical resolution, 62
path, 87
Pen tool, 88
PNG-24, 86
PNG-8, 86
Quick Mask tool, 79
Selection tool, 91
sheet-fed scanners, 61
single-lens reflex
  (D-SLR), 69
smooth point, 87
stroke, 90
Subselection tool, 91
tonal adjustments, 74
Unsharp Mask tool, 73

LEARNING AIDS

The Following learning aids can be found at the book's companion Web site.

Tonal Adjustments During Scanning

An interactive tutorial that explains and demonstrates why tonal optimization is necessary during scanning.

Worksheet: Making Sense Out of Megapixels

This worksheet guides you in looking up digital camera specifications and understanding how to calculate megapixels to suit your needs.

Image Retouching (Lab)

Use the example image (available from the book's Web site) and practice the retouching steps discussed.

Understanding and Applying Histograms

There are two parts of this learning aid: an interactive tutorial and practice exercises. The tutorial explains how to interpret an image's histogram and make tonal adjustments using histograms.

To test your knowledge of histograms, check out the two interactive exercises:

Exercise I: Reading Histograms. Practice relating the appearance of a histogram to the image characteristics.

Exercise II: Improving Image Contrast and Brightness. Identify the problem of the image by examining the histogram and improve it.

Image Alteration (Lab)

Use the example images (available from the book's Web site) to practice selectively altering areas.

Optical Color Mixing in Pointillism, Dithering, and Inkjet Printing

An interactive demonstration on optical color mixing.

Worksheet: Image PPI versus Printer DPI

Learn the difference between the printer DPI and image PPI by:

1. Experimenting with how the image PPI affects the output dimension of the image.
2. Experimenting with how the printer DPI affects the printing quality of the image.

Worksheet: JPEG versus GIF versus PNG

1. Learn to optimize files in JPEG, GIF, and PNG formats and to adjust the compression settings to achieve the balance between the file size and overall image quality.
2. Learn the type of images that each of these file formats is most effective at compressing.

REVIEW QUESTIONS

When applicable, please select all correct choices.

1. What are the different types of scanners?

2. What is the method of acquiring digital images besides a scanner?

3. Resampling an image is often referred to as _____ .

    A. rotating
    B. scaling
    C. translating
    D. repositioning

4. Why does scaling an image usually deteriorate the image quality somewhat? In three sentences or less, explain in terms of what happens to the pixels by scaling up and scaling down.

5. Show the math that an image of 1300 × 1950 pixels will give you an 8.7-inch × 13-inch print if it is printed at 150 ppi.

6. Suppose that you scan a 3-inch × 5-inch photograph in at a resolution of 300 dpi.

    i.   What are the pixel dimensions of the scanned image? _____ pixels × _____ pixels
    ii. What will the physical dimensions of the image be if you print it at 300 ppi, without changing the image's pixel dimensions? _____ inches × _____ inches

iii. What will the physical dimensions of the image be if you print it at 600 ppi, without changing the image's pixel dimensions? _____ inches × _____ inches

iv. What will the physical dimensions of the image be if you print it at 150 ppi, without changing the image's pixel dimensions? _____ inches × _____ inches

v. **True/False:** You gain image detail and quality if you print the image at 600 ppi as noted in (iii).

vi. **True/False:** You lose image detail and quality if you print the image at 150 ppi as noted in (iv).

7. **True/False:** When a digital image is printed, each image pixel is represented by one printer ink dot.

8. The "per inch" in the units dots-per-inch and pixels-per-inch are in _____.

   A. square inches
   B. linear inches

9. **True/False:** The optimization of tonal adjustment at the time of capturing images—scanning or digital photography—does not matter because you can always extend the tonal range of the image to any extent afterwards in Photoshop.

10. Given here are the general steps of image retouching of a scanned image.

   i. Order the steps by labeling 1 through 6.

      _____ Adjust the overall contrast or tonal range of the image
      _____ Crop and straighten the image
      _____ Fine-tune specific parts of the image using
      _____ Remove color casts
      _____ Remove dirt and dust
      _____ Sharpen the image

   ii. Explain your choice for the first step.

   iii. Explain your choice for the last step.

11. Suppose you want to scan part of a photograph to use in a digital collage. The part of the picture you want to scan is 2 × 2 inches² on the photograph. You want this scanned piece to appear as 6 × 6 inches² in the final collage that will be printed out at 300 ppi.

   If you scan the picture at a resolution insufficient to print it at a size of 6 × 6 inches² at 300 ppi, you will have to scale up the scanned image, which will deteriorate the image quality and make it look pixelated.

   What is the minimal scanning resolution (dpi) you should use to scan this 2 × 2-inch² area so that you do not have to resize the image to meet the printing requirement? Show your calculations.

   (*Tip*: First calculate the pixel dimensions of that piece of image needed in the final collage.)

12. What kind of images are GIF files most appropriate for?

   A. big areas of solid colors
   B. continuous tone photographs
   C. lots of gradients

13. What kind of images are JPEG files most appropriate for?

    A. big areas of solid colors
    B. continuous tone photographs
    C. lots of gradients

14. Shown here is a grayscale image and its histogram:

 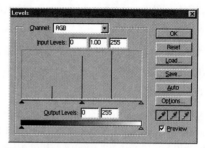

    i. Match each of the bars in the histogram to the color it represents. (Draw arrows linking each bar and the color in the grayscale image.)

    ii. To maximize the contrast and tonal range of this image, what changes of the sliders should be made? Show the new positions of the sliders.

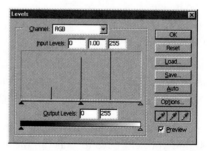

    iii. In each of the four outlines of the next image, predict the resulting grays that are caused by the adjustment made to the image (shown in each histogram to its right). Specify whether it is <u>black</u>, <u>white</u>, or <u>gray</u>. If it is gray, estimate an <u>RGB value for that gray</u>.

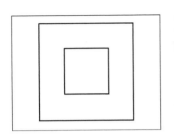
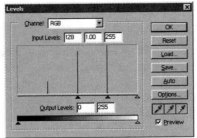

(a)

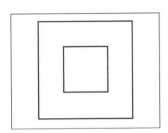
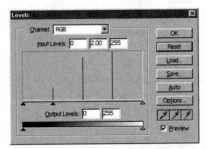

(b)

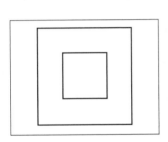
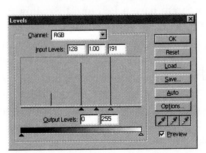

(c)

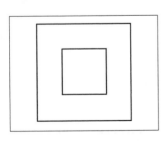
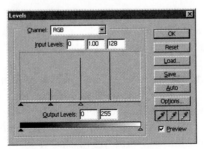

(d)

EXPLORING THE APPLICATIONS

1. Explore the selection tools of your image-editing program. Look up in the Help or the user manual to find out the following how-to's. Write down the answers. Use your notes as a quick reference guide and refer to them as needed. (If your image editing program is Adobe Photoshop, there is a worksheet on selection tools of Photoshop available at the book's Web site.)

- To select all
- To deselect
- To select the unselected parts of an image
- What are the different marquee tools available?
- What are the different lasso tools available?
- To add to a selection
- To subtract from a selection
- To select only an area intersected by other selections
- To expand or contract a selection by a specific number of pixels
- To feather the edge of a selection
- To save a selection
- To load a saved selection
- How do you make selection by color?
- Does your program have a Pen tool that allows you to draw paths to define the selection? If so, find out how it works.
- Does your program let you make a selection by painting a "mask"? If so, find out how it works.

2. Explore the use of layers in your image editing program. Look up in the Help or the user manual to find out information for the following. Note down the answers. Use your notes as a quick reference guide and refer to them as needed. (If your image editing program is Adobe Photoshop, there is a worksheet on layers of Photoshop available at the book's Web site.)

- To create a new layer
- To delete a layer
- To duplicate a layer
- To toggle the visibility of a layer
- To rename a layer
- To set opacity of a layer
- State in one to two sentences the advantage of using layers.
- How do you move the content of multiple layers simultaneously?
- How do you rearrange the order of layers?
- How does the stacking order of the layers affect the image?
- Does your program support layer masks? If so, how do layer masks work?
- Does your program support clipping groups? If so, how do clipping groups work?
- Does your program support adjustment layers? If so, how do layer adjustments work?

3. Explore your vector graphic program. Look up in the Help or the user manual to find out the information for the following. Note down the answers. Use your notes as a quick reference guide and refer to them as needed.
   - Find out the tools for creating paths
     - Pen tool
     - Freeform drawing tool
   - How do you add and delete points of a path?
   - How do you alter the curvature of a path?
   - How do you stroke a path?
   - How do you fill a shape?
   - Find out the selection tools for selecting the whole objects and for selecting the points and handles.
   - How do you create layers to organize the objects?
   - Find out the effects and filters available. Experiment with at least two.

4. Practice creating paths in a vector graphic program. If you are new to the vector graphic program, try to create simple paths like the following images—open and closed paths—using corner points and smooth points. Use the same number of points as shown in the paths.

Also, practice editing the paths by moving the points and their handles. If you are getting familiar with the program, try creating more complex vector shapes.

Fundamentals of Digital Audio

- Sound wave
- Frequency and pitch
- Digitizing sound
- Sampling rate and bit depth of digital audio
- Nyquist's theorem
- Dynamic range
- Audio file size optimization
- MIDI

GENERAL LEARNING OBJECTIVES

At the end of this chapter, you should be able to demonstrate that you understand

- The meaning of the common terms in audio.
- The common file types for digital audio.
- The properties of sound wave.
- The basic steps of digitization: sampling and quantization in digital audio.
- Sampling rate and bit depth of digital audio.
- The difference between digital audio recording and MIDI.
- Decibels in digital audio.
- The basic steps of digitization in digital audio.
- The general strategies for reducing digital audio file sizes.

4.1 INTRODUCTION

Sound is an integral part of our everyday sensory experience. It is also an analog phenomenon. But as is the case with most of our everyday sensory experiences, we seldom think of sound in its microscopic sense. However, in order to understand digital audio, you need to recognize the fundamental nature of sound as waves—the physics of sound. In this chapter we will explain and interpret the graphical depiction of sound as a *waveform*. A waveform serves as a means for us to "see" the information that we hear by providing quantitative properties of a sound, such as its amplitude and frequency.

4.2 THE NATURE OF SOUND WAVES

Sound is a wave that is generated by vibrating objects in a medium such as air. The vibrating objects can be the vocal cords of a person, a guitar string, or a tuning fork. Plucking a guitar string in the air causes the string to move back and forth. This creates a disturbance of the surrounding air molecules. When the string moves in one direction, it causes the air molecules to compress into a smaller space, raising the air pressure slightly in that region. The air molecules under higher pressure in that region then push the other air molecules surrounding them, and so forth. When the vibrating string moves in the reverse direction, it creates a gap between the string and the molecules. This lowers the air pressure in that region, causing the surrounding air molecules to move into that area. The displacement of air molecules propagates, radiating away from the string and causing periodic changes of air pressure—forming a sound wave. When this compression wave reaches your eardrums, it causes the eardrums to move back and forth. This sends a signal to your brain, which recognizes the changing air pressure as a sound. The harder you pluck the string, the greater the movement of the string, which causes greater displacement of the air molecules. This, in turn, causes higher pressure in the high pressure region and lower pressure in the low pressure region of the wave. The amplitude of the sound is higher when the string is plucked harder.

SOUND AS A MECHANICAL WAVE

Because the propagation of a sound wave in a medium relies on the mechanism of particle interactions, a sound wave is characterized as a mechanical wave. The implication of this property is that a sound wave does not propagate in a vacuum.

The motion of a particle in a sound wave is parallel to the direction of the wave. This type of wave is characterized as a longitudinal wave. Notice that it is the *motion* of the particles that propagates, not the particles themselves.

If you place a microphone in the path of the sound wave, the periodic air-pressure change will be detected by the recorder and converted into varying electrical signals. The changes of pressure in the propagating sound wave reaching the recorder are thus captured as changes of electrical signals over time. The sound wave can be represented graphically with the changes in air pressure or electrical signals plotted over time—a waveform (Figure 4.1). The vertical axis of the waveform represents the relative air pressure or electrical signals caused by the sound wave. The horizontal axis represents time.

A vibrating guitar string in the air causes the string to move back and forth, causing periodic changes of air pressure. The changes of pressure in the propagating sound wave reaching the recorder are captured as changes of electrical signals over time. The sound wave can be represented graphically with the changes in air pressure or electrical signals

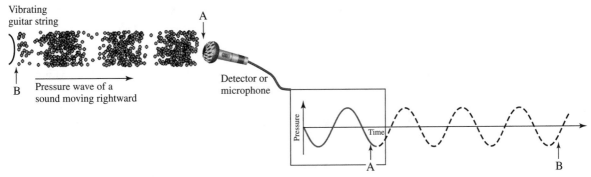

Figure 4.1 A pressure sound wave from a guitar string and its graphical representation

plotted over time—a waveform. Be careful *not* to interpret the waveform as a representation of the sound wave in *space*. The picture on the left in Figure 4.1 is a picture of the air molecules in space. On the right is a graph over *time*. The air-pressure information at point B is *not* where time is zero on the waveform graph. Instead, the pressure information of point B has not yet propagated to the microphone; it would have been after point A has been recorded—about three more cycles to the right of point A on the waveform.

A waveform is a graphical representation of the pressure–time fluctuations of a sound wave. The waveform may be misinterpreted if you are not careful. A sound wave propagates in space. The waveform matches the pressure changes in time at a fixed location. The crests correspond to the high pressure (compression of air molecules), and troughs correspond to the low pressure (rarefaction). The horizontal axis is time. However, looking at an illustration of a longitudinal pressure wave of sound placed side by side with its waveform can mislead you to think of the horizontal axis of the waveform as distance if you are not careful. Remember that the horizontal axis of a waveform is time, not distance. Therefore, when you read a waveform:

> **Sound as a Pressure Wave** An illustration of sound wave as longitudinal air-pressure wave.

1. Be careful *not* to interpret sound as a wave that has crests and troughs like in a transverse wave.
2. Be careful *not* to interpret the waveform as a representation of the sound wave in *space*. Instead, the waveform graph represents the pressure changes over *time*. For example, in Figure 4.1, the air-pressure information at point B is *not* where time is zero on the waveform graph. Instead, the pressure information of point B has not yet propagated to the microphone. It would have been after point A has been recorded—about three more cycles to the right of point A on the waveform.

What information—quantitative data—can we get from a waveform besides visualizing the pressure oscillation of the wave over time? The perceivable properties of sound are the pitch and loudness. The following sections discuss how these two properties are measured and derived from the waveform.

4.2.1 Frequency and Pitch

A sound wave is produced by a vibrating object in a medium, say air. No matter what the vibrating object is, it is vibrating or moving back and forth at a certain frequency. This causes the surrounding air molecules to vibrate at this same frequency, sending out the sound pressure wave. The *frequency* of a wave refers to the number of complete back-and-forth cycles of vibrational motion of the medium particles per unit of time. The common unit for frequency is *Hertz (Hz)* where the unit of time is one second.

$$1 \text{ Hz} = 1 \text{ cycle/second}$$

The period of a wave is the time for a complete back-and-forth cycle of vibrational motion of the medium particles. Shown in Figure 4.2a and b are two simple sine wave waveforms. If the short red line on the horizontal axis marks the first second, then the frequency of the wave in Figure 4.2a has a frequency of 2 Hz, because it completes two cycles within one second. In Figure 4.2b, the wave has a frequency of 4 Hz.

Two notes that are an octave apart correspond to sound waves whose frequencies are in a ratio of 2:1.

Sound frequency is referred to as the *pitch* of the sound. Higher frequencies refer to higher pitches. Generally speaking, the human ear can hear sound ranging from 20 Hz to 20,000 Hz.

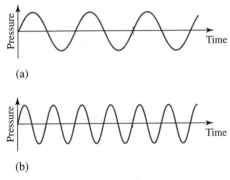

Figure 4.2 Simple waveforms representing two different frequencies (a) Lower frequency (b) Higher frequency

4.2.2 Sound Intensity and Loudness

Sound intensity is related to the perceived *loudness* of a sound, although the two are not exactly the same. Sound intensity is often measured in *decibels* (*dB*). A decibel is based on a ratio of a louder sound to a softer one. By definition,

$$\text{Number of decibels} = 10 \times \log (I_1/I_{ref})$$

(Equation 1)

I_1 and I_{ref} are the two sound intensity values in comparison.

$$\text{Number of decibels} = 20 \times \log (V_1/V_{ref})$$

(Equation 2)

V_1 and V_{ref} are the magnitudes of two electrical voltages or currents in comparison.

Notice that decibel is not an absolute unit. It is an expression of a ratio of two values. More precisely, it is a logarithm of the ratio of two values. The general implication of this is that doubling the sound intensity means an increase of about 3 decibels. Or, a louder sound that causes twice the magnitude of the electric voltages or currents as a softer sound is about 6 decibels higher than the softer one. Why 3 and 6? Let's plug some numbers into the previous equations.

Say that you have a sound whose pressure wave produces an electrical signal V_1, and this pressure is double the pressure of some reference sound (V_{ref}). This means

$$V_1 = 2 \times V_{ref}$$

Plugging this relationship into Equation 2, we get:

$$
\begin{aligned}
\text{Number of decibels} &= 20 \times \log (2 \times V_{ref}/V_{ref}) \\
&= 20 \times \log (2) \\
&\cong 20 \times 0.3 \\
&= 6
\end{aligned}
$$

Similarly, plugging numbers into Equation 1 for the sound intensity gives you 3 decibels. It may seem that this explanation presents more mathematics than you really need to know in order to work with digital audio-editing programs. Some application programs may have the option to let you use percentage for amplitude. However, in many audio-editing programs, the audio amplitude is measured in decibels. In addition, 3 and 6 decibels are given as preset values in amplification filters. Understanding what decibels mean and their relationship to audio signals helps you create predictable results in audio editing.

DECIBELS AND BELS

The unit called a *bel* was defined by scientists at Bell Labs to compare two power values. The unit was named after Alexander Graham Bell. By definition,

$$\text{Number of bels} = \log (P_1/P_0)$$

where P_1 and P_0 are the two power values in comparison. For sound, these can be considered the sound intensity.

A decibel (dB) is one tenth of a bel (i.e., one bel equals ten decibels.) So

$$\text{Number of decibels} = 10 \times \log (P_1/P_0)$$

Note that power equals voltage times current. This relationship leads to the following (which we present without going into the mathematical derivation).

$$\text{Number of decibels} = 20 \times \log (V_1/V_0)$$

where V_1 and V_0 are the two voltage or amplitude values in comparison.

The threshold of hearing is the minimum sound pressure level at which humans can hear a sound at a given frequency. It varies with frequency. Generally, 0 dB refers to the threshold of hearing at 1000 Hz. Note that 0 dB does not mean zero sound intensity or the absence of sound wave.

The threshold of pain is about 120 decibels, representing a sound intensity which is 1,000,000,000,000 (or 10^{12}) times greater than 0 decibels.

LOUDNESS VERSUS SOUND INTENSITY

The loudness of a sound is a subjective perception, but sound intensity is an objective measurement. Thus, loudness and sound intensity are not exactly the same properties.

To measure loudness, a 1000-Hz tone is used as a reference tone. The volume of the reference tone is adjusted until it is perceived by listeners to be equally as loud as the sound being measured. Sound intensity, on the other hand, can be measured objectively by auditory devices independent of a listener.

The age of the listener is one of the factors that affects the subjective perception of a sound. The frequency of the sound is also a factor because of the human ear's sensitivity to different sound frequencies. The loudness of sound (as perceived by human ears) is only roughly proportional to the logarithm of sound intensity. However, in general, the higher the sound intensity, the louder the sound is perceived.

4.3 ADDING SOUND WAVES

A simple sine wave waveform represents a simple single tone—single frequency. When two or more sound waves meet, their amplitudes add up, resulting in a more complex waveform (Figure 4.3). The sound we perceive every day is seldom a single tone. The waveforms representing speech, music, and noise are complicated waveforms that result from adding multiple waveforms of different frequencies. For example, Figure 4.4 shows a waveform of the spoken word "one."

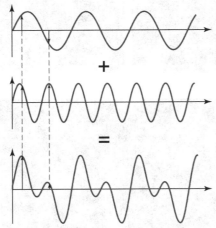

Figure 4.3 Addition of two simple sine wave waveforms results in a more complex waveform

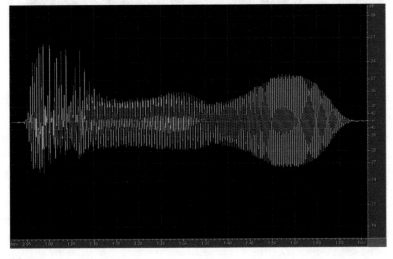

(a)

Figure 4.4 (a) A waveform of the spoken word "one" (*continued*)

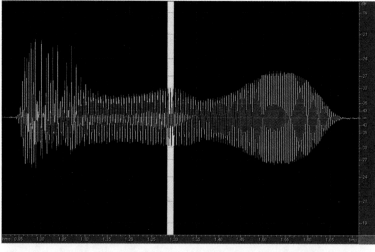

(b)

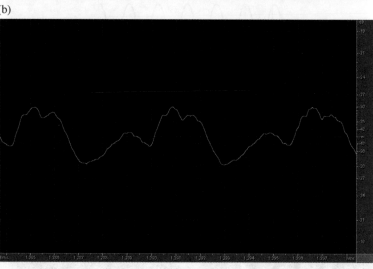

(c)

Figure 4.4 (*continued*) (b) The highlighted segment to be magnified
(c) The zoomed-in view of the segment of the waveform

The mathematical basis of the Fourier transform is discussed in the CS module.

DECOMPOSING SOUND

When we record a sound, such as the spoken word "one" in Figure 4.4, the waveform recorded is a complex one. Can a complex wave be decomposed into its simple component parts—the different sine waves that make up the complex wave? Yes! One of the mathematical methods to accomplish this decomposition is called the Fourier transform.

But why would you want to decompose a complex wave? One motivation is to filter out unwanted parts of complex sounds. When you want to remove certain sounds that can be characterized by a range of frequencies, such as low-pitched noise, you can apply filters using the Fourier transform. These filters are available in many digital audio-processing programs and are used for breaking down a sound and pulling out unwanted frequencies.

4.4 DIGITIZING SOUND

A sound wave is an analog phenomenon. In a sound wave, the amplitude changes continuously over time. Like the process of digitizing any analog information, the process of digitizing sound involves sampling and quantizing an analog sound wave.

4.4.1 Step 1: Sampling

In the *sampling* step, the sound wave is sampled at a specific rate into discrete samples of amplitude values. The higher the sampling rate, the higher the accuracy in capturing the data. However, a higher sampling rate will generate a larger amount of data, thus requiring more storage space and processing time. To give you a feel for the sampling rate for digital sound, the sampling rate for CD-quality audio is 44,100 Hz (i.e., 44,100 samples per second).

> ⏚ **Sampling and Quantizing in Digital Audio** An interactive tutorial illustrating the following sections on sampling and quantizing in digitizing a sound wave.

The common reconstruction of an analog wave from the discrete sample points is not done by keeping the sample values constant between sample points, as shown in Figure 4.5c. Instead, it is usually done by interpolation of the sample points using mathematical algorithms to regenerate a smooth curve. However, no matter what technique is used to reproduce the sound wave, the number of sample points, and thus the sampling rate, is the limiting factor for the accuracy of the reconstruction.

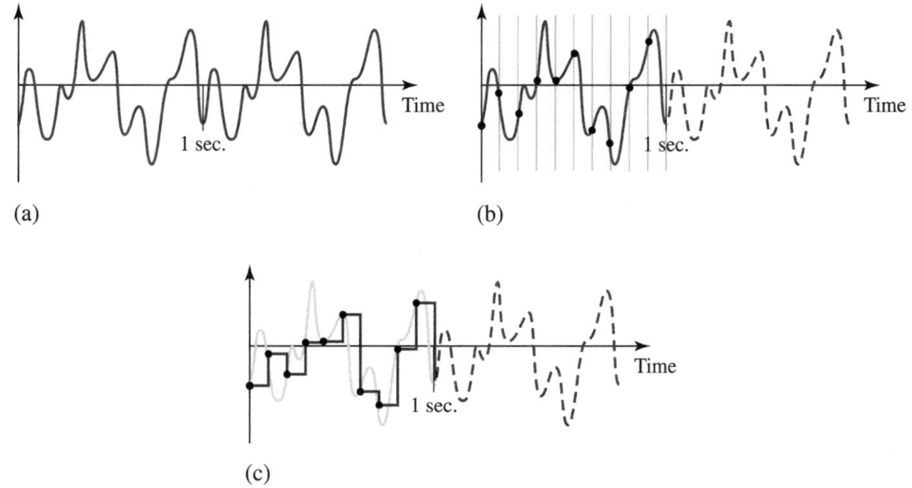

To keep the illustration simple and clear, our examples will use very low sampling rates. These rates are too low to be practical for digitizing sound in real life, but they are simple enough to demonstrate the point. Figure 4.5a represents a theoretical continuous soundwave signal. When we digitize the sound wave, we take discrete samples. Figure 4.5b shows a sampling rate of 10 Hz (that is, taking ten samples of the pressure per second). Figure 4.5c shows a simple reconstruction of the wave by keeping the pressure value a constant between sample points. As you see, any change—crest or trough—between sample points is missed.

Figure 4.5 (a) A theoretical continuous sound wave signal (b) Ten samples of the pressure are taken per second—a sampling rate of 10 Hz (c) A simple reconstruction by keeping the pressure value a constant between sample points

What if we raise the sampling rate to 20 Hz? Figure 4.6a shows a sampling rate of 20 Hz, and Figure 4.6c shows a simple reconstruction of the wave. The reconstructed wave now more accurately represents the original wave than the one sampled at 10 Hz. As you see, a higher sampling rate can increase the accuracy of the reproduction of a sound wave.

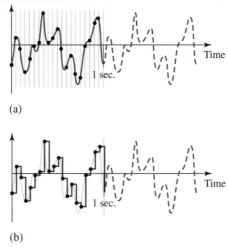

(a)

(b)

Figure 4.6 (a) A sampling rate of 20 Hz (b) A simple reconstruction of the sound wave

Because a higher sampling rate will produce more sample points, the file size of the resulting file will be larger. However, like in the 10 Hz example, any change—crest or trough—between the sample points is missed. This is an inherent limitation of the discreteness of digital data. No matter how high the sampling rate you adopt, there will always be missed points between those discrete sample points.

SAMPLING RATE VERSUS AUDIO FREQUENCY

Be careful not to confuse the sampling rate with the audio frequency. Both the sampling rate and the audio frequency are measured in Hertz (Hz), but they are not the same thing. The audio frequency relates to the pitch of the sound. The higher the frequency, the higher the pitch. The sampling rate refers to the number of samples taken per second for a sound wave. The sampling rate is a characteristic of the digitization process, but the audio frequency describes the sensory characteristics of the sound we perceive. You can set the same sampling rate for different audio frequencies. Also, for the same audio, you can use different sampling rates to create different digital audio files.

4.4.2 Step 2: Quantizing

In the *quantizing* step, each of the discrete samples of amplitude values obtained from the sampling step will be mapped and rounded to the nearest value on a scale of discrete levels. Therefore, the more levels available in the scale, the higher the accuracy in reproducing the sound. Having more levels means higher *resolution*. However, higher resolution will require more storage space. The number of levels in the scale is expressed in *bit depth*—the power of 2. For example, an 8-bit audio allows $2^8 = 256$ possible levels in the scale. To give you a feel of the bit depth for digital sound, CD-quality audio is 16-bit (i.e., $2^{16} = 65536$ possible levels in quantizing the samples of amplitude values).

For demonstration purposes, we use 3-bit as an example, which is a scale of eight discrete levels. Again, 3-bit is not a practical bit depth used in real life applications. The sampled data are mapped to the nearest level on the scale (Figure 4.7). Some samples may deviate more from their original amplitudes. With a low bit depth, data with different original amplitudes may be quantized onto the same level—for example, note the quantized sample points of the last six sample points in Figure 4.7b.

> 🔊 **Audio Examples (a Short Musical Sound and a Sound Effect) with Various Combinations of Sampling Rate and Bit Depth** Audio examples of a short musical sound and an explosion sound effect with various sampling rates (44,100 Hz, 22,050 Hz, and 11,025 Hz) and bit depths (8-bit and 16-bit) are used to demonstrate the impact of sampling rate and bit depth on (i) the audio quality and (ii) the file size. Review questions of the impact, the audio's waveforms, and frequency spectral views are also available.

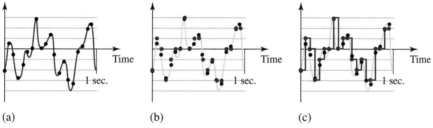

(a) (b) (c)

Figure 4.7 Quantizing with 3-bit resolution

4.5 DYNAMIC RANGE

In the quantization step, a scale of discrete levels of amplitude values is used to map the sample points. The range of the scale, from the lowest to highest possible quantization values in the scale, defines the *dynamic range* for digitizing audio. In the quantization example of the previous section, where a scale of eight levels (3-bit samples) is used, the lowest level of the scale is placed at about the lowest amplitude of the sound wave and the highest level at about the highest point of the sound wave. The remaining six levels are equally spaced in between these two levels. This scale is extended to include the highest and lowest amplitude values of the sound wave. That is, none of the sample points is outside of this range. The scale covers a full amplitude range of the sound wave, shown in Figure 4.8.

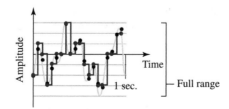

Figure 4.8 Quantization using a scale range equal to the full amplitude range of the sound wave

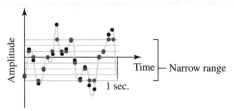

Figure 4.9 Quantization using a scale range narrower than the full amplitude range of the sound wave

If the dynamic range is smaller than the full amplitude range of the sound wave (Figure 4.9), some data will be lost. The digitized sound wave will be "chopped" off at the limit of the range, causing clipping of the sound wave. Clipping is an undesirable effect because of loss of data. The clipped amplitude values are not recoverable. However, with a reduced dynamic range, the accuracy can be improved for the data within the range. This is an advantage, especially if the majority of the sample points are within a smaller middle region of the range. By sacrificing the smaller number of highest and lowest amplitude values, the accuracy of the majority of the amplitude values of the sample points of the sound wave can be improved. In the simple example shown in Figure 4.9, you see that (with the same bit depth) reducing the dynamic range actually allows more subtle changes to be distinguishable (Figure 4.10). Instead of being quantized to the same value, more data can now be set apart on different levels.

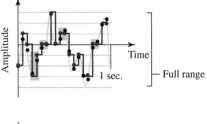

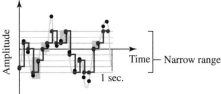

Figure 4.10 The quantized data (shaded in blue) in which subtle changes become more distinguishable in the reduced dynamic range than the full range

Dynamic range of a sound system refers to the range of the highest and lowest sound levels that the system can reproduce. In this context, a larger dynamic range is considered better because the sound system can then allow you to input audio components with wider ranges and it can output the audio within the full range with minimal distortion.

What if you extend the dynamic range to more than the amplitude range of the sound wave? Then you will get the opposite result of reducing the dynamic range—the accuracy will be lost. As you see in Figure 4.11, the amplitude of the sound wave is now within only six levels of the range. So, although this extended dynamic range has eight quantization levels available, only six levels are utilized for this sound wave.

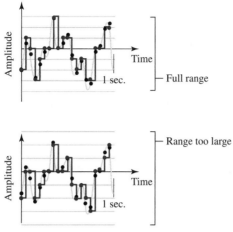

Figure 4.11 Comparing quantization using two ranges of scale: the full amplitude range of the sound wave, and one wider than the full amplitude range

4.6 FILE SIZE, FILE COMPRESSION, AND FILE TYPES OF DIGITAL AUDIO

Higher sampling rate and bit depth always deliver better fidelity of a digitized file—whether it is an image or audio. So the recurring question may come up again: If higher sampling rate and bit depth give better sound quality and less degradation, then why shouldn't we always choose the maximum possible values? Well, the answer to this question is always the file size. Large file sizes require more storage space, longer processing time, and longer transfer time. Especially if the digital media files are created for use on the internet, the network transfer time of a file is often a more important consideration than the storage space, which is becoming less expensive. The larger the file size, the longer it will take to download to another person's computer.

In addition to the sampling rate and bit depth, do not forget the duration of the audio as a factor of the file size, too. Audio is a time-based medium. Audio files (such as speech and music) require long, continuous playback. Therefore, the file size increases very rapidly with a higher sampling rate and bit depth. Let's look at an example of a one-minute CD-quality stereo audio. A stereo audio has two **channels**—a left channel and a right channel. The bit depth of CD-quality audio is 16-bit per channel—16 bits per sample for each channel. Its sampling rate is 44.1 kHz—that is, 44,100 samples per second.

$$1 \text{ minute} \times 60 \text{ seconds/minute} = 60 \text{ seconds}$$
$$60 \text{ seconds} \times 44,100 \text{ samples/second} = 2,646,000 \text{ samples}$$
$$2,646,000 \text{ samples} \times 16 \text{ bits/sample} = 42,336,000 \text{ bits}$$

Because stereo audio has two channels, the total bit size = 42,336,000 bits $\times$ 2 = 84,672,000 bits.

To convert the bit size into bytes,

$$84,672,000 \text{ bits}/(8 \text{ bits/byte}) = 10,584,000 \text{ bytes} \cong 10 \text{ MB}$$

In reality, because of other factors such as network traffic, you do not get a full 56 kbps with a 56K modem. It takes more than 25 minutes to transfer a 10-MB file with a 56K modem.

As you see, it requires about 10 MB for each minute of CD quality audio. An hour of such audio requires about 600 MB. If you post this one minute audio on the Web, the time it takes to download with 1.5 Mbps (mega bits per second) broadband speed is no less than

$$84{,}672{,}000 \text{ bits}/(1{,}500{,}000 \text{ bits/second}) = 56 \text{ seconds}$$

As you may recall from Chapter 1, the three general strategies of reducing a digital media file size include reducing the sampling rate, reducing bit depth, and applying file compression. As you see in the file size calculation,

File size = duration × sampling rate × bit depth × number of channels

The equation for calculating audio file size includes an additional factor—the number of channels. Therefore, by examining the equation of audio file-size calculation, you see four general strategies of reducing a digital audio file's size.

- Reduce the sampling rate
- Reduce the bit depth
- Apply compression
- Reduce the number of channels

Note that duration of the audio is also a factor in the equation for file-size calculation. We do not include reduction of audio duration in the listed strategies because, in most situations, you want to keep the duration of the audio. However, keep in mind that duration of the audio has a direct effect on the file size. You may want to remove the unnecessary silent segments in an audio file where possible. For example, most voice-over or speech contains unnecessary silence or pauses that may be removed to reduce the audio duration and thus the file size.

- **Reducing the number of channels.**
  Stereo audio has two channels. If you reduce a stereo audio file to mono—which becomes one channel—then you reduce the file size in half. This may suit speech and short sound effects for online games. Your decision to reduce the audio from stereo to mono is very much dependent on the nature of your project. Reducing a channel causes a noticeable difference unless your final product is expected to be listened to with a mono-speaker.
- **Reducing the sampling rate.**
  Reducing the sampling rate and bit depth sacrifices the fidelity of the digitized audio, which means it will not sound like the original. However, when working with digital media files, you often have to weigh the quality against the file size. No matter which strategy you use to preserve the optimal quality of the media while reducing the file size, you often need to take into consideration both human perception of the medium and how you're going to use the audio.

  First, let's consider that the human ear can hear sound ranging from approximately 20 Hz to 20,000 Hz. The range varies with individuals and their ages. Not all people can hear the two ends of the average range. The human ear is most sensitive in the range of about 2,000 to 5,000 Hz, not the two ends of the range.

  Second, according to a rule called *Nyquist's theorem*, we must sample at least two points in each sound wave cycle to be able to reconstruct the sound wave satisfactorily. In other words, the sampling rate of the audio must be at least twice of the audio frequency—called a *Nyquist rate*. Therefore, a higher pitch sound requires a higher sampling rate than the lower pitch sound. In reality, the sound we hear, such as music and speech, is made up of multiple frequency components. Then the sampling rate can be chosen as twice the highest frequency component in the sound in order to reproduce the audio satisfactorily. Reducing the sampling rate sacrifices the sound quality of the higher frequencies.

The most common sampling rates you may encounter in a digital audio editing program are:

11,025 Hz AM Radio Quality/Speech
22,050 Hz Near FM Radio Quality (high-end multimedia)
44,100 Hz CD Quality
48,000 Hz DAT (digital audio tape) Quality
96,000 Hz DVD-Audio Quality
192,000 Hz DVD-Audio Quality

Based on the human hearing range and the Nyquist theorem, the sampling rate for CD-quality audio of 44.1 kHz is reasonable. But can we reduce the sampling rate, and if so, to what extent? Since the human ear is most sensitive in the range of about 2 to 5 KHz, then 11,025 Hz and 22,050 Hz seem to be reasonable sampling rates, although 11,025 Hz causes more noticeable degradation to the music than speech, because music has higher frequency components than speech. Because the human voice in speech normally does not exceed 5 KHz, the sampling rate setting of 11,025 Hz is reasonable for speech. Depending on the nature of your final product, a sampling rate setting of 11,025 Hz may also suit short sound effects (such as breaking glass and explosions) which may not require high fidelity.

So, how much can we lower the file size by reducing the sampling rate? From the file size equation, the file size can be reduced in the same proportion as the reduction of the sampling rate. In the example of one minute of CD-quality stereo audio, lowering the sampling rate from 44.1 KHz to 22.05 KHz will reduce the file size from about 10 MB to about 5 MB.

- **Reducing the bit depth.**
The most common bit-depth settings you may encounter in a digital audio-editing program are 8-bit and 16-bit. According to the file-size equation, lowering the bit depth from 16 to 8 reduces the file size in half. In the example of a one minute CD-quality stereo audio, lowering the bit depth from 16 to 8 will reduce the file size from about 10 MB to about 5 MB. Say, the sampling rate of the audio has been lowered from 44.1 KHz to 22.05 KHz to a 5-MB file. Lowering the bit depth of this file from 16 to 8 will reduce the file size further, from 5 MB to 2.5 MB.

8-bit resolution is usually sufficient for speech. However, for music, 8-bit is too low to accurately reproduce the sound satisfactorily. Our ears usually can notice the degradation in playback. Typically, 16-bit is used for music.

- **Applying file compression.**
An audio file can be compressed to reduce the audio file size. Compression can be lossless or lossy. Lossy compression gets rid of some data, but human perception is taken into consideration so that the data removed causes the least noticeable distortion. The popular audio file format, MP3, uses lossy compression. It gives a good compression rate while preserving the quality of the audio. Keep in mind that a file compressed with a lossy compression method should not be used as a source file for further editing. To achieve the best result in editing an audio file, you should always start with a source file that is uncompressed or compressed with lossless compression.

TABLE 4.1	Common Audio File Types			
File Type	**Acronym For**	**Originally Created By**	**File Information & Type of Compression**	**Platforms**
.aiff	Audio Interchange File Format	Apple, adopted later by Silicon Graphics	Usually not compressed, but has a compressed version	Apple Macintosh and Silicon Graphics computers; now also supported on Windows
.wav		IBM and Microsoft	Supports uncompressed and a number of different compression formats	Primarily for Windows, but can be used on other systems
.au and .snd	Also called μ-law or Sun μ-law format	Sun and NeXT	μ-law encoding compresses the file at a ratio of 2:1; slow decompression	Sun, NeXT, Unix or Linux operating system
.ra or .rm	Real Audio	Real Systems	Can have very high degree of compression; allows you to choose the compression level in terms of network connection speed; files can be streamed with Real Server	Cross-platform; requires Real player
.mp3	MPEG audio layer 3	Moving Pictures Experts Group	Good compression rate with perceivably high quality sound	Cross-platform; many digital audio player can play it
.mov	QuickTime movie	Apple	• Not just for video • supports audio track and a MIDI track • a variety of sound compressors • files can be streamed with QuickTime Streaming Server • "Fast Start" technology also allows Users to listen to media as it is being downloaded	Cross-platform; requires QuickTime player
.wma	Windows Media Audio	Microsoft		
.swa	Shockwave audio	Adobe	Uses same compression as mp3	Requires Shockwave plug-in which is available for Mac and Windows
.asf	Advanced streaming format	Microsoft	Proprietary compression algorithm	Primarily used with Windows Media Player

No matter which file-size reduction strategies you want to apply to your audio file, you should always evaluate the acceptability of the audio quality of the reduced file based on the nature of your audio project and weigh the quality against the file size limitation. The intended use of your final audio dictates the acceptability of trade-offs.

Even working within a limitation of file size, you should record or digitize at a higher sampling rate and bit depth than you expect to need in your final product and then compress the file later, instead of digitizing at a lower sampling rate and bit depth in the first place. One reason is that compression algorithms are often designed to selectively remove data that will cause minimal impact on the audio quality perceivable by the human ear. Another reason is that by keeping a higher sampling rate and bit depth, you will have a choice of optimizing the file size by a combination of the file optimization strategies. You can weigh the file-size reduction against the quality at that point. However, if you do not digitize at a high enough sample rate or bit depth, you will get stuck with an unsatisfactory audio.

Many digital sound-editing programs let you choose the format in which you want to save your audio file. The common file types are listed in Table 4.1. Some file types already dictate the compression option to be used. Others allow you to choose whether you want to compress the file, and possibly the compression options.

Generally, the intended use of your audio file determines the file format. You should take into consideration the following factors.

- **The file size limits.** Is your audio intended to be used on the Web? If so, you may want to consider a file format that offers high compression or even a streaming audio file format.
- **The intended audience of your audio file.** How is your target audience going to listen to your audio? What equipment do they have? If they are listening on a computer, what is their operating system? If your audio will be played on multiple platforms, then the file should be a cross-platform format.
- **Keeping the file as a source file.** If you are keeping the file for future editing, then you should choose a file format that is uncompressed or allows lossless compression.

4.7 MIDI

So far in this chapter, we have been describing the digital audio of captured analog audio that is produced by the vibration of objects in air. The continuous fluctuation of pressure in a propagating pressure wave is captured by a device or microphone, then digitized by sampling and quantization. The audio can be speech, music, noise, or a combination of these.

There is another method of storing music information—in *MIDI* format. MIDI (Musical Instrument Digital Interface) defines the common interface for electronic digital musical instruments to communicate with computers or other instruments or devices containing microprocessors. It specifies the configurations of cables and cable plugs and the format of the data. MIDI is a communications protocol, not a physical object.

Many electronic keyboards have built-in synthesizers. A MIDI keyboard looks like a small piano, but upon receiving a signal such as a key being hit, its electronic device synthesizes sound using its own internal microprocessor (i.e., computer). Computers can be attached directly to a MIDI keyboard to capture the musical notes being played. There are also software programs that let you enter the notes directly via the computer's mouse and keyboard. The composed music also can be played through a MIDI keyboard that has a synthesizer.

MIDI signals are not digitized audio sample points but contain note *information* played with a virtual instrument. Such information includes the instrument being played, the note being played, the duration of the note, and how loud to play the note. Unlike the digital audio we have been describing in the previous sections of this chapter, MIDI music creation does not involve capturing, digitizing analog sound waves or any analog information. Therefore, it does not involve sampling and quantization; that is, there is no sampling rate or bit-depth option in storing a MIDI file.

Comparing to the sampled audio files, the MIDI format has both advantages and disadvantages. Its file size can be much more compact. For example, the file size of a one minute MIDI file can be about 2 KB, but, as you have seen in the file size calculations, a one-minute stereo, 16-bit audio with a sampling rate of 44.1 KHz is about 10 MB. If you convert this MIDI file into a 44.1 KHz, 16-bit, stereo digital audio file, it will become about

10 MB. In addition, because MIDI music can be edited like sheet music, the notation, timing, and instruments easily can be identified in the file, so it can be edited easily.

The composed music of a MIDI file requires a synthesizer to play. The quality of the sound depends on the quality of the synthesizer that plays back the composed music. The actual sound produced by different synthesizers may differ even for the same note of the same instrument. The composed music you hear from your MIDI keyboard may not sound the same on your friend's MIDI keyboard or computer synthesizer. For example, QuickTime has its own selection of high-quality MIDI instruments and thus can play MIDI without an external MIDI synthesizer. But it sounds different from a full-fledged synthesizer.

The analogy for MIDI music versus digitized audio may be a cake recipe versus the baked cake. It is much easier and lighter to send a cake recipe to other people. But how exactly the cake tastes and looks may vary depending on the exact ingredients the person uses—even the same temperature setting varies from oven to oven. On the other hand, a baked cake is more bulky to mail to your friends. But it ensures the cake's taste and look that you intend the recipient to experience.

4.8 SUMMARY

Sound is a wave that is generated by vibrating objects in a medium such as air. The vibrating objects can be the vocal cords of a person, a guitar string, or a tuning fork. The vibrating object creates a disturbance of the surrounding air molecules, causing periodic changes of air pressure—forming a sound wave.

No matter what the vibrating object is, the object is vibrating or moving back and forth at a certain frequency. This causes the surrounding air molecules to vibrate at this same frequency. The common unit for frequency is Hertz (Hz); 1 Hz refers to 1 cycle per second. The sound frequency is referred to as the pitch of the sound. Higher frequencies correspond to higher pitches.

Sound intensity is related to, but not exactly the same as, the perceived loudness of a sound. The loudness of a sound is a subjective perception, but sound intensity is an objective measurement. Sound intensity is often measured in decibels (dB). A decibel is based on a ratio of a louder sound to a softer one; it is not an absolute measurement.

When two or more sound waves meet, their amplitudes add up, resulting in a more complex waveform. The waveforms of the sound we perceive everyday (such as speech, music, and noise) are complicated waveforms that result when multiple waveforms of different frequencies are added together.

Like the process of digitizing any analog information, the process of digitizing a sound wave involves sampling and quantizing an analog sound wave. In the sampling step, the sound wave is sampled at a specific rate into discrete samples of amplitude values. The higher the sampling rate, the higher the accuracy in capturing the data. But a high frequency will generate a larger amount of data which will require more storage space and processing time. In the quantizing step, each of the discrete samples of amplitude values obtained from the sampling step will be mapped to the nearest value on a scale of discrete levels. Therefore, the more levels available in the scale, the higher the accuracy in reproducing the sound. Having more levels means higher resolution. But higher resolution requires more storage space.

Audio files, such as speech and music, usually require long continuous playback. Therefore, the file size increases very rapidly with higher sampling rate and bit depth. To reduce the file size, there are four general file optimization approaches: reduce the sampling rate, reduce the bit depth, apply compression, and reduce the number of channels. No matter which file size reduction strategies you want to apply to your audio file, you should always evaluate the acceptability of the audio quality of the reduced file based on the nature of your audio project, and weigh the quality against the file size limitation. The intended use of your final audio dictates the consideration of the acceptable trade-offs.

Even working within a limitation of file size, you will get better results by recording or digitizing at a higher sampling rate and bit depth than you expect to need in your final product and then compressing the file later.

Another method of storing music information is in MIDI format. MIDI stands for Musical Instrument Digital Interface. MIDI files do not contain digitized audio sample points but information about musical notes to be played with a virtual instrument. Such information includes the instrument being played, the note being played, the duration of the note, and how loud to play the note. Unlike digitized audio, MIDI music creation does not involve digitizing analog sound waves, or any analog information. Therefore, it does not involve sampling and quantization. MIDI music has the advantage of very small file size. Another advantage is that the file can be edited easily.

TERMS

bit depth, 111	loudness, 105	resolution, 110
channels, 113	MIDI, 117	sampling, 109
decibels (dB), 105	Nyquist rate, 114	sound intensity, 105
dynamic range, 111	Nyquist's theorem, 114	waveform, 102
frequency, 104	pitch, 104	
Hertz (Hz), 104	quantizing, 110	

LEARNING AIDS

The following learning aids can be found at the book's companion Web site.

⌐ Sound as a Pressure Wave
An illustration of sound wave as longitudinal air-pressure wave.

⌐ Sampling and Quantizing in Digital Audio
An interactive tutorial illustrating text sections on sampling and quantizing in digitizing a sound wave.

⌐ Audio Examples (a Short Musical Sound and a Sound Effect) with Various Combinations of Sampling Rate and Bit Depth
Audio examples of a short musical sound and an explosion sound effect with various sampling rates (44,100 Hz, 22,050 Hz, and 11,025 Hz) and bit depths (8-bit and 16-bit) are used to demonstrate the impact of sampling rate and bit depth on (i) the audio quality and (ii) the file size. Review questions of the impact, the audio's waveforms, and frequency spectral views are also available.

REVIEW QUESTIONS

When applicable, please select all correct answers.

1. A sound with higher _____ is perceived to have a higher pitch.

   A. volume
   B. frequency
   C. fidelity
   D. sampling rate
   E. bit depth

2. MIDI standard specifies _____.

   A. the sampling rate for the synthesized sound
   B. bit depth for the synthesized sound
   C. the configurations of cables and cable plugs
   D. the format of the data

3. **True/False:** 8-bit is generally considered to be more than adequate for recording music.

4. **True/False:** MP3 is a good file format to keep as a source file for further editing.

5. **True/False:** Zero decibels is when there is no sound wave.

6. Which of the following file extensions indicate audio files?

   BMP   WAV   JPEG   AIFF   MP3   GIF   JPG   PSD   TIFF   WMF

7. According to Nyquist's theorem, we must sample at least _____ points in each sound wave cycle to be able to reconstruct the sound wave satisfactorily. In other words, the sampling rate of the audio must be at least _____ of the audio frequency.

8. The reduction of a digital audio file size can be achieved by _____.

   A. reducing the sampling rate
   B. reducing the pitch of the audio
   C. reducing the bit depth
   D. reducing the amplitude of the audio
   E. applying file compression techniques

9. The _____ of a digitized sound affects the accuracy of the sampled amplitudes being stored.

   A. amplitude
   B. frequency
   C. sampling rate
   D. bit depth
   E. dynamic range

10. The _____ of a sound relates to the sound intensity or loudness.

   A. amplitude
   B. frequency
   C. sampling rate
   D. bit depth
   E. dynamic range

11. The unit used for measuring _____ is Hertz (Hz).

    A. amplitude
    B. frequency
    C. sampling rate
    D. bit depth
    E. dynamic range

12. In digital audio, the number of sample points taken per second is called _____.

    A. amplitude
    B. frequency
    C. sampling rate
    D. bit depth
    E. dynamic range

13. Higher _____ will result in larger file size.

    A. amplitude
    B. frequency
    C. sampling rate
    D. bit depth
    E. dynamic range

14. **True/False:** A waveform is a graphical representation of the pressure–time fluctuations of a sound wave.

15. The horizontal axis of a waveform is _____.

    A. distance
    B. time

16. How many levels of amplitude values does a 8-bit sound allow?

17. How many levels of amplitude values does a 16-bit sound allow?

18. Increasing the bit depth from 8-bit to 16-bit will _____ the file size.

19. Increasing the sampling rate from 22.05 KHz to 44.1 KHz will _____ file size.

20. Generally, audio CD music sampling rate is _____ and bit depth is _____.

Capturing and Editing Digital Audio

TABLE OF CONTENTS

KEY CONCEPTS
- Methods of acquiring digital audio
- Techniques of digital audio touch-up and alteration
- Delivery of digital audio

GENERAL LEARNING OBJECTIVES

At the end of this chapter, you should be able to demonstrate that you understand

- How to acquire sampled digital audio.
- The basic workspace of digital audio editing programs.
- The basic techniques of digital audio touch-up.
- The common techniques of digital audio alterations.
- The methods of creating music.
- How to embed audio on Web pages.

5.1 ACQUIRING DIGITAL AUDIO

Digital audio can be acquired by two methods: (1) recording sound directly into a digital format and (2) digitizing an existing analog audio media, such as analog audio tapes. In this section, we will discuss what hardware and software may be needed for each of these methods.

5.1.1 Recording

In order to record audio directly into digital format or to digitize analog audio, your computer needs to have a sound card. A **sound card** enables the playing and recording of sound on a computer. A sound card acts as an analog-to-digital converter that converts the electrical signals into digital format by sampling the signals based on the sampling rate and bit depth chosen. All new computers come with a sound card installed.

In order to record audio directly, you need a microphone. Most laptop computers have a built-in microphone. However, these built-in microphones (in general) do not produce sufficient sound quality for multimedia projects. Desktop computers usually do not have built-in microphones. Instead, an external microphone usually is needed for recording on a laptop or desktop computer.

Some microphones are designed to have a directional response to sound, unidirectional and omnidirectional, for example. Their sensitivity to sound varies with the angles of the sound approaching the microphone. A unidirectional microphone is most sensitive to the sound coming from the front. It has the advantage of isolating the sound source of interest from other noises coming from the rear. An omnidirectional microphone is equally

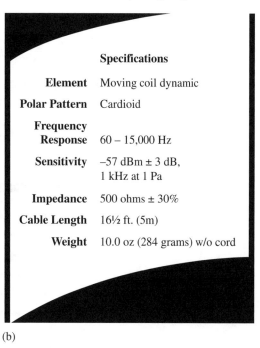

Specifications
Type: Dynamic microphone
Directivity: Uni-directional
Frequency response: 80 – 12,000 Hz
Output impedance: 600 ohms ± 30% at 1 kHz,
          unbalanced
Effective output level: –56.8 ± 3 dBm (0 dBm =
          1 mW/Pa, 1,000 Hz)
Dimensions: 54 mm (2⅛ inches) dia. × 211 mm
          (8³⁄₈ inches) length
Mass (Microphone incl. cord): Approx. 255 g (9.0 oz.)
Operating temperature: 0°C – 40°C
Design and specifications are subject to change
without notice:

(a)   (b)

Figure 5.1 Two examples of microphone specifications found on packaging (a) A unidirectional microphone (b) Cardioid polar pattern means unidirectional

sensitive to sounds coming from all directions. As a general rule for recording with a microphone, if you do not have access to the specifications of the microphone, place the sound source directly in front of the microphone. For example, if you are recording a voice-over, speak close to the front of the microphone; do not speak to the side of the microphone.

The specifications of a microphone (although some of them do not affect the quality of the recording) can give you useful information about its frequency range and its directivity. This helps you get the most out of the microphone. For example, the microphone with the specifications shown in Figure 5.1a has a frequency response range of 80 to 12,000 Hz. This covers human speech and musical instruments. This microphone is unidirectional.

The microphone with the specifications shown in Figure 5.1b has a frequency response range of 60 to 15,000 Hz. This has a little wider range than the one in Figure 5.1a. There is no directivity listed, but the polar pattern describes the pattern of the sound sensitivity around the microphone. Its polar pattern is cardioid. The cardioid pattern is roughly a heart shape, hence the name "cardioid". It is most sensitive to the sound coming from the front but not from the rear. The cardioid polar pattern is also unidirectional.

The software component is a digital audio recording program. Basically, all of the digital audio-editing programs, such as Adobe Audition, Sony Sound Forge, and Audacity, let you record audio. At the time of writing, Adobe Audition and Sony Sound Forge are Windows applications. Audacity is a free, open-source software available for Mac OS X, Microsoft Windows, GNU/Linux, and other operating systems. Audacity can be downloaded from the Web.

Cardioid shape: Imagine pinching the head of the microphone into a balloon. The shape of the pinched balloon approximates the cardioid shape. The volume of the balloon occupies the area where the microphone is most sensitive to where the sound is coming from.

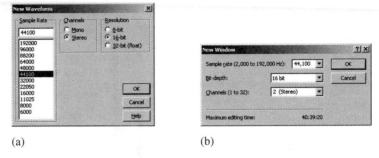

(a)   (b)

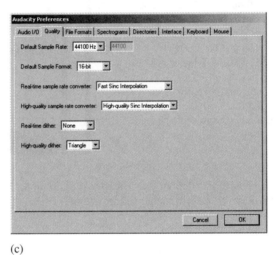

(c)

Figure 5.2 New file window prompts to set the audio sampling rate, bit depth, and number of channels (a) Adobe Audition (b) Sony Sound Forge (c) Audacity's Preference dialog box

Before you start recording, you need to specify the sampling rate, bit depth, and the number of channels you want to use (Figure 5.2). The available sampling rate and bit depth for recording are determined by the capability of the hardware—the sound card. Most sound cards are capable of recording at least CD-quality sound—i.e., a sampling rate of 44,100 Hz, a bit depth of 16, and two channels (stereo).

Audio software applications usually have an audio level meter that lets you monitor the sound input level during recording. By default, the level meter in Audition is located at the bottom of the window (Figure 5.3). In Sound Forge 9, its meter is vertical and is in a separate window (Figure 5.4). In Audacity, its meter is located at the top (Figure 5.5).

The input volume level can be adjusted so that the meter level stays below the red area (which is around −3 dB to 0 dB, as in Figure 5.3a). The loudest part of the audio may brush near the red area without going over it. Any data going over the limit of 0 dB will be given the value of zero. The areas of the waveform where this occurs will look chopped off and cause distortion of your recording (Figure 5.3b). This effect is called *clipping*. Too low of a recording level produces a recording that is too soft (Figure 5.3c).

The optimal range depends on the nature of your audio. As a general guide, the signals between −12 and −3 dB should have sufficient strength. The meter gives you the technical

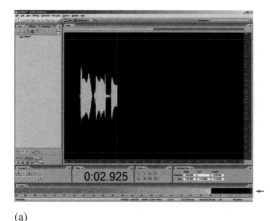

(a)

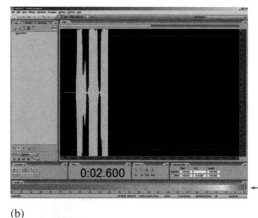

(b)

(c)

Figure 5.3 The audio level meter in Adobe Audition 2.0. The red arrow shows where the meter is, and the thin yellow line on the right side indicates the maximum level of the recording so far (a) The optimal level (b) The level is too high—going over the red area—causing undesirable clipping of the waveform (c) The level is too low

depiction of the strength of the signal, but your ear should be the final judge of the audio. Occasional signals peaking over 0 dB will be fine if the overall audio and the most important part of the audio maintains a desired level and those clipped signals do not produce noticeable distortion.

Before the actual recording, rehearse your recording, if possible, and watch the meter. Adjust the audio input level and experiment with how close the sound source to your microphone should be so that the level for the majority of the audio is not too low or going over the red area.

- In Windows, you can adjust the recording volume by setting the sound properties from the Control Panel.
    1. Double-click Sounds and Audio Devices.
    2. Under Device volume, click the Advanced . . . button to open the Master Volume dialog box.

> ⟢ **Setting Recording Controls in Windows** Screen capture movie that demonstrates how to set the recording device to microphone and adjust the volume in Windows.

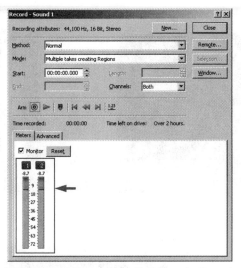

Figure 5.4 The audio level meter in Sound Forge 9.0

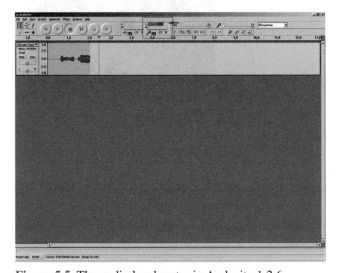

Figure 5.5 The audio level meter in Audacity 1.2.6

3. Select Options > Properties.
4. Check the Recording option (Figure 5.6a). Click OK. Then, adjust the microphone's volume level (Figure 5.6b).

• In Mac OS X,

1. Look at the System preferences, and select Sound.

2. Click on Input (Figure 5.7). You should see a list of devices for sound input, such as Internal microphone or External microphone.

3. Select the microphone and drag the Input volume slider bar to adjust the volume. You can test the Input volume setting by speaking into a microphone and watching the response of the Input level meter.

✏ **Recording Audio in Adobe Audition**
Screen capture movie that demonstrates the basic steps of recording audio in Adobe Audition.

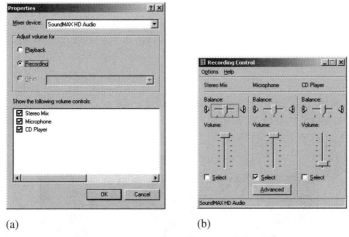

(a)   (b)

Figure 5.6 Windows audio Properties (a) Dialog box and (b) Volume controls

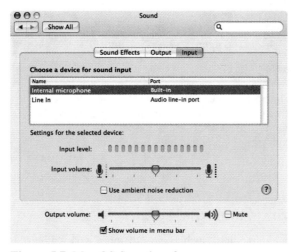

Figure 5.7 Mac OS Sound preferences

SOUND CARD

Instead of being installed as a separate card on a computer, the sound subsystem is now commonly built into the motherboard of the computer. In this chapter, the term *sound card* is used synonymously with such a sound subsystem, regardless of its physical form.

The role of sound card in the audio playback. During recording, a sound card acts as an analog-to-digital converter that converts the electrical signals into digital format. During playback, a sound card acts as digital-to-analog converter. This means that it can convert the discrete samples in the digital format of the audio into analog by reconnecting the samples to reconstruct a waveform. It then sends the analog signals through the line-out port to your speakers.

Working with a sound card. A basic sound card has line-out, line-in, and microphone-in ports (Figure 5.8). Some laptop computers do not have a line-in port. The line-out port is where the headphones or speakers are connected. The line-in and microphone ports are for recording. Sound cards that are capable of surround sound have more ports.

Figure 5.8 The back of a desktop computer showing the line-out (green), line-in (blue), and the microphone (red) ports. Similar ports can be found on laptop computers that have a sound card.

5.1.2 Digitizing Analog Medium

To digitize analog audio medium, such as cassette tapes, you will need to connect the line-out port of the cassette tape deck to the line-in port on your sound card using an audio cable. You will need to start the sound recording on the computer before playing the cassette tape. The starting and stopping of the recording do not have to be synchronized with the starting and stopping of the cassette tape. You should always digitize a little more before and after the segment that you need. The extra audio can be edited out later.

5.2 BASIC WORKSPACE ELEMENTS IN DIGITAL AUDIO-EDITING PROGRAMS

Examples of digital audio-editing application programs for Windows are Adobe Audition and Sony Sound Forge. Audacity is a free digital audio program available for Mac OS X, Microsoft Windows, GNU/Linux, and other operating systems.

5.2.1 Basic Editing: Working with One Audio At a Time

The two very basic elements you would find in these digital audio-editing programs are: (1) a waveform display window and (2) the transport controls where you find the play, record, rewind, and fast forward buttons. For example, Figure 5.9 shows screenshots of Adobe Audition, Sony Sound Forge 9, and Audacity 1.2.6 highlighting the areas of these two basic elements.

In the waveform display, the *x*-axis represents the time and the *y*-axis represents the amplitude value. The example shown in Figure 5.9 depicts two waveforms in the window because the audio is stereo, which means the audio has two channels. Each of the waveforms represents the waveform for that channel—the top waveform represents the left channel and the bottom one the right channel. If the audio is mono, there will be only one channel, and thus, there will be only one waveform depicted in the window. You can click inside the waveform window to position the playhead at a particular time.

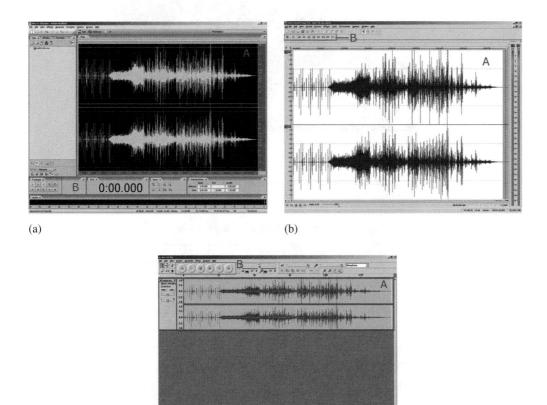

(a)   (b)

(c)

Figure 5.9 The area labeled **A** is the waveform display window. The area labeled **B** is the transport controls where you find the play, record, rewind, and fast forward button (a) Adobe Audition 2.0 workspace in the Edit View (b) Sony Sound Forge 9 workspace (c) Audacity 1.2.6

5.2.2 Audio Mixing: Working with Multiple Audio

Many programs also let you mix multiple audio. For example, Adobe Audition has the **Multitrack View** (Figure 5.10a) in addition to editing a single waveform in **Edit View**. Using Audacity, you can add audio tracks (Figure 5.10b) by choosing Project > Import Audio...

Multiple audio can be imported so that each audio is placed on an audio track. You can place different audio tracks at different times. Mixing multiple audio tracks is necessary and useful in situations such as when you want to mix a voice-over with background music,

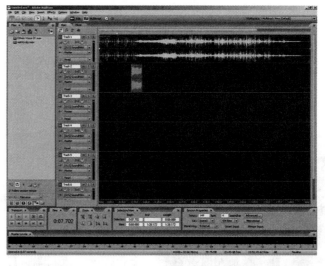

(a)

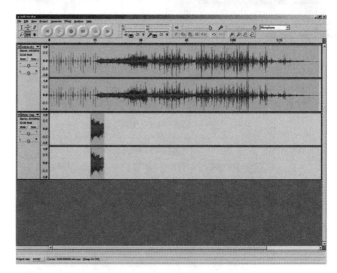

(b)

Figure 5.10 (a) Two different audio are placed on two separate tracks in Adobe Audition 2.0 Multitrack View (b) Audacity 1.2.6 with two audio tracks

compose different musical clips, or mix multiple instrumental playback where each is recorded as a separate audio.

It is advantageous to create or record audio separately and mix them later. This way you can adjust the volume level and apply effects (such as fade-in and fade-out) to each audio independently. For example, to record a voice-over with background music in one recording would require synchronization and control in matching the volume levels of voice-over with the background music all at once.

In addition, the synchronization and the relative volumes of the voice-over and background music would have already been fixed. What if later you find out that your project requires an extra few seconds of pause within the voice-over? If you record the voice-over and the background music in one recording, then you would have to record the whole audio again, because inserting a silence in the voice-over segment will also silence the background music. However, if the voice-over and background music are recorded separately as different audio files, then all you need to do is to insert a few seconds of silence in the voice-over where it is needed. The background music will be unaffected and can be mixed with the edited voice-over as usual. The background music will still be playing during the newly added silence portion of the voice-over.

5.2.3 Spectral View

The waveform representation is the most frequently used view in digital audio editing. However, many audio-editing programs also have a spectral view available. In the *spectral view* (Figure 5.11), the *x*-axis of the display is still time, like in the waveform display. However, the *y*-axis is the frequency of the audio, not the amplitude. The amplitude value is now represented using color. The spectral view can tell you the audio frequency information that you cannot get from the waveform view. For example, as you can tell from the spectral views shown in Figure 5.11, a middle section of the audio is missing sound that is higher than 3000 Hz.

In general, the higher amplitude is represented by brighter colors. The brightest color of the section that is capped at 3000 Hz occurs in the range of about 300 to 500 Hz. In the section after it, the brightest color occurs around 4000 Hz but the 300 to 500 Hz range is very dark (low in amplitude). This means that a sound amplitude in the range of 300 to 500 Hz is very low. You would not be able to discern such frequency information from the waveform view.

When working in the spectral view, you can still select audio data within a time range. Audition allows you to select the audio data in frequency in addition to time ranges (Figure 5.12). Thus, working in the spectral view also allows you to selectively edit a certain frequency range within a time frame. This is in contrast to selecting audio data in the waveform view where, when you make a selection, you select *all* the audio data within the selected time range, regardless of the frequency. Any change applied to the selection affects all frequencies within the selected time frame.

Spectral view is useful in analyzing the frequency range of the audio. It helps to give an idea of the most important frequency range of the audio, so that when you need to reduce the audio file size by downsampling, you can estimate the lowest sampling rate without causing serious distortion. This is also useful in situations when it is necessary to isolate the frequency range responsible for an audio anomaly.

Lowest sampling rate without serious distortion: Recall the implication of Nyquist theorem (Chapter 4)—the sampling rate of the audio must be at least twice the audio frequency. The audio with the highest amplitude usually is the most important part of the audio. If the frequency range that has the highest amplitude is around 4000 Hz, then resampling your audio to 8000 Hz would be acceptable.

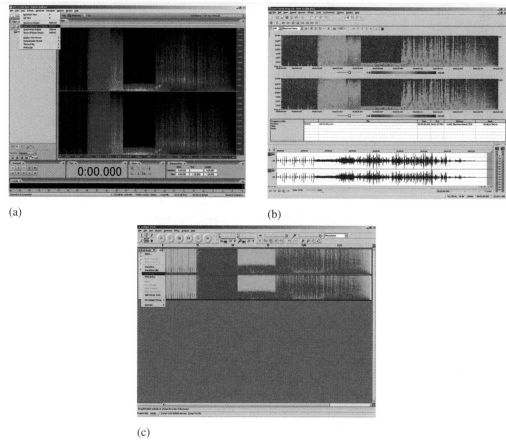

(a)

(b)

(c)

Figure 5.11 Spectral view of audio in Figure 5.9 (a) Adobe Audition 2.0: View > Spectral Frequency Display (b) Sony Sound Forge 9: View > Spectrum Analysis (c) Audacity 1.2.6: Spectrum

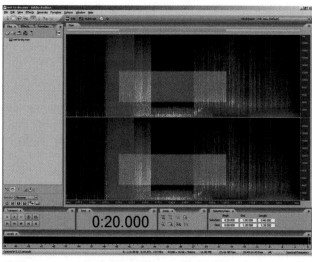

Figure 5.12 The frequency range of about 4000 to 12,000 Hz within the time frame between 20 second and 1 minute is selected (as indicated by the pale rectangle) in spectral view

5.3 BASIC DIGITAL AUDIO EDITING

In digital imaging, the scanned or digitally photographed image almost always needs retouching and editing, whether it is for cleaning up the image or artistic manipulation. This is also true for digital audio. Making connections across media with respect to the editing process will help you understand both the need for and the process of editing. So let's draw parallels from the common digital image-editing processes.

You can edit an image by copying and pasting; adjusting the tonal value; cleaning up dirt, dust, and scratches; resizing the image; reducing its color depth; and applying filters, such as blurring or embossing. The basic ideas of these processes are transferable to digital audio editing (Table 5.1). In both digital image and audio editing, the changes will be applied to the selected area. If there is not a selection made, the changes will be applied to the whole image or audio. These basic audio editing operations are described in the following sections.

TABLE 5.1	Parallels between Basic Digital Image and Digital Audio Editing
Basic Digital Image Editing	**Basic Digital Audio Editing**
Reassemble image content by cutting, copying, and pasting	Reassemble audio waveform by cutting, copying, and pasting
Adjust tonal value	Adjust volume
Clean up dirt, dust, and scratches	Noise reduction
Resize the image	Resample the audio
Reduce the image's color depth	Reduce the audio's bit depth
Apply filters for special effects	Apply filters for special effects, such as reverb and pitch changes
If you want to save your file as JPEG for the Web, wait until the last step because JPEG uses lossy compression	If you want to save your file as MP3 for the Web, wait until the last step because MP3 uses lossy compression

5.3.1 Reassembling Waveform

The audio waveform can be selected and then applied with operations such as Cut, Copy, or Delete. Selecting a segment of the waveform can be accomplished by simply dragging the cursor over the waveform.

Because the waveform is a visual representation of the audio amplitude in time, it is often possible to locate a sound segment in the waveform by looking for pauses or distinctive amplitude changes. You can edit out a specific word or pause from the audio. You can also click on a particular time on a waveform and paste a waveform segment that corresponds to a particular sound or speech. Figure 5.13a shows a waveform of the audio speech of 1-2-3-4. The second word is cut and pasted before the first word (Figure 5.13c). The audio now becomes 2-1-3-4.

Using the Cut or Delete operation, you can edit out an unwanted long pause in a voice recording and trim unnecessary extra time off the beginning and end of the recording.

> ✧ **Reassembling Waveforms in Adobe Audition** Screen capture movie demonstrating the selecting, cutting, and pasting of audio waveforms in Adobe Audition.

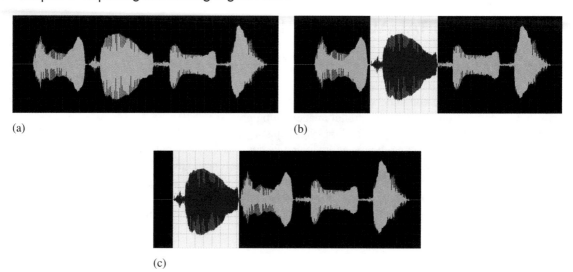

(a)

(b)

(c)

Figure 5.13 Reassembling an audio waveform (a) An original recording of speech saying 1-2-3-4 (b) The second word "2" is selected (c) The word "2" is cut and pasted before the first word

5.3.2 Changing Volume

You can adjust the volume or amplitude of an audio. This is necessary when the recorded volume is too loud or too low for the intended use of the audio in a project. Another situation where volume adjustment is needed is when assembling multiple recordings into a single sound track. In this case, you often need to adjust the volume of each recording to give a consistent volume level across the recordings. There are two menu items for the purpose of simple volume adjustment. *Amplify* lets you specify amplification in a dB (decibels) or percentage. *Normalize* lets you set a peak level for a file or selection, and it will amplify the entire file or selection so that the highest level is the peak level you specify. Use normalize instead of amplify to ensure the amplification does not result in clipping. For example, if you normalize an audio to 100%, you achieve the maximum amplitude that digital audio allows.

There are two extended applications of volume adjustment. The *fade-in* effect suppresses the volume at the beginning and gradually increases to 100% within the designated duration for the fade-in. Similarly, the *fade-out* effect lowers the volume level gradually to zero within the fade-out period.

The envelope graph allows you to control the volume changes over time using a curve. The *x*-axis of the envelope graph represents time and the *y*-axis amplification level. There are often presets available for Envelope graphs. You also can define your own curve. As you see in Figure 5.14, the fade-in and fade-out effects can be created by the Envelope graph.

5.3.3 Noise Reduction

Recordings often contain background noise, such as computer fan noise or hissing from the microphone. The two most useful features for noise reduction found in Adobe Audition are Hiss Reduction and Noise Reduction. The *Hiss Reduction* can be used to reduce hiss from the source, such as audio cassette tape or microphone. Hissing noise is often characterized by a certain frequency range. The basic idea of how hiss reduction works is that a threshold

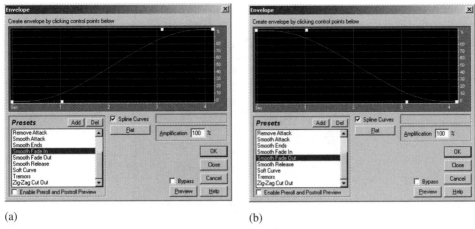

(a)   (b)

Figure 5.14 Examples of Envelope graphs (Adobe Audition) (a) Fade-in (b) Fade-out

amplitude for a frequency range, called the ***noise floor***, is defined—as preset or user-defined. If the audio amplitude within that frequency range falls below the threshold, the audio of that range will be greatly reduced. However, audio outside that frequency range and audio on that frequency range that is louder than the threshold will remain unchanged.

   Noise Reduction (Adobe Audition) or ***Noise Removal*** (Audacity) is another effect you can use to reduce noise that is constant throughout a waveform. This feature performs a statistical analysis of a pure noise segment, which is user-defined. Then it performs noise reduction on the whole audio based on this noise profile. Because it reduces noise based on a noise profile generated statistically, not a frequency range, the Noise Reduction can remove a wider range of noise. The downside of this effect compared to Hiss Reduction is that you need to have a sufficiently long segment (preferably more than one second) of pure noise for the statistical analysis to generate a representative profile for the noise. To get a pure noise segment, you can start the recording with a second or more of silence. That silence can be used as the Noise Reduction Profile for the final audio recording.

> ⬦ **Applying Noise Reduction in Adobe Audition** Screen capture movie demonstrating the application of the Noise Reduction effects to an audio recording in Adobe Audition.

5.3.4 Special Effects

There are many special effects or filters you can apply to an audio. Many audio programs let you alter the pitch of a sound file, alter the length (in time) of a sound file, and add echo or ***reverb*** to a sound (Figure 5.15). Reverb can be applied using presets or by adjusting the parameters to suit your needs.

5.3.5 Downsampling and Reduction of Bit Depth

It is advantageous to record and work with audio at CD-quality levels (i.e., 44,100 Hz sampling rate, 16-bit, and stereo) or higher. However, depending on the project, you may need to downsample the file to lower the file size for the final delivery. In Adobe Audition, you can alter the sampling rate, bit depth, and channel number by choosing Edit > Convert Sample Type ... Save the altered audio file as a different name. Always keep the original higher quality audio file for editing.

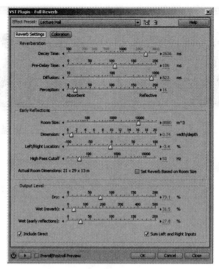

Figure 5.15 Applying reverb to an audio in Adobe Audition 2.0

See Chapter 4 for a detailed discussion on optimization audio files and effects of sampling rate, bit depths, and number of channels on the audio file size.

Another way of lowering file size is to save the audio file as a compressed file format, such as .mp3. MP3 files use a lossy but effective compression by applying a human perception of sound. This means that some audio data are removed and the audio data is approximated, but the data removed are basically imperceptible by humans. Because MP3 uses a lossy compression, you should avoid using MP3 files as the master copy for further editing. The file that you plan to use for editing should be saved using a lossless compression method, if possible.

5.3.6 General Steps of Digital Audio-Recording Touch-up

Even the most controlled studio recordings require touch-up before further manipulation of the audio. The general steps of touching up digital audio recordings are:

1. **Noise reduction:** Remove background noise by applying the noise reduction effect.
2. **Trimming:** Remove extra time at the beginning or end of the audio recording. You also may remove unwanted long periods of silence within the audio.
3. **Adjusting volume level** to the desired level.

 Audio Manipulation (Lab) Practice recording your voice, remove background noise, reassemble waveform, and apply audio effects.

The audio should be touched up before applying any special effect, such as reverb. Otherwise, the background noise and the unwanted silence will be mixed with the effects and become harder, if not impossible to remove.

5.4 MUSIC CREATION

Music scores can be created using sheet-music software in MIDI format. Creating an original music score requires musical composition skills. However, multimedia projects, such as games, product advertisements, and some digital art do not require a long musical score.

Loop music software and libraries are better solutions for non-music composers who are creating audio for such multimedia projects.

5.4.1 MIDI

MIDI and sampled digital audio are fundamentally different representations of digital sound. Therefore, the editing or creation of MIDI is also very different from sampled audio. MIDI is like sheet music in that it acts as an instruction for recreating the music. You edit notation and instrument assignment in a MIDI file.

MIDI messages: See Chapter 4 for an introduction of MIDI. CS module Chapter 4 contains a detailed description of MIDI messages.

Examples of software application programs are Cakewalk SONAR, Steinberg Cubase, and MakeMusic! Finale. Figure 5.16 show the different views available in Cakewalk SONAR for different creation and editing methods: **Staff view** for working with notation and staff; **Piano Roll view** for visualizing the notes as they would appear on a player-piano roll; **Event List view** for working with a sequence of MIDI information or MIDI messages.

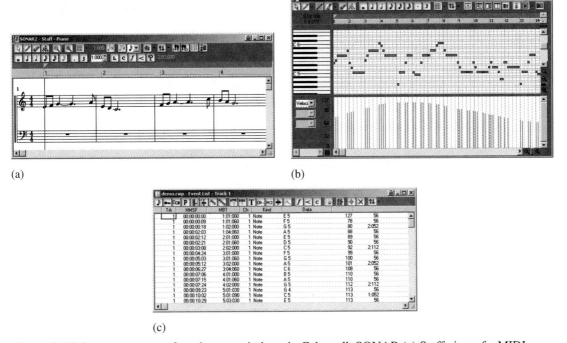

(a)

(b)

(c)

Figure 5.16 Screen captures of workspace windows in Cakewalk SONAR (a) Staff view of a MIDI track (b) Piano roll view of a MIDI track. The bottom pane shows the notes' velocity: The velocity corresponds to how hard the key is hit, and thus the note's loudness (c) Event List view of a MIDI track

Figure 5.17 shows the assignment of harmonica to a MIDI track in Cakewalk SONAR. If a MIDI keyboard is connected to the computer, you can also play on the MIDI keyboard to record your performance into a MIDI file with most MIDI programs.

During the MIDI file playback, the sound card uses the synthesizer to recreate the sound of the notes using the specified instrument. Because not all synthesizers are the same, the MIDI file will sound differently depending on the sound card that plays it.

✐ **Creating and Editing MIDI in Cakewalk SONAR** Screen capture movie that demonstrates creating and editing MIDI using Staff, Piano Roll, and Event List views in Cakewalk SONAR.

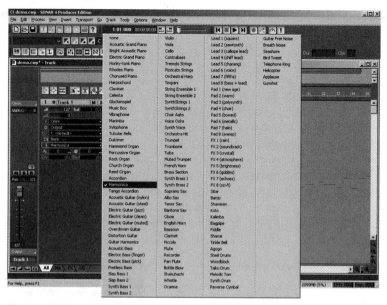

Figure 5.17 Assignment of harmonica to the instrument for a MIDI track in Cakewalk SONAR

5.4.2 Loop Music

Composing in MIDI allows you to create your own original score. This requires expertise in musical composition to build a good score. Although you can always hire someone to compose a score for you, you have to first clearly identify the role of the music for your project. If the music is used for a film production, you will probably need an original score that matches the mood and theme of your film. However, many multimedia projects, such as games and product advertisements, do not require an original score but often will require loop music.

Loop music is music that is created from short music clips that are repeated. These music clips usually are designed to loop seamlessly (i.e., without noticeable discontinuity between repetitions). There are many commercially available libraries of short sound effects and music clips designed to loop seamlessly. There are also fully orchestrated music pieces available for situations in which loops are not desirable.

> ⤸ **Working with Loops in Sony ACID Pro** Screen capture movie that demonstrates creating loop music in Sony ACID Pro.

> ⤸ **Working with Loops in Adobe Audition** Screen capture movie that demonstrates creating loop music in Adobe Audition.

Loop music application programs, such as Sony ACID Pro (for Windows) in Figure 5.18 and Apple GarageBand (for Mac OS) Figure 5.19, are designed to make the job of sequencing and mixing loop music easier. These programs often also support MIDI and let you import MIDI music.

Here is the basic idea of how these programs work. Loop music programs have multiple audio tracks. You can import an audio clip to place on a track. The audio clip is represented by a block. You create repetitions of the clip by dragging the right edge of the block to extend it.

Even programs, such as Adobe Audition and Audacity, that are not applications specific for loop music let you create loop music.

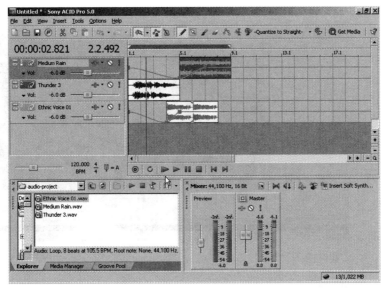

Figure 5.18 Sony ACID Pro with sound in track 3 set to loop twice simply by dragging the right edge of the sound clip to the right

Figure 5.19 GarageBand—a loop music creation program. The red arrows mark the end of cycle of the loop, for example, the clip in the fourth track (in blue) has about 2.5 repetitions

In Audition, you can set the loop option for a clip in Multitrack View, so that when you extend the duration of the clip, it will automatically repeat the clip without you having to manually copy and paste the clip multiple times (Figure 5.20). In Audacity, an effect called Repeat lets you repeat a selection of the audio for a specified number of times.

Figure 5.20 Adobe Audition Multitrack View where the sound is set to loop three times simply by dragging the right edge of the sound clip to the right

5.5 DELIVERY OF DIGITAL AUDIO

Digital audio can be created solely for audio CD production. However, in digital media production, digital audio is often combined with other media, for example, in video and multimedia presentation. It can be used for the Web, in which case the download time of the audio file is an important consideration. In addition, the audio can be embedded on a Web page or played in a window external to the browser window. You can control how the audio is played with HTML codes.

5.5.1 Video

If your audio is intended to import into a video editor, you will need to check the audio file format that is supported by your video editing software. Most video editing programs support .wav, .aif, and .mp3. Adobe Audition also lets you import video using the Multitrack View. As an audio-editing program, Adobe Audition does not have the video-editing capability you would find in a video-editing program. However, being able to import the video into the audio-editing program provides you the convenience of synchronizing video and audio without having to switch back and forth between editing programs.

5.5.2 Multimedia Authoring

Multimedia authoring programs often support a variety of audio file format. For example, the types of audio file you can import in Adobe Director and Flash include .wav, .aif, .au, .mp3, and audio-only QuickTime.

5.5.3 For the Web

To use audio on the Web, you can (1) integrate the audio by embedding it on the Web page or (2) simply link to the audio file. The second method will cause the audio file to play in a player window external to the Web page. The audio file format you can embed on the Web page is determined by the browser plug-in and audio player that the viewer has on the computer. At the time of writing, the common audio files used for embedding on a Web page are QuickTime, RealAudio, and WMA (Windows Media Audio). QuickTime movies can be used as audio-only movies that contain the audio track without the video track. Both the QuickTime and RealAudio require browser plug-ins—QuickTime and RealPlayer plug-ins. WMA files require Windows Media Player to play. Other audio formats, such as AIF, WAV, MP3, and MIDI files, also can be embedded on Web pages. Which player is used to play these audio files will depend on the viewer's browser setting. QuickTime can be used to play these audio files. However, the viewer's browser setting may not be set up for these files to use QuickTime player. You can use HTML coding—described later in this section—to force a browser to use the QuickTime to play a file no matter what its file type is. Otherwise, whether these files will be able to play on the viewer's browser or how these files will be played is unpredictable.

Fast download is a crucial criterion for any medium intended for use on the Web. Thus, audio files intended for the Web should be kept as small as possible in file size or in a format that allows streaming or progressive download. Both streaming and progressive download do not require the whole file being downloaded before playing. The audio starts playing once there has been enough audio data downloaded. Streaming requires a streaming server besides a Web Server but progressive download does not. QuickTime and RealAudio support streaming and progressive download.

QuickTime Audio-Only Movies

QuickTime audio-only movies can be exported using digital video-editing programs, such as Adobe Premiere Pro and Apple Final Cut Pro. You will need to check the option to export audio only. QuickTime movies that support progressive downloading are known as Fast-Start movies. One simple way to create a Fast-Start QuickTime is to save the QuickTime movie as a self-contained movie. To do so, you will need the Pro version of QuickTime Player, not the free version. First, open the QuickTime movie with QuickTime Pro. Then, select `File > Save As...` In the File Save dialog box, select the option "Make movie self-contained." If the option is not active, you give a different file name or save the movie in a different folder. You can replace the original QuickTime file with the Fast-Start movie later.

Including QuickTime Audio-Only Movies in a Web Page

To embed a QuickTime movie, whether an audio-only or one that contains a video track, you can use the `<object>` tag. The `src` parameter or `data` attribute specifies the file path to the QuickTime movie. There are many other parameters you can set to control how the embedded QuickTime is played on the Web page. Some examples are:

- `controller` parameter sets the visibility of the movie controller bar
- `loop` parameter sets whether the movie loops playback
- `autoplay` parameters set whether the QuickTime movie automatically starts. If it is set to false, the user would have to click on the play button to start the audio playback.

```
<html>
<head>
<title>Demo - Background Play QT Sound</title>
</head>

<body>
<object classid="clsid:02BF25D5-8C17-4B23-BC80-D3488ABDDC6B"
        codebase="http://www.apple.com/qtactivex/qtplugin.cab"
        width="0" height="0">
  <param name="src" value="ylwong-example.mov"/>
  <param name="controller" value="false"/>
  <param name="autoplay" value="true"/>
  <param name="loop" value="true"/>

  <object type="video/quicktime" data="ylwong-example.mov"
            width="0" height="0">
    <param name="controller" value="false"/>
    <param name="autoplay" value="true"/>
    <param name="loop" value="true"/>
    <a href="ylwong-example.mov">ylwong-example.mov</a>
  </object>

</object>
</body>
</html>
```

Figure 5.21 HTML code example 1 for embedding QuickTime

The HTML codes of two Web pages are shown here. The first example (Figure 5.21) demonstrates using a QuickTime audio-only movie as background audio. The display of controller is set to false and the movie dimensions are set to zero. Thus, there is no visual indication of a QuickTime movie on the Web page. The QuickTime movie has to be set to automatically start playing.

To use the example code for including your audio-only QuickTime movie in a Web page, you can copy the code of the <object> tags and change the values (in blue color) of parameters and attributes to suit your needs.

ABOUT THE EXAMPLE CODE FOR EMBEDDING QuickTime

At the time of writing, the <object> tags may not work properly in some browsers. If the browser or its plug-in can interpret the <object> tags, then the QuickTime movie will be played. Otherwise, the alternative content is displayed if an alternative content is specified.

In the example code shown in Figure 5.21, the alternative content inserted is a hyperlink to the QuickTime movie file:

```
<a href="ylwong-example.mov">ylwong-example.mov</a>
```

This creates a hyperlink to the file named ylwong-example.mov that will be displayed on the Web page if the browser cannot interpret the <object> tags in the code.

Any HTML code can be inserted as a alternative content. An image (such as a static image or a GIF animation) can be used as an alternative content.

```
<html>
<head>
<title>Demo - QT Sound with Controller</title>
</head>

<body>
<object classid="clsid:02BF25D5-8C17-4B23-BC80-D3488ABDDC6B"
        codebase="http://www.apple.com/qtactivex/qtplugin.cab"
        width="50" height="16">
   <param name="src" value="ylwong-example.mov"/>
   <param name="controller" value="false"/>
   <param name="autoplay" value="true"/>
   <param name="loop" value="true"/>

   <object type="video/quicktime" data="ylwong-example.mov"
              width="50" height="16">
      <param name="controller" value="false"/>
      <param name="autoplay" value="true"/>
      <param name="loop" value="true"/>
      <a href="ylwong-example.mov">ylwong-example.mov</a>
   </object>

</object>
</body>
</html>
```

Figure 5.22 HTML code example 2 for embedding QuickTime

(a)   (b)

Figure 5.23 QuickTime Controllers set at different widths (a) Width attribute set to 50 with only three buttons displayed (b) Width attribute set to larger than 50, say 100, so the progress slider will appear between the play/pause and options buttons

The second example (Figure 5.22) demonstrates embedding a QuickTime movie that displays a minimal height for the controller on the Web page. The width is set to allow displaying of three buttons: volume control, play/pause, and options (Figure 5.23a). The width attribute can be set longer to allow the audio progress slider (Figure 5.23b).

MP3 is a popular audio file format and has the advantage of a smaller file size compared to other formats. To use a QuickTime plug-in to play an mp3 file, you can use the code shown in Figures 5.21 and 5.22, but change the value of the type attribute in the <object> tag from "video/quicktime" to "audio/mpeg".

> ⌖ **Example Web Page of Including Audio-only QuickTime** Two Web pages that demonstrate embedding an audio-only QuickTime.

> ⌖ **Example Web Page of Including MP3** A Web page that demonstrates embedding a MP3.

RealAudio

RealAudio can be converted from a .wav file to a .ra or .rm file using RealProducer Basic (Figure 5.24). RealProducer Basic is freely available from the RealSystem Web site. There are

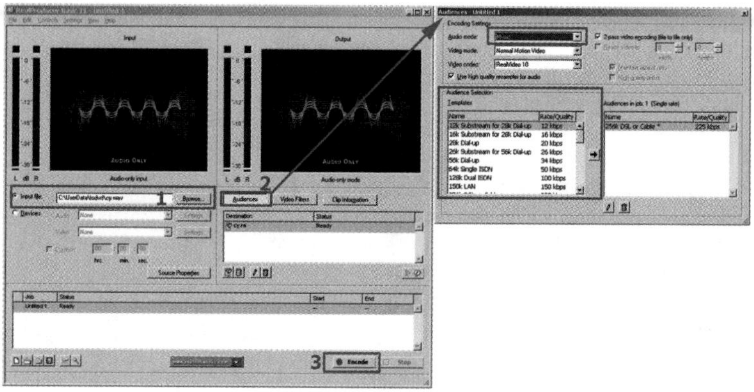

Figure 5.24 Creating RealAudio using Real Producer Basic 11 (1) Select the .wav file you want to convert to .ra or .rm (2) Click on the Audiences button and select the type of the audio and the target audiences' network connection speed (3) Click the Encode button to start the conversion

RealProducer Basic can also encode video into RealVideo.

also fee-based products, such as RealProducer Plus, that offer more features for encoding audio and video for streaming. For example, RealProducer Plus lets you create Real media with an unlimited number of different bit-rate streams, but the Basic edition is limited to three.

Embedding RealAudio on a Web Page

For more information about using RealAudio on the Web, visit Real-System's online chapter on Delivering a Presentation: http://service.real. com/help/library/ guides/production/ htmfiles/server.htm

RealAudio can be streamed. This will require a Real Server—a streaming server. However, RealAudio also can be used on the Web without streaming, and thus, a streaming server is not needed. The example shown in Figure 5.25 demonstrates how to embed a RealAudio file on a Web page where the RealAudio file will be played from a Web server, not from a RealServer.

To use the example code in Figure 5.25 for including your RealAudio file in a Web page, you can copy the code of the <object> tags and change the values (in blue color) of parameters and attributes to suit your needs.

The value of the parameter/attribute controls is set to "all" in this example. This makes the RealAudio player display a full player with all controls. There are other settings available for controls. For example, setting the value of controls to "PlayButton" will cause the player to display the play and pause buttons only, and setting it to "StatusBar" will cause the player to display the bar showing the audio status only.

> 🖱 **Example Web Page of Including RealAudio** A Web page that demonstrates embedding a RealAudio.

WMA

WMA files can be created using Microsoft's Windows Movie Maker 2. Movie Maker is a video editing tool, but it allows you to export audio as an .wma file. Other audio editing programs (such as Adobe Audition and Sony Sound Forge) and video editing programs (such as Adobe Premiere Pro) also let you save an audio as a .wma file. An HTML code example for embedding a WMA file is shown in Figure 5.26.

```
<html>
<head>
<title>Demo - Embed RealAudio</title>
</head>

<body>
<object classid="clsid:CFCDAA03-8BE4-11cf-B84B-0020AFBBCCFA"
        width="100" height="50">
   <param name="type" value="audio/x-pn-realaudio-plugin"/>
   <param name="src" value="ylwong-realaudio-example.rm"/>
   <param name="autostart" value="true"/>
   <param name="controls" value="all"/>

   <object type="audio/x-pn-realaudio-plugin" data="ylwong-realaudio-example.rm"
           width="100" height="50"
           autostart="true"
           controls="all">
     <param name="autostart" value="true"/>
     <param name="controls" value="all"/>
     <a href="ylwong-realaudio-example.rm"> ylwong-realaudio-example.rm</a>
   </object>

</object>
</body>
</html>
```

Figure 5.25 HTML code example for embedding RealAudio

```
<html>
<head>
<title>Demo - Embed WMA</title>
</head>

<body>
<object classid="CLSID:22D6F312-B0F6-11D0-94AB-0080C74C7E95"
        width="200" height="44">
   <param name="type" value="application/x-oleobject"/>
   <param name="fileName" value="ylwong-example.wma"/>
   <param name="autoStart" value="true"/>
   <param name="showControls" value="true"/>

   <object type="application/x-oleobject" data="ylwong-example.wma"
           width="200" height="44">
     <param name="autostart" value="true"/>
   <param name="showControls" value="true"/>
     <a href="ylwong-example.wma">ylwong-example.wma</a>
   </object>

</object>
</body>
</html>
```

Figure 5.26 HTML code example for embedding Windows Media Audio

🖰 **Example Web Page of Including WMA** A Web page that demonstrates embedding a WMA file.

To use the example code from Figure 5.26 for including your .wma file in a Web page, you can copy the code of the <object> tags and change the values (in blue color) of parameters and attributes to suit your needs.

5.5.4 Audio CD

Audio editing programs (such as Adobe Audition) also let you create audio CD projects in which you can specify a title and artist for each track. CD players that support CD Text can display such information during playback. It also lets you designate the length of pauses between tracks, enable or disable copy protection, and add an ISRC (International Standard burning software Code) number—a code that is used for commercial distribution. Many CD burning software programs let you create audio CDs. However, these programs usually do not have these options.

Audio on CDs must use 44,100 Hz sampling rate, 16-bits and stereo. If you are creating audio CDs, you should plan to acquire audio sources that are recorded or generated at at least these settings. If you insert a track with a different sample type in Adobe Audition or a CD recording program, the program automatically will convert the audio to these CD settings for you. However, such conversion does not boost the audio quality.

5.5.5 Podcast

A *podcast* is a collection of files available on a Web server. The files in a podcast are usually audio and video, but they also can be Web pages, text, PDF, images, or any file type. Each file is referred to as an *episode* of the podcast. The internet addresses of the files are listed in a text file, known as the *feed*.

The feed is posted on a Web server. People can subscribe to a collection by subscribing its feed, so that whenever new episodes or files become available in the collection, the files will automatically be downloaded to their computers or devices (i.e., portable media players such as iPod).

The subscriber's computer or device will need to have a software program that checks the collection periodically for new files and automatically downloads the new items. Such software is called the *aggregator*. For example, iTunes is a podcast aggregator. The aggregator also is used to subscribe to and playback podcasts.

The files in a podcast can be any file type. These are the same file types that you would find posted on the Web. You do not have to make your audio files or any other media files a podcast in order to deliver them on the Web. The key difference between podcasting and posting the media files on the Web is the automatic mechanism of podcasting. When you post files on the Web, you depend on the audience coming to your site to check new updates and download the files. In podcasting, once the audience has subscribed to your feed, the aggregator will periodically go to your site to check the feed file for updates and automatically download any new items. Of course, you would need to add the information of the new items to the feed text file in addition to posting the new items on the Web.

How to Podcast Audio[*]

To create a podcast, you will need to have at least two files.

- Your audio content must be saved in a file format that is supported by the aggregator used by your target subscribers. MP3 is the most commonly supported format for podcast aggregators.
- Your podcast feed file is a text file and an XML file that lists the information of the items in your podcast. A feed file usually has a file extension .rss or .xml. An example of a feed file is shown in the following step-by-step guide.

Step 1 Create Your Audio Content in MP3

In this chapter, you have learned how to create digital audio. Almost all digital audio editing programs let you export your audio content to MP3 format.

- Adobe Audition 2.0: File > Save As ... and choose MP3PRO® (FhG)(*.mp3) for the file type (Figure 5.27a).
- Sony Sound Forge 9: File > Save As ... and choose MP3 Audio (*.mp3) for the file type (Figure 5.27b).
- Audacity 1.2.6: File > Export As MP3... (Figure 5.27c).
- Sony ACID Pro 6: File > Render As... and choose MP3 Audio (*.mp3) for the file type (Figure 5.27d).

Step 2 Put Your MP3 Files on a Web Server

Upload your MP3 files onto a Web server. Note their internet address or URLs.

Step 3 Create Your Podcast Feed File

A feed file is a text file that provides links to your MP3 files. You can use any text editor to create the feed file. However, there is specific format for how the links and other information of the podcast are written in the feed file. There are programs that you can use to generate the feed file. A feed file may look like that in Figure 5.28.

The <channel> element is used to describe the whole podcast. The example in Figure 5.28 includes only <title>, <link>, <description>, and <item> within the <channel>. You can also include <pubDate> to indicate the publication date of the whole podcast, <copyright> to include copyright information, and <language> to indicate the language used in the podcast.

The <item> elements are the most important elements in a channel. Each <item> element contains information about each podcast episode, for example, where the aggregator can download the media file from. The <enclosure> element specifies the internet address or URL of the media file. The length attribute of <enclosure> is the audio's file size in bytes. Within <item>, there is also a <title> tag. It is used to give the episode a name. The <link> gives the URL of the Web page that discusses the episode.

Apple GarageBand 3.0 lets you publish audio podcasts from your Garage-Band project without having to write your feed file and create a MP3 file.

Don't forget that MP3 uses lossy compression. You should save your audio content using an uncompressed format or a file format that uses lossless compression, such as Windows PCM WAV or AIFF. After you have finished with the audio content, you can export the audio as an MP3 file.

For information on other tags for the channel element, look up the RSS specifications on the Web.

---

[*]Useful resources to podcast audio:

Make Your First Podcast:
http://www.podcastingnews.com/articles/How-to-Podcast.html
Understanding RSS News Feeds:
http://www.podcastingnews.com/articles/Understanding_RSS_Feeds.html
Podcasting Software (Publishing): http://www.podcastingnews.com/topics/Podcasting_Software.html

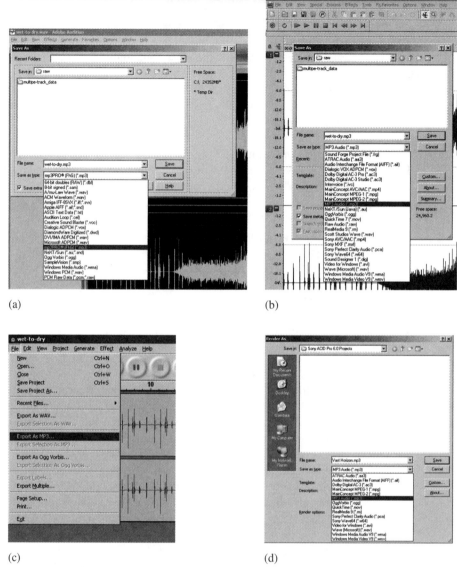

Figure 5.27 Saving an audio in MP3 format (a) Adobe Audition (b) Sony Sound Forge (c) Audacity (d) Sony ACID Pro

Step 4 **Publish Your Podcast Feed**

Post your feed file to a Web server and make a link to the feed file like you would post and link any other content. Many sites use an icon, usually orange in color, like those shown in Figure 5.29 to indicate that a news feed is available.

Figure 5.30 shows how the example feed file (shown in Figure 5.28) is displayed in iTunes, a podcast aggregator. The titles and the descriptions for the channel and items that are displayed in iTunes are specified in the code (highlighted in the code in Figure 5.30).

```
<?xml version="1.0"?>
<rss version="2.0">
    <channel>
        <title>Demos of Podcast</title>
        <link>http://digitalmedia.wfu.edu/</link>
        <description>This is a demo for podcasting.</description>

        <item>
           <title>Episode 1: Analog vs. Digital</title>
           <link>http://digitalmedia.wfu.edu/primer/chapter1.html</link>
           <author>Yue-Ling Wong</author>
           <description>Analog is continuous while digital is discrete. Analog information
           is also infinite. However, computers deal with discrete data and have finite
           capacity. </description>
           <enclosure url="http://digitalmedia.wfu.edu/podcast/media/analog-digital.mp3"
           length="352128" type="audio/mpeg"/>
           <pubDate>Tue, July 24, 2007</pubDate>
        </item>

        <item>
           <title>Episode 2: Sampling and Quantizing</title>
           <link>http://digitalmedia.wfu.edu/primer/chapter1.html</link>
           <author>Yue-Ling Wong</author>
           <description>The digitization is a 2-step process: sampling and quantizing</description>
           <enclosure url="http://digitalmedia.wfu.edu/podcast/media/sampling-quantizing.mp3"
           length="73240" type="audio/mpeg"/>
           <pubDate>Sun, July 29, 2007</pubDate>
        </item>

    </channel>
</rss>
```

Figure 5.28 An example feed file

Figure 5.29 Icons used on the Web to indicate news feed is available

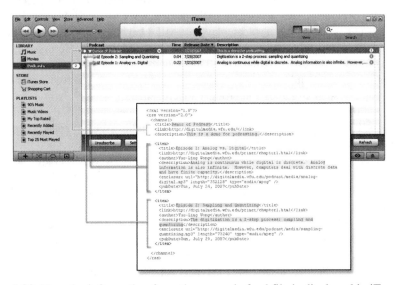

Figure 5.30 How the information from the example feed file is displayed in iTunes

151

5.6 SUMMARY

Digital audio can be acquired by two methods: (1) recording sound and directly storing it in digital format and (2) digitizing an analog audio media, such as analog audio tapes. To record audio directly into digital format or digitize analog audio, your computer needs to have a sound card. All new computers nowadays come with a sound card installed.

In order to record audio directly, you also need a microphone. For the software requirement, you need a digital audio-recording program. Most, if not all, digital audio-editing programs are capable of recording audio. Before you start recording, you need to specify the sampling rate, bit depth, and number of channels you want to use. Monitor the sound level meters during recording. Adjust the input volume level so that the meter level stays below the red area, occasionally brushing near the red area without going over it. Going over the red area will cause clipping and distortion of your recording.

To digitize analog audio medium, such as cassette tapes, you do not need a microphone but you will need to connect the line-out port of the cassette tape deck with the line-in port on your sound card using an audio cable.

The two very basic elements you would find in a digital audio-editing program are (1) a waveform display window and (2) the transport controls where you find the play, record, rewind, and fast forward buttons.

In the waveform display, the *x*-axis represents the time, and the *y*-axis represents the amplitude value. Many audio-editing programs also have a spectral view available. The *y*-axis in the spectral view represents the audio frequency. The amplitude information is color-coded in the spectral view.

You can reassemble an audio by cutting and pasting the waveform. You can enhance the audio by adjusting the volume of the audio using amplify, normalize, or envelope effects. Some programs have built-in functions for noise reduction to clean up background noise and hiss. Special effects, such as reverb and pitch change, also are available for altering the audio.

Programs such as Adobe Audition, Sony Sound Forge, and Audacity let you mix multiple audio tracks in addition to editing a single waveform.

MIDI and loop music are two common methods for creating music for digital media projects. Music scores can be created using sheet music software in MIDI format. MIDI creation software often provides three views for MIDI creation and editing: Staff view, Piano Roll view, and Event List view. You also can play on a MIDI keyboard (if connected and set up properly with the software) to record your performance into a MIDI file. Composing in MIDI allows you to create your own original score, but it requires some musical composition skills.

Loop music software and libraries provide a solution for non-music composers to create audio for projects, such as games and product advertisement.

Digital audio can be created for audio CD production, video production and multimedia presentations. It can be used for the Web. To use audio on the Web, you can (1) embed the audio on the Web page or (2) create a hyperlink to the audio file. The second method will cause the audio file to play in a player window external to the Web page. How the audio is going to play is determined by the browser plug-in and audio player that the viewer has on the computer. This chapter shows several examples of HTML code for embedding QuickTime, RealAudio, and WMA files.

Podcasting is another way to deliver digital audio on the Web. The key difference between podcasting and posting media files on the Web is from the automatic mechanism of podcasting. A podcast is a collection of files available on a Web server. The files in a podcast are usually audio and video, but they can be any file type. Each file is referred to as an episode of the podcast. The internet addresses of the files are listed in a text file, known as the feed. The feed is posted on a Web server. People can subscribe to a collection by subscribing to its feed. The subscriber's computer or device will need to have a software that checks the collection periodically for updates and automatically downloads the new items. Such software is called the aggregator. The aggregator also is used to subscribe to and playback podcasts.

TERMS

aggregator, 148	feed, 148	Piano Roll view, 139
Amplify, 136	Hiss Reduction, 136	podcast, 148
clipping, 126	loop music, 140	reverb, 137
Edit view, 132	Multitrack view, 132	sound card, 124
Envelope, 136	noise floor, 137	spectral view, 133
Event List view, 139	Noise reduction, 137	Staff view, 139
fade-in, 136	Noise removal, 137	
fade-out, 136	Normalize, 136	

LEARNING AIDS

The following learning aids can be found at the book's companion Web site.

Setting Recording Controls in Windows
Screen capture movie that demonstrates how to set the recording device to microphone and adjust the volume in Windows.

Recording Audio in Adobe Audition
Screen capture movie that demonstrates the basic steps of recording audio in Adobe Audition.

Reassembling Waveforms in Adobe Audition
Screen capture movie demonstrating the selecting, cutting, and pasting of audio waveforms in Adobe Audition.

Applying Noise Reduction in Adobe Audition
Screen capture movie demonstrating the application of the Noise Reduction effects to an audio recording in Adobe Audition.

Audio Manipulation (Lab)
Practice recording your voice, remove background noise, reassemble waveform, and apply audio effects.

Creating and Editing MIDI in Cakewalk SONAR
Screen capture movie that demonstrates creating and editing MIDI using Staff, Piano Roll, and Event List views in Cakewalk SONAR.

Working with Loops in Sony ACID Pro
Screen capture movie that demonstrates creating loop music in Sony ACID Pro.

Working with Loops in Adobe Audition
Screen capture movie that demonstrates creating loop music in Adobe Audition.

Example Web Page of Including Audio-only QuickTime
Two Web pages that demonstrate embedding an audio-only QuickTime.

Example Web Page of Including MP3
A Web page that demonstrates embedding a MP3.

Example Web Page of Including RealAudio
A Web page that demonstrates embedding a RealAudio.

Example Web Page of Including WMA
A Web page that demonstrates embedding a WMA file.

REVIEW QUESTIONS

When applicable, please choose all correct answers.

1. The x-axis of the waveform view represents the _____ .

   A. amplitude value
   B. frequency
   C. time

2. The y-axis of the waveform view represents the _____ .

   A. amplitude value
   B. frequency
   C. time

3. The x-axis of the spectral view represents the _____ .

   A. amplitude value
   B. frequency
   C. time

4. The y-axis of the spectral view represents the _____.

   A. amplitude value
   B. frequency
   C. time

5. Which view allows you to inspect the audio frequency distribution over time?

   A. waveform view
   B. spectral view

6. **True/False:** The optimal meter level for recording is going past the red area of the meter.

7. **True/False:** Application of special effects, such as reverb, to a noisy audio should be done before the noise reduction.

8. The fade-in and fade-out effects can be created by applying the _____ effect.

   A. amplify
   B. envelope
   C. noise reduction
   D. normalize
   E. reverb

9. **True/False:** In order to use RealAudio on the Web, you have to have a RealServer to stream the audio.

10. The HTML tag that you can use to place a QuickTime on a Web page is _____ .

    A. <object>
    B. <qt>
    C. <rpm>
    D. <mov>
    E. <src>

11. Which of the following parameters needs to set to true so that a QuickTime embedded in a Web page will start playing automatically?

    A. autoplay
    B. controller
    C. loop
    D. src

EXPLORING THE APPLICATIONS

1. Explore the workspace of your audio editing program.
   - Locate the transport control.
   - Locate the recording level meter.
   - Find out if your program has spectral view.
   - Find out if your program supports multitrack audio mixing.

2. Explore the audio editing functionalities of your audio editing program. Locate the commands for:
   - Resampling the audio, altering bit depth, and changing the number of channels
   - Amplify
   - Normalize
   - Reverb
   - Noise reduction
   - Using an envelope graph
   - Creating fade-in and fade-out

3. Practice:
   (i) Recording your voice
   (ii) Reassemble the waveform of your recording
   (iii) Apply noise reduction to clean your recording
   (iv) Normalize your waveform to a satisfactory amplitude
   (v) Apply effects such as reverb, fade-in, and fade-out
   (vi) Export your recording to audio-only QuickTime or MP3
   (vii) Include your audio on a Web page

Fundamentals of Digital Video

CHAPTER

6

KEY CONCEPTS

- Interlaced and progressive scan
- Overscan and safe zones
- Frame rate
- Frame size and frame aspect ratio
- Pixel aspect ratio
- Counting frames with timecode
- Data rate
- Video compression methods
- MPEG
- GOP, I-frame, P-frame, and B-frame
- Standard definition and high definition digital video
- Streaming video and progressive download

GENERAL LEARNING OBJECTIVES

At the end of this chapter, you should be able to demonstrate that you

- Know the common terminology used in digital video.
- Know the common terminology for DTV.
- Comprehend the influence of analog broadcast standards on digital video.
- Distinguish the different implications of data rate and file size.
- Determine the suitable video data rate for a playback device.
- Comprehend the relationship among frame size, frame aspect ratio, and pixel aspect ratio.
- Comprehend how pixel aspect ratio affects the display of video picture.
- Read video timecodes.
- Comprehend the general strategies for video file size optimization.
- Comprehend video general compression strategies.
- Distinguish true streaming and progressive download.
- Comprehend GOP, I-frame, P-frame, and B-frame, and the M and N parameters.
- Comprehend motion compensation and motion vector in MPEG compression.
- Distinguish the frame size and frame aspect ratio of standard and high definition digital video.

6.1 THE NATURE OF MOTION AND BROADCAST VIDEO

In the natural world, we perceive motion as a continuous flow of events. It is a combination of visual, auditory, and temporal experience. Video cameras have long been available to capture motion on analog media, such as films, VHS tapes, and Hi-8 tapes.

Conceptually, motion is captured as a sequence of pictures at a constant time interval. Each picture is called a *frame*. How fast the pictures are captured or how fast the frames are played back is determined by the *frame rate*, which is measured in *frames per second (fps)*.

There are broadcast standards for digital video's resolution, color spaces, and frame rate to adhere to. The digital video standards have been influenced by the existing analog television broadcast standards. In order to understand the rationale behind digital video standards, it is necessary to learn about analog television broadcast standards.

6.1.1 Broadcast Standards

There are three sets of broadcast standards for analog color televisions. These standards pertain to the technical details of how color television pictures are encoded and transmitted as broadcast signals. Each standard is also characterized by its specific frame rate and the number of scan lines in each frame. These important attributes are translated into digital video standards. The number of lines in each frame in the analog broadcast standard is translated to the pixel height of a frame in digital video.

NTSC was named after United State's National Television Systems Committee, which designated this standard. It is used in North America, Japan, Taiwan, and parts of the Caribbean and South America. *PAL* stands for Phase Alternating Line, which refers to the way the signals are encoded. It is used in Australia, New Zealand, and most of Western Europe and the Asian countries. *SECAM* stands for Séquentiel Couleur avec Mémoire, which translates as sequential color with memory. It is used in France, the former Soviet Union, and Eastern Europe. The standards adopted in Africa and parts of Asia are mostly influenced by their colonial histories.

> The implications of the scan lines in a frame will be discussed in Section 6.1.3.
>
> Not all digital video formats have to conform to broadcast standards. Some digital video formats are intended mainly for computer playback—not for television. For example, QuickTime movies do not have to conform to a standard resolution or frame rate. On the other hand, videos intended for DVD playback need to conform to DVD-video standards, which are based on broadcast standards.

6.1.2 Frame Rate

Table 6.1 lists the frame rate of different systems. The frame rate for NTSC was originally 30 fps for black-and-white television broadcast. In order to accommodate additional color information for color pictures, the frame rate was lowered to 29.97 fps.

TABLE 6.1	Frame Rates of Different Video Types
Video Type	**Frame Rate (frames per second or fps)**
NTSC	29.97
PAL	25
SECAM	25
Motion-picture film	24

6.1.3 Interlaced and Progressive Scan

A picture displayed on a television or a computer CRT monitor is made up of horizontal lines. These lines are traced across the screen one line at a time. An NTSC frame contains 525 lines, of which about 480 are picture. Each PAL or SECAM frame contains 625 lines, of which about 576 are picture.

Video Display: Interlaced Scan versus Progressive Scan An interactive animation that illustrates two-pass scanning in interlaced scan and one-pass scanning in progressive scan.

Upper Field and Lower Field An interactive demo shows the upper field and the lower field of a video frame.

Fast-Action Digital Video Showing the Interlace Artifact A soccer practice video clip of Figure 6.1 shows the comb-like interlace artifact.

Video Recording: Interlaced Mode versus Progressive Mode An interactive animation that illustrates how the interlace artifact may be produced in fast-action videos.

Computer monitors display the picture by displaying the lines from top to bottom in one pass. Analog television standards for NTSC, PAL, and SECAM display the picture in two passes: for NTSC, the first pass traces the even-numbered lines and the second pass traces the odd-numbered lines to fill in the alternating gaps left by the first pass. The set of the lines in the same pass (i.e., the set of even lines or odd lines) is called a *field*. The field containing the topmost scan line (i.e., the first scan line) is called the *upper field*, and the other field is the *lower field*. This display method of using two alternating fields is called *interlaced scan*. Displaying all lines in one pass on computer monitors is called *progressive scan*.

Because the two fields in a frame are captured at a slightly different moment in time, discontinuities will become apparent for fast moving objects in video shot in the interlaced mode. Such discontinuities appear as comb-like artifacts, as shown in Figure 6.1. The lower field of the frame is shown in Figure 6.1c and the upper field in Figure 6.1e. The interlace artifact is usually not apparent in normal playback. It is discernible in slow motion or freeze frame.

(a)

(b)

(c)

(d)

Figure 6.1 (a) A digital video frame showing comb-like artifact caused by fast action and camera panning (b) Close-up of the small red area in (a) (c) The upper field of the video frame (d) Close-up of the small red area in (c). (*continued*)

(e)   (f)

Figure 6.1 (*continued*) (e) The lower field of the video frame (f) Close-up of the small red area in (e)

DEINTERLACE

The interlace artifact can be removed by discarding one field and filling in the gaps by duplicating or interpolating the other field (Figure 6.2). Either way will degrade the image quality.

During normal playback, the interlace artifact is not discernible. Deinterlacing is normally not necessary. However, if you need to capture a freeze frame and the interlace artifact is discernible, you may need to deinterlace the image.

(a)   (b)

Figure 6.2 (a) The video frame deinterlaced by eliminating the upper field and interpolating the lower field to fill in the gaps (b) Close-up of the small red area

6.1.4 Overscan and Safe Zones

When a video is displayed on a consumer analog television set, the border of the image extends beyond the screen; not the entire image is visible on screen. The area that is outside of the screen is called the ***overscan***. Overscan is necessary for television to conceal, for example, the edge distortion and nonimage signals. The signals are not actually "lost." For example, if you record a digital television program, such as satellite TV, and play it back on a computer monitor, you will see the whole image as well as other nonimage

Figure 6.3 (a) Outlines of the safe action area (b) Outlines of the safe title area

signals which look like noise at the edges of the frame. If you watch a DVD movie on a computer, you can see a whole frame. However, if the same DVD movie is played on a consumer analog television set, the content outside the border may not be seen on screen due to the overscan.

As a consequence of overscan, you should not place the important content too close to the edge when framing your shots, especially if your target audience will be watching your video on consumer television. But how close is "too close"? There is no one exact number to fit all televisions, because the overscan area is not consistent across consumer television sets. However, there are two common guides that can help you frame your shots: the safe action area and the safe title area.

The *safe action area* is where the significant action takes place. The *safe title area* is where you should place critical text titles and critical content. The safe title area is visible on the majority of the television sets. In general, it is recommended the center 90% of the frame size as the safe action area and 80% as the safe title area (Figure 6.3). This means that the safe action area leaves an approximately 5% border all around the frame and the safe title area leaves about a 10% border around. In Figure 6.3, it is very likely that the soccer player on the right edge of the frame—outside of the safe action area—will not be visible on an analog television screen. Also, depending on the overscan of the television that plays the video, the soccer ball which lies at the border of safe title area may not show up whole.

6.1.5 Color Format

RGB is a common color model for still digital images, but for video, the luminance-chrominance color models are used (for example, *YUV* and *YIQ* color models). These color models divide color into one *luminance* (brightness) component (Y) and two *chrominance* (color or hue) components (U and V in YUV, or I and Q in YIQ).

The luminance-chrominance color model was invented at the same time as color television for adding color signals to the television broadcast. By using this color model, the same signal could be used for both black-and-white and color television sets: the black-and-white television uses only the luminance (Y) signal, while the color set uses both the luminance and chrominance signals.

YUV was originally the color model for analog television broadcasts of the PAL system. YIQ is the model adopted by the National Television System Committee (NTSC) in the United States.

In addition, another luminance-chrominance model called YC_bC_r, which is closely related to YUV, is used in MPEG compression. MPEG compression is used in DVD videos. MPEG compression will be discussed later in this chapter.

RELATIONSHIPS BETWEEN RGB AND YUV/YIQ

The CS module discusses the conversion between color spaces in details. But to show you that the Y, U, and V, and Y, I, and Q can be derived from RGB values, here are the equations:

$$Y = 0.299R + 0.587G + 0.114B$$
$$U = 0.492(B - Y) = -0.147R - 0.289G + 0.436B$$
$$V = 0.877(R - Y) = 0.615R - 0.515G - 0.100B$$

$$Y = 0.299R + 0.587G + 0.114B$$
$$I = 0.596R - 0.275G - 0.321B$$
$$Q = 0.212R - 0.523G + 0.311B$$

The reason we introduce the analog broadcast's color models in this chapter is that the YUV color models are also used in the standards for digital video.

When you edit digital video, you do not need to explicitly set the color space to YUV or YIQ. If you create digital images for use in video, they can be kept in RGB format. The digital video-editing program will convert the images to the correct color format.

6.2 SAMPLING AND QUANTIZATION OF MOTION

Each frame in a video is an image. Conceptually, in digital video, these images are digitized in a way similar to digital images by sampling and quantization. The image for each frame is sampled into a grid of discrete samples—the sampling process. Each sample becomes a pixel. The digital video frame size is still measured in pixels, like digital still images. Each pixel is assigned with a color value from a finite list of color—the quantization process. The finite list of color is within the video's color space.

See Chapter 1 for the general concept of sampling and quantization and Chapter 2 for the sampling and quantization in the digital image.

Besides the image frame, the sampling process also occurs in the temporal dimension of video. The sampling rate of the temporal dimension is the frame rate of the video. The higher the frame rate, the more accurate the motion is sampled. However, higher frame rate also means more frames for the same video duration, which results in a larger file size.

6.3 MEASURING FRAME SIZE AND RESOLUTION OF DIGITAL VIDEO

Because digital videos are basically a sequence of digital images, many aspects of digital images discussed in Chapters 2 and 3 can be applied to a video frame. For example, in digital video, the *frame size* is referred to as *resolution* and is measured in pixel dimension.

However, unlike digital images, pixel per inch (ppi) is not really applicable in digital video. As discussed in Chapters 2 and 3 , the ppi value matters *only* when the image is printed—ppi is meaningless for images intended for Web or on-screen display. You never find the ppi attribute in digital video. The implication of this is that if you are creating a digital image to use in a digital video, you should set the image size based on the pixel dimension only—the ppi setting does not matter.

Another attribute used to describe the video frame size is its aspect ratio. As you will see in the following sections, a frame aspect ratio is not simply the ratio of its pixel width to its pixel height. This is because of an attribute called the pixel aspect ratio.

6.3.1 Frame Size

The *video frame size* (also referred to as resolution) is measured in the pixel dimension of a frame—its width by its height, expressed in number of pixels; for example, 640 × 480 pixels.

The terms DV and HDV may appear to be simple abbreviations for digital video and high definition digital video respectively. However, DV format and HDV format refer to specific video standards. In this chapter, the terms DV and HDV refer to those specific standards, not shorthands for digital video and high definition digital video.

- For a NTSC standard definition DV format, the frame size is 720 × 480 pixels. The frame size for a PAL standard DV frame is 720 × 576 pixels.
- For NTSC high definition digital video, there are several formats. For **HDV** format, there are two frame sizes at the time of this writing: 1280 × 720 pixels and 1440 × 1080 pixels. Other formats support different frame sizes. For example, AVCHD supports 1920 × 1080.

6.3.2 Frame Aspect Ratio

The *frame aspect ratio* is the ratio of its *viewing* width to height; it is not equivalent to the ratio of the frame's pixel width to height. For example, the frame aspect ratio for the standard format of standard definition NTSC video is 4:3, while the wide-screen format is 16:9 (Figure 6.4). The frame aspect ratio for high definition digital video and high definition TV (HDTV) are 16:9. Note that the grid in Figure 6.4 is used as a visual aid only to help you easily tell the width to height ratio. The grid cells are *not* representing the image pixels and the number of cells is *by no means* the number of pixels.

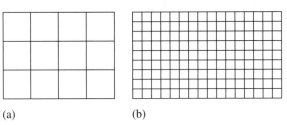

(a)   (b)

Figure 6.4 (a) A frame using an aspect ratio of 4:3
(b) A frame using an aspect ratio of 16:9

6.3.3 Pixel Aspect Ratio

The frame size of a NTSC standard definition DV frame is 720 × 480 pixels. However, based on these numbers, its width to height ratio is 720:480, i.e, 3:2. It does not match the frame aspect ratio quoted above; it is neither 4:3 nor 16:9. What is missing here?

In digital image editing, images use square pixels by default. However, some video formats use non-square pixels to make up the frame. The shape of the pixel can be described by an attribute called *pixel aspect ratio*. It is the ratio of a pixel's width to its height. For a square pixel, its pixel aspect ratio is equal to 1. A pixel aspect ratio of less than 1 depicts a tall pixel while a pixel aspect ratio of greater than 1 depicts a wide pixel.

For standard DV format, the pixel aspect ratio is 0.9, while the pixel aspect ratio for the wide-screen DV format is 1.2. The pixel aspect ratio for HDV 720p is 1.0 and HDV 1080i and 1080p is 1.333. Let's see if this makes sense for the DV frame size and its frame aspect ratio.

- For pixel aspect ratio = 0.9,
$$\text{width} : \text{height} = 720 \times 0.9 : 480 \cong 640 : 480 = 4:3$$
- For pixel aspect ratio = 1.2,
$$\text{width} : \text{height} = 720 \times 1.2 : 480 \cong 852 : 480 = 16:9$$

For HDV, its frame aspect ratio is 16:9.

- For 720p, pixel aspect ratio = 1.0,

$$\text{width : height} = 1280 \times 1.0 : 720 = 16:9$$

- For 1080i and 1080p, pixel aspect ratio = 1.333,

$$\text{width : height} = 1440 \times 1.333:1080 = 16:9$$

A video should be displayed on a system with the matching pixel aspect ratio, otherwise the image will be distorted. Figure 6.5 illustrates the effects of various pixel aspect ratios displayed on systems with different pixel aspect ratios. Figure 6.5a, d, and g show how video frames of pixel aspect ratios of 1.0, 0.9, and 1.2, respectively, are supposed to look when displayed correctly on a system with the same pixel aspect ratio as the frame's. Figure 6.5b, c, e, f, h, and i show the distorted frames displayed on systems with a pixel aspect ratio different from the frame's intended pixel aspect ratio.

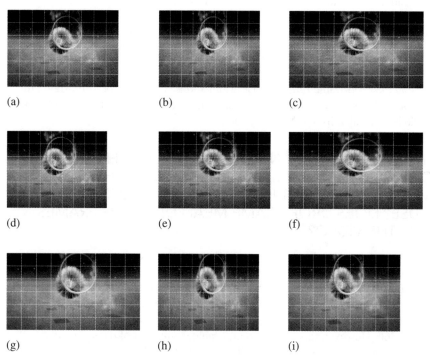

(a)   (b)   (c)

(d)   (e)   (f)

(g)   (h)   (i)

Figure 6.5 The images in the first column show how they look when displayed with the correct pixel aspect ratio. The other six images demonstrate how they are distorted when displayed with an incorrect pixel aspect ratio (a) A frame of pixel aspect ratio 1.0 displayed correctly (b) A frame of pixel aspect ratio 1.0 displayed incorrectly with a pixel aspect ratio of 0.9 and the ring is elongated vertically (c) A frame of pixel aspect ratio 1.0 displayed incorrectly with a pixel aspect ratio of 1.2 and the ring looks squashed (d) A frame of pixel aspect ratio 0.9 displayed correctly (e) A frame of pixel aspect ratio 0.9 displayed incorrectly with a pixel aspect ratio of 1.0 and the ring looks slightly wider than it should (f) A frame of pixel aspect ratio 0.9 displayed incorrectly with a pixel aspect ratio of 1.2 and the ring looks squashed (g) A frame of pixel aspect ratio 1.2 displayed correctly (h) A frame of pixel aspect ratio 1.2 displayed incorrectly with a pixel aspect ratio of 0.9 and the ring is elongated vertically (i) A frame of pixel aspect ratio 1.2 displayed incorrectly with a pixel aspect ratio of 1.0 and the ring is elongated vertically

A frame displayed on a system with a pixel aspect ratio larger than the frame's will stretch the image horizontally, and a frame displayed on a system with a smaller pixel aspect ratio will elongate the image vertically. The larger the difference between the frame's pixel aspect ratio and the system's, the greater the distortion.

SMPTE, founded in 1916, is an organization to develop standards in the motion picture industry. Their Web site is http://www.smpte.org

6.4 COUNTING TIME IN DIGITAL VIDEO

Video editing requires precise synchronization and hence precise measurement of time. The smallest timing unit in video is a frame which is usually only a fraction of a second. Therefore, our usual measurement of time in hours, minutes, and seconds is not precise enough for video. *Timecode* is used to number frames. *SMPTE* (Society of Motion Pictures and Television Engineers) video timecode, the most common timecode for digital video, numbers frames in hours, minutes, seconds, and frames. For example, 00:02:32:07 refers to the duration of 2 minutes, 32 seconds, and 7 frames.

There are two types of timecode: drop-frame and non-drop-frame. For example, the following indicates video time at 0 hours, 2 minutes, 51 seconds, and 20 frames.

Drop-frame timecode   00;02;51;20
Non-drop-frame timecode   00:02:51:20

Notice that the drop-frame timecode uses semicolons while the non-drop-frame timecode uses colons. This is how you can tell which timecode a system is using. The drop-frame timecode is preferable for the NTSC system.

WHAT IS THE DIFFERENCE BETWEEN DROP-FRAME AND NON-DROP-FRAME TIMECODES? WHY ARE THERE TWO TIMECODE FORMATS? HOW DO YOU CHOOSE WHICH ONE TO USE? DOES DROP-FRAME MEAN DELETING FRAMES FROM THE VIDEO?

To help you understand the need for two different timecodes, let's look at an analogous situation in our daily life—the purpose of leap years.

The time it takes for the Earth to orbit the Sun is about 365.242199 days, according to the Encyclopedia Britannica. Because it is not an exact number of days, we need leap years.

How? 365 days are designated for a year because the number 365.242199 is closer to 365 than 366. However, this causes an inevitable slight shift of days—about a 0.24 day each year or about 24 days for every 100 years. Without leap years, the seasons would shift. By adding one extra day to every fourth year, we get $(356 \times 3 + 366)$ days for four years, i.e., an average of 365.25 days per year. This offsets the shift very closely.

Why do we need to offset the shift? It is because we want to keep the seasons the same at the same time of the year every year. By using leap years, do we skip or delete time from our lives? No, of course not. We have the same amount of time no matter whether we have leap years or not; it is just a different way of counting days.

A similar situation arises with the NTSC-standard timebase. The NTSC-standard timebase is 29.97, not exactly 30 frames per second (fps). This fractional discrepancy will accumulate to make a significant difference between the actual frame duration and the time duration. Using the drop-frame timecode eliminates this error.

TABLE 6.2	Examples of How the Drop-Frame and Non-Drop-Frame Timecodes Count Frames, where the Length in Minutes Is Calculated by Dividing the Number of Frames by the Frame Rate			
Number of Frames	Length (minutes) for 29.97 fps	Length (minutes) for 30 fps	Drop-Frame Timecode	Non-Drop-Frame Timecode
1799	1.0004	0.9994	00;00;59;29	00:00:59:29
1800	1.001	1	00;01;00;02	00:01:00:00
17981	9.999	9.989	00:09:59:29	00:09:59:11
17982	10	9.990	00;10;00;00	00:09:59:12

When you use a drop-frame timecode, the program renumbers the first two frames of every minute except for every tenth minute. To demonstrate what this means, Table 6.2 shows the comparison of the two timecode formats with the length of video calculated based on different frame rates. For example, the drop-frame timecode increments from 00;00;59;29 to 00;01;00;02 in stepping one frame from the 1799th frame to the 1800th. The timecode skips 00;01;00;00 and 00;01;00;01—*renumbers two frames*—but *no* frame is actually discarded or dropped. On the other hand, the non-drop-frame timecode increments from 00;00;59;29 to 00;01;00;00.

For video of 29.97 fps, the 1800th frame is actually a little longer than 1 minute; it is about 1.001 minutes (1800/29.97). The drop-frame timecode 00;01;00;02 represents the duration of the 29.97-fps video more accurately than the non-drop-frame timecode 00:01:00:00.

However, the drop-frame timecode increments from 00;09;59;29 to 00;10;00;00 in stepping one frame from the 17981st frame to the 17982nd. The timecode now does not renumber any frame because it is the tenth minute—the first tenth. For the 29.97-fps video, the drop-frame timecode represents exactly the length of the video.

The discrepancy between the drop-frame and non-drop-frame timecodes seems very small. However, the discrepancy grows as the frame number progresses. If you have a separate audio created for the video, the discrepancy in video length will cause problems synchronizing the separate audio track with the video.

In working with digital video-editing programs, you need to choose a timecode format—drop-frame or non-drop-frame—for your project. However, you do not need to compute the timecode. The explanation provided in this section on how drop-frame timecode is computed is intended to help you understand the rationale to use the drop-frame timecode for the NTSC video and how it counts frames to maintain the time accuracy. It also helps you understand why some timecodes, such as 00;01;00;00 and 00;01;00;01, are skipped—not an abnormality. No frame is discarded in the process.

DROP-FRAME TIMECODE: WHY RENUMBER THE FIRST TWO FRAMES OF EVERY MINUTE? AND WHY SKIP THE RENUMBERING EVERY TENTH MINUTE?

It sounds complicated at first, but let's do a calculation to demonstrate the rationale behind it, so it does not seem complicated anymore.

Question

1. *Why renumber the first two frames of every minute?*

Let's first find out the number of frames in a video of exactly one minute.

- If the timebase for counting frames is 30 fps:

$$30 \text{ fps} \times 60 \text{ seconds} = 1800 \text{ frames}$$

- If the timebase for counting frames is 29.97 fps:

$$29.97 \text{ fps} \times 60 \text{ seconds} = 1798.2 \text{ frames}$$

For a one-minute video clip, the frame difference between the 30 fps and 29.97 fps is:

$$1800 - 1798.2 = 1.8 \text{ frames, or } \textit{approximately two frames}$$

Now you see why the first *two frames* of every minute need to be renumbered in the drop-frame timecode for NTSC-standard timebase.

Question

2. *Why does such renumbering skip every 10th minute?*

At exactly ten minutes, for 30 fps, it is the $18,000^{th}$ frame. It is denoted as 10:00:00 in non-drop-frame timecode.

But if counted for 29.97 fps, the 18000th frame is a little over ten minutes—it is 10 minutes and 18 frames (18,000 frames/29.97 fps).

In the first nine minutes, drop-frame timecode has already renumbered 18 frames (two frames each minute) to offset the shift. 18 frames are the offset necessary for ten minutes. Therefore, when it comes to the 10th minute, it should not renumber another two frames, otherwise, it will overcompensate.

6.5 DIGITAL VIDEO STANDARDS

6.5.1 Standard Definition

The term DV is often used as an abbreviation for digital video. However, *DV compression* or DV format refers to specific types of compression. For example, *DV25* is the most common DV compression for *standard definition digital video*.

DV25 is used by many digital video camcorders. These camcorders compress the video directly inside the camcorder. The video you get on tapes is already compressed into DV format.

Table 6.3 lists the specifications for the DV25 format.

TABLE 6.3	Part of the Specifications of DV25 Format		
Pixel Dimensions		720 × 480 (NTSC)	
Frame Aspect Ratio		4:3	16:9
Pixel Aspect Ratio		0.9	1.2
Data Rate	Total (video + audio + control information):	3.6 megabytes per second (MB/s), i.e. about 4.6 minutes of video per gigabyte of storage space	
	Video data only:	25 megabits per second (Mbps); compressed at a fixed rate of 5:1	
Color Sampling Method		YUV 4:1:1	
Audio setting	Sampling rate and bit depth:	Two options: • 48 kHz, 16-bit • 32 kHz, 12-bit	

DV25 compresses the video at a fixed data rate of 25 mega bits per second (Mbps) for the visual component of the video—hence the 25 in its name. This means 3.125 MB per second. The total data rate for video, audio, and other control information is about 3.6 MB per second The color space and color sampling method for NTSC is YUV 4:1:1. For NTSC, the frame size of the video is 720 × 480 pixels, and the frame rate is 29.97 fps.

WHAT DOES YUV 4:1:1 MEAN?

YUV is a luminance-chrominance color model that digital video uses to represent the color of each pixel.

The human eye is more sensitive to changes of the luminance (brightness) than it is to chrominance (color or hue) changes. Digital video systems exploit this phenomenon to reduce the storage of information by assigning fewer bits to storing the chrominance components. In other words, some chrominance data is discarded. This method is called the *chroma subsampling* or color subsampling.

There are several subsampling formats, depending on the ratio of the chrominance information to be discarded. The format is designated with three numbers separated by colons, for example, 4:2:2, to represent the ratio of the Y-component to the two chrominance components, Y:U:V.

The full-color information for each pixel contains one sample each of Y, U, and V. There are a total of three samples per pixel related to color information.

4:4:4

This means for each group of four pixels, four samples of Y-components and four samples each of the two chrominance components will be stored, i.e., total 12 samples for each group of four pixels. In other words, there is no saving in storage (no compression), i.e., no subsampling.

4:2:2

This subsampling method means that for every four pixels, it will use:

- 4 samples of Y
- 2 samples of U
- 2 samples of V

The total of samples used for every four pixels is now reduced from 12 to 8. This means a one-third reduction in storage.

This subsampling method is used in Digital Betacam video format.

4:2:0

This subsampling method means that for every four pixels, it will use:

- 4 samples of Y
- 2 samples of either U or V

The total of samples used for every four pixels is now reduced from 12 to 6. This results in a 50% reduction in storage requirement.

The selection of U and V are alternated by scan lines. In one scan line, the samples from the U are used. In the next scan line, the samples from the V are used.

This subsampling format is used in HDV, MPEG-1, DVD MPEG-2, PAL DV.

4:1:1

This subsampling method means that for every four pixels, it will use:

- 4 samples of Y
- 1 sample of U
- 1 sample of V

The total of samples used for every four pixels is now reduced from 12 to 6. This means a 50% reduction in storage.

This subsampling method is used in NTSC DV. The DV format is used in the miniDV digital video camcorder, which is the most common consumer and prosumer digital video camcorder.

6.5.2 High Definition

There are different high definition standards. HDV is one of the standards and currently supported by most high definition video cameras. The current HDV format specifies two recording systems: the 720p (progressive) method and the 1080i (interlaced) method. Table 6.4 lists

TABLE 6.4	Part of the Specifications of HDV Format		
Video Signal		720/25p, 720/30p, 720/50p, 720/60p	1080/50i, 1080/60i*
Pixel Dimensions		1280 × 720	1440 × 1080
Frame Aspect Ratio		16:9	
Pixel Aspect Ratio		1.0 (square)	1.33
Data Rate	Video data only:	approx. 19 Mbps (megabits per second)	approx. 25 Mbps (megabits per second)
Color Sampling Method		YUV 4:2:0	
Audio setting	sampling rate and bit depth:	48 kHz 16-bit	
	bit rate after compression	384kbps	

* Although currently there is no 1080p standard in HDV format, there are HDV cameras that support 1080/24p and 1080/30p.

HDV PICTURE FORMAT NOTATION

When describing the HDV picture format, it is often written in a form such as 1080/60i and 720/30p. Figure 6.6 explains the notation.

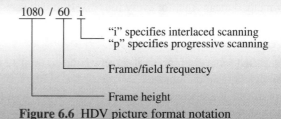

Figure 6.6 HDV picture format notation

part of the specifications of **HDV** format. The pixel dimensions for the 720p is 1280 × 720 pixels and for the **1080i** is 1440 × 1080 pixels. The number designates the height of the frame size, and the letters "p" and "i" specify the video's scan type—progressive and interlaced, respectively. The numbers 25, 30, 50, and 60 that follow the slashes specify the frame rate.

One of the key differences between high definition and standard definition DV is their frame size (resolution). To give you an idea of how the frame sizes of HDV differ from standard definition DV, Figure 6.7 shows a comparison of the frame sizes. Note that the pixel dimensions of a frame may be different from its viewing size because some high definition digital video standards (for example, HDV 1080i and 1080p) and standard definition DV use non-square pixels for displaying the frame.

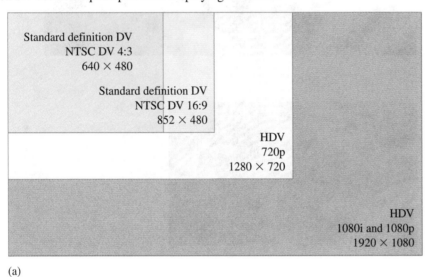

(a)

(b)

Figure 6.7 Comparison of frame sizes of standard definition and high definition digital video (a) Comparison by the viewing frame sizes (b) Comparison by the pixel dimensions

(a)

(b)

(c)   (d)

Figure 6.8 Frame size comparison (a) A frame from a 1080i video
(b) The same frame as 720p (c) The same frame as standard definition DV
wide-screen (16:9) format (d) The same frame as standard definition DV
standard 4:3 format.

To give you a feel of the relative frame sizes of different digital video formats and how
the different frame sizes may affect the details of the image, Figure 6.8 shows a comparison of the viewing frame sizes. Figure 6.8a is a frame from an 1080/60i video. Its pixel
dimensions are 1440 × 1080. The figure shown is scaled based on its pixel aspect ratio
to make the frame conform to the frame aspect ratio 16:9. Figures 6.8b through 6.8d are

scaled to show you how the frame would have looked if shot at the resolution for 720p, standard definition DV 16:9, and standard definition DV 4:3 format.

At the time of writing, there are several HDV camcorders available. For example, JVC has models that record in 720p format, Canon has several models of 1080i format, and Sony has models for both 1080i and 1080p formats. HDV can be shot on miniDV cassette tapes that are used with standard definition DV.

6.5.3 Digital Television (DTV)

The signals of DTV are broadcast over the air or transmitted digitally by a cable or satellite system. In order for the consumer to watch DTV, a decoder is needed to receive and use the signal, which is in digital form, to directly drive the digital TV set.

At the time of this writing, in the United States, **Advanced Television Systems Committee**, Inc. (**ATSC**)—an international, nonprofit organization that develops voluntary standards for digital television (DTV)—has developed a total of 18 DTV formats: twelve formats for **standard definition television (SDTV)** and six for **high definition television (HDTV)**.

For more information about ATSC and their standard development, visit their Web site at http://www.atsc.org

Table 6.5 lists the 18 formats. Again, the letter "p" or "i" next to the frame rate designates the scan mode: p for progressive and i for interlaced. The frame rate for the progressive scan refers to frames per second. The number for the interlaced scan is actually in

TABLE 6.5	The 18 ATSC Formats for DTV		
	Frame Size	Display Aspect Ratio	Frame Rate and Scan Mode
SDTV	704 × 480	16:9	24p
			30p
			60i
			60p
		4:3	24p
			30p
			60i
			60p
	640 × 480	4:3	24p
			30p
			60i
			60p
HDTV	1920 × 1080	16:9	24p
			30p
			60i
	1280 × 720		24p
			30p
			60p

fields per second. 60i refers to 30 frames per second, because each interlaced frame consists of two fields. HDTV has a higher resolution than both the traditional analog TV and SDTV. It uses MPEG-2 format. The frame aspect ratio of all six HDTV formats is 16:9.

For more information, visit http://www.dtv.gov/consumercorner.html

The Federal Communications Commission (FCC) has mandated that all television stations be capable of broadcasting digital television (DTV) by 2007. At the time of writing, the date of ending analog broadcasts is extended to Feb 17, 2009.

In order for the consumers to watch DTV, there are several equipment requirements on different parties, for example:

- TV stations will need new production and transmission equipment.
- Consumers will need new equipment for reception of the DTV signals.

6.6 FILE TYPES OF DIGITAL VIDEO

Many digital video-editing programs let you choose the video format in which you want to export your video file. The common file types are listed in Table 6.6. The file types often already dictate the available codecs.

Generally, the intended use of your video file determines its file format. Here are several considerations:

- **The file size limits.**
  - If your video is intended for use on the Web, then you may want to consider a file format that offers high compression or a streaming video file format.
  - If your video is intended for CD-ROM or DVD-DOM playback, you will need to consider a data rate that can be handled by your target audience's computer.
  - If your video is intended to be DVD-video, then you need to export it into DVD MPEG-2.
- **The intended audience of your video file.**
  - If your video will be played on multiple platforms, then the file format should be cross-platform. The cross-platform formats (see Table 6.6) include Apple QuickTime, MPEG, Flash video, and RealVideo.
  - How is your target audience going to watch your video? What equipment do they have?
    - If they are playing it on a set-top DVD player, then you need to make a DVD-video.
    - If they are playing it on a computer, then what kind of computer are they using—older or newer? This dictates the data rate for your video.
- **Files that are intended to be source files for future editing.**
  You may want to choose a file format that is uncompressed (provided that the frame size is small, the video duration is extremely short, and you have enough disk storage) or allows lossless compression.
  - An uncompressed file or even a file using lossless compression will require large amount of storage space.
  - If the original footage is shot in DV format, you can also export the video sequence as DV format, which allows you to export it onto DV tapes. The DV format uses lossy compression but provides acceptable quality for further editing.

Table 6.6	Common Video File Types for Windows and Mac OS			
File Type	**Acronym For**	**Originally Created By**	**File Information & Codecs**	**Platforms**
.mov	QuickTime movie	Apple	• Not just for video, but there is also audio-only QuickTime • Also supports MIDI • Files can be streamed with QuickTime Streaming Server • "Fast Start" technology also allows users to play the video as it is being downloaded • Common codecs available are: Animation, Sorenson Video, H.264, PlanarRGB, and Cinepak.	Apple QuickTime player, which is available for Mac and Windows
.avi	Audio Video Interleave	Intel	Common codecs available are: Microsoft RLE, Intel Indeo Video, and Cinepak.	Primarily used on Windows but Apple QuickTime player can play AVI files
.rm	Real Video	Real Systems	• Can have very high degree of compression • Allows you to choose the compression level in terms of network connection speed • Files can be streamed with Real Server	• Cross-platform • Requires Real player
.wmv	Windows Media	Microsoft		Primarily used with Windows Media Player
.mpg .mpeg	MPEG	Motion Picture Experts Group	For DVD-video, export the final sequence to DVD MPEG-2 format	Cross-platform
.flv	Flash Video	Adobe	• Supports progressive download from a Web server • Can be streamed if the file is hosted on Adobe Flash Media Server Three choices of codec: • Sorenson Spark • On2 VP6: This also supports alpha channel, which means the video can have transparency • H.264	• Cross-platform • Requires Flash Player to play a SWF file that calls or contains the FLV file

6.7 DIGITAL VIDEO FILE SIZE AND OPTIMIZATION

Chapter 2 shows that the file size of an uncompressed high resolution image can be very large. For example, the file size of an uncompressed 3000 × 2000-pixel, 24-bit image is 18,000,000 bytes, i.e., about 17 MB.

For digital video, the frame size is not as large. For example, the frame size for the HDV 1080i and 1080p is 1440 × 1080 pixels. However, video comprises of a sequence of images (24 to 30 frames per second), which add up the file size fast. For example, a one-minute video at a frame rate of 30 fps comprises 1800 frames! Even if each frame takes up only 1 MB, 1800 frames mean almost 2 GB of data!

Let's look at the size of a video with the following properties:

- 1440-by-1080-pixel frame size
- 24-bit color
- 30 fps
- 1-second
- Audio: stereo, i.e. 2 channels
- Audio: 48,000 Hz sampling rate and 16-bit.

The *uncompressed* file size can be computed as follows:

For the video:
Total pixels in each frame:

$$1440 \times 1080 \text{ pixels} = 1,555,200 \text{ pixels/frame}$$

File size in bits for each frame:

$$345,600 \text{ pixels/frame} \times 24 \text{ bits/pixel} = 37,324,800 \text{ bits/frame}$$

File size in bits for 1 second video:

$$37,324,800 \text{ bits/frame} \times 30 \text{ frames/second} \times 1 \text{ second} = 1,119,744,000 \text{ bits}$$

File size in bytes:

$$1,119,744,000 \text{ bits}/(8 \text{ bits/byte}) = 139,968,000 \text{ bytes} \cong \textbf{133 MB}$$

For the audio:
File size of an uncompressed audio file:

Sampling rate $\times$ length of the audio $\times$ bit-depth $\times$ number of channels
$$= 48,000 \text{ samples/second} \times 1 \text{ second} \times 16 \text{ bits/sample} \times 2$$
$$= 15,36,000 \text{ bits}$$
$$= 15,36,000 \text{ bits}/(8 \text{ bits/byte})$$
$$= 192,000 \text{ bytes}$$
$$\cong \textbf{188 KB}$$

This one-second uncompressed video would require 133 MB + 188 KB (video + audio) of storage space, which is about 133 MB!

6.7.1 Data Rate

The file size is one of the considerations for video files—a larger file requires more storage space. But an important factor related to the smoothness of the video playback is its data rate.

The *data rate* refers to the amount of video data to be processed per second. The average data rate of a video is calculated by dividing the file size by the total length of the video in seconds.

In the one-second video example, the data rate is 133 MB/s. To play a video smoothly would require computer equipment capable of handling this data rate. For instance, the data rate of a 48x-speed CD-ROM drive is about 7 MB/s, which is not high enough to handle the data rate of this video. In other words, the playback of this video on a 48x-speed CD-ROM drive will be very choppy.

VIDEO FILE SIZE AND DATA RATE

Video file size and data rate are closely related, but they do not have the same implication. File size pertains to the *total* amount of the data. Large file size requires more disk space and longer transfer time.

Data rate refers to the amount of data to be processed *per second*. Hence, a very long video, even with low data rate, can have a large file size.

Data rate affects the smoothness of the video playback. If the data rate is too high for a computer to handle, the data will not be processed fast enough for continuous playback. The playback will be choppy.

HOW DO I FIND OUT IF THE DATA RATE OF MY VIDEO CAN BE HANDLED BY THE AUDIENCE'S CD-ROM DRIVE?

The data rate information and other information of a QuickTime movie is available in the Movie Info, which can be accessed by selecting Window > Show Movie Info. As shown in the Movie Info in Figure 6.9b, the file size (Data Size) of the QuickTime movie example shown in Figure 6.9a is 252.29 MB, and its average data rate is 9.65 MB/s. Where does the 9.65 MB/s come from? Here is how the average data rate is calculated:

The movie's total length (Duration) is 26 seconds and 3 frames (i.e., approximately 26.1 seconds). Its data size (i.e., file size) is 252.29 MB. Thus, its data rate can be calculated as 252.29 MB/26.1 seconds = 9.67 MB/s

The data rate (reading data) of a 48x-speed is about 7200 KB/s, about 7.2 MB/s. If this QuickTime movie is played on an 48x CD-ROM drive, it may not play smoothly.

The QuickTime movie in Figure 6.9c is compressed using the same compressor as 6.9a but with 70% of its picture quality. As shown in the Movie Info (Figure 6.9d), its file size (Data Size) is 138.1 MB and its data rate is 5.28 MB/s. Now that you know how the data rate is calculated, can you verify the data rate of this movie? This movie should be played smoothly on a 48x-speed CD-ROM drive.

Because video is comprised of a sequence of images and audio, the strategies for reducing the file size of digital images and audio are also applicable for digital video.

Recall that, as discussed in Chapter 2, the strategies for reducing image file sizes are: reduction in pixel dimension, lowering the bit depth, and file compression. Similarly, the strategies for reducing audio file size, as discussed in Chapter 4, are: reducing the audio sampling rate, reducing the audio bit depth, file compression, and reducing the number of channels.

There is an additional type of video file compression that are different from those of image file compression. This type of the compression methods exploits the temporal nature of video. The general concepts of video file compression will be discussed in the next section.

Let's first look at how the general strategies for reducing image file size can be applied to reduce the video data rate. Reducing the video file size can be achieved by reducing the

(a)

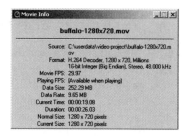

(b)

(c)

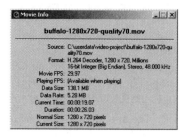

(d)

Figure 6.9 Two QuickTime movies, same frame size (1280 × 720 pixels) and frame rate (29.97 fps), but different picture quality (a) The movie compressed with 100% picture quality (b) Movie Info shows that the average data rate is 9.65 MB/s (c) The movie compressed with 70% picture quality (d) Movie Info shows that the average data rate is 5.28 MB/s

data rate and/or reducing the length of the video. The following discussion on file size optimization assumes that the length of the video is fixed. In this situation, reducing file size also means reducing the average data rate.

- **Lower the frame size of the video.**

  In general, the frame size is proportional, though not necessarily directly proportional, to the file size. Exactly how much the file size can be reduced by reducing the frame size depends upon the compression methods.

  For example, for an uncompressed video, reducing its width and height of to half will reduce the file size to a quarter of the original. However, for a compressed video, the resulting file size is often more than a quarter of the original that is applied with the same compression.

  Although the frame size of digital video footage captured by a camera are often fixed, you can export your final video to a smaller frame size in the video editing program.

- **Lower the frame rate of the video.**
  In general, the frame rate is directly proportional to the file size. Reducing the frame rate to half will reduce the file size to half of the original. Again, the file type and format, and thus the frame rate, of digital video footage captured by a video camera are often fixed. However, in the video-editing program, you can export your final video using a lower frame rate.

  Lowering the frame rate affects the smoothness of fast-action content more than those talking-head types. For CD-ROM projects, you can start at 15 fps and lower the frame rate as much as possible without making the video too choppy. Sometimes, the talking-head type videos may work fine at a frame rate of as low as 10 or 8 fps.
- **For QuickTime or AVI, choose a video compressor that supports higher compression.**
  Sorenson Video 3 and H.264 for QuickTime usually gives good compression with optimal picture quality. QuickTime Animation and PlanarRGB compressors are good for computer-generated animation, but the resulting file is less compressed.
- **Lower the picture quality of the video.**
  Most compressors let you set the picture quality. The lower the picture quality, the lower the data rate. Some, such as Sorenson (Figure 6.10), also let you set a limit on data rate.

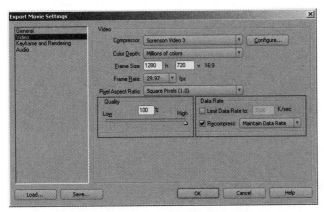

Figure 6.10 Adobe Premiere Pro CS3's Export Movie Settings dialog box with a Sorenson compressor chosen

The two QuickTime movies shown in Figure 6.9 are compressed with the same compressor, H.264, but one with a picture quality set to 100% and the other at 70%. The file size of the 70% quality movie is about half of the 100% one, but there is not much perceivable image degradation.
- **Lower the color depth if appropriate.**
  This is a least used strategy because:
  - Most digital video standards (DV, HDV, DVD) have specifications of color space.
  - Live videos usually need 24-bit to look good. They may not work well with 8-bit color.
  - Some compressors support 24-bit color only.

However, reducing color depth may work well for some computer-generated graphics or presentations that contain less than 256 colors. A compressor that supports 8-bit color is QuickTime Graphics.

- **Lower the sampling rate, bit depth, and number of channels of the audio.**

  This is another least used strategy because:

  - Lowering the quality of the audio generally has much less impact on the file size than lowering the image quality, frame size, and frame rate of the video. For example, in the previous file size calculation, we see that the audio takes up less than 200 KB per second. The video portion for a HDV 1080i or 1080p takes up 25 Mbps (megabits per second) (Table 6.4), i.e., about 3 MB per second, which is about 15 times the rate of the audio portion. This means that even if you totally discard the whole audio, only one-sixteenth of the file size would be saved.

  - Many the many digital video standards (DV, HDV, DVD) have specifications for the audio sampling rate and bit depth.

    If you really need to reduce the file size as much as possible (even by lowering the quality of the audio), here are some general rules. The setting for a CD-quality audio is a 44,100 Hz sampling rate, 16-bit, stereo (two channels). If the content of the audio is speech, then a 22,050 Hz sampling rate should be acceptable. If the target audience will be playing the video with low-end speakers, then making the audio to mono (i.e., reducing the number of channels to one) may be acceptable.

Lowering the data rate sacrifices the video quality. You will need to experiment with the settings and judge whether the resulting quality meets the intended use of the final video.

6.8 GENERAL CONCEPTS OF VIDEO FILE COMPRESSION METHODS

A compressed file must be decompressed before it can be used in normal applications. Think of compressing a file like packing a suitcase.

- Packing your clothes neatly in a suitcase makes it more compact to transport, but it takes time to pack.
- The clothes will need to be unpacked or even ironed before you wear them.
- How the clothes are unpacked often depends on how they are originally packed.

Similarly, it takes time to compress a video file. In addition, a compressed video file must be decompressed before it is played. Compression and decompression always go together as a pair. The term *codec* comes from abridging *co*mpressor/*de*compressor.

The general idea behind the file compression method is to represent the same content by using less data. Some involve discarding original data (lossy compression), while others preserve the original data (lossless compression) by encoding them specially.

Many codecs adopt more than one method. In general, you do not encounter the name of these compression methods directly in video-editing programs. Instead, you are provided with a list of available codecs from which to choose when you export the final video sequence. The following description of the common compression strategies intends to help you make an educated decision in choosing a codec by understanding what the different compression methods do to the file and correlating them to the common codec names.

6.8.1 Spatial Compression

The general goal of **spatial compression** is to compact *individual frames*. This means that the pixel information of each frame is compressed independently from the content of other frames.

Some digital image compression algorithms, such as Run-length encoding (RLE) and JPEG compression are used. Codecs that use spatial compression and RLE are QuickTime Animation, QuickTime PlanarRGB, and Microsoft RLE. RLE works well for video with large areas of solid colors, such as most cartoon animation.

6.8.2 Temporal Compression

In a typical video sequence, the changes from frame to frame are often very small. **Temporal compression** exploits the repetitious nature of the image content *over time* and the possibility of predicting one frame from the other.

Instead of describing the pixel information of *every* frame, temporal compression only does so in *selected* frames. These frames generally are referred to as **keyframes**. For all other frames, only the *difference* from the previous keyframes is described. If the change between the current frame and the previous keyframe is small, the file size requirement for storing the difference will be small.

Temporal compression works well for video that contains continuous motion. Videos with frequent flickering and scene changes, may not be compressed too well. Many codecs use temporal compression, for example, Sorenson Video and H.264 are both used for QuickTime.

6.8.3 Lossless and Lossy Compression

Lossless compression preserves the original data. One of the strategies to do so is to exploit the pattern and repetition of the data, such as the run-length encoding (RLE) method. Examples of lossless codecs are QuickTime Animation and PlanarRGB—set at the maximum quality setting.

Lossy compression discards or alters some of the original data. This will lower the video quality. However, the algorithms often take human perception into account when deciding which data will be discarded, so the video will maintain its perceptual quality as much as possible.

Usually, lossy compression results in a much smaller file size than lossless compression. In addition, lowering the quality setting for the lossy compressor lowers the data rate by discarding more original data. The discarded data cannot be recovered.

6.8.4 Symmetrical and Asymmetrical Compression

A **symmetrical codec** requires about the same amount of time and processing to compress as to decompress a video. In contrast, the amount of time and the complexity required to compress and decompress are significantly different in **asymmetrical codecs**.

Fast decompression is preferable for video, because it makes the playback much better—less wait time. In fact, many codecs fall into the asymmetrical category because it takes much longer to compress a video than to decompress.

Run-length encoding (RLE): Recall the discussion in Chapter 2, RLE compacts a file by replacing a sequence of the same repeated value by one instance of the value followed by the number of times it is repeated. For example, imagine that the color blue is represented in 8 bits as 00001010. If there is a section of sky in a digital image where blue is repeated for 100 pixels, then without any compression, this section would require 800 bits. With run-length encoding, we could encode this section as one instance of blue—00001010—followed by the number 100 in binary (1100100). Instead of 800 bits, we've now used 16 bits—16 digits for 00001010 and 1100100.

The implication of this type of compression pertains to your time management during production. You may choose a fast compression during a time crunch or a fast preview of the work-in-progress video sequence. When you are ready to export the final video, you will need to plan for a much longer time for compression using a more efficient codec. For example, QuickTime Animation codec compresses faster than Sorenson Video. But the video file using QuickTime Animation codec is generally a lot larger than using the Sorenson Video codec.

6.9 MPEG COMPRESSION

MPEG stands for **Moving Pictures Experts Group**. This committee derives standards for encoding video. MPEG file format allows high compression. There are several variations of MPEG: MPEG-1, MPEG-2, and MPEG-4.

WHAT HAPPENED TO MPEG-3?

Do not be confused MPEG-3 with MP3. MP3 uses MPEG-1 audio layer-3 encoding format. MPEG-3 is *not* the MP3 audio format.

MPEG-3 was intended as an extension of MPEG-2 to accommodate the standard for HDTV (high definition television). However, the HDTV specification was then merged into the MPEG-2 standard. And the task for deriving the MPEG-3 standard was ended.

6.9.1 MPEG-1

MPEG-1 provides video quality comparable to VHS and is useful for video intended for the Web and CD-ROM playback. It supports frame sizes up to 352×240 pixels. It is also the file format for VCD (VideoCD) which was popular before DVD become more widespread.

6.9.2 MPEG-2

MPEG-2 supports the DVD-video, HDTV, and HDV standards. Without going into the details of the specifications of the standard, what this means to digital video production is:

- If your final video is intended for DVD video, you will need to export the final video into DVD MPEG-2 format. There are different variants of MPEG-2, but only the ones that conform to the DVD specifications can be used for DVD-video.

  Most digital video-editing programs provide template settings for DVD export, so you do not need to memorize all of the specification details in order to export a correct MPEG-2 for DVD-video.

- If your final video is intended for HDV format, you will need to export the final video into HDV's MPEG-2 format.

How Compression Works

In a typical video sequence, neighboring frames often have a great deal of similarity. This means that there is *temporal redundancy*. MPEG compression exploits the temporal redundancy by looking for motion differences from one frame to the next in order to reduce

This section intends to introduce you a very basic and general explanation of MPEG compression, so you will understand the key parameters that you see in digital video-editing programs when exporting your video to DVD MPEG format.

A detailed description of the MPEG standards and MPEG compression algorithms are covered in the CS module.

file size. The technique it uses is called ***motion compensation***. The basic idea of motion compensation is:

1. An image is read in as a reference frame, and then the next image is read.
2. The image of this current or target frame is compared one block of pixels at a time with the reference image. There are two possibilities.
   - If the pixels of the two blocks at the same location in the frame are identical, then there will be no need to encode the pixel information of the current block. An instruction will be included to tell the decoder to use the block from the reference image. This will save more storage size than encoding the whole block.
   - If the two blocks are not identical, then it will search the reference image at different locations for a match. A match may or may not be found.
     - If no match is found, then it will encode that block fully. In this case, there is no file size saved.
     - However, if a match is found, then the data of the block from the reference image plus the displacement information of the block will be encoded.

       The displacement information of the current block is called a ***motion vector***. It has a two-dimensional value, normally represented by a horizontal component and a vertical component. It tells the decoder exactly where in the reference image to get the data.

The example in Figure 6.11a represents a reference image and Figure 6.11b its subsequent frame. In comparing Figure 6.11b with Figure 6.11a, some pixel blocks in Figure 6.11b can be found in Figure 6.11a; for example, the blocks highlighted in blue in Figure 6.11f. However, some pixel blocks, such as those highlighted in yellow, cannot be found in Figure 6.11a.

Figures 6.12a and 6.12b show frames 1 and 2 of the previous example. The block highlighted in blue in frame 2 (Figure 6.12b) has a match in the reference frame (frame 1). The motion vector is represented by a red line connecting the two blocks in Figure 6.12c. It provides the displacement information of the pixel block.

The example in Figure 6.11 is a very simple situation where all of the objects in the scene are flat and static. In a typical video, the movement of the subjects is much more complex. The subjects move and rotate in three dimensions, and the movement is not limited to a flat plane parallel to the camera. Identical matches are rarely obtained. Instead, closest matches are usually what the encoder will find.

How does the encoder determine whether it is a match? The basic idea is to measure the differences (color value, pixel by pixel) between the block in the reference frame and the block in the current frame. The one with the minimum difference will be the closest match.

The color difference between the closest match from the reference frame and the actual pixel block of the current frame will be calculated. If the bits required to store the difference are fewer than encoding the actual pixel block, then the difference and the motion vector will be encoded. Otherwise, the actual pixel block will be encoded.

Group of Pictures (GOP)

In the earlier explanation of motion compensation, a frame is compared with a reference frame. But how are reference frames chosen? To answer this question, we need to discuss an important concept in MPEG-1 and MPEG-2—the ***group of pictures*** (***GOP***). It defines the grouping structure of different frame types.

A typical MPEG consists of a repeating GOP structure. There are three frame types in terms of the information used for encoding the frame: I-frames, P-frames, and B-frames.

I-frames stand for ***intraframes***. An I-frame is encoded using only the information within that frame. It is called ***intracoding***. In other words, I-frames use spatial compression but no temporal compression.

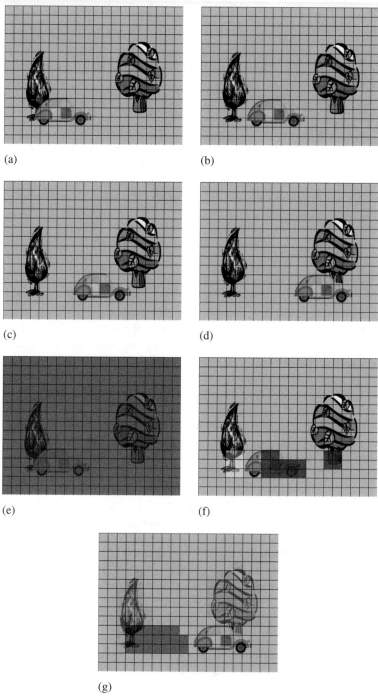

Figure 6.11 (a) through (d) The first four frames of a video: (a) Frame 1, being the reference frame or the I-frame (b) Frame 2, being a B-frame (c) Frame 3, being a B-frame (d) Frame 4, being a P-frame (e) through (g) Areas highlighted in red are original pixel information and highlighted areas in blue are from the previous I-frame, in cyan are from the previous I-frame at the same location, and in yellow are from the next P-frame

Note: Not all the blocks are labeled for their encoding method; only some are highlighted to illustrate the points.

(a)   (b)

(c)

Figure 6.12 (a) Frame 1 of the example in Figure 6.11 where the block outlined in black matches the block highlighted in blue in (b) (b) Frame 2 of the same example where the block highlighted in blue is the block under motion search (c) The location difference is indicated by a red line—the motion vector

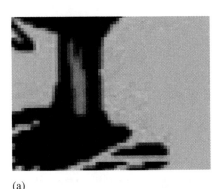

(a)   (b)

Figure 6.13 (a) MPEG artifact, discernible at the intersect area of black and light gray (b) The original image before MPEG compression

The encoding of an I-frame is very similar to JPEG compression. Artifacts similar to the artifacts in JPEG images can be seen in MPEG videos (Figure 6.13).

A GOP starts with an I-frame; there is only one I-frame in a GOP. The number of frames, including the I-frame, in a GOP is specified by the parameter N of the GOP. The value of N for DVD-compliant MPEG-2 is 15. HDV also supports $N = 15$. Because the I-frame is encoded using spatial compression without temporal compression, it is the least compressed frame type among the three types of frames.

P-frames are *predicted frames*. A P-frame is encoded by using the previous I- or P-frame as the reference frame. It is possible that a pixel block in a P-frame will use intracoding when a match to the reference is not found, or the intracoding will use fewer bits than using the match.

B-frames are the frames between the I- and P-frame, the P- and P-frame, and the P- and next GOP's I-frame. B-frames are *bidirectional frames*, which means a B-frame is encoded by using the previous and subsequent I- and/or P-frame as the reference frames.

The parameter **M** of the GOP specifies the number of these frames between the non-B-frames plus one. For DVD-compliant MPEG-2, the **N** and **M** parameters for the GOP are 15 and 3 respectively. In other words, the frames in a GOP are structured as

I B B B B P B B P B B P B B

The two B-frames are encoded using the previous I-frame and the subsequent -frame as the reference frames.

The example in Figure 6.11 is based on this GOP structure. This means that:

- Frame 1 in the example in Figure 6.11a is the I-frame. The whole frame is intracoded (Figure 6.11e).
- Frame 4 (Figure 6.11d) is the first P-frame in the GOP.
- Frames 2 (Figure 6.11b) and 3 (Figure 6.11c) are B-frames.

Some blocks in frame 4 are intracoded (highlighted in red in Figure 6.11g). Some blocks (highlighted in blue in Figure 6.11f) in frame 2 (a B-frame) uses the I-frame (frame 1) as the reference frame. However, part of a tree trunk is only available in the subsequent P-frame (frame 4) and those blocks (highlighted in yellow) use frame 4 as the reference frame.

You may encounter the **N** and **M** settings for the GOP when you export your video to MPEG-2. Some video-editing programs hide the GOP settings from you. Some, such as Adobe Premiere Pro CS3, let you check out or even change the **N** and **M** settings of the GOP when you export a MPEG-2 (Figure 6.14).

Consequences of GOP Structure

There are at least two consequences of using GOP structure in video: one pertains to the file size and the other to the video editing.

For file size, consider these:
- A MPEG-2 consists of a repeating GOP structure.
- Each GOP contains one I-frame.
- I-frames are the least compressed among the three types of frames, and thus take up more storage space.

What this means to the MPEG-2 file size is that the shorter the GOP (i.e., lower value of **N**), the more I-frames a video will have. This, in turn, means that the overall file size is larger with a smaller value of **N**.

For video editing, consider these:
- The information for a P-frame depends on the information of its previous I-frame.
- A B-frame depends on the information of its previous and subsequent I- or P-frames.

Because of this dependency, frame-accurate editing for MPEG-2 is more complex than in standard definition DV that uses the DV25 format. Editing MPEG-2 has been difficult. Any alteration made on the frame sequence requires decompression and recompression (lossy and could be slow). However, digital video-editing application programs now are designed to work seamlessly.

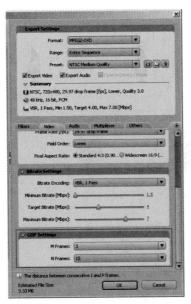

Figure 6.14 Adobe Premiere Pro CS3's DVD MPEG-2 movie export window with the red rectangle highlighting the GOP's **M** and **N** parameters

6.9.3 MPEG-4

MPEG-4 is the newer standard in the MPEG family. It differs from MPEG-1 and MPEG-2 in the coding approach and the range of target data rate. The new coding approach uses **media objects**. For example, if the car and the two trees from the scene in Figure 6.11 are each a media object, then even if the car is blocking part of a tree trunk in one scene, as in Figure 6.11a, the tree trunk information is still available. This approach allows better motion prediction.

As you see in Figure 6.15d, it is easier to locate an exact match for the pixel block for the back of the car than with traditional frame-based coding (Figure 6.15e) in MPEG-1 and MPEG-2.

The object-based coding also supports content-based manipulation of the scene and thus user interaction with the media objects.

Each object in a scene does not have to be separated into a media object in order to produce a MPEG-4 video. A conventional frame-based video—from a digital camcorder—can be converted to MPEG-4 format. In this case, the whole frame, as a rectangular bitmap image, is treated as an object—a degenerated case.

The data rate of MPEG-4 standard covers a wide range. The low-end of the range targets the mobile applications, such as cell phones, that MPEG-1 and MPEG-2 standards do not support. The high-end supports the video quality for high definition TV (HDTV). MPEG-4 is also the movie file format supported by many handheld and portable game devices, such as Sony Playstation Portable (PSP).

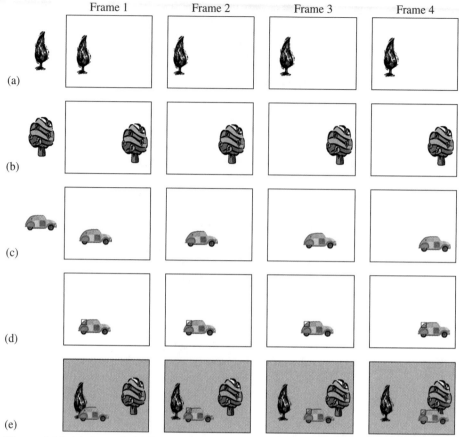

Figure 6.15 (a) through (c) Rows illustrate the concepts of how elements would be treated as media objects (d) through (e) The same pixel block for the back of the car can be easier to find a precise match in row (d) than in row (e)

6.10 STREAMING VIDEO AND PROGRESSIVE DOWNLOAD

There are two modes of video delivery (i.e., two ways of playing videos).

1. **Play from disk.**

   In this mode of delivery, an entire clip needs to be already on disc before it can be played. The file can be on a hard drive or an optical disc (such as CD and DVD). And, if the video needs to be obtained from a Web site or any remote network site, then the entire file needs to be downloaded before it can start playing. This is the most common mode of digital video delivery. All video file types support this mode of delivery.

2. **Play over a network.**

In this mode, the video will be displayed while it is being downloaded. The video file does not need to be downloaded in entirety before it can be played. Streaming video and progressive download fall into this mode of video delivery.

The common file formats of *streaming video* are: Streaming QuickTime, Real Networks' RealVideo, and Windows Media Video (WMV). Streaming video files can also be played from disc. However, in order to stream the video over a network, it requires a streaming server.

All of the streaming file formats allow saving several different compression levels of a movie in a single file to match the requirements of different connection speeds. The server chooses the appropriate one to fit the speed of the user's connection. For example, Figure 6.16 shows some choices of different target connection speeds that you can add to the RealVideo file when you export your video in Adobe Premiere Pro CS3. This technology of RealMedia is called *SureStream*.

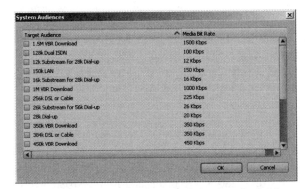

Figure 6.16 System Audiences dialog box in Adobe Premiere Pro CS3 showing a list of target connection speeds you can choose from for RealVideo

Streaming does not guarantee continuous playback; it still takes time for the data stream to arrive. If the network connection is too slow, there still may be wait time every few frames. When this happens, you usually see a message about "buffering . . ." in your media player.

Unlike other modes of video delivery, true streaming video is never stored on the user's disk. If you want to watch the video again, the video will be streamed all over.

An alternative method of streaming is *progressive download* or *pseudostreaming*. For example, QuickTime's fast-start feature allows playback as soon as enough of the data stream has arrived. A simple way to convert a QuickTime movie into a fast-start movie is to save the QuickTime movie as a self-contained movie in QuickTime Pro, a professional version of QuickTime player.

Progressive download does not require a streaming server. The file is transferred to the user's disk as with non-progressive download. The file usually remains on the user's hard disk after playback, for example, in their Web browser's cache if the video is played in the

Web browser. Therefore, after the entire video has been played once, it can be played again from the Web browser's cache on the user's hard drive without having to wait for download again.

6.11 SUMMARY

Video intends to capture our temporal experience of sights and sounds. Conceptually, video captures motion as a sequence of pictures at a constant time interval. Each picture is called a frame. How fast the pictures are captured or how fast the frames are played back is determined by the frame rate which is measured in frames per second (fps).

Sampling and quantization apply to digital video. The concepts of sampling and quantization for images apply to the visual component of the video, and those for the digital audio apply to the auditory component. The frame size or resolution relates to the sampling step, and the bit-depth relates to the quantization step. Like stand-alone digital audio, the quality of the audio component in digital video is determined by its sampling rate and bit depth.

In many situations, the available choices in digital video settings, such as frame size and frame rate, are influenced by digital video standards, which in turn, are influenced by the analog television broadcast standards. There are three sets of broadcast standards for analog color televisions: NTSC, PAL, and SECAM. They differ in frame sizes, frame rates, and color spaces.

In digital video, the frame size also is referred to as resolution. It is measured in the pixel dimensions of a frame—its width by its height, expressed in number of pixels. For a NTSC standard definition DV frame, the frame size is 720 × 480 pixels. The frame size for a PAL standard DV frame is 720 × 576 pixels. For a NTSC high definition digital video, the HDV format has two frame sizes: 1280 × 720 pixels and 1440 × 1080 pixels.

The frame aspect ratio is the ratio of its width to height dimensions. For example, the frame aspect ratio for the standard format NTSC DV is 4:3, while the wide-screen format is 16:9. The frame aspect ratio for high definition digital video and high definition TV (HDTV) are 16:9.

Some video formats use non-square pixels to make up the frame. The shape of the pixel can be described by an attribute called pixel aspect ratio. For a square pixel, its pixel aspect ratio is equal to 1. A pixel aspect ratio of less than 1 depicts a tall pixel, while a pixel aspect ratio of greater than 1 depicts a wide pixel. For standard DV format, the pixel aspect ratio is 0.9, while for the widescreen DV, the pixel aspect ratio is 1.2. A video should be displayed on a system with the matching pixel aspect ratio, otherwise the image will be distorted.

Timecode is used to number frames in video. The two common formats of timecode used in digital video are drop-frame and non-drop-frame. No frame is dropped or lost in the drop-frame timecode. The drop-frame timecode is preferable for the NTSC system to maintain the time accuracy.

A picture displayed on a television or a computer CRT monitor is made up of horizontal lines. These lines are traced across the screen one line at a time. Computer monitors display the picture by displaying lines from top to bottom in one pass—progressive scan. Analog television standards for NTSC, PAL, and SECAM display the picture in two passes. For NTSC, the first pass traces the even-numbered lines, and the second pass traces the odd-numbered lines to fill in the alternating gaps left by the first pass. The set of the lines in the same pass (i.e., the set of even lines or odd lines), is called a field. This display method of using two alternating fields is called interlaced scan.

Digital television (DTV) refers to television signals that are broadcast or transmitted digitally. At the time of this writing, in the United States, there are 18 DTV formats developed by the Advanced Television Systems Committee, Inc. (ATSC). The 18 formats include twelve formats for standard definition television (SDTV) and six for high definition television (HDTV). There are two frame aspect ratios for the SDTV format—4:3 and 16:9—while the frame aspect ratio of all six HDTV formats is 16:9. HDTV has higher resolution than the traditional analog TV and SDTV. It uses MPEG-2 format.

The data rate refers to the amount of video data to be processed per second. The average data rate of a video is calculated by dividing the file size by the total length of the video in seconds. It provides a measure for predicting the smoothness of the video playback on devices. If a video's data rate is too high for a playback device to handle, the playback of the video will be choppy. Lowering the video data rate can be achieved by reducing the video file size. The general strategies to reduce video file size include: (1) lowering the frame size of the video, (2) lowering the frame rate of the video, and (3) using a compressor that allows higher compression.

MPEG stands for Moving Pictures Experts Group. It is a file format that allows high compression. There are several variations of MPEG: MPEG-1, MPEG-2, and MPEG-4. MPEG-1 supports VideoCD format while MPEG-2 supports the DVD-video, HDV, and HDTV standards. MPEG-4 is the newer standard of the MPEG family. It differs from MPEG-1 and MPEG-2 in the coding approach and the range of target data rate. MPEG-4's low-end range of data rate targets the mobile applications, such as cell phones, that MPEG-1 and MPEG-2 standards do not support. The high-end supports the video quality for high definition TV (HDTV) and HDV.

There are two modes of video delivery: play from disk and play over a network. When playing from a disk, an entire clip needs to be already on the disk before it can be played. In playing over the network, the video will be displayed as the data stream arrives. In other words, a video file does not need to be downloaded in entirety before it can be played. Streaming video and progressive download or pseudo-streaming fall into this mode of video delivery. True streaming requires a streaming server.

TERMS

1080i, 171
4:1:1, 170
4:2:0, 169
4:2:2, 169
4:4:4, 169
720p, 170
Advanced Television
    Systems Committee, Inc.
    (ATSC), 173

asymmetrical codecs, 181
B-frames, 186
bidirectional frames, 186
chroma subsampling, 169
chrominance, 162
codec, 180
data rate, 176
DV compression, 168
DV25, 168

field, 160
frame, 159
frame aspect ratio, 164
frame rate, 159
frame size, 163
frames per second (fps), 159
group of pictures (GOP), 183
high definition television
    (HDTV), 173

LEARNING AIDS

The following learning aids can be found at the book's companion web site.

⌐ **Video display: Interlaced Scan versus Progressive Scan**

An interactive animation that illustrates two-pass scanning in interlaced scan and one-pass scanning in progressive scan.

⌐ **Upper Field and Lower Field**

An interactive demo shows the upper field and the lower field of a video frame.

◇ **Fast-Action Digital Video Showing the Interlace Artifact**

A soccer practice video clip of Figure 6.1 shows the comb-like interlace artifact.

⌐ **Video recording: Interlaced Mode versus Progressive Mode**

An interactive animation that illustrates how the interlace artifact may be produced in fast-action videos.

⌐ **Pixel Aspect Ratio**

An interactive demo lets you see the effect of an incorrect pixel aspect ratio on an image.

REVIEW QUESTIONS

When applicable, please choose all correct answers.

1. Which of the following is the television broadcast standard for the U.S. and Japan?

   A. NTSC
   B. PAL
   C. SECAM

2. Which of the following is the television broadcast standard for most of the Asian countries?

   A. NTSC
   B. PAL
   C. NSTC
   D. SECAM

3. Which of the following compression methods works best with large areas of solid color, such as in a cartoon animation?

   A. QuickTime Animation
   B. Cinepak
   C. MPEG-1
   D. MPEG-2

4. Which of the following compression methods achieves higher compression for videos without much motion difference, such as for talking heads?

   A. spatial compression
   B. temporal compression
   C. lossless compression
   D. asymmetric compression

5. Which of the following is the most common color model for video?

   A. RGB
   B. HSV
   C. CIE XYZ
   D. luminance-chrominance

6. In the YUV color model, the Y-component is _____, the U-component is _____, and V-component is _____.

   A. luminance; luminance; chrominance
   B. luminance; chrominance; luminance
   C. luminance; chrominance; chrominance
   D. chrominance; chrominance; luminance
   E. chrominance; luminance; luminance

7. The frame rate for the NTSC system is _____ fps.

   A. 24
   B. 25
   C. 28.9
   D. 29.97
   E. 30

8. The frame rate for the PAL system is _____ fps.

   A. 24
   B. 25
   C. 28.9
   D. 29.97
   E. 30

9. The frame rate for motion-picture film is _____ fps.

   A. 24
   B. 25
   C. 28.9
   D. 29.97
   E. 30

10. The scan mode of a CRT computer monitor is _____.

    A. interlaced
    B. progressive

11. The scan mode of a CRT television set is _____.

    A. interlaced
    B. progressive

12. Interlaced scan displays the frame by scanning the lines of a frame _____.

    A. in one pass from top to bottom
    B. in two passes: even-numbered lines in one pass and odd-numbered lines in the second

13. Progressive scan displays the frame by scanning the lines of a frame _____.

    A. in one pass from top to bottom
    B. in two passes: even-numbered lines in one pass and odd-numbered lines in the second

14. The comb-like artifact in a digital video, as shown here, occurs in the _____ video.

    A. interlaced
    B. progressive
    C. both A and B

15. Overscan is _____.

    A. the area where critical content and text titles should be placed
    B. the area where the significant action takes place
    C. the area that is outside of the television screen

16. It is recommended that _____ of the frame size be the safe title area.

    A. 10%
    B. 20%
    C. 50%
    D. 80%
    E. 90%

17. It is recommended _____ of the frame size be the safe action area.

    A. 10%
    B. 20%
    C. 50%
    D. 80%
    E. 90%

18. True/False: There is no sampling and quantization involved in capturing motion in digital video.

19. The frame size of a video refers to the video's _____.

    A. aspect ratio
    B. pixel aspect ratio
    C. resolution
    D. ppi

20. **True/False:** The pixel per inch (ppi) is an important attribute for video resolution and should be set correctly when working with digital video in video-editing programs.

21. Pixel aspect ratio means _____.

    A. the ratio of a frame's width (in pixels) to the height (in pixels)
    B. the ratio of a frame's height (in pixels) to the width (in pixels)
    C. the ratio of a pixel's width to its height
    D. the ratio of a pixel's height to its width

22. The pixel aspect ratio of a wide-screen format DV is _____.

    A. 4:3
    B. 16:9
    C. 1.0
    D. 0.9
    E. 1.2

23. The pixel aspect ratio of a standard format DV is _____.

    A. 4:3
    B. 16:9
    C. 1.0
    D. 0.9
    E. 1.2

24. The frame aspect ratio of a wide-screen format DV is _____.

    A. 4:3
    B. 16:9
    C. 1.0
    D. 0.9
    E. 1.2

25. The frame aspect ratio of a standard format DV is _____.

    A. 4:3
    B. 16:9
    C. 1.0
    D. 0.9
    E. 1.2

26. If a frame with pixel aspect ratio 1.2 is displayed on a device using a pixel aspect ratio of 1.0, the image will be _____.

    A. squashed horizontally
    B. elongated vertically
    C. cropped at the left and right edges
    D. cropped at the top and bottom
    E. displayed correctly

27. **True/False:** The timecode representing the 35th frame is either 00:00:00:35 or 00;00;00;35.

28. **True/False:** The drop-frame timecode drops or discards frames to preserve the time accuracy of a video.

29. Which of the following is the drop-frame timecode format?

   A. 00:00:00:00
   B. 00;00;00;00

30. Which timecode format is preferable for the NTSC system?

   A. drop-frame
   B. non-drop-frame

31. Chroma subsampling reduces the storage of pixel information by assigning fewer bits to store the _____ components.

   A. RGB
   B. luminance
   C. chrominance

32. The format of chroma subsampling is designated with three numbers separated by colons (for example, 4:2:2) to represent _____.

   A. the ratio of red : green : blue
   B. the ratio of the luminance to the two chrominance components
   C. the ratio of the number of three different types of pixels
   D. hours : minutes : seconds

33. Standard definition DV camcorders support audio of _____.

   A. 32 kHz
   B. 44.1 kHz
   C. 48 kHz
   D. all of the above
   E. A and B only
   F. A and C only
   G. B and C only

34. **True/False:** The signals of digital television are broadcast or transmitted digitally.

35. **True/False:** The frame aspect ratio of all six HDTV formats is 16:9.

36. HDTV is in _____ format.

   A. MPEG-1
   B. MPEG-2
   C. MPEG-3
   D. MPEG-4
   E. QuickTime
   F. AVI

37. The frame size for NTSC standard definition DV is _____ pixels, and _____ pixels for the PAL system.

A. 720 × 480; 720 × 480
B. 720 × 576; 720 × 576
C. 720 × 480; 720 × 576
D. 720 × 576; 720 × 480

38. Several high definition video camcorders are available to record 720p and 1080i formats. The number in the format name—720 or 1080—designates the _____.

A. data rate of the video
B. width (in pixels) of the frame size
C. height (in pixels) of the frame size
D. ppi of the video
E. none of the above; they are model numbers of different companies

39. Several high definition video camcorders are available to record 720p and 1080i formats. The letters "p" and "i" in each format name stand for _____ and _____ respectively.

A. pixels; inches
B. proprietary; infrastructure
C. progressive; interlaced
D. ppi; ppi

40. **True/False:** A long video, even with low data rate, can have a large file size.

41. For a one-minute QuickTime video file with a file size of 100 MB, its playback on a 48x CD-ROM drive very likely will be _____. (*Hint*: The data rate for a 48x CD-ROM drive is about 7 MB/s.)

A. smooth
B. choppy

42. For a five-second QuickTime video file with a file size of 100 MB, its playback on a 48x CD-ROM drive very likely will be _____. (*Hint*: The data rate for a 48x CD-ROM drive is about 7 MB/s.)

A. smooth
B. choppy

43. What is the maximum file size for a 30-second QuickTime movie to have a smooth playback on a 48x CD-ROM drive? Show your calculations. (*Hint*: The data rate for a 48x CD-ROM drive is about 7 MB/s.)

44. If the file size of a QuickTime movie takes up an entire CD, estimate the minimum length of the movie to have a smooth playback on a 48x CD-ROM drive? Show your calculations. (*Hint*: The data rate for a 48x CD-ROM drive is about 7 MB/s.)

45. Which of the following factors has the most direct impact on the smoothness of video playback? If the value of that property is too high for the playback device to handle, the playback of the video will be choppy.

    A. file size
    B. frame size
    C. frame rate
    D. frame aspect ratio
    E. pixel aspect ratio
    F. data rate

46. What does the term codec stand for?

47. _____ refers to the type of compression method that aims at compacting individual frames.

    A. asymmetric compression
    B. lossless compression
    C. lossy compression
    D. spatial compression
    E. temporal compression

48. _____ refers to the type of compression method that exploits the repetitious image content over time.

    A. asymmetric compression
    B. lossless compression
    C. lossy compression
    D. spatial compression
    E. temporal compression

49. _____ refers to the type of compression method that preserves the original data.

    A. asymmetric compression
    B. lossless compression
    C. lossy compression
    D. spatial compression
    E. temporal compression

50. _____ refers to the type of compression method that discards or alters some of the original data.

    A. asymmetric compression
    B. lossless compression
    C. lossy compression
    D. spatial compression
    E. temporal compression

51. _____ refers to the type of compression method in which the amount of time and the complexity required to compress and decompress are significantly different.

    A. asymmetric compression

    B. lossless compression

    C. lossy compression

    D. spatial compression

    E. temporal compression

52. Which of the following types of video can be compressed the most with temporal compression?

    A. fast action

    B. slow continuous motion

53. **True/False:** The MP3 audio is a MPEG-3.

54. Which of the following provides a video quality comparable to VHS and is the file format for VCD?

    A. MPEG-1

    B. MPEG-2

    C. MPEG-3

    D. MPEG-4

    E. QuickTime

    F. AVI

55. Which of the following support the DVD-video, HDV, and HDTV standards?

    A. MPEG-1

    B. MPEG-2

    C. MPEG-3

    D. MPEG-4

    E. QuickTime

    F. AVI

56. Which of the following also targets the mobile applications, such as cell phones?

    A. MPEG-1

    B. MPEG-2

    C. MPEG-3

    D. MPEG-4

    E. QuickTime

    F. AVI

57. **True/False:** A typical MPEG-2 consists of a repeating GOP structure.

58. Motion compensation is a key technique in _____.

A. asymmetric compression
B. lossless compression
C. lossy compression
D. spatial compression
E. temporal compression

59. Which of the following frame types is encoded using only the information within that frame?

A. B-frame
B. I-frame
C. P-frame

60. Which of the following frame types is encoded using only the previous I- or P-frame as the reference frame?

A. B-frame
B. I-frame
C. P-frame

61. Which of the following frame types is encoded using the previous and subsequent I- and/or P-frame as the reference frames?

A. B-frame
B. I-frame
C. P-frame

62. Which of the following frame types is the least compressed?

A. B-frame
B. I-frame
C. P-frame
D. none of the above; all are compressed at the same level

63. The M parameter of the GOP refers to _____.

A. the number of B-frames in a GOP
B. the number of I-frames in a GOP
C. the number of P-frames in a GOP
D. the total number of frames in a GOP
E. one plus the number of frames between the I- and P-frame, the P- and P-frame, and the P- and next GOP's I-frame

64. The N parameter of the GOP refers to _____.

A. the number of B-frames in a GOP
B. the number of I-frames in a GOP
C. the number of P-frames in a GOP
D. the total number of frames in a GOP
E. one plus the number of frames between the I- and P-frame, the P- and P-frame, and the P- and next GOP's I-frame

65. **True/False:** There is only one I-frame in a GOP structure.

66. **True/False:** Progressive download requires a streaming server.

67. **True/False:** True streaming requires a streaming server.

68. **True/False:** Progressive download allows the video to start playing as soon as enough of the video data has arrived.

69. **True/False:** For streaming video, the file usually remains on the user's hard disk after playback, for example, in their Web browser's cache.

70. **True/False:** In progressive download, the file usually remains on the user's hard disk after playback, for example, in their Web browser's cache.

71. "After the entire video has been played once in a Web browser, it can be replayed without having to wait for download again."
    Which of the following modes of video delivery match(es) this description?

    I. True streaming
    II. Progressive download or pseudo-streaming

    A. **I** only
    B. **II** only
    C. **I** and **II**
    D. none of the above

72. Verify that an one-hour miniDV tape can store about 13 GB of DV25 or HDV format video. (*Hint*: See Tables 6.3 and 6.5 for the data rate of DV25 and HDV, respectively, for calculation.)

73. Explain why in general, the longer GOP structure allows more file size compression. (*Hint*: Consider the number of I-frames in a GOP structure and the different levels of compression for different frame types.)

Digital Video: Post-Production

TABLE OF CONTENTS

KEY CONCEPTS
- Capturing and digitizing video
- Common workspace and workflow in digital video-editing programs
- Tools and techniques in digital video editing
- Common workspace and workflow in DVD authoring programs

GENERAL LEARNING OBJECTIVES
At the end of this chapter, you should be able to demonstrate that you understand
- The steps for acquiring digital video.
- The common workspace and workflow in digital video-editing programs.
- The common workspace and workflow in DVD authoring programs.
- The output and distribution options for digital video.
- Digital video-editing processes, tools, and techniques.
- The output and distribution options.
- How to apply digital video-editing tools and techniques.

7.1 ACQUIRING DIGITAL VIDEOS

In digital imaging, there are two ways to acquire digital images—by taking digital photos with a digital camera or by scanning an analog print. The latter method is digitizing—converting analog images to digital. It is the same with digital video—by shooting digital video footage using a digital video camera or by digitizing the video from an analog source, such as VHS, 8 mm and Hi-8 tapes.

7.1.1 Analog Sources

Videotapes, such as VHS and Hi-8, and motion-picture films are analog media. Digitizing converts them into a form that a computer can store and process. For hardware requirements in the digitizing process, you need an appropriate video capture card on your computer to digitize the analog video. You will also need an analog video device, such as an analog video camera or tape deck, to output the analog video signal to the capture card. In addition to hardware, digitizing videos requires video capture programs. Many capture cards bundle with such programs. Many video capture programs also have video-editing capability.

Digital video cameras are widely available nowadays. Analog video cameras, especially the consumer to prosumer types, are dying out. Almost all new video footage are now shot directly in digital format. It is unlikely to have a need to digitize new footage from analog tapes, but there still may be a need for digitizing older videos or documentaries that were shot in analog format.

7.1.2 Digital Video

Videos shot with a digital video camera are already captured in a digital format. They can be transferred directly onto a hard drive if shot on tape. Some newer model camcorders can record digital video directly to a memory card, DVD disc, or hard drive. Unlike analog videos, digital video does not require "digitizing".

Adobe Premiere Pro, Apple Final Cut, iMove, and Ulead Video Studio are examples of digital video programs that allow you to capture and edit both standard definition and high definition digital videos.

Basic Steps of Capturing Digital Video

Although there are many different digital video programs available on the market, they share some basic workflow techniques for video capturing and editing. This chapter intends to give you an overview of the basic steps of capturing digital video. Although Adobe Premiere Pro will be used for examples, the basic ideas of the workflow can be generalized to other digital video-editing programs.

1. Connect a DV or HDV camera or a DV tape deck to the computer. This can be done by connecting the camera or the tape deck to the computer via FireWire. Three common types of FireWire connectors are shown in Figure 7.1.

   Turn on the camera before starting up the video capturing program, although many programs may recognize the camera if the camera is turned on after the program is started.

FireWire

IEEE 1394 is a standard for high speed data transfer between computers and peripheral devices. *FireWire* is Apple's trademarked name for their implementation of this standard. It is also known as *i.Link* (Sony's name).

FireWire lets you easily connect different pieces of equipment and transfer data quickly between them. It also features simple cabling and hot-pluggable ability, which means that you can connect the device to the computer without having to turn off the computer first.

Most, if not all, of the DV and HDV cameras nowadays are equipped with FireWire or i.Link. Many new computers already have such port(s). For computers that do not have an appropriate port, FireWire cards are available and can be installed on the computer, provided the computer supports such installation.

At the time of writing, there are three common types of FireWire connectors in dealing with digital video: 4-pin, 6-pin, and 9-pin (Figure 7.2).

- 4-pin: on digital video cameras (Figures 7.2a and 7.2b), many laptop computers, and some desktop computers
- 6-pin: on most FireWire cards for desktop computers (Figure 7.2c) and Apple MacBook Pro (Figure 7.2d)
- 9-pin: on Apple MacBook Pro (Figure 7.2d)

(a)   (b)   (c)

Figure 7.1 FireWire connectors: (a) 4-pin (b) 6-pin (c) 9-pin

(a)

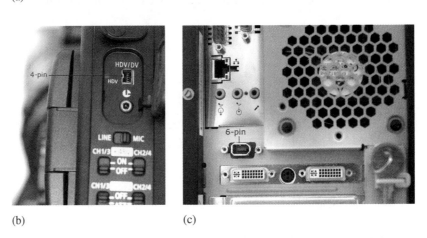

(b)   (c)

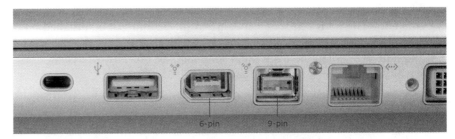

(d)

Figure 7.2 FireWire connectors on devices (a) A 4-pin FireWire DV IN/OUT port on a standard definition DV camcorder (b) A 4-pin FireWire HDV IN/OUT port on a HDV camera (c) A 6-pin FireWire port on a desktop computer (d) 6-pin and 9-pin FireWire ports on an Apple MacBook

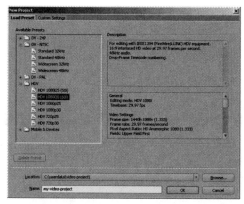

Figure 7.3 The New Project dialog box of Adobe Premiere Pro CS3

2. If you are prompted to select a project setting when the project starts, select the settings that match your video footages. Many programs provide you with a list of presets to choose from (Figure 7.3).

Standard definition DV.
- Select NTSC for U.S.
- Select either widescreen (16 : 9) or standard (4 : 3). This has to match the camera setting when you shoot the video you are going to capture.
- For audio, select the sample rate of 48 kHz if you shoot the video using 16-bit; select 32 kHz for 12-bit. Again, this setting has to match the camera setting when you shoot the video.

High definition digital video.
Select the correct frame size, scanning mode (interlaced or progressive), and frame rate that match your video sources.

3. Customize the device control for the digital video device. Specify the manufacturer brand and the model if the program provides a built-in device control for your device.
4. Open the movie capture window.
5. Use the *device controller* provided by the program to control the playback of the device while watching the video in the preview window. Use the record button on the device controller to start recording. Use the stop button to stop the recording. Then, give a file name to the captured video.

> **Setting the Device Control for Video Capture** Screen capture movies demonstrate setting the device control for video capture in Adobe Premiere Pro.

Programs such as Adobe Premiere Pro and Apple Final Cut Pro also let you *batch capture* by letting you save a list of *In and Out points* for each clip. You can start the batch capture later at your convenience. The clips on the batch list will be captured automatically during the batch capture.

In setting up a batch capture list, you can fast forward to search for the In and Out points you want to record on the list and let the batch capture perform the capture automatically. Without a batch capture, you will have to be at the computer the

The In and Out points define the beginning and the end time of the segment you want to capture.

> **⊘ Batch Capturing Digital Video**
> Screen capture movies demonstrate the basic
> steps of batch capturing a digital video in two
> digital video editing application programs:
> Adobe Premiere Pro and Apple Final Cut Pro.

whole time to watch for the end of the clip in order to push the stop button.

In capturing videos, you should capture at least a few seconds extra at the beginning and the end of the clip segment you want.

7.2 TYPES OF DIGITAL VIDEO CAMERAS

In this section, the types of digital video cameras are discussed based on the factors that matter the most in general digital media production. These factors are: (1) the video file format in which the digital video camera records and (2) the image quality of the video.

7.2.1 Video File Format and Recording Media

The video file format in which the digital video camera records often is related to the camera's recording medium. The recording medium can be looked up in the camcorder's specifications. Because camcorders are recording-media specific, it is important to choose the type that best suits your needs. Currently, the four most common types of camcorder media are tapes, DVDs, memory cards, and hard drives.

Digital-8 uses the same DV codec technology as miniDV but can record to Hi-8 tapes. It helps analog camcorder users to transition to digital video. At the time of their inception in 1998, Digital-8 models were usually cheaper than their miniDV counterpart.

Tapes

At the time of writing, most tape-type digital camcorders (standard definition DV and HDV formats) record video to *miniDV* tapes (Figure 7.4).

Figure 7.4 A miniDV tape

A second digital tape format is ***Digital-8***, which was invented by Sony. There is another type of digital tape format by Sony called ***DVCAM***. A DVCAM camcorder can record video to miniDV tapes or DVCAM tapes. Digital videotapes (such as miniDV, DVCAM, and Digital-8) record the video as DV format, which is a preferable choice for digital video projects.

DVDs

As the DVD player becomes more common as a computer peripheral—and as a part of the family entertainment center—DVD-recording camcorders are becoming popular. These camcorders record videos in MPEG format. Some of these camcorders allow in-camera editing; you can delete scenes, reorder and trim the footages. However, MPEG-2 and MPEG-4 recorded by these camcorders are not the preferable format for further editing for digital media/art production projects that require high quality source footage.

Memory Cards and Hard Drives

As the capacity of memory cards (such as the SD card) are reaching gigabytes, some newer camcorders record video onto them.

Some camcorder models let you record video directly to a hard drive. This saves the time and work for capturing the video into the hard drive for editing.

Other Media

Some digital still cameras allow recording videos in QuickTime, MPEG-1, or MPEG-4. The video resolution of these videos is often about 320 × 240 pixels, and the frame rate is about 15 frames per second. The quality of these videos is often sacrificed for a smaller file size. These types of video are acceptable for Web and e-mailing but do not match the quality, resolution, and frame rate of the DV and high definition digital video format.

7.2.2 Image Quality: The Number of CCD and Resolution

In general, the image quality of a video depends on the quality of the video camera and the lighting of the original scene. The quality of a video camera, in turn, depends on the quality of the optics, number of CCD, video resolution, and the camera's signal processing. The number of CCD and the video resolution are two quantifiable parameters that can be looked up in the camera's specifications.

Number of CCD

CCD is short for ***charge coupled device***. Like in a digital still camera, CCD converts the light intensity into an electronic signal, which is then processed by the camcorder and stored to the recording medium. Consumer camcorders typically have one CCD and professional camcorders have three CCD. The colors from a 3-CCD camcorder are much brighter and more vivid than those from a 1-CCD camcorder. The number of CCD can be looked up in the camcorder's specification.

Resolution

Standard definition DV.

- NTSC: 720 × 480 pixels
- PAL: 720 × 576 pixels

High definition HDV format.

There are two formats available at the time of this writing.

- 720p: 1280 × 720 pixels; progressive
- 1080i, 1080p: 1440 × 1080 pixels; interlaced, progressive

At the time of this writing, the manufacturers that offer HDV cameras include JVC, Sony, Canon, and Panasonic.

Distinguishing between DV and DVD:

Generally, DV is used as an abbreviation for digital video. However, DV format is a specific video format that uses the DV codec. MiniDV-camcorders record video in DV format. DV format is suitable for further editing.

DVD stands for digital versatile disc. DVD does not necessarily mean videos; there is DVD-audio too. Generally, DVD-type camcorders record videos in MPEG-2 format on DVD-R or DVD-RW discs. MPEG-2 format is not a suitable format for further editing.

Some camcorders use CMOS, instead of CCD, as the light sensor. CMOS stands for complementary metal-oxide semiconductor.

7.3 BASIC WORKSPACE ELEMENTS IN DIGITAL VIDEO EDITING PROGRAMS

Examples of professional digital video-editing programs are Adobe Premiere Pro, Apple Final Cut Pro, Sony Vegas, and Avid. There are some basic workspace elements that many of these programs share, which usually are divided into four main areas:

1. *Asset list* manages the imported source materials for the video project. They include the captured or digitized video footage, audio, still images, titles, and graphics. The source materials imported are not embedded in the video project file itself; the source files are linked. This means that if you move the source files to another folder or delete the source files later, you will be prompted to locate these linked source files the next time you open the video project.

2. *Preview window* lets you preview your entire video project. Adobe Premiere also has a Dual View Monitor window that you can use to view, edit, and trim the individual source clip.

3. *Timeline* is where you can arrange your source clips in sequence. It usually has video tracks and audio tracks.

4. *Effects* and *transitions* can be found in a separate palette or menu item. Effects can include video and audio effects. Many of the video effects work very similar to the image filters that you may find in image-editing programs. Examples of video effects include altering the color balance of the video clip, desaturating, resizing, clipping, blurring, sharpening, distorting, and stylizing the video clip. The most commonly used video transition is cross dissolve. Other transition types include 3-D motion, page peel, slide, wipe, zoom, and stretch.

Figures 7.5 through 7.7 show the screenshots of the workspace of Adobe Premiere Pro, Apple Final Cut Pro, and Sony Vegas 6, respectively.

Figure 7.5 An Adobe Premiere Pro CS3 workspace (a) Asset list (b) Preview windows (c) Timeline (d) Effects and transitions

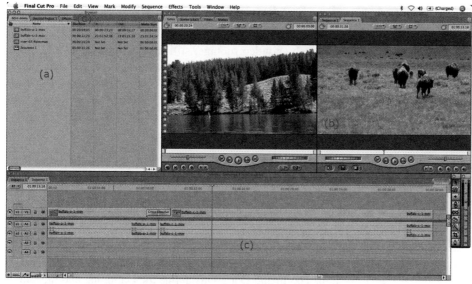

Figure 7.6 An Apple Final Cut Pro 6 workspace (a) Asset list (b) Preview windows
(c) Timeline (d) Effects and transitions can be accessed in a different tab

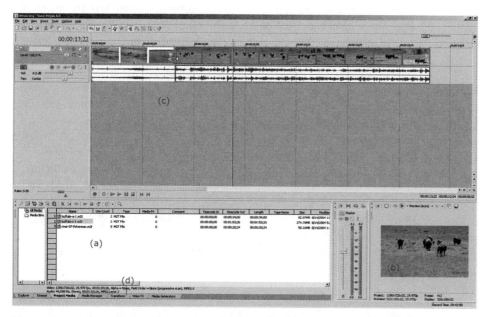

Figure 7.7 A Sony Vegas 6 workspace (a) Asset list (b) Preview window (c) Timeline
(d) Effects and transitions can be accessed in a different tab

7.4 BASIC STEPS OF DIGITAL VIDEO EDITING

After you have collected the raw materials, you will need to import them into a project in a
digital video program. Then, you edit the footage, trim away the parts that you don't need,
and apply audio, transitions, visual effects, and audio effects.

The basic steps of creating a final digital video are:

Step 1   **Import the source materials in the video project as assets.**

These source files (such as video footage, still images, titles, and audio) are usually linked—they are not embedded in the project. Therefore, you will need to keep the files stored on the hard drive or an external storage device if you are going to work on the video project later.

Step 2   **Arrange these assets on the timeline.**

When you shoot video footage, you should always shoot more than you will actually use in the video project; it is natural that this will happen anyway. You capture at least a few seconds before and after the actual segment you want to use. When you use the footage for your video project, you will need to remove the unnecessary parts using the following methods.

Trimming.

- There are several ways to trim video footage. For example, many video-editing programs let you set In and Out points for a source clip. The In and Out points define the beginning and the end of the segment you want to use. The segment before the In point or after the Out point will not be used on the timeline.

Setting In and Out points is not a destructive method for trimming clips. The segments outside of the In/Out range are not really deleted from the original source clip. You can always include them later, if needed, by adjusting the edit points.

- Another way to trim a clip is splitting. Using Premiere, you can split a clip with a Razor tool into multiple segments which then can be arranged on the timeline independently. This tool is nondestructive. It is not physically splitting the source clip *file* into multiple files. The original file is still intact. Only the *copy*—like an alias—of that clip on the timeline is split. If you drag the source clip file from the asset list onto the timeline again, the clip will still have the original length.

When you alter the length of a clip that has adjacent clips on the timeline, it will cause one of the following changes in terms of the duration of the entire video sequence.

- The duration of the entire video sequence is changed to accommodate the length change of a clip.
- The duration of the entire video is maintained by altering the length or the In/Out points of the adjacent clips.

There are several useful editing tools available in video editing programs to deal with such situations in *nonlinear editing—ripple edit, rolling edit, slip edit,* and *slide edit.* With these tools, you can edit the length of a clip or its In/Out points on the timeline without having to manually adjust the location of the adjacent clips on the timeline.

For example, if you have three video cuts sequenced on the timeline, like the one illustrated in Figure 7.8a, and you later want to lengthen the middle clip (the blue clip in Figure 7.8), you can use ripple edit to lengthen the middle clip. The subsequent clip (shown in dark gray) will be pushed to the right. Without using the ripple edit tool, you would have to move the dark gray clip to

---

> ✏ **Trimming a Clip by Setting In and Out Points, and Applying a Video Transition to Video Clips** Screen capture movies demonstrate the basic steps of setting In and Out points for video clips, and applying a video transition in two digital video-editing application programs: Adobe Premiere Pro and Apple Final Cut Pro.

Nonlinear Editing (NLE):

With NLE, the video can be assembled in any order, and changes can be made anywhere in the sequence at any time. In linear editing, a video must be assembled from the beginning, and the shots are laid down in the story order. An analogy for NLE versus linear editing in video is the word processor versus the typewriter in publishing.

> 🖰 **Nonlinear Editing Techniques in Digital Video** An interactive tutorial demonstrates the characteristics of ripple edit, rolling edit, slip edit, and slide edit.

Figure 7.8 Illustration of the effect of four nonlinear video-editing tools. (a) A video sequence consisting of three video clips (indicated by different colors) placed side-by-side on a timeline (b) After ripple edit (c) After rolling edit (d) After slip edit (e) After slide edit

Video effects and transitions should be used judiciously and as carefully as selecting your source materials. Transitions add temporal changes or "motion" that is not part of the source footage. Video effects integrate extra visual elements into the video. Indiscriminate use of video effects and transitions can lower the artistic value and dilute the story or statement of the final video.

the right to leave room for the blue clip to extend its length. Then, after you extended the duration of the blue clip, you would have to move the dark gray clip back to the end of the blue clip.

Rolling edit maintains the duration of the entire video sequence. For example, the middle clip (blue color) is lengthened at the end by using rolling edit (Figure 7.8c). The adjacent clip (purple color) is shortened to maintain the duration of the entire video sequence. Using slip edit (Figure 7.8d), the middle clip's In and Out points are altered. There is no duration change on any of the clips. The duration of the entire video sequence remains the same. In slide edit, the middle clip can slide to the left or right. In Figure 7.8e, this causes the change in the Out point of the previous clip (orange color) and the In point of the subsequence clip (purple). The duration of the entire video sequence and the blue clip remains the same.

These editing tools may not seem useful to simple video sequence. However, these tools are indispensable time-saver in editing complex sequence of clips.

Step 3 **Apply transitions, video effects, and audio effects, if needed.**

Two of the most commonly used transitions are straight-cut and dissolve. *Straight-cut* transitions can be achieved by arranging the two clips next to each other—there is not really a "transition" effect applied to these clips. There are several types of dissolve. In general, the *cross dissolve* transition gives the smoothest fade between two clips.

Many video-editing programs come with a variety of video effects. The most common effects include transformation (e.g., resizing and cropping) and image adjustment (e.g., tonal and color adjustment).

⟋ **Straight-cut versus Cross Dissolve Transitions** A short video clip shows side-by-side two different transitions: straight-cut and cross dissolve.

⟋ **Applying a Video Effect to Video Clips and Animating the Effect by Keyframing** Screen capture movies demonstrate the basic steps of applying a Gaussian blur video effect to a clip and keyframing the effect in two digital video-editing application programs: Adobe Premiere Pro and Apple Final Cut Pro.

> **Chroma Keying Video Clips** Screen capture movies demonstrate the basic steps of chroma keying a video clip using two digital video-editing application programs: Adobe Premiere Pro and Apple Final Cut Pro.

Video clips can be *superimposed* on top of each other by placing them on different video tracks. Adjusting the opacity of the top clip allows the clip underneath to show through. This affects the entire frame. However, an alpha channel created in the top clip can be used to define the areas that you want to remain transparent.

Another way to designate transparent areas is *keying*. Keying can make the pixels in an image that match the specified range of color or brightness transparent. In many digital video-editing programs, various keys are found under the video effects. For example, the *Blue Screen* and *Green Screen keys* can be used to key out blue or green screens when creating composites. The *Chroma Key* lets you select the color to be keyed out. For example, if a steaming geyser video clip is chroma keyed with the color range of the mist, the transparent areas will follow the flow of the steam in the air.

Although audio effects can be created separately with audio editing programs, video editing programs may come with audio effects that let you create audio effects without having to switch to a separate audio program. The basic audio editing includes trimming the audio, volume adjustments, audio fade-in/out, and panning. More advanced audio effects may include creating echoes, envelop, and an audio mixer that lets you create audio mix with multiple audio tracks.

7.5 OUTPUT AND DISTRIBUTE YOUR FINAL VIDEO

After you have finished assembling your video project, you can output the final video to a different file format. The choice of file format depends on how you want to distribute your final video to your audience. Some common choices of delivery media include:

DVD-video: MPEG-2 for DVD
Web:
- QuickTime for progressive download
- QuickTime, RealVideo, Windows Media, and Flash Video also support streaming on the Web

Optical discs, such as CD or DVD: QuickTime, AVI, MPEG-1
Tapes

7.5.1 DVD Playback

Standard definition DVD-videos can be played back on set-top players or on computers that have the DVD-ROM drive and software player.

Basically, there are two ways to create a DVD-video disc.

Some DVD authoring programs require the DVD MPEG-2 format for the video titles to be imported into a DVD project. Others do not have this requirement, and may accept AVI and QuickTime files. But the resolution and frame rate still need to be compliant with the NTSC DV or PAL DV (for example, 720 × 480 pixels and 29.97 fps for NTSC).

1. **Export your final video as a DVD-compliant MPEG-2 file and then author a DVD project using DVD authoring programs.**
   In Adobe Premiere Pro CS3, you can export your video to MPEG-2 DVD-compliant file using Adobe Media Encoder (Figure 7.9).

   Recall that, as discussed in Chapter 6, a MPEG consists of a repeating GOP (Group of Pictures) structure. The **N** parameter specifies the length of a GOP, and the **M** parameter specifies the number of the B-frames between the non-B-frames plus one. Now, you see these **N** and **M** parameters in the MPEG-2 export settings (Figure 7.9). For a DVD-compliant MPEG-2, **N** is 15 and **M** is 3.

Figure 7.9 Exporting DVD-compliant MPEG-2 file using Adobe Media Encoder in Adobe Premiere Pro

Notice that there is a section of Bitrate Settings (Figure 7.9). The bitrate, or bit rate, is the data rate. Recall that, as discussed in Chapter 6, data rate affects the video file size and quality. A video with higher picture quality often requires a higher data rate. Higher data rate increases file size. The preset shown in Figure 7.9 sets the target bitrate to 4 Mbps (mega bits per seconds), i.e., approximately 500 kB/s. This means that for a 4.7-GB disc, it can fit over two hours of the video.

You can import the MPEG-2 file into a DVD-authoring program, such as Adobe Encore, Apple DVD Studio Pro, Sony DVD Architect, and Ulead DVD Workshop. You can add menus and multiple videos on a DVD. The general steps to authoring a DVD-video disc will be discussed in the next section.

> **Export Video to DVD MPEG-2**
> Screen capture movies demonstrate the basic steps of exporting videos to DVD MPEG-2 in Adobe Premiere Pro.

2. **Export your final video directly to DVD.**
Some digital video-editing programs let you export your final video directly to DVD. This way, you do not need to export your video to MPEG-2 as an intermediate step. The resulting DVD is a simple single-movie DVD without any menu navigation. The video will start playing when the disc is inserted into the DVD player.

7.5.2 High Definition Video Disc

There have been two formats for high definition video disc: HD-DVD and Blu-ray. However, HD-DVD has been discontinued. DVD-writers and the authoring software for

Note that the term HD-DVD refers a specific high definition video disc format; it is not an abbreviation for high definition video disc in general.

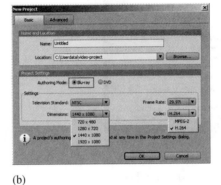

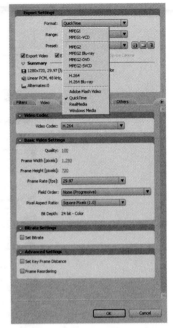

(a)   (b)

Figure 7.10 Blu-ray export (a) Adobe Premiere Pro CS3 supports Blu-ray MPEG-2 exporting using presets provided in Adobe Media Encoder (b) Adobe EncodeDVD CS3 has Blu-ray authoring mode in addition to DVD

Figure 7.11 Adobe Premiere Pro CS3's Adobe Media Encoder lets you export your video to various formats for Web

high definition video disc are starting to become available. For example, Adobe Premiere Pro CS3 and Apple Final Cut Pro 6 let you export Blu-ray format (Figure 7.10a). Adobe Encore CS3 and Apple DVD Studio Pro 4 support Blu-ray DVD authoring (Figure 7.10b).

7.5.3 The Web

Many digital video programs let you export your video to QuickTime and Windows Media formats.

For RealVideo, you can use the free software Real Producer Basic from Real Systems to convert your video. Chapter 5 shows how you can use Real Producer Basic to create streaming audio. The same procedure applies to creating RealVideo.

In Adobe Premiere Pro CS3, you can export your video to various formats by choosing File > Export > Movie. . . . You can also export your video for the Web using Adobe Media Encoder (File > Export > Adobe Media Encoder . . .), as in Figure 7.11, where you can choose from various formats, such as QuickTime, Adobe Flash Video (FLV), RealAudio, and Windows Media.

QuickTime PROGRESSIVE DOWNLOAD

QuickTime supports progressive download of movies, known as Fast-Start movies. The Fast-Start QuickTime movie starts playing before the entire file has been transferred over a network. The experience seems like streaming but Fast-Start is not video streaming.

One simple way to create a Fast-Start QuickTime is to save the QuickTime movie as a self-contained movie. To do so, you will need the Pro version of the QuickTime player, not the free version. First, open the QuickTime movie with QuickTime Pro. Then, select File > Save As. . . . In the File Save dialog box, select the option "Make movie self-contained" (Figure 7.12). If the option is not active, you give a different file name or save the movie in a different folder. You can replace the original QuickTime with the Fast-Start movie.

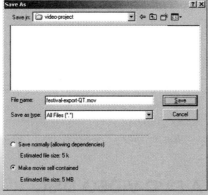

Figure 7.12 QuickTime Pro File Save dialog box

7.5.4 CD-ROM or DVD-ROM Playback

For videos intended for CD-ROM or DVD-ROM playback, the common options for the output file format include QuickTime and AVI. You may need to consider the operating system of your audience's computers. QuickTime players are available on Mac OS and Windows. AVI is for Windows but requires an extra player on Mac OS.

> ✎ **Export Video to QuickTime Movie**
> Screen capture movies demonstrate the basic steps of exporting videos to QuickTime movies in two digital video-editing application programs: Adobe Premiere Pro and Apple Final Cut Pro.

You need to find out the speed of your target audience's CD-ROM or DVD-ROM drive. From that, you can estimate the data rate. The data rate of your video should be no higher than the data rate of your target audience's playback device. If the data rate of your video is higher than the audience's CD-ROM or DVD-ROM drive can handle, your video will skip frames and become choppy.

Recall that the average data rate is equal to the file size divided by the length of the video. Thus, reducing file size can reduce the data rate. In addition, you can reduce the video file size by reducing its frame size, frame rate, and by lowering picture quality in the compressor settings. Here are some suggested steps to determine export settings for your video.

Step 1 **Start with the desired frame size, frame rate, and compressor.**
Of course, the frame size and frame rate should not exceed the original video's. If you do not know which compressor you want to use, start with H.264 or Sorenson

Video 3. They are commonly used codecs and give satisfactory compression without much visible degradation in image quality.

Step 2 **Export your video.**

After you have exported your video (or a test segment of your video), look up its file size and calculate the data rate.

If the data rate is higher than your target audience's device can handle, then try reducing the frame size, lowering the frame rate, or lowering the picture quality. The nature of your video dictates which strategy you should try first. For example, for a fast-action video, reducing frame rate may be the last option. If your video contains many fine details that you do not want to lose, then reducing frame size is not the best option.

Step 3 **Always test your final production on the computer equipment as close to the target audience's as possible.**

7.5.5 Tapes and Other Media

Exporting final sequence onto miniDV tapes is usually for backup or archival purposes.

When you export your video to tapes, you can record the final video directly onto miniDV tapes.

You can also export a selected frame of your final video into a still image, or export your final video (in entirety or a segment) into a sequence of still images.

7.6 CREATING A DVD-VIDEO DISC

7.6.1 Menu Structures and Navigation Hierarchy

A DVD-video can be as simple as a single-movie DVD that will automatically start playing after the disc is inserted in the player. It also can need a menu system.

Menus

A *menu* is made up of a background and buttons. A background can be a still image or a video. A button can be just text, a still image, or a video clip (with or without text). A menu that contains video clips as either a background or buttons is called a ***motion menu.***

Buttons

A *button* can be linked to a video or another menu. That is, when the button is clicked, whatever is linked to it—a video or a menu—will be played. As a user-friendly design, each button should be set up to have some kind of highlight when it is selected. This is especially critical if the intended viewing environment is set-top players. Without visual feedback, the set-top viewer will not know which button is the current selected choice when they are navigating among the buttons on a menu.

Submenus

A menu structure contains a main menu which can then branch out to other ***submenus***. Each submenu can have a button to let the viewer return to the main menu and/or move one level up. It also can have a button that leads to another submenu.

If the items for a menu do not fit on one screen, they can be divided into multiple "pages." Each of these pages is created as a menu, with buttons to let the viewer step through all of the pages.

A flowchart or storyboard type of approach may be used to lay out and visualize the menu hierarchy and the associated content materials of each menu. It also helps to make sure that no content or menu is left orphaned. An orphaned file or menu is one that is included on the disc but not linked or accessible from any other menus. Content that is not linked or used in any menu does not need to be included on the disc. However, having orphaned content may mean something originally planned is missing from the navigation design. The navigation design needs to be reexamined to make sure all of the necessary contents are properly incorporated and linked in order to be accessible by the viewer.

Although DVD remote controls have options for the viewer to return to the title menu or root menu directly, you may want to consider whether you want to include buttons on a submenu to let the viewer return to the main menu or navigate from one menu to the other directly without having to return to the main menu.

The navigation hierarchy and menu structure should be ready before you start authoring a DVD. It would be best to also have all of the content (such as the graphics for the background and buttons) for the menu ready. If the graphics are not finalized, then at least create placeholders with matching pixel dimensions.

Whether your DVD has a menu system or not, you can add chapter points in a video. *Chapter points* are like built-in bookmarks of the video. They allow the viewer to quickly jump to a particular location in the video at any time without having to rewind or fast forward.

7.6.2 Authoring a DVD Project

There are many off-the-shelf DVD authoring programs available. Some examples include Adobe Encore CS3 (Figure 7.13), Apple DVD Studio Pro 4 (Figure 7.14), Sony DVD Architect 3 (Figure 7.15), and Ulead DVD Workshop. Different programs have different

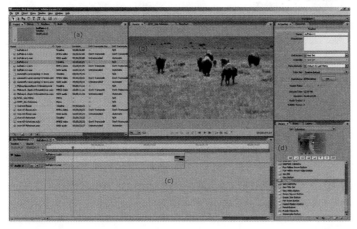

Figure 7.13 An Adobe Encore CS3 workspace with four basic panels (a) Project window (b) Monitor (c) Timeline (d) Library

Figure 7.14 An Apple DVD Studio Pro 4 workspace with four basic panels (a) Assets (b) Viewer (c) Track or timeline (d) Template library

Figure 7.15 A Sony DVD Architect 3.0 workspace (a) Project Overview Window shows a hierarchical view of the menus and titles (b) Workspace Window displays the current menu or title (c) Timeline (d) Library

workspaces and different workflows to follow. However, there are some basic elements in the workspace and in the workflow that many of these programs share. This section intends to give you a general idea how to work with these DVD authoring programs.

The common elements you find in the workspace of these programs are:

(a) *Asset lists* manages the imported source materials for your DVD project. The types of assets include videos, audio, menus, still images.

(b) *Preview window* lets you preview your video and menus.

(c) *Timeline* or *Track* lets you add audio tracks and chapter points. Some programs, such as Sony DVD Architect 3.0, supports *multiple angles* (Figure 7.16). You can add multiple video tracks on the timeline to create multiple angles. During playback of a

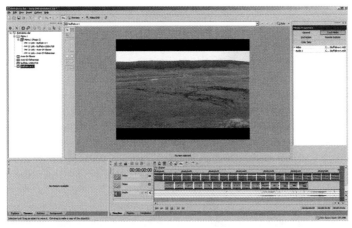

Figure 7.16 A Sony DVD Architect 3.0 workspace showing two
video tracks on the timeline for creating multiple angles

multi-angle DVD, the user can press the Angle button on the remote control to switch
between the two angles.

(d) *Library* and *Templates* are preset features containing menus, buttons, and background
images to use for building your DVD menus.

Described below are the general steps for authoring a DVD project with these programs.

Step 1 **Set Project Settings.**
When you start a DVD authoring project, you need to specify your target audience
standard—for example, standard definition (NTSC or PAL) or high definition.

Step 2 **Import Content as Assets.**
You then import the content materials to be included on the disc, such as video,
audio, images, menus, and buttons.

Many DVD authoring programs have a preset library of menus and buttons to
choose from, but also allow you to import custom-created images as buttons and
background for the menu. Imported menus and buttons are usually listed in a
separated window or tab from the video and audio content in a DVD project.

Note that these imported media are all externally linked; they are not embedded within the DVD project. This means that you need to keep those media files
available whenever you need to edit the DVD project.

Step 3 **Put Things Together.**
You start creating new menus by defining the background image (or video, if it is
a motion menu) and by putting buttons on the menu.

Before designing the navigation structure, you need to consider what kind of
built-in navigation is already available on a DVD player. The generic menu built
into a DVD player lets the viewer pause or resume playback, move forward or
backward frame by frame, jump to a chapter, return to the title menu or root menu,
or switch between camera angles. Without authoring a menu structure for a DVD,
a simple DVD that contains only video and audio can still have the nonlinear

viewing possibility because the viewer can access any point of a DVD title at any time. However, a menu structure allows you to integrate a higher level of interaction and nonlinearity to your DVD project.

Menu creation may be done in a menu editor window or on the "stage" area. Some programs have a separate menu editor window for menu creation, while others may have a stage area that you can directly drag and drop the background image and the buttons on.

You can also add static nonclickable text as titles or description on the menu. Then, you need to link each button to a video, audio or another menu. Many programs allow you to simply drag a video from the Asset list onto the menu. It will create a button automatically that is linked to that video with a thumbnail image from the video.

Some programs come with preset menu templates that include placeholders of buttons. You can simply drag and drop a video onto a placeholder. If you have more than one menu, you will need to set one as the first play. Figure 7.17 shows an example of a menu and a submenu created in Adobe Encore CS3 using a template. The videos can be dragged and dropped onto the button to create thumbnails for the buttons.

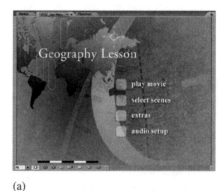

(a)

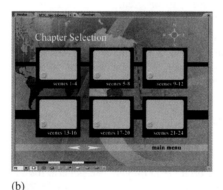

(b)

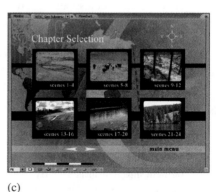

(c)

Figure 7.17 A menu and submenu created in Adobe Encore CS3 using a menu tempate (a) A main menu set as the first play (b) A submenu template (c) A submenu is linked to the button "select scenes" on the main menu shown in (a)

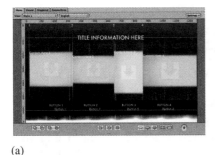 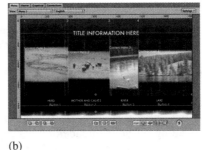

(a)   (b)

Figure 7.18 A menu created in Apple DVD Studio Pro 4 using a template (a)
A template (b) Video thumbnails are used for the buttons

Figure 7.18 shows another example of a menu created in Apple DVD Studio Pro 4 using a template. Similarly, a video can be dragged and dropped onto the button to create a thumbnail of the video on the button.

When you export your video into an MPEG-2 DVD-compliant file using your video-editing program, you may have the multiplex option. If the multiplex option is off, it means your video and audio will be exported into two separate files: a MPEG-2 file for the video (a file with a file extension of .m2v, .mpg, or .mpeg) and an audio file (.wav file). If you turn on the multiplex option, then both video and audio will be combined in one file.

Some DVD authoring programs may support the multiplexed media but others may not. Before you export your final video to the MPEG-2 file, you should check the supported media file formats in the user manual or Help of the DVD authoring program.

If the video and the audio are separated into two files, how would the audio be associated with the video? Many DVD authoring programs use Timeline or Track for the video used in a DVD project. Timeline has video and audio tracks. You can add the audio that has been imported into the Asset list onto the audio track of the timeline.

Some programs support multiple audio tracks, which can be used for multiple languages. Some even support multiple video tracks for multiple-angle video production. Some programs let you define chapters by adding chapter points on the timeline.

Limited edition or consumer-type DVD authoring programs often support only a single video track and a single audio track. These programs usually let you simply drag and drop the video and audio onto a button on a menu.

Step 4   **Preview and Test Play Your Project.**
Test play your DVD project thoroughly within the DVD authoring program using its Preview feature.

Step 5   **Build a DVD Volume and Make a DVD Disc.**
Many DVD authoring programs let you choose whether to build the DVD to a folder or directly onto a disc. Building the DVD to a folder has at least two advantages:

- It gives you a chance to test the DVD volume before you write it to a disc.
- The computer you are authoring the DVD project with does not have to have a DVD-writer available at the time you build the DVD.

You can write the DVD volume to a disc later if you do not have a blank DVD disc on hand or if a DVD-writer is not available. You can transfer the DVD volume with an external hard drive to another computer that has a DVD-writer.

The DVD volume contains two folders: VIDEO_TS and AUDIO_TS. For the video DVD, all of the files are in the VIDEO_TS folder. The AUDIO_TS is empty. The AUDIO_TS folder is for the audio DVD. To make a DVD-video disc, write the VIDEO_TS folder onto a disc. It is fine to also include the empty AUDIO_TS.

Depending on your intended audience playback device and the size of your DVD volume, you can write the DVD volume to a CD or a DVD disc. The VIDEO_TS and the AUDIO_TS folders have to be written to the disc in its root (i.e., topmost) directory. Do not place them in a subfolder on the disc, or the player will not automatically start playing your video on the disc.

7.8 SUMMARY

Digital videos can be acquired by shooting digital video footage using a digital video camera or by digitizing the video from an analog source, such as VHS, 8 mm and Hi-8 tapes.

The video file format that the digital video camera records in is often related to the camera's recording medium. Currently, the four most common types of camcorder media are tapes, DVDs, memory cards, and hard drives. At the time of writing, most tape-type digital camcorders (standard definition DV and HDV formats) record video to miniDV tapes.

Examples of digital video-editing programs are Adobe Premiere Pro, Apple Final Cut Pro, Sony Vegas, and Avid. The basic workspace elements that many of these programs share are:

- Asset lists
- Preview window
- Timeline or Track
- Effects and transitions

The basic steps of creating a final digital video are:

1. Import the source materials in the video project as assets.
2. Arrange these assets on the timeline.
3. Apply transitions, video effects, and audio effects, if needed.
4. Output and distribute your final video.

After you have finished assembling your video project, you can output the final video to a different file format. The choice of file formats depends on how you want to distribute your final video to your audience. Some common choices of delivery media include:

DVD-video: MPEG-2 for DVD
Web:
- QuickTime for progressive download
- QuickTime, RealVideo, Windows Media, and Flash Video also support streaming on the Web

Optical disc, such as CD or DVD: QuickTime, AVI, MPEG-1
Tapes

Standard definition DVD-videos can be played back on set-top players or on computers that have a DVD-ROM drive and player.

Basically, there are two ways to create a DVD-video disc:

- Export your final video as a DVD-compliant MPEG-2 file and then author a DVD project using DVD authoring programs.
- Export your final video directly to DVD.

There have been two formats for high definition video disc: HD-DVD and Blu-ray. Blu-ray has become the choice of the market. DVD-writers and the authoring software for the high definition video disc are starting to become available. For example, Adobe Premiere Pro CS3 and Apple Final Cut Pro let you export Blu-ray format. Adobe Encore CS3 and Apple DVD Studio Pro 4 support Blu-ray DVD authoring.

The general steps to authoring a DVD project are:

1. Set project settings
2. Import content as assets
3. Put things together
4. Preview and test play your project
5. Build a DVD volume and make a DVD disc

For videos intended for CD-ROM or DVD-ROM playback, you need to find out the speed of your target audience's CD-ROM or DVD-ROM drive. From that, you can estimate the data rate. The data rate of your video should be no higher than the data rate of your target audience's playback device. If the data rate of your video is higher than the audience's CD-ROM or DVD-ROM drive can handle, your video will skip frames and become choppy.

Here are some suggested steps to determine export settings for CD-ROM or DVD-ROM playback.

1. Start with the desired frame size, frame rate, and compressor.
2. Export your video. Look up its file size and calculate the data rate.
   If the data rate is higher than your target audience's device can handle, then try reducing the frame size, lowering the frame rate, or lowering the picture quality. The nature of your video dictates which strategy you should try first.
3. Finally, always test your final production on the computer equipment as close to the target audience's as possible.

TERMS

LEARNING AIDS

The following learning aids can be found at the book's companion Web site.

✎ Setting the Device Control for Video Capture

Screen capture movies demonstrate setting the device control for video capture in Adobe Premiere Pro.

✎ Batch Capturing Digital Video

Screen capture movies demonstrate the basic steps of batch capturing a digital video in two digital video editing application programs: Adobe Premiere Pro and Apple Final Cut Pro.

✎ Trimming a Clip by Setting In and Out Points, and Applying a Video Transition to Video Clips

Screen capture movies demonstrate the basic steps of setting In and Out points for video clips, and applying a video transition in two digital video-editing application programs: Adobe Premiere Pro and Apple Final Cut Pro.

⊕ Nonlinear Editing Techniques in Digital Video

An interactive tutorial demonstrates the characteristics of ripple edit, rolling edit, slip edit, and slide edit.

✎ Straight-cut versus Cross Dissolve Transitions

A short video clip shows side-by-side two different transitions: straight-cut and cross dissolve.

✎ Applying a Video Effect to Video Clips and Animating the Effect by Keyframing

Screen capture movies demonstrate the basic steps of applying a Gaussian blur video effect to a clip and keyframing the effect in two digital video-editing application programs: Adobe Premiere Pro and Apple Final Cut Pro.

✎ Chroma Keying Video Clips

Screen capture movies demonstrate the basic steps of chroma keying a video clip using two digital video-editing application programs: Adobe Premiere Pro and Apple Final Cut Pro.

✎ Export Video to DVD MPEG-2

Screen capture movies demonstrate the basic steps of exporting videos to DVD MPEG-2 in Adobe Premiere Pro.

✎ Export Video to QuickTime Movie

Screen capture movies demonstrate the basic steps of exporting videos to QuickTime movies in two digital video-editing application programs: Adobe Premiere Pro and Apple Final Cut Pro.

REVIEW QUESTIONS

When applicable, please choose all correct answers.

1. **True/False:** The only way to acquire digital video footage is to shoot video directly in digital format.

2. **True/False:** A DVD-video project has to have a menu structure.

3. A DVD volume, built with a DVD authoring program, contains two folders, called _____ and _____ .

4. Which of the following is the best way to capture digital videos?

   A. Capture at least a few seconds extra at the beginning and the end of the clip segment you expect you will need.
   B. Capture at least a few seconds extra at the beginning of the clip segment you expect you will need, but no extra seconds at the end of the clip.
   C. Capture at least a few seconds extra at the end of the clip segment you expect you will need, but no extra seconds at the beginning of the clip.
   D. Capture exactly only the clip segment you expect you will need; no extra seconds at the beginning or the end of the clip.

5. In most digital video-editing programs, the imported source footage and images to be used in a video project are listed in the _____ .

   A. Asset list window
   B. Effects and transitions window
   C. Preview window
   D. Timeline window

6. In most digital video-editing programs, _____ has video and audio tracks, and it is where you can arrange and compose your raw footage in sequence.

   A. Asset list window
   B. Effects and transitions window
   C. Preview window
   D. Timeline window

7. Which of the following is NOT an option for the final digital video output?

   A. CD-ROM playback
   B. DVD playback
   C. Web delivery
   D. miniDV tape playback
   E. none of the above

8. Most digital video cameras support FireWire. Which of the following is a FireWire cable adapter AND fits the FireWire DV IN/OUT port found in most of the digital video cameras?

   A.    B.   C.

D. E.

9. The first figure shows a video sequence consisting of three video clips placed side-by-side on a timeline. Which nonlinear editing tool lets you lengthen the middle clip (blue color) while pushing the adjacent clip down? The second figure shows the resulted video sequence.

A. Ripple edit
B. Rolling edit
C. Slip edit
D. Slide edit

10. The first figure shows a video sequence consisting of three video clips placed side-by-side on a timeline. Which nonlinear editing tool lets you lengthen the middle clip (blue color) while maintaining the duration of the entire video sequence by pushing the In point of the adjacent clip? The second figure shows the resulted video sequence.

A. Ripple edit
B. Rolling edit
C. Slip edit
D. Slide edit

EXPLORING THE APPLICATIONS

1. Find the following information about your **video-editing program** from its user manual or online Help.
- Workspace:
  - Identify the Asset list, Timeline, Preview window, Transitions and Effects palette/menu
- Capturing videos:
  - How to capture digital video
  - How to batch capture if it is available
- Editing captured clips:
  - Methods of trimming source clips:
    - Does the program let you set In and Out points? If so, how?
    - What are the other methods of trimming clips? Write down the instructions and the characteristic features for each method.
  - How to change the speed and duration of a clip

- How to create titles
- Composing video sequences:
  - Find out the available transitions, and how to apply transitions
  - Find out the available video effects, and how to apply them to the clip—for example, resizing and cropping a clip or applying tonal and color adjustments to a clip
  - Locate the ripple edit, rolling edit, slip edit, and slide edit tools, if available
  - Find out the available audio effects, and how to apply them to the audio
  - How to create a simple fade-in and fade-out of an audio
  - How to set transparency of a clip
  - How to superimpose a clip over another
- Exporting video:
  - How to output your final video
  - Find out the supported output video format

2. Find the following information about your **DVD authoring program** from its user manual or online Help.

- Workspace:
  - Identify the Asset list, Timeline, Preview window, and Media Library window
- Starting a new project:
  - How to start a new project and set the proper project settings, such as NTSC or PAL, frame size, and aspect ratio
- Media:
  - Find out the file types supported by the program
  - How to add a media file to your project
- How to create a simple single-movie DVD project (i.e., without a menu)
- How to set the single-movie or a menu to loop
- Creating menu:
  - How to create a menu
  - How to add text and graphics for the menu
  - How to link the text and graphics of a menu to a video or another menu
- How to preview or test play your DVD project within the program
- Exporting your DVD project:
  - How to build a DVD volume on a hard drive
  - How to burn the DVD volume onto a DVD disc

Interactive Multimedia Authoring with Flash: Animation

KEY CONCEPTS
- Frame-by-frame, tweened, and scripted animation
- Flash basics

GENERAL LEARNING OBJECTIVES

At the end of this chapter, you should be able to demonstrate that you understand

- The basic workspace and terminology of Flash to get you started on animation and ActionScript.
- Symbols and shapes in Flash.
- Animation with Flash.
- Frame-by-frame, tweening, and scripted animation.
- When it is best to use these different types of animation.
- Creating tweened animation using motion guide in Flash.
- Creating mask and animated mask in Flash.
- How to publish Flash movies as projector and SWF.

8.1 WHAT IS MULTIMEDIA AUTHORING?

Multimedia authoring is the process of creating a multimedia production. It involves assembling or sequencing different media elements, adding interactivity, and then packaging the production for distribution to the *end users*. The end users are the target audience who will be viewing your final production.

Business presentations, advertising kiosks, games, and educational products are just a few examples of multimedia productions. These multimedia projects can be delivered to end users over the Internet (played in a Web browser or as a download) or as a stand-alone executable program suitable for distribution through CD-ROM and DVD-ROM.

Multimedia authoring programs allow you to combine text, images/graphics, audio, video, and animation into an interactive presentation. Many programs also have their own scripting language that lets you add interactivity to your production. Adobe Flash and Director are examples of commercial multimedia authoring programs. Flash has its scripting language called *ActionScript*, and Director's scripting language is called Lingo. You also can develop a multimedia production by programming in languages that are not specific formultimedia authoring, for example, C++, Visual Basic, JavaScript, or DHTML.

This book's multimedia authoring chapters cover the basics of Flash animation and ActionScript. ActionScript shares the same basic programming terms and concepts of other programming languages. Hence, you will be able to apply the fundamentals you learn in these chapters to other programming projects.

8.2 THE MULTIMEDIA PRODUCTION PROCESS

Multimedia authoring refers to the *assembly* of media elements. The actual creation of the necessary media elements is a separate process. Digital images, video, and audio can be created with programs that are specialized for producing and editing these media.

For example, if you want to use video clips in your multimedia project, you can shoot digital videos with a DV camera, transfer the video to a computer with a video-editing program (such as Adobe Premiere Pro), and then edit the video by adding transitions, adjusting durations, adding voice or music to the audio tracks, performing color correction, and adding special effects. Finally, you export the video into a format, such as QuickTime, AVI, or a series of images, that you can import into your multimedia authoring program.

In the authoring process, you specify when your video will show up and how the video should interact with other media elements on the screen when the multimedia production plays.

This section discusses the basic steps of creating an interactive multimedia production to give you a big picture of the multimedia authoring process. The details of working with Flash are covered later in this chapter.

Step 1 **Collect and assemble the media elements**
Media elements include text, bitmapped images, vector graphics, digital videos, digital audio, and animation. These elements usually are created outside of the multimedia authoring program, using programs that are specific to the media type.

Flash is a vector graphic-based multimedia authoring program. It has simple tools for creating and modifying vector graphics to be used in a movie. You can also import other types of media files to use.

Shown here are some of the common file formats that are supported by Flash.

Bitmap images: Photoshop (PSD), BMP, GIF, JPEG, PNG, TIFF
Vector graphics: Flash Movie (SWF), Adobe Illustrator, WMF
Digital Videos: QuickTime (MOV), AVI, Flash Video (FLV)
Digital Audio: WAV, MP3, AIFF, AU

WMF Files: Many vector graphic cliparts, such as Microsoft Office cliparts, are in WMF format.

Step 2 **Assemble the media elements**
In Flash, you can create vector graphics using the pencil and brush tools. You can also import various types of media elements. These elements can be arranged on a timeline to control the order and timing of their appearance.

Step 3 **Add interactivity**
Interactivity can be added, for example, by programming in ActionScript in a Flash project.

Step 4 **Package the movie for distribution to the end users**
The two most common forms of distributing multimedia productions are stand-alone executables and movies that play back in a Web browser. Publishing your multimedia project in either of these two formats allows others to view your finished project without the authoring environment. For example, they do not need to have a copy of Flash installed in order to view your Flash movies.

- The Web version of Flash movies is a SWF file. SWF has a smaller size than the stand-alone executable and is designed for the Web. It is playable on Windows, Macintosh, and Linux computers, as long as the Flash player or the browser plug-in is installed.

To create a version of your movie playable through a Web browser, you need to publish the movie as SWF. Selecting the file format for the published movie can be set in the Publish Settings (File > Publish Settings . . .). In the Publish Settings dialog box (Figure 8.1), you can check to select the format(s) of the published movie(s). SWF and HTML with embedded SWF are the default selection.

Figure 8.1 Flash's Publish Settings dialog box

- A stand-alone executable does not require a plug-in to play. Stand-alone executables usually are created for distribution on CD-ROM or DVD-ROM. The file size for an executable is larger than a Web version, and you need to create separate executables for different operating systems.

    To create a standalone executable in Flash, you publish your movie as a ***projector***.

8.3 ANIMATION

Conceptually, animation is very much like video. It is a sequence of images that create the illusion of movement when played in succession. Many multimedia projects make use of animation, and many multimedia authoring programs, such as Flash and Director, allow you to create animation. These programs are frame-based. This means that you can sequence the animation content visually on a timeline as a sequence of frames.

There are several different ways to create animations with these programs: frame-by-frame, tweening, and scripting. These methods are not exclusive of each other in a project; they can be used in combination in creating an animation sequence.

8.3.1 Frame-by-Frame Animation

Frame-by-frame animation involves explicitly placing or creating different visual content for each frame. Each frame is a ***keyframe***, which is a frame that explicitly specifies the content.

For example, Figure 8.2 shows a character running sequence.

Figure 8.2 An example of frame-by-frame animation

Figure 8.3a shows a simple nine-frame animation of a bird flying. The visual content of all nine frames are explicitly placed. Figure 8.3b shows an example of a tweened animation, which is discussed next.

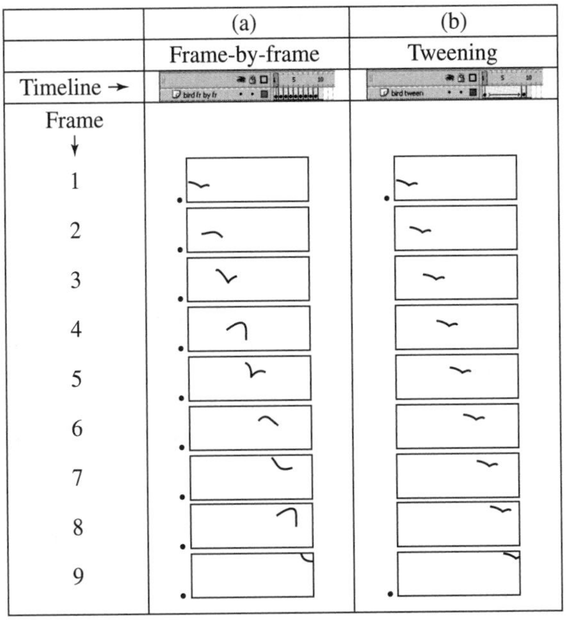

	(a) Frame-by-frame	(b) Tweening
Timeline →		
Frame ↓		
1		
2		
3		
4		
5		
6		
7		
8		
9		

Figure 8.3 Frame-by-frame versus tweening showing the • next to the image frame to indicate that the image is created manually (a) Frame-by-frame (b) Tweening

8.3.2 Tweened Animation

Tweening also requires keyframes. You need two keyframes for any tweened segment: one at the beginning and the other at the end. Frames that are between keyframe are called *in-between frames*.

When tweening is applied to the first keyframe, the content in these in-between frames will be filled in by interpolating the values of the object's properties. What this means is that you do not manually draw or paste the bird into these in-between frames.

Suppose you want to animate a bird moving across the screen from left to right in nine frames. In the first keyframe (frame 1), place the bird on the left side of the screen, and in the last keyframe (frame 9) place it on the right side of the screen (Figure 8.3b). The content in frames 2 through 8 (the in-between frames) are filled in automatically.

In this simple example, the property of the bird that changes in each keyframe is its position. In addition to position, other common properties that can be animated by tweening in animation programs include rotation, size, color, and opacity. The shape of an object also can be tweened in Flash.

8.3.3 Scripted Animation

You will learn how to create scripted animation in Chapter 10.

Scripted animation does not rely on a sequence of frames on the timeline. The animation can be scripted to respond to the user's interaction. In the previous example of bird flying animation, the bird can be scripted to follow the mouse cursor or to start flying after the user has clicked on a button. In such cases, the bird is not always at the middle of the frame at the two-second point. When the bird reaches the middle of the frame varies in different playback sessions and for different users. If the bird is scripted to follow the mouse cursor, the bird may not even move to the middle of the image frame.

8.3.4 Frame-by-Frame versus Tweened versus Scripted

Frame-by-frame and tweening rely on creating a fixed sequence of images on the timeline. The appearance of a particular image in such sequence is deterministic. For example, if a bird is animated to reach the middle of the image frame two seconds after the animation starts, then it will *always* reach the middle at a two-second point, assuming the computer playing the animation is fast enough to sustain the frame rate specified in the animation.

Frame-by-frame and tweening techniques do not require scripting. However, the animated sequence is fixed at the authoring time. The scripted animation can be more dynamic and interactive because the property of the object can be changed in response to user interaction during playback.

Creating frame-by-frame animation is usually more time-consuming than tweening. However, tweening does not always create the sophisticated effect that you might want. In addition, because the in-between frames are computed, it results in smooth motion. Such smoothness sometimes may give a mechanical feeling to the animation. On the other hand, frame-by-frame animation in which each frame is drawn manually can give an organic touch to the animation, such as in the simple bird flying example in Figure 8.3a.

Frame-by-Frame, Tweening, and Scripted Animation A side-by-side comparison of frame-by-frame, tweening, and scripted animation using the bird flying example shown in Figure 8.3.

8.3.5 Frame Rate and Frame Size

Frame size refers to the width and height dimensions of the animation. For digital video, the dimensions are in pixels. In Flash and Director, the size of a frame is the stage dimension of the movie, also in pixels.

The default frame rate of a Flash file is 12 fps. 30 fps is an acceptable rate for most computers.

Frame rate specifies the playback speed of the animation. It is in frames per second (fps). Like video, a low frame rate will make the animation choppy. Too high a frame rate may also cause choppiness if the computer playing the animation is not fast enough to process and display the frames.

The presentation of an animation is controlled by frame size and frame rate. Multimedia authoring programs, such as Flash and Director, allow you to set the frame rate for your animation project. The frame rate setting in these programs usually defines the *maximum* rate.

This means that the program will not exceed the frame rate you specify in your animation project, but it does not guarantee that your animation will be kept at that frame rate. Slower computers may not be able to keep up with a high frame rate.

8.4 ADJUSTING THE SPEED OF ANIMATION PLAYBACK

For the frame-based animation, both the number of frames and its frame rate affect the speed of the motion.

- To speed up the motion: Reduce the number of frames or increase the frame rate (preferred)
- To slow down the motion: Add more frames (preferred) or reduce the number of frames

Whether you want to slow down or speed up the motion, the basic guideline is to do so without reducing the number of frames. Eliminating frames in an animation sequence means eliminating the content that makes up the motion. This reduces the continuity of the motion and may break it up—causing noticeable jerkiness. Elimination of frames should be used only as a last resort for adjusting the speed of the animation playback.

8.4.1 Slowing Down Motion by Adding More Frames

Suppose after you have created a tweened animation, you feel that the motion seems a little too fast. A good way to slow down the motion is to add more frames between keyframes instead of lowering the frame rate. The exception to this is when your frame rate is already too high—for example, higher than 30 frames per second.

The example shown in Figure 8.4 demonstrates the different effects of adding more frames versus lowering the frame rate. The original sequence (Column A) contains five frames and its frame rate is 20 fps. This means the animation sequence finishes in 0.4 seconds.

Column B and Column C show two different approaches to slow down the animation. The approach shown in Column B (Approach #1) maintains the frame rate but slows down the animation by increasing the number of frames, allowing the motion to stretch over a longer period of time. The animation now finishes in one second.

The approach shown in Column C (Approach #2) slows down the animation by lowering the frame rate. The animation still finishes in one second. However, as you see, using Approach #1, the motion of the ball in the resulting animation changes every 0.05 seconds while it updates every 0.2 seconds using Approach #2. Therefore, Approach #1 gives a smoother motion than Approach #2.

> ✐ **Adjusting the Speed of an Animation: Frame Rate versus Number of Frames** A side-by-side comparison of the original sequence and two approaches shown in Figure 8.4.

8.4.2 Speeding up Motion

If you want to speed up a frame-based animation, in most situations you may consider increasing the frame rate. The exception for this guideline is when the frame rate is already too high for the target audience's computer to play. In this case, you can try reducing the number of frames in the animation sequence.

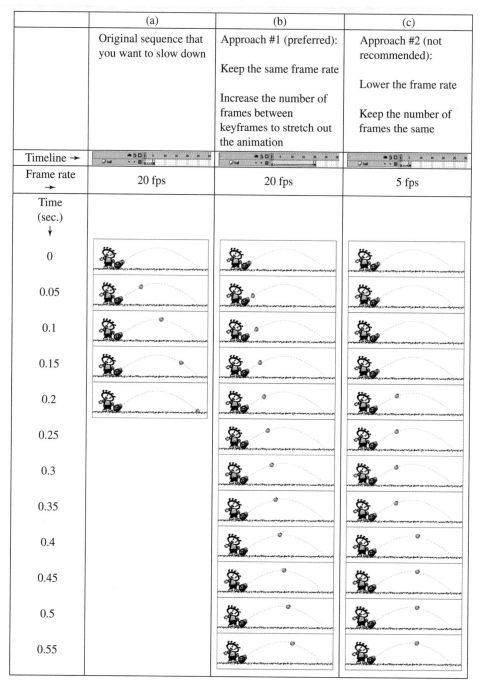

Figure 8.4 Different approaches to slowing down an animation illustrated by showing the frame of an animation at each time interval (*continued*)

0.6	
0.65	
0.7	
0.75	
0.8	
0.85	
0.9	
0.95	

Figure 8.4 (*continued*)

8.5 FLASH CS3 WORKSPACE

The Flash workspace or authoring environment has a variety of panels. This section gives you an overview of the most essential workspace elements: Tools, Stage, Timeline, Property Inspector, and Library (Figure 8.5). You are encouraged to explore the workspace on your own and use Help for more detailed information.

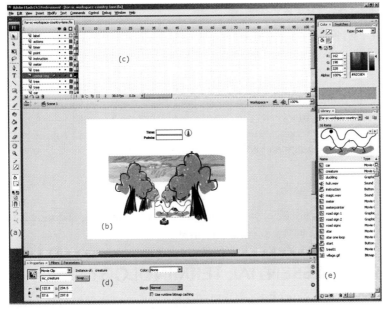

Figure 8.5 Workspace of Flash CS3 (a) Tools panel (b) Stage (c) Timeline (d) Property Inspector (e) Library panel

8.5.1 Tools Panel

By default, the Tools panel (Figure 8.5a) is located on the far left. It contains tools to select, draw, scale, and modify the content used in the Flash document.

8.5.2 Stage

The Stage (Figure 8.5b) is the area where a Flash movie plays. By default, it is a rectangle in the center of the window. Its color is defined by the background color of the project (Modify > Document...). The outside of the stage rectangle is marked in gray color. Any object placed outside of the stage is not visible by the user when the movie is played using a player, even though it is visible at the authoring time.

8.5.3 Timeline

The Timeline (Figure 8.5c) is made of a series of frames in a row and a stack of layers. Flash is a frame-based authoring program. The media contents are organized on a timeline (Figure 8.5c) over time in frames and layers. The content on the top layer will cover the one beneath it.

The appearance of a frame indicates whether it is a keyframe, a regular frame, or an empty frame.

- A solid black circle in a frame indicates it is a keyframe.
- A circle means it is an empty keyframe.
- A shaded frame without any circle is a regular frame that contains the same content as the previous keyframe in the same layer.
- A frame with an empty rectangle is also a regular frame, but it is the end frame of a frame sequence.

8.5.4 Property Inspector

By default, the Property Inspector (Figure 8.5d) is located at the bottom of the window. It displays the information and properties to be edited for the object that is currently selected on the Stage.

When you select *a frame on the Timeline*, the Property Inspector displays the *frame property*. If the frame selected is a keyframe, then this is where you can assign a frame label and a tweening to that frame.

If *an object on the Stage* is selected, then you can alter *the object's properties*, such as its *x* and *y* position or width and height, by entering numbers.

8.5.5 Library Panel

The Library panel (Figure 8.5e) stores symbols, imported bitmaps, and sounds to be used in the project. Symbols are explained in the next section.

8.6 FLASH: ESSENTIAL TERMINOLOGY

The visual items used on the Stage in a Flash file can be categorized in two types: shapes and symbols. They have different properties, purposes, and requirements.

Beware of What is Selected:

Selecting the frame is different from selecting the objects on the Stage. To select a frame, you click on the frame on the timeline. This will cause all of the objects in that frame to be selected. Because a frame is selected, the Property Inspector shows the properties of that frame only. This includes the tweening option and the frame label name.

If you mean to select an object in a frame to apply a color effect, then make sure you select the object by clicking on the object on the Stage— not by clicking on the frame on the Timeline.

8.6.1 Shape

A *shape* is made up of strokes and/or fills.

- *Strokes* are lines that are created with the Pencil, Pen, and Ink Bottle tools (Figure 8.6a through c). A stroke's properties, such as width, color, and style of the line, can be modified in the Property Inspector.
- A *fill* is an area of filled content. It can be created by using the Paint Bucket and Brush tools (Figure 8.6d through e).

The section on vector graphic programs in Chapter 3 discusses how to create strokes and fills. The techniques of working with anchor points and handles to create and edit paths also apply to Flash.

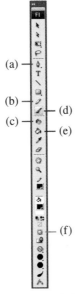

Figure 8.6 Tools panel of Flash CS3 (a) Pen tool (b) Pencil tool (c) Ink Bottle tool (d) Brush tool (e) Paint Bucket tool (f) Object Drawing

There are two drawing models for drawing shapes: Object Drawing and Merge Drawing. When you select the Pencil, Brush, Pen, Line, or Rectangle tools, you have an option called Object Drawing (Figure 8.6f). You turn on the Object Drawing option to use Object Drawing, turn it off to return to Merge Drawing.

Merge Drawing model is the default drawing model. The shapes that overlap are merged. In the *Object Drawing model*, the shapes you create are self-contained objects.

The drawing objects differ from the shapes drawn in the Merge Drawing model in two ways:

- When you click to select a drawing object on the Stage, you select the whole shape. You see a box around the drawing object.

    For example, Figure 8.7 show two head drawings: (i) the one on the left is made up of drawing objects; (ii) the one on the right is made up of regualr shapes. Figure 8.7a shows that they are selected. As you see, each brush stroke in (i) is an individual drawing object.

You cannot selectively select an individual area of the fill or a segment of the stroke. You can double-click on the drawing object to edit its shapes, like you would regular shapes (Figure 8.7b).

- The overlapped drawing objects do not alter one another.

For example, you can change the color of a drawing object (Figure 8.7c(i)) without altering the other objects that it overlaps with. If you fill the same part of the shape, Figure 8.7c(ii), the color in the contiguous shape with the same color will be changed. If you reposition drawing objects, such as the two eyes (Figure 8.7d(i)), the previously overlapping hair (also a drawing object) is not altered. On the other hand, holes are created in the shapes on the right (Figure 8.7d(ii)).

Depending on how you want to create your content, object drawing mode may or may not suit your needs. An empty enclosed space created in a merged shape can be filled easily.

For example, the empty space can be filled with a green color in Figure 8.7e(ii) using the Paint Bucket tool. However, to make the same area filled with a color in the one made up of drawing objects (Figure 8.7e(i)), you would need to create another shape or drawing object of that color.

> ✏ **Creating Shapes in Flash** A screen-capture movie shows how to create a simple shape using Pencil, Pen, Ink, and Paint Bucket tools.

> ✏ **Modifying Shapes in Flash** A screen-capture movie shows how to modify of a shape.

If you find that you have unintentionally drawn drawing objects on the Stage, select the Pencil, Brush, Pen, Line, of Rectangle tool and make sure Object Drawing is turned off, so that the new shapes are not drawn. Turning off Object Drawing does not automatically convert the existing objects on the Stage to shapes. The existing objects still remain, but you can convert them into shapes by selecting the objects and choosing `Modify > Break Apart`.

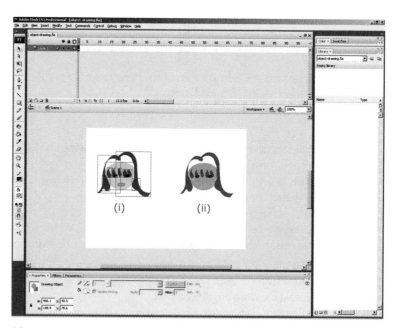

(a)

Figure 8.7 Drawing object (i) versus merge shape (ii) (*continued*)

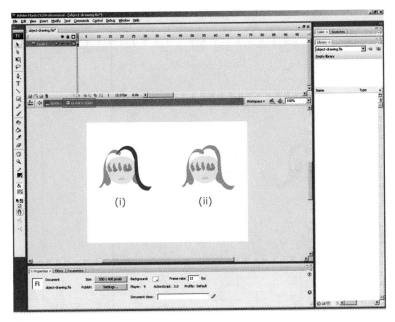

(b)

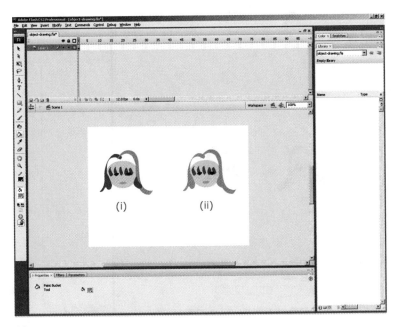

(c)

Figure 8.7 (*continued*)

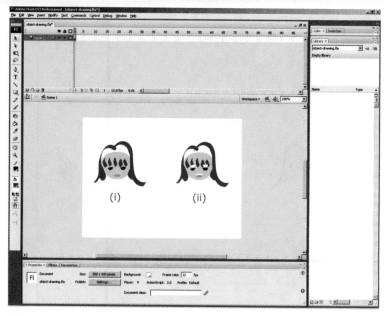

(d)

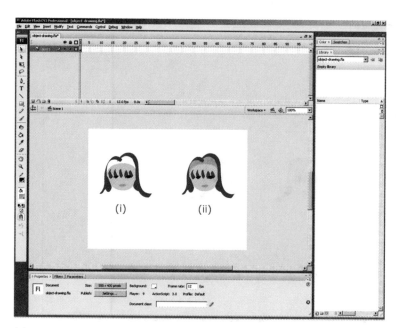

(e)

Figure 8.7 (*continued*)

8.6.2 Symbol

Symbols are stored in the Library panel and can be reused throughout the project.

To create a symbol, you can either: (1) convert an existing shape into a symbol or (2) create a blank symbol and then start creating shapes and/or place other symbols inside it.

New symbols are automatically added to the Library panel. To place a symbol on the Stage, you can drag the symbol from the Library panel onto the Stage.

When you select a symbol that is placed on the Stage, a rectangular bounding box appears around the symbol (regardless of the symbol's shape), as shown in the puppy on the left in Figure 8.8. If you want to edit the shape of the symbol, you will need change to the editing mode of the symbol by double-clicking on the symbol's instance on the Stage or the symbol itself in the Library. You can tell a symbol from a shape on the Stage by looking at the Property Inspector. In Figure 8.8, the puppy selected on the left is a copy of a symbol. The blue rectangular box around it indicates the selection is a copy of the symbol. The puppy selected on the right is a merged shape, indicated by patterned dots.

Chapters 10 will explain how to assign actions to an object on the Stage.

Figure 8.8 Symbol and shapes

There are three types of symbols: graphic, button, and movieclip. The characteristics and purposes of each type are described briefly here:

1. **Graphic.**
   - Purposes: To be used as static graphics. It can be placed in other graphic, button and movieclip symbols in addition to the main timeline.
   - Interactive controls and sounds won't work in a graphic symbol's timeline.
2. **Button.**
   - Purposes: To be used as interactive buttons in the movie to respond to mouse clicks and rollovers. It can be placed in movieclip symbols in addition to the main timeline.
   - There are only four special-purpose frames in a button symbol. They correspond to the various states of the button: up, over, down, and hit. Hit is to define the hot spot

Movieclips versus Buttons: Because movieclips can offer more possibilities in interactivity, all of the ActionScript examples in this book use movieclips instead of buttons. However, the ActionScript code in most of the examples also will work for buttons.

of the button if you only want a certain area of the button to respond to the mouse. You can add different graphic symbols, movieclips, or just shapes to define the appearance of the different button states.

- You can use ActionScript to control a button that is placed on the timeline.

3. **Movieclip.**

- Purposes: To be used as reusable pieces of animation. Movieclips can have their own timeline that play independently from the main movie's timeline. You can think of movieclips as mini-Flash movies inside a main movie.

    Like buttons, movieclips can be controlled using ActionScript in response to mouse clicks and rollovers. However, unlike a button, each movieclip has a timeline for frame-based animation. A button's timeline only has four special-purpose frames.

- A movieclip can contain copies of other symbols (graphic, buttons, and other movieclips), ActionScript, and sounds.

- You also can place movieclip copies inside the timeline of a button symbol to create animated buttons.

- If you use movieclips in your movie, you need to select Control > Test Movie to preview them, not just Control > Play.

- The animation of a movieclip will start playing automatically unless you use an ActionScript to stop it at its first frame.

Using symbols is not a technical requirement for basic Flash animation. Depending on the complexity of a project, some projects can be worked on without using symbols, using only shapes. However, symbols offer at least two advantages.

1. Reusability: Using a symbol multiple times on the Stage will not increase the Flash file size. On the other hand, if you duplicate a shape on the Stage, it will increase the file size.
2. The symbol stored in the Library is a master copy of all the copies used on the Stage. The copies used on the Stage are called the *instances* of that symbol. Changes made to the content of the master copy will be reflected automatically in all of its copies used on the Stage. For example, as shown in Figure 8.9, there are three movieclip instances of the puppy symbol on the Stage. Each instance can be resized independently. By changing the one master copy of the puppy symbol in the Library panel to a Dalmatian puppy, all three instances of the puppy symbol on the Stage become Dalmatians.

> ✎ **Creating Symbols in Flash** A screen-capture movie shows show to create (1) a new symbol and (2) a symbol by converting from a shape.

In situations where the authoring process starts before the visual content of the symbols are ready, symbols with temporary content can be used while waiting for the actual content. Once the final designs of the symbols are ready, each symbol will need to be updated only once in the Library panel. All of the instances used on the Stage will reflect the new content automatically.

8.6.3 Tweening

Tweening is an effective way to create movement and changes over time. It requires two keyframes for each tweened sequence. To create a keyframe, use one of the following methods:

- Select a frame, select Insert > Timeline > Keyframe
- Right-click (Windows) or Control-click (Macintosh) a frame on the Timeline, and select Insert Keyframe.

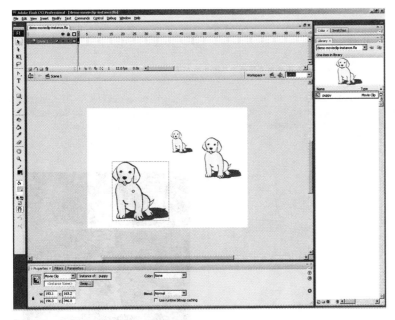

(a)

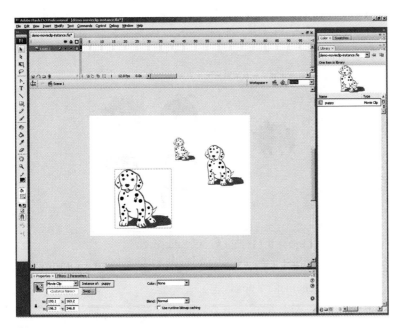

(b)

Figure 8.9 Symbol and its instances (a) Three instances (copies) of the movieclip symbol named puppy are placed on the Stage (b) When the master copy of the symbol puppy, which is stored in the Library panel, is modified to a Dalmatian puppy, all of the instances placed on the Stage are updated automatically

🖰 **Practice Drawing (Lab)** Practice Flash drawing and painting tools, and create movieclip symbols. Create two files:

1. x-ray (Figure 8.10)

2. hair styles (Figure 8.11)

The x-ray file will be used to create tweened animation in a lab later in this chapter. The hair styles file will be used in a lab in Chapter 10 where you will learn how to add interactivity to allow the user to change the hair style on the character's head by clicking on one of the hair style choices.

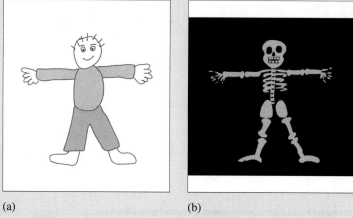

(a)   (b)

Figure 8.10 File #1: Create two symbols and put each on a separate layer

Figure 8.11 File #2: Create seven symbols: a character's head (without hair), five hair styles, and one hair to put on the character's head

There are two types of tweening in Flash: ***motion tween*** and ***shape tween***. They serve different purposes and have different requirements. Comparisons of these two different tweening techniques are summarized in Table 8.1.

Figure 8.12 shows an example of creating a three-keyframe motion tweened animation. In each of the three keyframes, the position, scale, and rotation of the leaf symbol instance

TABLE 8.1	Comparison between Motion Tween and Shape Tween	
Motion Tween		**Shape Tween**
Works with **symbols** only.		Works with **shapes** only.
Not for creating morphing animation.		Can be used to create a shape morphing animation.
No more than one symbol is allowed on a single layer that is going to be motion tweened.		Technically, more than one shape can be placed on a single layer that is going to be shape tweened. However, if you want more control over which shape to morph to which destination shape, you should separate the shape onto separate layers, which is almost always the case when you create a shape tween.
Can be used in combination of **motion guide**.		It does not work with motion guide.
The frames of the motion tween sequence are colored in **blue** on the timeline (Figure 8.12).		The frames of the shape tween sequence are colored in **green** on the timeline (Figure 8.14).

If you applied an incorrect tweening type or use multiple symbols in the same layer for motion tween, the tweened sequence will not work and it will be indicated as a dash-line (instead of a solid-line arrow) on the timeline.

Motion guide will be explained in Section 8.6.4.

are altered. Motion tween is applied to each of the keyframes except the last one. (Only the beginning keyframe of each tween segment is needed to be applied with the tweening.)

The in-between frames are filled in automatically by interpolating the position, scale, and rotation of two immediate keyframes.

> ◇ **Creating Motion Tween in Flash** A screen-capture movie shows how to create a motion tween animation.

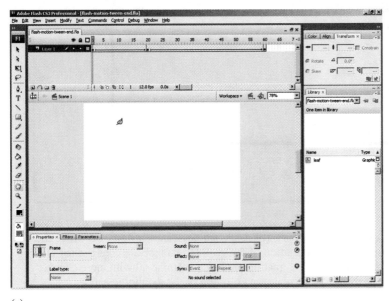

(a)

Figure 8.12 A motion tweened animation with the frame color shown on the timeline in blue (a) Keyframe at frame 1 (*continued*)

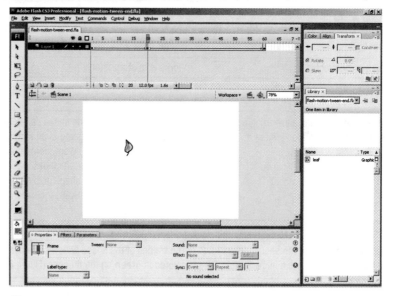

(b)

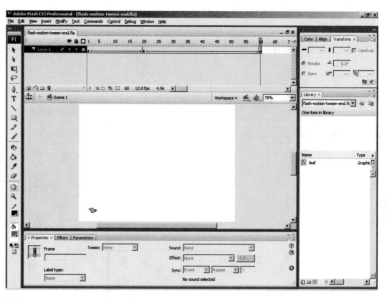

(c)

Figure 8.12 (*continued*) (b) A second keyframe at frame 20 where the position, scale, and rotation of the symbol instance are changed (c) The last keyframe of this animation sequence at frame 60 with more changes made to the position, scale, and rotation of the symbol instance

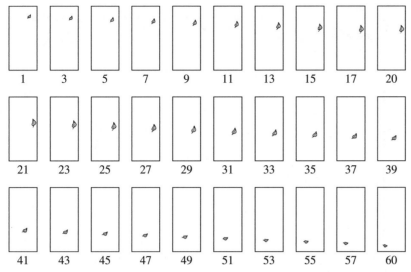

1	3	5	7	9	11	13	15	17	20
21	23	25	27	29	31	33	35	37	39
41	43	45	47	49	51	53	55	57	60

Figure 8.13 The example motion tweened animation (Figure 8.12) is shown in approximately every other frame with the corresponding frame number.

Figure 8.13 shows the results of this animation sequence in approximately every other frame. Although not being demonstrated in this example, the color and opacity of the symbol instance also can be animated with motion tween.

Figure 8.14 shows an example of creating a three-keyframe shape tweened animation. In each of the three keyframes, the shape and color are altered. The first keyframe contains

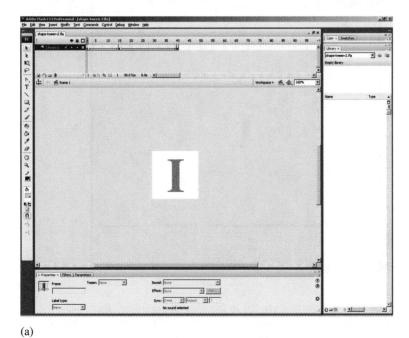

(a)

Figure 8.14 A shape tweened animation with the frame color shown on the timeline is green (a) Keyframe at frame 1 *(continued)*

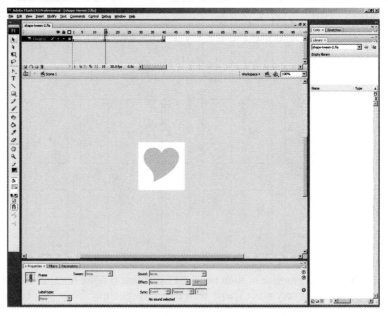

(b)

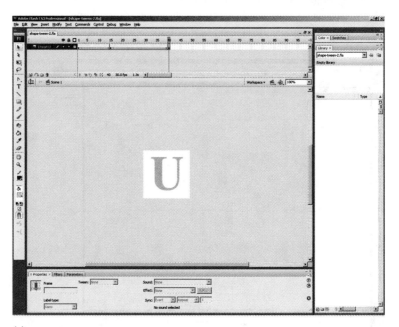

(c)

Figure 8.14 (*continued*) (b) In the second keyframe (frame 15), the shape and color are altered (c) In the last keyframe of this animation sequence (frame 40), the shape and color are further altered

a shape of the letter "I" in blue; the second keyframe contains a heart shape in pink; the third keyframe contains a shape of the letter "U" in green.

Shape tween is applied to the first keyframe of each segment. The in-between frames then are filled in automatically by interpolating the shape and color of the shape in two keyframes.

Figure 8.15 shows the results of this animation sequence in every other frame. This example demonstrates the shape tweening of the shape and color. Position, scale, rotation, and opacity of the shape also can be tweened in a shape tweened sequence.

◇ **Creating Shape Tween in Flash** A screen-capture movie shows how to create a shape tween animation.

⏚ **Creating an Animation in Flash—Tweening (Lab)** A lab practice exercise to: (1) practice creating shapes and symbols; (2) create an animation using shape and motion tween.

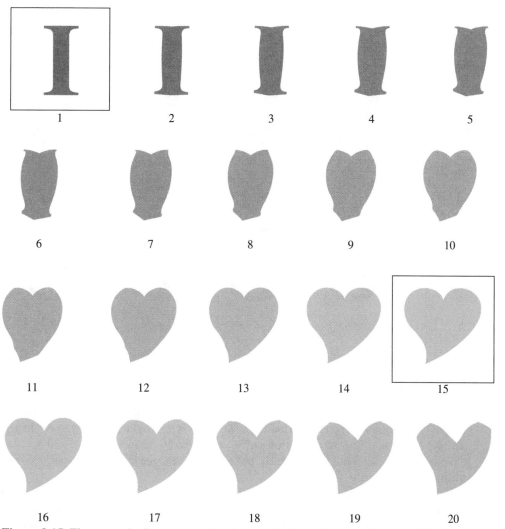

Figure 8.15 The example shape tweened animation is shown in every frame with the corresponding frame number, where frames 1, 15, and 40 are the keyframes where changes to the shape are made

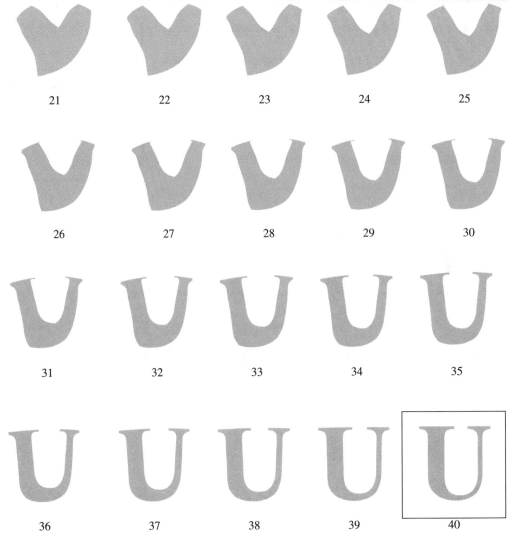

Figure 8.15 (*continued*)

8.6.4 Motion Guide

The ***motion guide*** allows you to animate objects along a path that you draw. The path is placed on a motion guide layer. Motion guide works with symbols, but not with shapes. The symbol instance whose animation path is controlled by the motion guide still needs to have at least two keyframes. The symbol instance in each of the keyframes is snapped onto the motion guide path.

The example in Figure 8.16 uses two keyframes. In each keyframe, the leaf is snapped to one end of the path. However, more than two keyframes can be used. You can use middle keyframes to specify the object reaching a certain point on the path. In addition, the object at the beginning and ending keyframes can be snapped to the middle of the path; it does not have to be snapped at either end of the path.

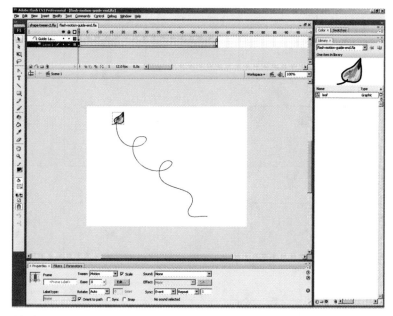

(a)

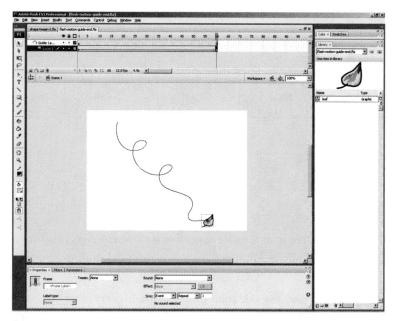

(b)

Figure 8.16 A motion guide animation where the black line across the stage is the path used as a motion guide on the layer above the leaf layer on the timeline (a) Keyframe at frame 1: The leaf symbol instance is snapped at the beginning of the motion path (b) A second keyframe at frame 60: The leaf symbol instance is snapped at the end of the motion path

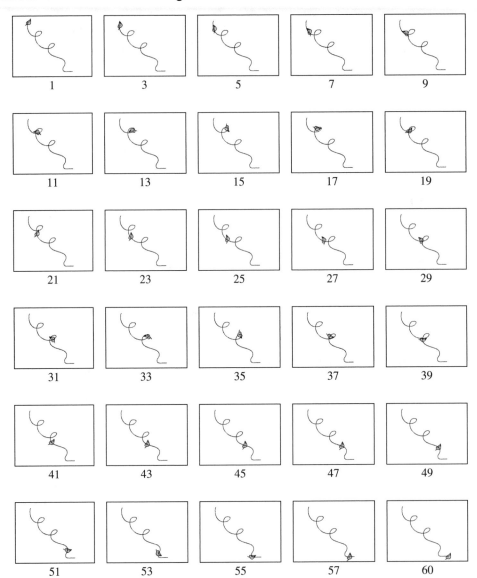

Figure 8.17 The example motion guide animation is shown in every other frame with the corresponding frame number

The sequence of this motion guide animation is shown in every other frame with the corresponding frame number in Figure 8.17. Frames 1 and 60 are the keyframes where the leaf object is snapped to the two ends of the path. The rotation of the leaf in all the in-between frames is interpolated while following the motion path. The motion path, whether it is made hidden in Flash or not, does not appear in the published movie. This example duplicates the path onto a non-motion-guide layer so that the path shows up to give you a visual reference of the motion of the leaf object. You do not need to worry about making the guide invisible on the timeline.

◇ **Creating Motion Tween using Motion Guide in Flash** A screen-capture movie shows how to create a motion tween animation using motion guide.

8.6.5 Mask

A *mask* defines areas to reveal the linked layers (maskee layers). The ***maskee layer*** is the layer being masked. Think of the content in the mask layer as creating a hole that lets the underlying maskee layers show through.

To create the mask effect:

Step 1 Arrange the maskee layer immediately below the layer that you want to be the mask layer.

Step 2 Right-click on the mask layer on the timeline, and select Mask. You will see the maskee layer is indented (Figure 8.18a). It is now linked to the mask layer.

In the example shown in Figure 8.18, the mask layer contains a black circular shape (Figure 8.18b). Figure 8.18c shows the resulted mask effect after the mask layer is locked. You can unlock the mask layer any time to edit the mask.

The mask layer can be linked with one or more maskee layers. You can add maskee layers to a mask layer by dragging and dropping the layer that you want to be a maskee onto the mask layer.

The mask layer can contain shapes and symbol instances. The color of the shape or symbol instance does not matter; the color of the mask will not show up anywhere in the resulted mask effect and will not affect the mask effect.

The shapes or symbol instances in the mask layer can be animated to create interesting effects. In this example, the black circular shape could have been animated to move across the stage using tweening. This will create a spotlight effect revealing only a small part of the underlying writing at a time. Mask can be used creatively in combination with tweening to create interesting animation. Let's look at the following two examples.

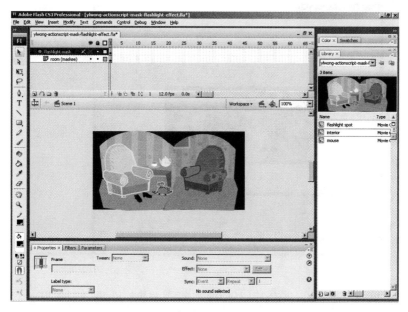

(a)

Figure 8.18 Mask in Flash (a) The visual content on a maskee layer, which is the layer being masked (*continued*)

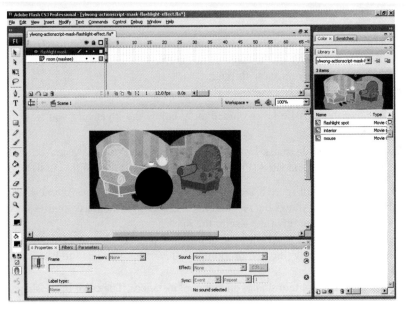

(b)

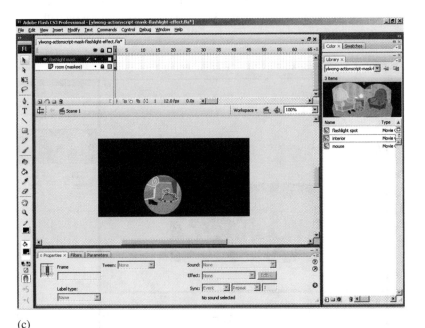

(c)

Figure 8.18 (*continued*) (b) The black circle is the content on the mask layer in this example (c) The resulted effect after the mask is turned on by locking the mask layer

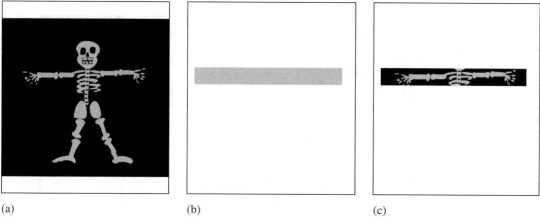

Figure 8.19 (a) The skeleton is the maskee (b) A rectangular bar representing a scanner bar used as the mask (c) The resulted mask effect

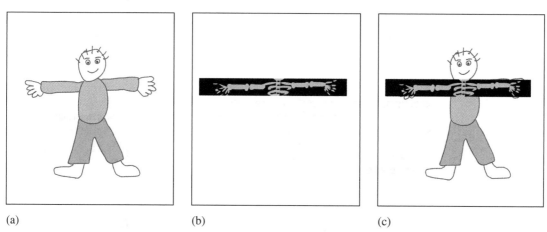

Figure 8.20 (a) Graphic of a man (b) Resulted mask effect of the scanner bar masking the skeleton. (c) The mask effect overlays on top of the man graphic, giving an illusion that the man is being x-rayed

Mask Animation Example 1: X-ray

In this example, a skeleton created on a black rectangle (Figure 8.19a) serves as the maskee. The rectangle (Figure 8.19b) which represents the scanner bar is the mask. Figure 8.19c shows the resulted mask effect.

If a man graphic (Figure 8.20a) is placed in a layer beneath the mask effect (Figure 8.20b) and aligned with the skeleton position, it will create an illusion that the scanner bar is letting you see through the man (Figure 8.20c).

Mask Example 2: Beaming Up and Down

In this example, an animated mask is created to animate the appearance and disappearance of an alien from a spaceship (Figure 8.21).

⬦ **Animating a Mask in Flash** A screen-capture movie shows how to create the x-ray animation example by motion tweening the mask.

Note that the man graphic in this example is not a mask or a maskee. It is not part of the mask effect at all. It is on a regular layer. The mask effect works without the man graphic. However, with the man graphic placed beneath the mask effect, it creates the desired illusion and gives more meaning to the animation.

🖱 **Animating a Mask in Flash: X-ray Effect (Lab)** An exercise to: (1) create a mask and (2) animate a mask for interesting effects.

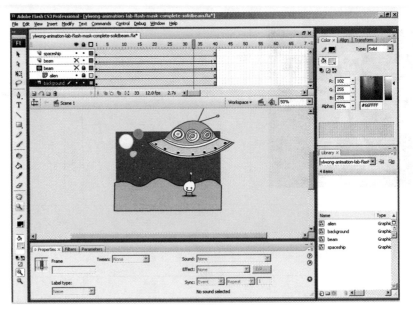

(a)

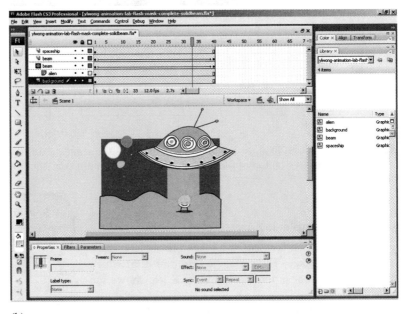

(b)

Figure 8.21 An animated mask used in conjunction with non-mask animation to create interesting effects (a) A spaceship and an alien stay static throughout this beaming sequence (b) The cyan rectangle is the mask. The mask is turned off in the figure to show you its position (*continued*)

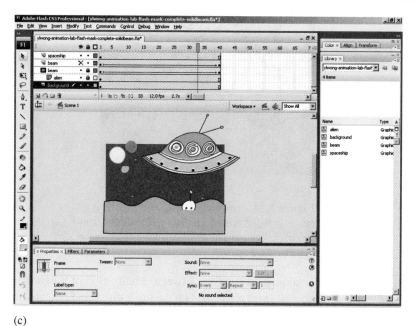

(c)

The opacity setting of the graphics used for the mask does not affect the mask effect at all. The resulted mask effect will be the same as shown in Figure 8.21c regardless of the opacity of the mask graphic. The soft-edged light beam shown in Figure 8.21e is produced by over-laying the light beam (regular, non-mask) on the mask effect shown in Figure 8.21c.

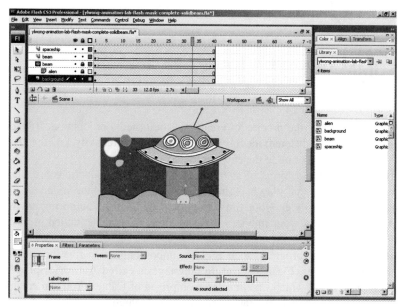

(d)

Figure 8.21 (*continued*) (c) The mask is turned on, so the alien is showing through the area defined by the cyan mask (d) A layer (regular, non-masking, and non-masked) contains a rectangle filled with semi-transparent cyan color is placed on top of the mask layer (*continued*)

(e)

Figure 8.21 (*continued*) (e) The overlaying beam is filled with a gradient instead of a solid color

---

🖰 **Animating a Mask in Flash: Beaming Up and Down (Lab)** A lab exercise to: (1) create a mask; (2) animate a mask; and (3) create another layer for the light beam that is visible and synchronizes the motion of the mask.

To add the light beam, a tweened animation of a light beam on a separate layer is overlaid on the mask effect and synchronized with the mask's animation to create an illusion of the alien is being beaming up and down. Instead of a solid color, the overlaying beam can be filled with a gradient of different opacities to make it look more like a beam of light (Figure 8.21e).

8.7 SUMMARY

Multimedia Authoring

Multimedia authoring is the process of creating a multimedia production. It involves assembling or sequencing different media elements, adding interactivity, and then packaging the production for distribution to the end users.

The two most common forms of distributing multimedia productions are stand-alone executables and movies that play back in a Web browser. Publishing in any of these two formats allows others to view your finished project without the authoring environment. Flash lets you publishing your movie as a stand-alone executable, called projector, or a SWF file for the Web.

Multimedia authoring programs such as Flash support animation creation and have their own scripting languages. Flash's scripting language is called ActionScript. Flash is a frame-based program in which timelines are comprised of frames. You can create frame-based animations using frame-by-frame and tweening techniques. With scripting support, you also can create animation using scripts. Scripting lets you incorporate interactivity and non-linearity in your multimedia project.

Flash's Workspace

This chapter gives you an overview on Flash's workspace, and introduces you the Tools panel, Stage, Timeline, Property Inspector, and Library panel.

Shapes and Symbols

The visual items used on the Stage in a Flash file can be categorized by two types: shapes and symbols. They have different properties, purposes, and requirements.

- A shape is made up of strokes and/or fills.
- A symbol is an encapsulated object in Flash. They are stored in the Library panel and can be reused throughout the project. To place a symbol on the Stage, you can drag the symbol from the Library panel onto the Stage.

There are three types of symbols: graphic, button, and movieclip. Graphic symbols are mainly used for static graphics. It can be placed inside another graphic, button, or movieclip symbol. Instances of button and movieclip can be controlled using Action-Script in response to mouse clicks and rollovers. A button's timeline only has four special-purpose frames. Unlike a button, each movieclip has a timeline for frame-based animation.

Tweening

Tweening is an effective way to create movement and changes over time. It requires at least two keyframes. There are two types of tweening in Flash: motion tween and shape tween. Motion tween works with symbols and can be used with motion guide. Shape tween works with shapes and can create an animation of morphing between two shapes.

Motion Guide

The motion guide allows you to animate objects along a path that you draw. The path is placed on a motion guide layer. Motion guide works with symbols, but not with shapes. The symbol instance whose animation path is controlled by the motion guide still needs to have at least two keyframes, each of which is snapped onto the motion guide path.

Mask

A mask defines areas to reveal the linked layers (maskee layers). The maskee layer is the layer being masked. The mask layer can be linked with one or more maskee layers. The shapes or symbol instances in the mask layer can be animated to create interesting effects, such as a spotlight effect.

TERMS

LEARNING AIDS

The following learning aids can be found at the book's companion Web site.

Frame-by-frame, Tweening, and Scripted Animation
A side-by-side comparison of frame-by-frame, tweening, and scripted animation using the bird flying example shown in Figure 8.3.

Adjusting the Speed of an Animation: Frame Rate vs. Number of Frames
A side-by-side comparison of the original sequence and two approaches shown in Figure 8.4.

Creating Shapes in Flash
A screen-capture movie shows how to create a simple shape using Pencil, Pen, Ink, and Paint Bucket tools.

Modifying Shapes in Flash
A screen-capture movie shows how to modify of a shape.

Creating Symbols in Flash
A screen-capture movie shows show to create (1) a new symbol; (2) a symbol by converting from a shape.

Practice Drawing (Lab)
Practice Flash drawing and painting tools, and create movieclip symbols. Create two files:

1. x-ray (Figure 8.10)
2. hair styles (Figure 8.11)

The x-ray file will be used to create tweened animation in a lab later in this chapter. The hair styles file will be used in a lab in Chapter 10 where you will learn how to add interactivity to allow the user to change the hair style on the character's head by clicking on one of the hair style choices.

Creating Motion Tween in Flash
A screen-capture movie shows how to create a motion tween animation.

Creating Shape Tween in Flash
A screen-capture movie shows how to create a shape tween animation.

Creating an Animation in Flash—Tweening (Lab)
A lab practice exercise to: (1) practice creating shapes and symbols and (2) create an animation using shape and motion tween.

Creating Motion Tween using Motion Guide in Flash
A screen-capture movie shows how to create a motion tween animation using motion guide.

Animating a Mask in Flash
A screen-capture movie shows how to create the x-ray animation example by motion tweening the mask.

🖰 **Animating a Mask in Flash: X-ray Effect (Lab)**
An exercise to: (1) create a mask and (2) animate a mask for interesting effects.

🖰 **Animating a Mask in Flash: Beaming Up and Down (Lab)**
A lab exercise to: (1) create a mask; (2) animate a mask; and (3) create another layer for the light beam that is visible and synchronizes the motion of the mask.

REVIEW QUESTIONS

When applicable, please choose all correct answers.

1. If you have an outline of a shape and want to fill its inside with a color, you should use _____ tool.

   A. bucket
   B. ink bottle

2. If you have a fill of a shape and want to create an outline around it, you should use _____ tool.

   A. bucket
   B. ink bottle

3. Which tweening can be used to animate *symbols*?

   A. motion tween
   B. shape tween

4. Which tweening can be used to animate *shapes*?

   A. motion tween
   B. shape tween

5. What is the color of a *motion tween* sequence on the timeline?

   A. blue
   B. green

6. What is the color of a *shape tween* sequence on the timeline?

   A. blue
   B. green

7. If a tweening sequence has problems, it is indicated as a _____ on the timeline?

   A. solid-line arrow
   B. dash line

8. **True/False:** You can have multiple symbols in the same layer for motion tween.

9. What are stored in the Library panel?

   A. symbols
   B. shapes
   C. all of the above

10. Motion guide can be used in _____.

A. motion tween
B. shape tween
C. all of the above

11. Which of the following is correct about mask?

A. The mask item *conceals* the area of linked layers that lie beneath it. The rest of the mask layer reveals everything except what shows through the mask item.
B. The mask item acts as a window that *reveals* the area of linked layers that lie beneath it. The rest of the mask layer conceals everything except what shows through the mask item.

12. You can tween the position of a symbol or shape. Name three other properties of a symbol or shape that you can animate using tweening.

13. What is the menu item you should select if you want to change the Stage size, frame size, and Stage color?

14. If you use movieclips in your Flash movie, what is the menu item you should select in order to preview your movie properly?

A. `Control > Play`
B. `Control > Test Movie`

15. Interactive controls, sound, and animation work in _____.

A. graphic symbols
B. movieclip symbols
C. all of the above

16. _____ can contain other graphic symbols.

A. A graphic symbol
B. A movieclip symbol
C. all of the above

17. _____ can contain other graphic, button, *and* movieclip symbols.

A. A graphic symbol
B. A movieclip symbol
C. all of the above

18. To publish a Flash movie intended for the *Web*, you should publish your Flash movie as a _____.

A. .swf
B. projector
C. .fla

19. To publish a Flash movie intended as a *stand-alone program*, you should publish your Flash movie as a _____.

A. .swf
B. projector
C. .fla

20. A movieclip placed on the Stage is called a(n) _____ of that movieclip.

A. keyframe
B. shape
C. symbol
D. instance
E. motion guide

Interactive Multimedia Authoring with Flash: ActionScript—Part 1

KEY CONCEPTS
- programming fundamentals

GENERAL LEARNING OBJECTIVES
At the end of this chapter, you should be able to demonstrate that you
- understand the computer programming basics that multimedia authoring languages share.
- are prepared for programming in ActionScript.

9.1 PROGRAMMING LANGUAGES VS. SCRIPTING LANGUAGES

A *programming language* specifies the rules for writing instructions that can be followed by a computer. There is a programming language that communicates with a computer through 0s and 1s. It is called *machine language*. Other programming languages that look more like natural language are called *high-level languages*. They are easier for humans to read and write, but they require more translation behind the scenes to make the instructions understandable by the computer. C++ and Java are examples of high-level programming languages.

Scripting languages are examples of very high-level programming languages. Compared to full-fledged programming languages such as C++ and Java, scripting languages do not have a complex array of features that give the programmer control over the details of memory allocation and program execution efficiency. The advantage of scripting languages; however, is that they are easier for nonprogrammers to learn because they use keywords and syntax that look more like natural language, but they still provide enough features for the programmer to be creative in putting together a complex interactive project.

Multimedia authoring programs such as Macromedia Flash and Director have their own scripting languages. Flash's scripting language is called ActionScript and Director's is called Lingo. ActionScript and Lingo let you add interactivity to your multimedia projects. The user can interact with your program through mouse clicks or keystrokes on the keyboard. What the movie does in response to such interaction is determined by your script.

Movie: A multimedia production created in Flash or Director is often referred to as a movie. It does not mean video or film.

9.2 PROGRAMMING AND SCRIPTING FUNDAMENTALS—PART A

Sample ActionScript and Flash projects are widely available on the Web and in books. You may be able to use them in your project "as is." However, if these sample scripts do not do exactly what you have in mind, you will need to compromise your ideas in order to use them. With the knowledge of basic programming concepts and techniques, you will be able to read and modify the sample scripts to suit your need. You can also write your own scripts from scratch.

ActionScript shares the programming concepts and constructs that are common to all high-level programming languages—for example, variables, functions, conditions, loops, mouse events, and keyboard events. Learning how to program with ActionScript helps you learn other programming languages, and vice versa.

This section will first go over definitions of terms that are common to computer programming languages. These basic terms are interconnected. You may find that the further elaboration of a term may involve other terms that have not been introduced but will be covered later in the section. You may want to read through this section once and then come back and review to get a thorough understanding of these basic terms.

9.2.1 Syntax

The *syntax* of a programming or scripting language prescribes the ways in which statements must be written in order for them to be understood by the computer. The syntax of a programming language is like the rules of grammar and punctuation in human language, but the difference is that these rules must be followed precisely in computer programming.

Syntax defines things such as whether a statement must end in some kind of punctuation, how long names can be, and what operator symbols are used for arithmetic operations such as addition or subtraction.

Here are two of the rules of ActionScript 3.0:

- Case-sensitivity: Most programming languages are case-sensitive, and this includes ActionScript. This means that when you use the language's keywords and commands, or any custom-defined variables, their cases have to match exactly how they are originally defined.

  Keywords and variables will be explained later in this section. For now, to give you an idea of the case-sensitivity, a name score is different from Score.
- Each statement ends with a semicolon (;). This is optional if a single line of code contains only one statement. However, because many programming languages require ending each statement with a semicolon, all the ActionScript examples in this text enforce this rule.

9.2.2 Data Types

The value assigned to a variable could be of many different types, such as integers, individual characters from the alphabet, and strings of text. The type of the value is called its *data type*.

Many programming languages require that you explicitly declare the data type of a variable when the variable is first created. It is called *strict data typing*. Earlier versions of ActionScript (1.0 and 2.0) are *loosely typed* languages. This means that you do not have to specify the data type of a variable when you declare it, and data types are converted automatically as needed during script execution. The current ActionScript 3.0 is strictly typed.

Table 9.1 lists the data types used in the ActionScript 3.0 examples in this book. You will be able to find more inforamtion about these data types and other data types in Flash Help.

TABLE 9.1	A List of Data Types Used in the ActionScript Examples in This Book
Data Type	**Description**
int	Stands for ***integers***, which means whole numbers.
	Many values stored in programs are whole numbers that may be positive or negative, for example, scores in a game. In some situations where a value can be a floating-point number, but you want to store it as a whole number. For example, in keeping time in seconds, it is possible to keep the time as 5.2 seconds. However, depending on the situation, you may only want to keep the time in whole number, for example, simply round 5.2 seconds to 5 seconds. In this case, you would need to declare the variable that keeps the time as int, or better yet, uint (see below) if it will only have non-negative values.
	There is a limit on how large an integer can be stored. (Recall that, as discussed in Chapter 1, computers deal with finite data.) For introductory level examples and projects, you seldom exceed this limit. However, if you are interested to know the limit of an integer in Actionscript, an int variable is stored as a 32-bit integer and valid integers that can be stored range from $-2,147,483,648$ (-2^{31}) to $2,147,483,647$ $(2^{31}-1)$, inclusive.
uint	Stands for ***unsigned integers***, which means nonnegative integers.
	Like int, an uint variable is also stored as a 32-bit integer but nonnegative only. This means that the valid integers that can be stored range from 0 to $4,294,967,295$ $(2^{32} - 1)$, inclusive.
	Examples where values stored in programs are nonnegative whole numbers are number of people, number of collected items, number of bullets fired in a game, and number of trials.
Number	This can be an integer, unsigned integer, and floating-point number. You can think of a floating-point number as a number with a decimal point, for example, 1.1, 20.849, and 0.2157.
	Like int and uint, Number data type also has a limit and you seldom exceed the limit for introductory projects. The Number data type uses 53 bits to store integers. Thus, the range of integer values it can store ranges from $9,007,199,254,740,992$ (-2^{53}) to $9,007,199,254,740,992$ (2^{53}).
	(Recall the eye signal analogy discussed in Chapter 1, the more bits you use to represent information, the more distinct numbers of values you can represent. Now you see why Number data type (53 bits) has a wider range than int and uint (32 bits).)
	However, for better efficiency, you should use the Number data type only for (1) floating-point numbers or (2) integer values larger than the 32-bit int and uint types can store.
String	Simply speaking, the String data type represents a sequence of characters.
	The values are enclosed within quotation marks, for example, "This is a text string.".
	An empty text string is written as "".
	Note: The default value for a variable declared with the String data type that has not been initialized is null. The value null is not the same as the empty string ("").
Boolean	The Boolean data type has only two possible values: true and false.
	The default value of a Boolean variable that has not been initialized is false.

9.2.3 Variables

Variables are elements used to store values in your program. You can also update and retrieve the value of a variable.

There are three properties associated with a variable: name, value, and data type.

- **Variable name:** Data is stored in memory as bits (recall the discussion in Chapter 1). A variable name lets you refer to the data's memory location by name.
- **Value:** The value of a variable is the actual data stored.
- **Data type:** Data type specifies the type of data stored.

To use a variable, you need to first declare a variable—give the variable a name. To declare a variable in ActionScript 3.0, you use the var statement with the variable name. Append the variable name with a colon (:), followed by the variable's data type.

The general syntax to declare a variable in ActionScript 3.0 is like this:

```
var variableName:dataType;
```

For example, the following statement declares a variable called highScore. It is an integer (int).

```
var highScore:int;
```

You can also assign a value to the variable at the declaration, like this:

```
var highScore:int = 0;
```

Variable Naming

All languages have rules about what constitutes a legal name for a variable. Here is a list of ActionScript rules, which also apply to many programming languages. Variable names

- must contain only letters, numbers, and underscore (_) characters.
- cannot begin with a number.
- can include the dollar sign ($) in ActionScript only, even as the first character of the name.
- do not include spaces.

The general naming convention is that when variable names consist of more than one word, they are written in *camel case*, like this: sheepCount and highScore. This means

- the variable name starts with a lowercase letter, and
- an uppercase letter is used for every new word.

This is the most common practice. This naming convention is used in all the Action-Script examples in this book.

Another common naming convention is to use all lowercase letters and separate each word with an underscore (_) like this: sheep_count and high_score.

> ### ❓ Self Test Exercise: Variable Names
>
> Which of the following variable names are legal?
> 1. myScore
> 2. my_score
> 3. my score
> 4. my-score
> 5. my4score
> 6. 4score
>
> Answers to Self Test Questions
> 1. legal
> 2. legal
> 3. illegal; no space is allowed
> 4. illegal; no dash is allowed
> 5. legal
> 6. illegal; cannot start with a number

Giving a Value to a Variable

Giving a value to a variable is called *assigning a value*. The statement that assigns a value to a variable is called an *assignment statement*. Finding out the current value of a variable is called *accessing the variable*.

VARIABLES VS. STRING LITERALS

score (without quotation marks) and "score" in the code mean different things.

score (without the quotation marks) is a variable name. A variable has a value. The value of a variable score can be an integer or a text string, depending on its data type.

If score has a value of 3, then the expression score + 9 gives you a value of 12.

A text string is enclosed within quotation marks, for example, "score". "score" is a string literal, and it is a value by itself.

The expression "score" + 9 gives you a concatenated text string "score9".

❓ Self Test Exercise: Variables vs. String Literals

Suppose the value of the variable **score** is equal to 3.

1. An expression score + score gives a _____ (text string or number?) equal to _____.
2. An expression score + "score" gives a _____ (text string or number?) equal to _____.
3. An expression "score" + "score" gives a _____ (text string or number?) equal to _____.

Answers to Self Test Questions

1. number, 6
2. text string, "3score"
3. text string, "scorescore"

9.2.4 Statements

Statements are instructions that can be executed. Statements can be used to:

- give values to variables—assignment statements, which will be explained in the next subsection.
- cause things to happen only under certain conditions—for example, if-statements, which will be explained later in the Control Structure section.
- cause instructions to repeat—for example, for-loop, which will also be explained later in the Control Structures section.

9.2.5 Assignment Statements

An *assignment statement* assigns a value to a variable. In most languages, you use the = (equals) operator to assign a value to a variable. For example, the statement:

```
score = 0;
```

is used to assign a value of 0 to a variable named score.

It is possible for a variable to appear on both the left- and right-hand sides of an assignment statement. For example:

```
score = score + 1;
```

This statement increments the value of the variable score by 1. Suppose the variable score has a value of 10 before this statement is executed. Then after it is executed, it has a value of 11.

There are more assignment operators in addition to the = operator. They will be discussed in the next section on Operators.

9.2.6 Operators

Operators are symbols that cause a new value to be calculated from one or more other values (operands). This section introduces five common types of operators.

Arithmetic Operators: +, −, *, /, %

An arithmetic operator takes two other values (or operands) and performs an arithmetic calculation to give a new value.

For example, the + (addition) operator is used to add two or more values together to produce a new value. 2 + 3 gives a value of 5.

Other common operators are - (subtraction), * (multiplication), / (division), and % (modulo). All of these five operators, +, -, *, /, and %, are available in ActionScript.

The modulo (%) operator gives the remainder in a division. For examples:

- 20 % 2 gives 0, because the remainder of 20 divided by 2 is 0.
- 20 % 11 gives 9 because the remainder of 20 divided by 11 is 9

The modulo operator is useful in determining whether the value of a variable is even or odd by dividing the variable by 2. The value is an even number if the remainder is 0; odd number if the remainder is 1.

Assignment Operators: =, +=, −=, *=, /=, %=

You have seen the usage of = operator in assignment statements. This section will show you more assignment operators (Table 9.2) that let you write some types of assignment statements in shorthand forms.

TABLE 9.2 Assignment Operators	
	Equivalent Statements
score += 3;	score = score + 3;
score -= 3;	score = score - 3;
score *= 3;	score = score * 3;
score /= 3;	score = score / 3;
score %= 3;	score = score % 3;

For example, the statement,

```
score = score + 1;
```

can be written using the *addition assignment operator* (+=) operator as:

score += 1;

Similarly,

score = score - 1;

is equivalent to:

score -= 1;

using the *subtraction assignment operator* (-=). += and -= are useful because increment and decrement are very common steps in a program.

There are also *multiplication assignment operator* (*=), *division assignment operator* (/=), and *modulo assignment operator* (%=).

Postfix Operators: ++, −−

The *postfix operators* (++ and --) take only one operand and either increase or decrease its value by one. Table 9.3 shows the usage of these operators and the equivalent statements.

TABLE 9.3	Equivalent Statements for Postfix Operators
	Equivalent Statements
score++;	score = score + 1;
score--;	score = score - 1;

Comparison Operators: >, >=, <, <=, ==, !=

A *comparison operator* (>, >=, <, <=, ==, !=) takes two other values (or operands) and performs a comparison to give one of the two possible values: true or false. For example, 2 > 3 gives a value of false.

Table 9.4 shows a list of the comparison operators with a brief description for each.

TABLE 9.4	A List of the Comparison Operators
Comparison Operator	**Description**
>	greater than
>=	greater than or equal to
<	less than
<=	less than or equal to
==	equal to
!=	not equal to

Suppose the current value of a variable score is equal to 15.

- The expression score > 10 gives true.
- The expression score >= 10 gives true.

- The expression score > 15 gives false.
- The expression score >= 15 gives true.
- The expression score == 15 gives true.

Note that the equal to (==) operator for comparison has two equal signs. It is different from the assignment operator (=).

- The == operator performs a comparison on two operands and gives a value of true or false. The values of the two operands are not altered.
- The = operator assigns the value on the right-hand side of the = sign to the variable on the left-hand side of the = sign. The value of the operand on the left is changed to the value of the operand on the right of the = sign.

Table 9.5 demonstrates the differences by comparing player == 1 and player = 1.

TABLE 9.5	Differences between Two Operators: Comparison for Equality (==) and Assignment (=)	
	player == 1	player = 1
Type of operation performing	Comparison for equality It is like getting an answer to the question: Is player equal to 1?	Assignment It is an action to be carried out: Assign a value to player.
Results from the operation	The expression player == 1 will give one of the two possible values: true or false. If the value of the variable player is 1, then the expression player == 1 gives the value true. Otherwise, it will give the value false. The value of the variable player is not changed.	The value of the variable player becomes 1.

It is important to understand (and remember) the difference between == and = operators. To see the significance of the difference, let's look at an example. In a tic-tac-toe game, two players take turns. Suppose you use a variable named player to keep track of player's turn. Each time after a player marks a cell on the game board, you check the value of player. If player is equal to 1, the value of player is switched to 2 and it becomes the player 2's turn to mark a cell. Otherwise, the value of player is switched to 1 and the player 1 can mark a cell. If you mistakenly use player = 1 instead of player == 1 in checking who's turn it is, the variable player will always be assigned with 1 regardless of the current value of the player. This means that your program will always think it has been player 1's turn and switch to player 2's turn.

Logical Operators: &&, ||, !

The three commonly used logical operators are:

&&   logical AND
|| logical OR
!   logical NOT

Logical operators operate on two Boolean values to give a new Boolean value. This may sound complicated, but you have been using this type of operators in daily life, for example:

> If it rains *and* you have to go out, bring an umbrella.

With an "and" in this if statement, both conditions have to be true in order to carry out the instruction. You bring an umbrella only when both of these conditions are true. If it rains but you are not going out, you would not bring an umbrella. If you have to go out but it is not raining, you would not bring an umbrella, either.

However, if you say:

> If it rains *or* you have to go out, bring an umbrella.

Then you bring an umbrella whenever it rains regardless of whether you are going out or not. You also bring an umbrella whenever you are going out whether it is raining or not.

The logical operators are often used in conditional statements. It will make more sense when you see examples in the section of if statements later in this chapter.

9.2.7 Constants

Constants are elements that do not change in a program. You can think of constants as "read-only variables". The number 0 itself is a constant. Aside from numeric constants, many languages have predefined constants in the form of words, such as the constants true and false in ActionScript. Constants like this generally have the obvious meaning.

ActionScript 3.0 also has predefined constants such as Keyboard.UP, Keyboard.DOWN, Keyboard.LEFT, Keyboard.RIGHT and Keyboard.SPACE to represent the *keycodes* (a number associated with each key on the keyboard) for the up, down, left, and right arrow keys, and space bar respectively. You can use these constants by calling these defined names, saving you time from looking up the numeric keycode values.

You can also declare constants in ActionScript 3.0. To declare a constant in ActionScript 3.0, you use the const statement with the constant's name. Append the constant name with a colon (:), followed by the its data type.

The general syntax to declare a variable in ActionScript 3.0 is like this:

```
const constantName:dataType = value;
```

For example, the following statement declares a constant called PENALTY. It is an unsigned (nonnegative) integer (uint).

```
const PENALTY:uint = 50;
```

Constant Naming

Like variables, spaces are not allowed in constant names. The common naming convention for constants is to use

- all uppercase letters, and
- underscore (_) to separate the words, if the name consists of more than one word.

For example:

```
GRAVITY
MAX_SHEEP
```

This book uses this naming convention for constants in all ActionScript examples.

9.2.8 Keywords

In general, *keywords* are reserved words that have a special meaning in a programming language. These words are not to be used for any other purpose, such as variable or function names, because they are predefined with special meanings in the language. For example, `if` is a keyword in most programming languages. Giving a variable the name `if` will result in an error message.

The following list is a small set of keywords in ActionScript. You will see these keywords in the examples throughout the multimedia authoring chapters of this book.

```
break
case
const
default
else
false
for
function
if
null
return
switch
this
true
var
void
while
```

9.2.9 Expressions

An *expression* is any part of a statement that produces a value. Example expressions and the values produced by these expressions are shown in Table 9.6.

TABLE 9.6	Example Expressions and the Values That the Expressions Produce
Expression	**Value That the Expression Produces**
`2 + 2`	4
`(a + b + c)/3`	the value of the sum of the values of the three variables, a, b, and c, divided by 3
`a > b`	`true` or `false`, depending on whether the value of the variable a is greater than the value of b

? Self Test Exercise: Identify Programming Constructs

Before moving on to Part B of programming fundamentals, let's do a self test exercise to review the materials you have learned so far.

Introduction

The purposes of this exercise are:

(1) to let you look at the complete code of a program to get an idea of how the programming elements you have learned so far are placed together in a program, and

(2) to serve as a self test by identifying the programming elements you have learned.

Figure 9.1 shows the complete code in ActionScript 3.0 for a simple shoot-them-up game. You are *not* expected to understand the code now. Most of the concepts and programming constructs used in the code have not been covered yet. So don't worry about understanding the complete code for now. All you need to do in this self test is to identify the programming constructs you have learned so far, such as variables, constants, expressions, and operators. Think of this self test exercise as a *Where's Waldo?* game.

```
1    const PENALTY:int = 50;
2    const MISSILE_SPEED:int = 7;
3    const SPACESHIP_SPEED:int = 5;
4
5    var isFired:Boolean = false;
6    var isHit:Boolean = false;
7    var missed:int = 0;
8
9    reset();
10
11   addEventListener(Event.ENTER_FRAME, onLoopFrame);
12   stage.addEventListener(KeyboardEvent.KEY_DOWN, onKeyControl);
13
14   function onLoopFrame(evt:Event):void
15   {
16       mc_spaceship.x += SPACESHIP_SPEED;
17
18       if (isFired == true)
19       {
20           mc_missile.y -= MISSILE_SPEED;
21       }
22
23       if (mc_spaceship.hitTestPoint(mc_missile.x, mc_missile.y, true) &&
         isHit == false)
24       {
```

Figure 9.1 A complete code for a simple shoot-them-up game shown in Figure 2. (*continued*)

```
25          isHit = true;
26          missed--;
27          mc_spaceship.gotoAndPlay("explosion");
28       }
29
30       if (mc_spaceship.x > stage.stageWidth + 100 || mc_missile.y < -50 ||
         mc_spaceship.currentFrame == mc_spaceship.totalFrames
31       {
32          reset();
33       }
34    }
35
36    function onKeyControl(evt:KeyboardEvent):void
37    {
38       if (isFired == false)
39       {
40          if (evt.keyCode == Keyboard.RIGHT)
41          {
42             mc_missile.x += MISSILE_SPEED;
43          }
44          else if (evt.keyCode == Keyboard.LEFT)
45          {
46             mc_missile.x -= MISSILE_SPEED;
47          }
48          else if (evt.keyCode == Keyboard.SPACE)
49          {
50             isFired = true;
51          }
52       }
53    }
54
55    function reset():void
56    {
57       if (isHit == false)
58       {
59          missed++;
60       }
61
62       isHit = false;
63       isFired = false;
64       mc_spaceship.x = -100;
65       mc_spaceship.y = missed * PENALTY;
66       mc_spaceship.gotoAndStop(1);
67       mc_missile.y = stage.stageHeight - 20;
68    }
```

Figure 9.1 (*continued*)

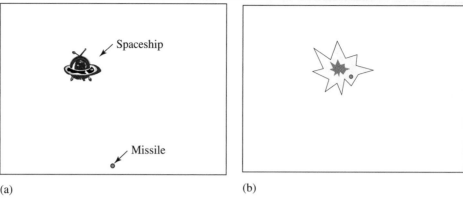

(a)   (b)

Figure 9.2 How the game works (a) A spaceship is moving across the screen from left to right; the user can control the horizontal position of the blue missile by using the left and right arrow keys (b) Hitting the space bar will fire the missile; if it hits the spaceship, an explosion animation will play

To do this self test, you do not need to know the logic behind the code. However, knowing how the game plays may help you understand the roles of some of the variables and constants in this program. Below is a description of how the game works. The Flash file can be downloaded from the book's Web site.

Figure 9.2 shows two screen shots of how this game works. When the game starts, a spaceship moves horizontally from left to right. The blue circle at the bottom of the screen is the missile (Figure 9.2a). The user can use the left and right arrow keys on the keyboard to move the missile horizontally. Hitting the space bar will fire the missile, which will move up. If the missile hits the spaceship, you will see an explosion animation (Figure 9.2b). Then, the spaceship will start again from the left of the screen, but higher. On the other hand, if the missile misses the spaceship, the spaceship will start again from the left and move down 50 pixels closer to the missile—this is a penalty.

Questions

1. **Identify variables**

   There are three custom-defined variables defined in the code (Figure 9.1).
   (a) What are the names of these variables?
   (b) Where are they declared? Give the line number for each.
   (c) What is the data type of each variable?
   (d) What is the initial value assigned to each variable at declaration?
   (e) Where are these variables accessed or modified in the code? Give the line numbers for all the occurences.

2. **Identify custom-defined constants**

   There are five custom-defined constants defined in the code (Figure 9.1).
   (a) What are the names of these constants?
   (b) Where are they declared? Give the line number for each.
   (c) What is the data type of each constant?
   (d) What is the value assigned to each constant?

3. **Identify ActionScript predefined constants**

   There are five predefined constants used in the code (Figure 9.1).

   (a) What are the names of these constants?

   (b) Where are they used? Give the line number for each.

4. **Identify assignment operators**

   Circle in the code all the occurences of the following operators. Mark "none" for those that are not used in the code at all.

   (a) addition assignment $(+=)$

   (b) subtraction assignment $(-=)$

   (c) multiplication assignment $(*=)$

   (d) division assignment $(/=)$

   (e) postfix increment $(++)$

   (f) postfix decrement $(--)$

5. **Read expressions**

   If the value of the variable missed is equal to 3, then the resulting value from the expression missed * PENALTY (see line 65) will be _____.

Answers to Self Test Questions

1. **Variables**

   (a) isFired, isHit, and missed

   (b) isFired: line 5;   isHit: line 6;   missed: line 7

   (c) isFired: Boolean;   isHit: Boolean; missed: int

   (d) isFired: false;   isHit: false;   missed: 0

   (e) isFired: lines 18, 38, 50, 63

       isHit: lines 23, 25, 57, 62

       missed: lines 26, 59, 65

2. **Custom-defined constants**

   (a) PENALTY, MISSILE_SPEED, SPACESHIP_SPEED

   (b) PENALTY: line 1;   MISSILE_SPEED: line 2; SPACESHIP_SPEED: line 3

   (c) PENALTY: uint;   MISSILE_SPEED: uint;   SPACESHIP_SPEED: uint

   (d) PENALTY: 50;   MISSILE_SPEED: 7;   SPACESHIP_SPEED: 5

3. **Predefined constants**

   (a) KEYBOARD.RIGHT, KEYBOARD.LEFT, KEYBOARD.SPACE, true, false

   (b) KEYBOARD.RIGHT:line 40;

       KEYBOARD.LEFT: line 44;

       KEYBOARD.SPACE: line 48

       true: lines 18, 23, 25, 50;

       false: lines 5, 6, 23, 38, 57, 62, 63

4. **Assignment operators**

   (a) +=: lines 16, 42

   (b) -=: lines 20, 46

   (c) *=: none

   (d) /=: none

   (e) ++: line 59

   (f) --: line 26

5. 150, because PENALTY is equal to 50 (line 1) and missed is equal to 3.

9.3 PROGRAMMING AND SCRIPTING FUNDAMENTALS—PART B

9.3.1 Control Structures

A program is written as a sequence of statements (i.e., instructions). The program executes the instructions sequentially—one instruction after the other, in the order in which they appear in the code. However, using *control structures*, you can write statements that cause your program to execute instructions nonsequentially. For example:

- Loop: A set of statements is executed repeatedly until a certain condition is met. The statements that let you execute instructions repeatedly—loops—will be introduced in Chapter 11.
- Conditional: A set of statements is executed only if some conditions are reached. There are two types of statements that let you define conditions under which a set of instructions will be executed: if *statements* and switch *statements*. Here we will cover if statements only.

if **Statement**

The general syntax of an if statement is as follows:

```
if (logical expression(s))
{
    statement(s)
}
```

Here is an example of if statement in ActionScript:

```
if (score > 60)
{
    grade = "pass";
}
```

This if statement checks to see whether the value of a variable score is greater than 60. The expression score > 60 is a logical expression, which will give a value of true or false. If the condition is satisfied—i.e., the expression score > 60 is evaluated to be true—then the value of another variable named grade will be set to "pass".

If there is only one statement to be executed, the curly braces are optional. Thus, the example above can also be written like this:

```
if (score > 60)
    grade = "pass";
```

or, like this, on a single line:

```
if (score > 60) grade = "pass";
```

if...else **Statement**

In the simple if statement above, there is not a specified statement to be executed when score is not greater than 60. To specify an alternative set of instructions for the condition being false, you can use an if...else statement.

The general syntax of an if...else statement is like this:

```
if (logical expression(s))
{
    statement(s)
}
else
{
    statement(s)
}
```

Here is an example of if...else statement:

```
if (score > 60)
{
    grade = "pass";
}
else
{
    grade = "fail";
}
```

if...else if Statement

The if...else if statements let you test for more than one condition.

Here is an example of if...else if statement:

```
if (score > 90)
{
    grade = "A";
}
else if (score > 80)
{
    grade = "B";
}
else if (score > 70)
{
    grade = "C";
}
else if (score > 60)
{
    grade = "D";
}
else
{
    grade = "F";
}
```

Self Test Exercise: if Statements vs. if . . . else if Statements

Question

Suppose the variables a and b are both greater than 0. What are the resulting values of s from the following two code segments?

```s = 0;```
```if (a > 0) s++;```
```if (b > 0) s++;```
	```s = 0;```
	```if (a > 0) s++;```
	```else if (b > 0) s++;```

Answer to Self Test Question

In the case on the left, s will be equal to 2 because s will be increased twice. In the case on the right, s is equal to 1.

 Self Test Exercise: if . . . else if Statements and Comparison Operators

Question

In which of the following if...else if statements does the order of the tests matter?

```if (score == 1) x = n;```
```else if (score == 2) x = n*n;```
```else if (score == 3) x = n*n*n;```
```else x = -1;```
	```if (score <= 1) x = n;```
	```else if (score <= 2) x = n*n;```
	```else if (score <= 3) x = n*n*n;```
	```else x = -1;```

Answer to Self Test Question

In the case on the left, the order does not matter. In the case on the right, the order matters.

In the first case, for each logical expression in the if...else if statement, there is only one value for the variable score that can return true. In the second case, for each logical expression in the if...else if statement, there is a range of values for the variable score that can return true. Note that there is some overlap among these three ranges, score <= 1, score <= 2, and score <= 3. The values that are <= 1 all satisfy these three conditions. The values that are <= 2 all satisfy the latter two conditions. The order of the tests matters in determining which statement is to be executed.

Suppose score is equal to 1, the table below highlights the statement that will be executed.

`if (score == 1) x = n;`
`else if (score == 2) x = n*n;`
`else if (score == 3) x = n*n*n;`
`else x = -1;`
	`if (score <= 1) x = n;`
	`else if (score <= 2) x = n*n;`
	`else if (score <= 3) x = n*n*n;`
	`else x = -1;`

`if (score == 3) x = n*n*n;`
`else if (score == 2) x = n*n;`
`else if (score == 1) x = n;`
`else x = -1;`
	`if (score <= 3) x = n*n*n;`
	`else if (score <= 2) x = n*n;`
	`else if (score <= 1) x = n;`
	`else x = -1;`

Nested if statements

if statements can be placed inside another if statement to create different combinations of conditions for different sets of instructions.

Example 1:
```
if (age < 40)
{
    if (weight < 150)
    {
        x = 2;
    }
    else
    {
        x = 3;
    }
}
```

Example 2:
```
if (age < 40)
{
    if (weight < 150)
    {
        x = 2;
    }
}
else
{
        x = 3;
}
```

Be aware of the placement of the closing curly braces. Note that the nested if statements in Example 1 and Example 2 have different meanings. Table 9.7 shows the different results from these two examples of nested if statements.

TABLE 9.7	Different Results Are Generated from Two Different Nested if Statements		
age	weight	Statement Executed in Example 1	Statement Executed in Example 2
38	145	x = 2	x = 2
38	157	x = 3	none; x is not set
46	145	none; x is not set	x = 3
46	157	none; x is not set	x = 3

Logical Operators in *if* Statements

Recall that there are three common logical operators: logical AND (&&), logical OR (||), and logical NOT (!). Table 9.8 shows the general syntax of each, with descriptions of the new Boolean values generated.

TABLE 9.8	General Syntax for the Logical Operators and the New Boolean Values Generated
General Syntax	**New Boolean Value Generated**
logicalExpression1 && *logicalExpression2*	true: *only when both* logicalExpression1 and logicalExpression2 are true false: *when either* logicalExpression1 or logicalExpression2 is false
logicalExpression1 || *logicalExpression2*	true: *when either* logicalExpression1 or logicalExpression2 is true false: *only when both* logicalExpression1 and logicalExpression2 are false
!logicalExpression1	true: when logicalExpression1 is false false: when logicalExpression1 is true

Let's look at some examples.

Example 1:
```
if (age < 40 && weight < 150)
{
    x = 2;
}
else
{
    x = 3;
}
```

Example 2:
```
if (age < 40 || weight < 150)
{
    x = 2;
}
else
{
    x = 3;
}
```

Table 9.9 shows the new Boolean values generated from the logical operators in different scenarios. The new Boolean value determines which set of statements are executed.

TABLE 9.9		Different Results Are Generated from if Statements Using Different Logical Operators			
age	weight	**Boolean Value for** age < 40 && weight < 150	**Statement Executed in Example 1**	**Boolean Value for** age < 40 || weight < 150	**Statement Executed in Example 2**
38	145	true	x = 2	true	x = 2
38	157	false	x = 3	true	x = 2
46	145	false	x = 3	true	x = 2
46	157	false	x = 3	false	x = 3

? Self Test Exercise: if...else if Statements and Comparison Operators

(a)
```
i = 1;
n = 2;
if (choice == 1 && positive == true)
{
    i = n;
}
else if (positive == false)
{
    i = n * n;
}
else if (choice == 3)
{
    i = n * n * n;
}
else
{
    i = 0;
}
```

(b)
```
i = 1;
n = 2;
if (choice == 1)
{
    if (positive == true)
        i = n;
    else
        i = -n;
}
else
{
    if (positive == true)
        i = n * n;
    else
        i = -n * n;
}
```

Question

Predict the value of i for each of the scenario.

		What is the value of i after executing the code shown in (a)?	What is the value of i after executing the code shown in (b)?
(i)	choice = 1 positive = true		
(ii)	choice = 2 positive = true		
(iii)	choice = 3 positive = true		
(iv)	choice = 1 positive = false		
(v)	choice = 2 positive = false		
(vi)	choice = 3 positive = false		

Answers to Self Test Question

For code segment **(a)**: (i) 2   (ii) 0   (iii) 8   (iv) 4   (v) 4   (vi) 4
For code segment **(b)**: (i) 2   (ii) 4   (iii) 4   (iv) −2   (v) −4   (vi) −4

9.3.2 Functions and Procedures

A *function* is a block of program instructions (also called *code*) that form a discrete unit with a name. This discrete unit is the function's definition. The instructions in a *function definition* are not executed immediately when the program runs. They will be executed only when the function is called or invoked.

To define a function, you use the keyword `function`. The general syntax for defining a function looks like this:

```
function functionName():dataType
{
        statement(s)
}
```

For example:

```
function startGame():void
{
        score = 0;
        health = 100;
}
```

In ActionScript, a *function call* invokes the function and is simply a statement with the function name followed by a pair of parentheses, which looks like this:

```
startGame();
```

When a statement containing a function call is executed, the program jumps to the block of code that constitutes the function's definition and then executes its block of code. When it is finished with the function block, it returns to execute the statement after the one in which the function call has occurred.

Returning a Value

Before going into further explanation of functions vs. procedures, let's look at an analogy. Suppose you work as a manager in a company and you need a signature from your supervisor on a contract. So you send your assistant to take the contract to your supervisor to sign. When your assistant takes the contract to your supervisor, he may need to go to a different floor, talk to your supervisor's secretary, etc. However, you only need to give him a simple "command" to get the contract signed. You did not need to go through with your assistant all these details of how to get to your supervisor's office because your assistant can look up the detailed directions that are kept elsewhere. Your simple "command" is like the function call. The set of exact steps to get to your supervisor's office and get the signature are like the block of code defined in the function.

Once the supervisor has signed the contract, the task is complete. However, you can either have your assistant bring the signed contract back to you or leave the contract with your supervisor. Whether your assistant brings back the signed contract or not, the contract is signed—a task has been performed.

The assistant bringing back the signed contract is analogous to what we called returning a value in a function. A function *returns a value* to the calling statement. In this analogy, the returned value is the signed contract that the assistant brings back. The calling statement is your "command" sending your assistant to get the signature.

If the assistant does not need to bring back the signed contract, the contract is still signed. The supervisor may continue on to whatever he is supposed to do with the contract.

The assistant getting the job done without bringing something back for you is analogous to a *procedure* in the terminology of most programming languages.

How to Write Procedure and Function Definitions in ActionScript

Procedures are closely related to functions. In common usage, a ***procedure*** is exactly like a function except it does not return a value. A procedure still does some useful activities, such as sorting a list of numbers or displaying values on the screen. In the previous analogy, the activity is to get the supervisor's signature.

While the terms function and procedure are sometimes used interchangeably, most programming languages reserve the word *function* specifically for procedures that return a value. In ActionScript, functions and procedures are all referred to as functions. The keyword `function` is used to define functions and procedures. Here, definitions of function and procedure will be referred to as function definitions.

The data type of the return value has to be specified in the function definition. If the function does not return a value, then its data type is `void`.

Here is an example of a function definition in ActionScript that returns a value:

```
function calcTax():int
{
        var tax:int = sales * taxRate;
        return tax;
}
```

The previous code defines a function name `calcTax`. The function name is followed by a pair of parentheses. The block of code is enclosed within the curly braces {}. The last statement is a `return` statement. It returns the value of the variable tax.

Here is an example of a function definition in ActionScript that does not return a value:

```
function startGame():void
{
        score = 0;
        health = 100;
}
```

The previous code defines a function (or a procedure) named `startGame`. This function simply sets two variables to some values: `score` to zero and `health` to 100. It performs activities, but does not return any value.

How to Call a Function That Does Not Return a Value

The calling statements for a procedure and a function are different. To call a procedure—a function that does not return a value—in ActionScript, you simply use the name of the function followed by a pair of parentheses. For example, the following statement calls the procedure `startGame`:

```
startGame();
```

How to Call a Function That Returns a Value

What about a function that returns a value? Where would the returned value go? The function call is generally used on the right-hand side of an assignment statement.

For example, the following statement causes the calcTotal() function to be executed to calculate the tax and returns the calculated value.

```
newBalance = calcTotal();
```

Then the returned value is assigned to the variable newBalance.

The function call can also be used in a logical expression. For example, the following statement causes the calcTotal() function to be executed—calculating the tax and returning the calculated value. Then the returned value is used to compare to the value 100 in the if statement.

```
if (calcTotal() > 100)
{
    discount = 10;
}
```

Most programming languages have predefined functions and procedures. This means that you can call these functions and procedures. The code for these functions and procedures is already built into the language—you just need to know what functions exist and how to use them.

9.3.3 Parameters and Arguments

A function or procedure can be defined to have **parameters** so that it receives values when it is called, and these values can be used in its computation. Values that are passed into functions or procedures are called **arguments**.

The general syntax for defining a function that takes arguments look like this:

```
function functionName(parameter1:dataType1, parameter2:dataType2,...):dataType
{
        statement(s)
}
```

In the function definition, the parameters are listed inside the parentheses that follow the function name. The data type of each parameter needs to be specified there. The parameter name is followed by a colon (:) and then its data type.

For example, the function, calcTotal(), shown next has two parameters named sales and taxrate. The data types for these two parameters are int and Number, respectively. What this function does is that it adds the values passed into these two parameters, and assigns the sum to the variable named total.

```
function calcTotal(sales:int, taxrate:Number):void
{
    total = sales * (1 + taxrate);
}
```

This function would be called with a statement like this:

```
calcTotal(90, 0.07);
```

There are two arguments that are passed into the function call: the values of 90 and 0.07. When the function is executed as a result of this function call:

- the parameter sales gets the value 90 and taxrate gets the value 0.07;
- the two values are used in the statement total = sales * (1 + taxrate) and total gets the sum of 96.3.

Parameters can also be used in functions that return a value. For example,

```
function calcTotal(sales:int, taxrate:Number):Number
{
    var total:Number;
    total = sales * (1 + taxrate);
    return total;
}
```

This function would be called with a statement like this:

```
newBalance = calcTotal(90, 0.07);
```

9.3.4 Comments

Comments allow you to provide descriptive notes for your codes. In ActionScript, there are two ways to signify the comments:

- // for a single-line comment, and
- /* and */ for a multiline comment.

Two forward slashes // signify the text following the two slashes until end of the line is comment and will not be executed. For example:

```
function calculateScore()               // to increment the score by 1
{
        score = score + 1;
}
```

and

```
function calculateScore()
{
        // This function is to increment the
        // score by 1.
        score = score + 1;
}
```

To make multiline comments in a block, use /* at the beginning and */ at the end of the comments. For example:

```
function calculateScore()
{
        /* This function is to increment the
        score by 1. */
        score = score + 1;
}
```

The /* and */ do not have to be on the same lines as the comment. The previous example can also be written like this:

```
function calculateScore()
{
        /*
        This function is to increment the
        score by 1.
        */
        score = score + 1;
}
```

Parameters vs. Arguments:

Arguments are the actual values that are passed into the function. In the current example, the arguments are the values 90 and 0.07. The two parameters of the function calcTotal() are sales and taxrate. The terms *parameter* and *argument* are often used interchangeably.

The indentation in the script, including the comments, is not a syntactical requirement, but the indentation makes the code easier to read.

> ### ❓ Self Test Exercise: Identify if Statements, Function Definitions, Function Calls, and Parameters
>
> Let's return to the example code from the previous Self Test. This time, you are asked to identify if statements, function definitions, function calls, and parameters.

```
 1   const PENALTY:int = 50;
 2   const MISSILE_SPEED:int = 7;
 3   const SPACESHIP_SPEED:int = 5;
 4
 5   var isFired:Boolean = false;
 6   var isHit:Boolean = false;
 7   var missed:int = 0;
 8
 9   reset();
10
11   addEventListener(Event.ENTER_FRAME, onLoopFrame);
12   stage.addEventListener(KeyboardEvent.KEY_DOWN, onKeyControl);
13
14   function onLoopFrame(evt:Event):void
15   {
16       mc_spaceship.x += SPACESHIP_SPEED;
17
18       if (isFired == true)
19       {
20           mc_missile.y -= MISSILE_SPEED;
21       }
22
23       if (mc_spaceship.hitTestPoint(mc_missile.x, mc_missile.y, true) &&
         isHit == false)
24       {
25           isHit = true;
26           missed--;
27           mc_spaceship.gotoAndPlay("explosion" );
28       }
29
30       if (mc_spaceship.x > stage.stageWidth + 100 || mc_missile.y < -50 ||
         mc_spaceship.currentFrame == mc_spaceship.totalFrames
31       {
```

Figure 9.3 The complete code for the simple shoot-them-up game from the previous self-test exercise (*continued*)

```
32      reset();
33      }
34   }
35
36   function onKeyControl(evt:KeyboardEvent):void
37   {
38      if (isFired == false)
39      {
40         if (evt.keyCode == Keyboard.RIGHT)
41         {
42            mc_missile.x += MISSILE_SPEED;
43         }
44         else if (evt.keyCode == Keyboard.LEFT)
45         {
46            mc_missile.x -= MISSILE_SPEED;
47         }
48         else if (evt.keyCode == Keyboard.SPACE)
49         {
50            isFired = true;
51         }
52      }
53   }
54
55   function reset():void
56   {
57      if (isHit == false)
58      {
59         missed++;
60      }
61
62      isHit = false;
63      isFired = false;
64      mc_spaceship.x = -100;
65      mc_spaceship.y = missed * PENALTY;
66      mc_spaceship.gotoAndStop(1);
67      mc_missile.y = stage.stageHeight - 20;
68   }
```

Figure 9.3 (*continued*)

Questions

1. **Identify function definitions and function calls**

There are three custom-defined functions in the code (Figure 9.3).

(a) What are the names of these functions?

(b) Where are they defined? Give the line numbers for each.

(c) For each function, what is the data type of the returned value?

(d) Which functions take argument(s)? How many argument(s) do they take?

(e) Where are these functions called? Give the line numbers.

2. **Identify function calls of predefined functions**

   There are some function calls to predefined function (Figure 9.3). You can tell by the parentheses. (Recall that a function call uses the name of the function followed by a pair of parentheses. If the function takes arguments, then you will also see arguments within the parentheses.)

   (a) What are the names of these functions? Give the line number for each of these function calls.

   (b) Which functions take argument(s)? How many argument(s) do they take?

3. **Identify if statements**

   Give the line numbers where if statements (including if...else and if...else if) are used.

4. **Identify logical operators**

   Circle in the code all the occurences of the following operators. Mark "none" for those that are not used in the code at all.

   (a) logical AND (&&)

   (b) logical OR (||)

   (c) logical NOT (!!)

Answers to Self Test Questions

1. function definitions and function calls

   (a) onLoopFrame, onKeyControl, and reset

   (b) onLoopFrame: lines 14–34; onKeyControl: lines 36–53; reset: lines 55–68

   (c) onLoopFrame: void; onKeyControl: void; reset: void

   (d) onLoopFrame: 1 parameter; onKeyControl: 1 argument

   (e) reset: lines 9 and 32

2. Function calls to predefined functions

   (a) addEventListener: lines 11 and 12

   hitTestPoint: line 23

   gotoAndPlay: line 27

   gotoAndStop: line 66

   (b) addEventListener: 2 arguments

   hitTestPoint: 3 arguments

   gotoAndPlay: 1 argument

   gotoAndStop: 1 argument

3. if **statements**

   if statements: lines 18–21, 23–28, 30–33, lines 38–52, 57–60

   if...else if statements: lines 40–51

4. **Logical operators**

   (a) &&: line 23

   (b) ||: 2 occurrences in line 30

   (c) !: none

⚓ Flash File Used in the Self Test Exercise

You can download the Flash file that is used in the Self Test. Run it to see how it works. Experiments you can try in the code:

- Change the values of the variables and constants.
- Rewrite some of the assignment statements that use += or -= operator to use = operator.

9.4 SUMMARY

Multimedia authoring programs, such as Flash, support animation creation and have scripting languages. The scripting language for Flash is called ActionScript. Scripting lets you incorporate interactivity and nonlinearity into your multimedia project.

ActionScript shares many programming concepts and constructs that are common to all high-level programming languages—for example, variables, functions, conditions, loops, mouse events, and keyboard events. This chapter gives an overview of these concepts and terms to prepare you to start scripting in ActionScript 3.0 in the subsequent chapters.

Syntax: The syntax of a programming or scripting language prescribes the ways in which statements must be written in order for them to be understood by the computer. ActionScript is case sensitive.

Data Types: The type of a value is called its data type. This chapter introduces several basic data types that are commonly used in introductory level Actionscript. They are: `int` (integer), `uint` (unsigned integer), `Number`, `String` (text string), and `Boolean` (true or false).

Variables: Variables are elements used to store values that are used in your program, so that you can also update and retrieve values. There are three properties associated with a variable: name, value, and data type. The general syntax to declare a variable in ActionScript 3.0 is as follows:

```
var variableName:dataType;
```

Statements: Statements are instructions that can be executed.

Assignment Statements: An assignment statement assigns a value to a variable. In most languages, you use the = (equals) operator to assign a value to a variable. For example, the statement:

```
score = 0;
```

Operators: Operators are symbols that cause a new value to be calculated from one or more values (operands). This text introduces five common types of operators:

- Arithmetic operators: +, -, *, /, %
- Assignment operators: =, +=, -=, *=, /=, %=
- Postfix operators: ++, --
- Comparison operators: >, >=, <, <=, ==, !=
- Logical operators: &&, ||, !

Constants: Constants are elements in a program that do not change. You can think of constants as "read-only variables." ActionScript 3.0 also has predefined constants such as `Keyboard.UP`, `Keyboard.DOWN`, `Keyboard.LEFT`, `Keyboard.RIGHT` and `Keyboard.SPACE` to represent the key code values (a number associated with each key on the keyboard) for the up, down, left, right arrow keys, and space bar respectively. You can also declare constants in ActionScript 3.0. The general syntax to declare a variable in ActionScript 3.0 is like this:

```
const constantName:dataType = value;
```

Keywords: In general, keywords are reserved words that have a special meaning in a programming language. You are not allowed to use these words for any other purpose, such as variable or function names, because they are predefined with special meanings in the language. For example, `if` is a keyword in most programming languages. You are not allowed to give a variable the name `if`; it will result in an error message.

Expressions: An expression is any part of a statement that produces a value, for example:

```
2 + 2, (a + b + c) /3, a > b
```

if statements: The general syntax of an if statement is as follows:

```
if (logical expression(s))
{
    statement(s)
}
```

The general syntax of an if..else statement is as follows:

```
if (logical expression(s))
{
    statement(s)
}
else
{
    statement(s)
}
```

The general syntax of an if..else if statement is as follows:

```
if (logical expression(s))
{
    statement(s)
}
else if (logical expression(s))
{
    statement(s)
}
```

Functions and *Procedures*: A function is a block of program instructions (also called code) that form a discrete unit with a name. This discrete unit is the function's definition. The instructions in a function definition are not executed immediately when the program runs. They will be executed only when the function is called or invoked. A procedure is exactly like a function except that it does not return a value.

In ActionScript, this type of construct is referred to as function whether the function returns a value or not.

To define a function in ActionScript 3.0, you use the keyword function. The following shows the general syntax for defining a function:

```
function functionName():dataType
{
        statement(s)
}
```

Parameters and *Arguments:* A function or procedure can be defined to have parameters so that it receives values when it is called—and these values can be used in its computation. Values that are passed into functions or procedures are called arguments. The terms parameter and argument are often used interchangeably.

The general syntax for defining a function that takes arguments is as follows:

```
function functionName(parameter1:dataType1, parameter2:dataType2,...):dataType
{
        statement(s)
}
```

Comments: Comments allow you to provide descriptive notes for your codes. For ActionScript, two forward slashes // signify the text following the two slashes until end of the line is a comment that will not be executed. To make multiline comments in a block, use /* at the beginning and */ at the end of the comments.

TERMS

LEARNING AIDS

The following learning aids can be found at the book's companion Web site.

⌨ **Flash File Used in the Self Test Exercise**
You can download the Flash file that is used in the self test. Run it to see how it works. Experiments you can try in the code:

- Change the values of the variables and constants.
- Rewrite some of the assignment statements that use += or -= operator to use = operator.

REVIEW QUESTIONS

Programming Fundamentals

1. **True/False:** If it is strict data typing, a programming language requires that you explicitly declare the data type of a variable when the variable is first created.

2. The type of the value is called a(n) _____ .

    A. variable

    B. function or procedure

    C. argument

    D. statement

    E. data type

3. _____ are used to store values, which can be updated and retrieved.

    A. Variables

    B. Functions and Procedures

    C. Arguments

    D. Statements

    E. Data types

4. A(n) _____ contains a block of program instructions, which form a discrete unit with a name.

    A. variable

    B. function or procedure

    C. argument

    D. statement

    E. data type

5. Values passed into functions or procedures are called _____.

    A. variables

    B. arguments

    C. statements

    D. data types

6. _____ can be used to make the program execute nonsequentially.

    A. If statements

    B. Loops

    C. Both of the above.

7. True/False: A function definition is executed automatically when the program runs.

8. True/False: A function is executed only when it is called within the program.

9. The difference between a function and a procedure is that a _____ returns a value to the calling statement.

    A. function

    B. procedure

10. True/False: Another difference between a function and a procedure is that one takes parameters while the other does not.

11. `sum = addTogether(2,5);`

    By looking at the previous statement, you can tell that `addTogether()` _____ .

    A. returns a value

    B. does not return a value

    C. It is not possible to tell whether or not it returns a value.

12. `sum = addTogether();`

By looking at the previous statement, you can tell that `addTogether()` _____.

A. returns a value

B. does not return a value

C. It is not possible to tell whether or not it returns a value.

13. `addTogether(2,5);`

By looking at the previous statement, you can tell that `addTogether()` probably _____.

A. returns a value

B. does not return a value

14. `addTogether();`

By looking at the previous statement, you can tell that `addTogether()` probably _____.

A. returns a value

B. does not return a value

ActionScript

15. ActionScript is a _____ language.

A. strictly typed

B. loosely typed

16. The statement in ActionScript ends with a _____.

A. colon (:)

B. semi-colon (;)

C. closing parenthesis ())

D. closing curly brace

17. **True/False:** ActionScript syntax is case sensitive.

18. Which of the following is a valid variable name for ActionScript?

A. 3 high score

B. 3_high_score

C. high_score

D. high-score

19. To declare a variable, you use the keyword _____.

20. To declare a constant, you use the keyword _____.

21. To define a function, you use the keyword _____.

22. Write an `if` statement to do the following. (Assume the variables have been declared. You do not need to declare the variables. Simply construct an `if` statement.) Hint: You will need to use comparison operators and a logical operator.

If both variables `a` and `b` are greater than 0, then increment the value of variable `c` by 1.

23. Write an `if` statement to do the following. (Assume the variables have been declared. You do not need to declare the variables. Simply construct an `if` statement.) Hint: You will need to use comparison operators and a logical operator.

If either variable `a` or `b` is equal to 0, then increment the value of variable `c` by 1.

Interactive Multimedia Authoring with Flash: ActionScript—Part 2

KEY CONCEPTS
- ActionScript basic terminology
- syntax errors and logical errors in scripts

GENERAL LEARNING OBJECTIVES
At the end of this chapter, you should be able to demonstrate that you
- are prepared for programming in ActionScript.
- are able to distinguish syntax errors and logical errors.
- know how to read and fix syntax errors in ActionScript in Flash IDE.

10.1 ActionScript: ESSENTIAL TERMINOLOGY AND BASIC CONCEPTS

The basic programming concepts introduced in the previous sections apply to ActionScript and other programming languages. However, when it comes to programming in Flash's authoring environment, there are elements—such as symbols, stage, and timeline—that are specific to Flash and ActionScript. To prepare you for programming in ActionScript in the next chapter, the remaining sections of this chapter will discuss these specific aspects of ActionScript.

The movieclip symbol is particularly useful when you want to add interactivity to control animated objects whose animation is timeline-based. For example, the spaceship and missile in the self test exercises in Chapter 9 are movieclip symbols. The spaceship movieclip symbol contains an animated sequence of the explosion on its timeline. It is programmed to play the animation when the missile hits the spaceship.

To be able to control these movieclip objects on the stage, you need to know how to refer to them in your script. This section will discuss how to refer to movieclip objects on the stage by names.

10.1.1 Movieclips: Instances and Naming

Movieclip symbols and other symbols are stored in the library panel. When you drag a movieclip from the library onto the stage, an instance of that movieclip symbol is created. An *instance* means a copy or an occurrence of the original movieclip symbol.

A movieclip can be used multiple times on the stage in the same frame. A movieclip instance placed on the stage can be controlled by ActionScript. Such instance needs to be assigned with a name so that you can refer to the instance by name in your code. Within the same frame on a timeline, each instance—whether it is from the same symbol or not—should have a unique name. The same name may be used again in a different frame.

It is important to remember: it is the movieclip's instance name—not the movieclip's symbol name that appears in the library—that you should use in the code to refer to the object on the stage.

To assign a name to an instance, select the movieclip instance on the stage, and enter a name in the Property Inspector (Figure 10.1). Note that in Figure 10.1 the name of the movieclip symbol, as listed in the Library, is character and the two instances are named mc_tommy and mc_joe, as shown in the Property Inspector. You may notice that the sizes of these two instances can be altered independently. Other properties of an instance such as position, rotation, color, and alpha can also be adjusted independently. Thus, you can, for example, program to move mc_tommy on stage, rotate, change size, change color, change opacity without affecting mc_joe.

10.1.2 Movieclips: Each Has Its Own Timeline

Each movieclip has its own timeline and it is different from the main timeline of a scene—another key point to remember. The significances of having multiple timelines in a Flash movie are that:

- There can be more than one frame with the same frame number, say Frame 2.
- Hence, you need to be specific about which timeline when sending a playhead to another frame using ActionScript.

When you refer to a certain frame in the codes, make sure you specify which timeline. Referring to the timeline of a particular movieclip will need a little more explanation because movieclips can be nested, i.e., a movieclip can be placed inside another movieclip. The next subsection will discuss this in detail.

10.1.3 Nesting Movieclips and Dot Syntax

Added to the complication of existence of multiple timelines in the same project—one for each movieclip—is the ***nesting movieclips***. A movieclip can contain other symbols—graphics, buttons, and movieclips. Therefore, one movieclip can be placed inside another movieclip, i.e., one timeline containing an animation can be placed inside another timeline.

Although it may seem confusing at first, this is a very useful feature and commonly used in projects. With more than one timeline, how do you specify in ActionScript which timeline's animation should be played? The answer is to use a target path to specify the address of the instance you want to target. A ***target path*** is constructed by stringing together the instance names using periods (.) according to their hierarchical relationship—***dot syntax***.

Let's return to the example shown in Figure 10.1. Suppose:

- In the movieclip character, there is an instance of another movieclip as the head. This head is assigned with an instance name mc_head.
- Inside this head movieclip symbol, you place other movieclip instances: mc_hair, mc_eyeL, mc_eyeR, and mc_mouth (Figure 10.2).
- The timeline of the mouth movieclip contains a mouth moving animation.

Now, suppose you want to let the user click on the character instance mc_tommy to start the talking animation. You need to be able to specify the mouth timeline to start playing the animation. The target path for the mouth instance is:

mc_tommy.mc_head.mc_mouth

Movieclip Instance Naming Convention used throughout this chapter: The movieclip instance names in all the examples start with mc_. This is not a technical requirement in ActionScript. However, it helps identify that the name refers to a movieclip instance, rather than a custom-defined object or a variable in the code. - Another common naming convention is ending with _mc.

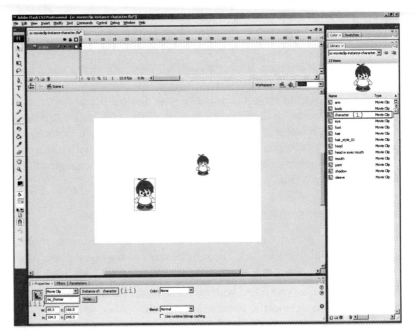

(a)

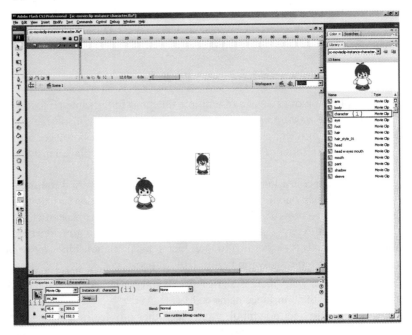

(b)

Figure 10.1 Two instances, (a) mc_thomas and (b) mc_joe, of the same movieclip symbol, named character; symbol name of master copy in Library (i) and in the Property Inspector; assigning the instance name (ii) in the Property Inspector

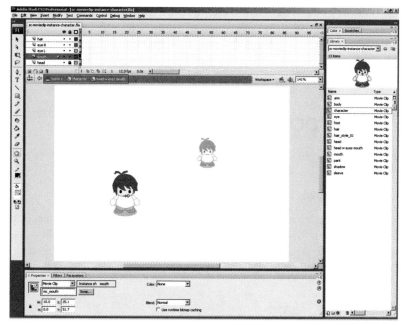

Figure 10.2 The movieclip symbol named head w eyes mouth contains an instance of the movieclip symbol name mouth; this instance's name is mc_mouth, and it is on the timeline of movieclip symbol head w eyes mouth, not the main timeline

and the statement to make the mouth to start playing animation is:

```
mc_tommy.mc_head.mc_mouth.play();
```

The ActionScript function, play() causes the playhead on the timeline—the one specified by the path—to start. The timeline that the above path refers to is the mc_mouth that is inside mc_head, which in turn is inside mc_tommy.

Let's look at another organization of the mouth. Suppose the mc_mouth is placed on the main timeline instead of the mc_head's. Visually, it is not different from the previous example, but the target path for the mouth instance now is:

```
mc_mouth
```

and the statement to make the mouth to start playing animation is:

```
mc_mouth.play();
```

Dots can be used for more than constructing paths to a movieclip instance. Dots can be used to:

- denote the target path to a timeline;
- invoke a method for a specific movieclip instance (tell the object to do something, such as play() in the example above);
- denote the property of a movieclip, such as position and size.

The previous examples demonstrate the first two usages of dots. You will see more examples for the third usage in the section of controlling objects in Chapter 11. For example, the lines of codes to change the size of the mouth to 60% are:

```
mc_tommy.mc_head.mc_mouth.scaleX = 0.6;
mc_tommy.mc_head.mc_mouth.scaleY = 0.6;
```

10.2 WHERE DO SCRIPTS GO?

The script should be added to a keyframe. The code is entered in the Actions panel.

10.2.1 Keyframe

The script is placed in a frame on the timeline. The frame has to be a keyframe. If the frame you want to place a script in is not a keyframe, you will need to convert it into a keyframe first. In the examples throughout Chapters 10 and 11, the script will be placed in the first frame only. The script will be executed when the playhead reaches that frame.

10.2.2 Actions Panel

You can create or edit ActionScript code in the Actions panel (Figure 10.3(i)). To open the Actions panel, choose Window > Actions, or press the F9 key. Before you do so, you need to select the frame first. If you are creating a new script, select a keyframe and then open the Actions panel. If you are editing an existing script, select the keyframe that has the script and open the Actions panel. The keyframe that has a script will show an "a" above the

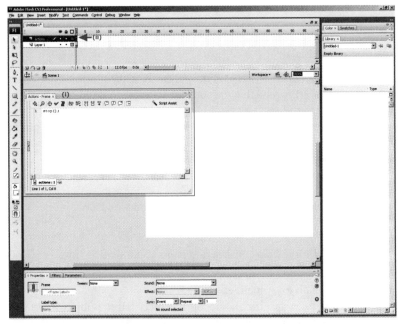

Figure 10.3 (i) Actions panel (ii) A keyframe that has a script; the "a" displayed in the frame indicates that the frame has a script

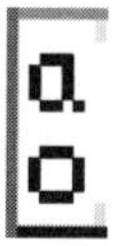

Figure 10.4 A keyframe that has a script shows an "a" on top of the circle

circle (Figure 10.3(ii) and Figure 10.4). You can tell whether or not a frame has a script simply by looking at the timeline.

10.2.3 "actions" Layer

Although ActionScript can be placed in any keyframe in any layer, it is a best practice to create a layer dedicated to hold the script. By doing so, the ActionScript keyframes will not interfere with the keyframes that are created for visual or audio content, and the placement of the keyframes for frame scripts is independent of the animation keyframes.

It is a common practice to name the layer that is dedicated to hold the script "actions" or "action." This layer is arranged as the topmost layer, or the second topmost layer if there is a topmost layer for the frame label. All the ActionScript examples in this book follow this convention.

10.3 SCRIPT ERRORS

Do not feel frustrated when your first programs do not run properly or even at all. Even when writing an essay, there are often errors, such as spelling and grammatical mistakes. Even if you have had your essay go through a spelling and grammar checker, your reader or proofreader may still find some parts of the essay difficult to understand. Then you will need to analyze the essay's logic and flow, and make adjustments. These errors are experienced by writers of all levels.

Scripting errors are experienced by scripters of all skill levels, too. There are tools and techniques to help you fix the errors. But first, let's look at two main types of errors: syntactical errors and logical errors.

10.3.1 Syntactical Errors

Syntactical errors are analogous to the spelling and grammatical errors in essay writing. When you test or export a movie, Flash's compiler analyzes the code. The Compiler Errors panel will display a list of descriptions of any syntactical errors. It tells you the location of the error by giving you the scene name, layer name, frame number, and line number.

You can also check syntax by clicking the Check Syntax button (Figure 10.5) in the Actions panel.

The code shown in Figure 10.6 is missing a closing parenthesis. The Output panel lists two errors. This tells you the location of the source: Scene 1, Layer 'action', Frame 1, Line 32. Both errors are related to the same typo: missing closing parenthesis in Line 32. Once you have fixed the closing parenthesis, both errors will go away.

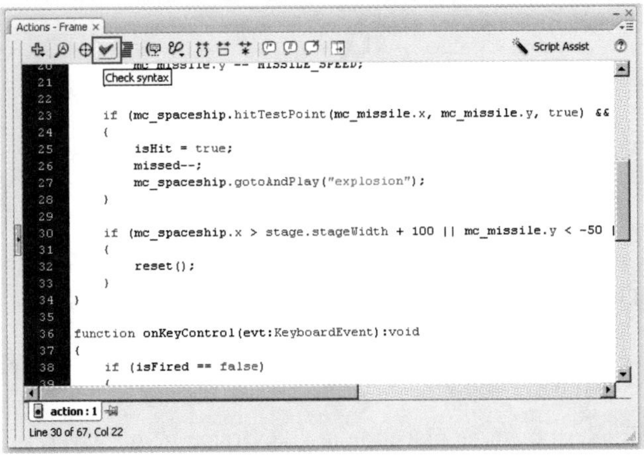

Figure 10.5 The Check Syntax button in the Actions panel

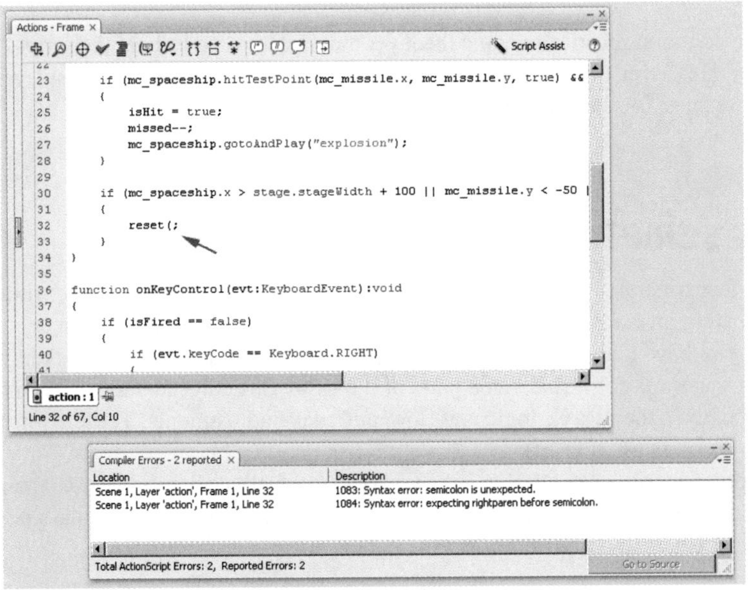

Figure 10.6 A closing parenthesis is missing in Line 32; the Compiler Errors panel (bottom window) lists two errors

As you see from this example:

- One syntax error can lead to more than one reported error.
- The error description may not (and often is not sufficient to) pinpoint the exact problem. But it leads you to the "area" where the faulty code is.

A strategy to locate and fix syntax errors is:

1. Fix the errors one at a time from the first one on the error list.
   Look at the first error on the list to discern the line number. Read the explanation of the error. Return to your code and look at the reported line number. Based on the description of the error, try to identify the actual location and the cause of the error.

2. Every time you have made one change in the code, test the movie *immediately*. See if the error has been fixed. Fixing one error may clear up more than one problem. If you do not fix the correct error, then more errors or different errors may come up.

   Do not wait until you have made multiple changes before testing the movie again. If you do and there are still errors or even more errors, it will be difficult to determine which of your changes actually fix the errors, and which changes cause new errors.

10.3.2 Logical Errors

When there are *logical errors* in your code, the movie simply does not work properly. For example:

- Nothing happens when you click on a button.
- Objects are not displayed at the correct position or are not displayed at all.
- The problem may seem random at times.

There are no errors reported in the Compiler Errors panel. It may take some logical deduction to locate the source of the logical error and fix it. There are two tools that can help you perform these deductive tasks. They are the trace() function and the Debugger. While the Debugger is a very powerful debugging tool, it is beyond the scope of this introductory text. We will look at trace().

10.3.3 trace() Statement

trace() lets you display a specified message in the Output panel. The message can be a string or the value of a variable used in the movie. It is a very useful function to help you debug your program and trace the progress of your program by displaying messages in the Output panel while testing your Flash movie.

To determine where to put a trace() statement, you need to first identify the possible sources of an error.

- If it is a variable or movieclip property, then trace it at various places in the code where the variable or the property get changed. See if it is changing as expected.
- If it is a code segment, such as a for loop or if statement, then trace a fixed text message. See if the code segment is actually executed as expected.

  Here are some examples of how you may use trace() to help you track down the errors.

- If you are not sure whether a function is executed when you click on a button, you can put a trace() statement as the first statement inside the function definition. The expression to be traced out can be just a simple string, for example:

```
trace("OK");
```

If the function is executed, the word "OK" will appear in the Output panel.

- Similarly, if you are not sure whether an if statment is executed correctly, you can put a trace() statement as the first statement inside the statement block. For if...else or if...else if statement, you may need to put a trace() statement in each of the statement block, like this:

```
if (score > 90)
{
    trace(90);
    grade = "A";
}
```

```
    else if (score > 80)
    {
        trace(80);
        grade = "B";
    }
    else if (score > 70)
    {
        trace(70);
        grade = "C";
    }
    else if (score > 60)
    {
        trace(60);
        grade = "D";
    }
    else
    {
        trace("less than 60");
        grade = "F";
    }
```

In this particular example of an if...else if statement, all the conditions use the variable score. Thus, if the message traced is different from what you expect, it may mean that there are errors in the value of the score. In this case, you should try adding a trace() statement like this:

```
trace(score);
```

right before the if statement.

- You can trace a variable, as just shown. Here is an example. Suppose you have a variable called score to keep track of the player's score in a shoot-them-up game, and the value of score is supposed to be incremented by one every time a missile hits a spaceship. However, you see the score shown on the screen is not incrementing correctly. You can output the value of score by placing the following statement in the code right *before* and *after* the statement that increments the score.

```
trace("before: " + score);
score++;
trace("after: " + score);
```

Notice that in these trace() statements, we are not simply tracing the value of the variable score. We also add a short text string to label the message, so that we can distinguish the two score values at different times: before and after the increment. An example output is shown in Figure 10.7a. Figure 10.7b shows the same example without adding the string "before: " and "after: " to label the score. As you see, the output is much easier to read with the added text to label the score (Figure 10.7a).

Note that the text string "before: " is enclosed within quotation marks. The value of the variable score is appended to the string using the operator +.

- You can trace a property of a movieclip instance. For example, if a movieclip instance named mc_ball is not moving across the Stage properly, then you can place the

You will learn more about the syntax for the movieclip's properties, such as position and size, in Chapter 11.

(a)

(b)

Figure 10.7 An example of tracing the value of a variable
(a) Tracing the value of the variable with text added
(b) Same trace with no text added

trace() statement as shown next:

trace(mc_ball.x);

at several places in the code to help you see how the *x*-coordinate of mc_ball changes.

10.3.4 Lists of Common Errors

The following is a list of some common errors in writing code. Knowing the common errors will help you avoid and identify errors in ActionScript programming.

- Missing or mismatching closing curly braces or parentheses
  Every open curly brace must have a matching closing brace, and the same for parentheses.
- Misspelling variable and function names
  Don't forget that ActionScript is case sensitive. Be aware of the plural forms of the names. numFlower is different from numFlowers. If you find it difficult to remember which names use the plural form, then you may want to make all names singular.
- Missing quotation marks for text strings
  Recall that "score" is a literal string—a text string—which is a value itself, but score is a variable name that has a value.
- Forgetting to declare and initialize a variable before using it
- Using = (an assignment operator) for == operator (the comparison for equality) in an if statement

---

Practice Using Compiler Errors Panel and trace() Statement for Debugging (Lab) Objectives of this lab:

- Get acquainted with Flash ActionScript authoring environment.
- Use trace() to output custom messages.
- Distinguish variables and literal strings.
- Learn to read syntax error report.
- Locate and fix syntax errors.
- Identify pairing curly braces and parentheses.

10.4 SUMMARY

Movieclip Instances: Movieclip symbols and other symbols are stored in the Library panel. When your drag a movieclip from the Library onto the Stage, an instance of that movieclip symbol is created. An instance means a copy or an occurrence of the original symbol. You use the movieclip's instance name, not the movieclip's symbol name that appears in the Library, in the code to refer to the object on the Stage.

Dot Syntax: Dots can be used to: (1) denote the target path to a timeline; (2) invoke a method for a specific movieclip instance (for example, tell the object to do something, such as `mc_tommy.mc_head.mc_mouth play()`); (3) denote the property of a movieclip, such as position and size—for example, `mc_tommy.mc_head.mc_mouth.xscale = 60`

Where Do Scripts Go? The script is placed in a keyframe on the timeline. To create or edit the code, select the keyframe and open the Actions panel (Window > Actions or press the F9 key). Although the script can be placed on any layer, it is a common convention to dedicate the topmost layer to hold the script (or the second topmost if there is a topmost layer for the frame labels), and this layer is named "actions".

Script Errors: There are two main types of script errors: syntactical errors and logical errors. Syntactical errors are often detected by the compiler when you test or export your movie. The errors are listed in the Compiler Errors panel, giving you information that helps you locate and fix the errors. You can also click the Check Syntax button in the Actions panel to check the syntax.

Logical errors are not detected by the compiler. You may notice that the movie simply does not work properly. It may take some logical deduction to locate the source of the logical error and fix it. There are two tools that can help you to perform these deductive tasks. They are the `trace()` function and the Debugger. `trace()` lets you display a specified message in the Output panel. This chapter discusses how you may use `trace()` statements to help you debug, for example, by tracing the variable in question, the property of a movieclip instance that is not behaving as expected, or a simple text message from a function or `if` statement that is in question.

TERMS

dot syntax, 305	nesting movieclips, 305	target path, 305
instance, 304	syntactical errors, 309	trace(), 311
logical errors, 311		

LEARNING AIDS

The following learning aids can be found at the book's companion Web site.

🖱 **Practice Using Compiler Errors Panel and trace() Statement for Debugging (Lab Manual)** Objectives of this lab:

- Get acquainted with Flash ActionScript authoring environment.
- Use trace() to output custom messages.
- Distinguish variables and literal strings.
- Learn to read syntax error report.
- Locate and fix syntax errors.
- Identify pairing curly braces and parentheses.

REVIEW QUESTIONS

1. The ActionScript function that can be used to show a specified message or a result of a specified expression in the Output panel is _____. This is a very useful tool to debug.

   A. alert()
   B. trace()
   C. output()
   D. out()
   E. print()

2. An ActionScript is placed _____.

   A. on a keyframe on the timeline
   B. on a movieclip instance
   C. on the Stage

3. It is the _____ that you use in the code to refer to the object on stage.

   A. movieclip's instance name
   B. movieclip's symbol name that appears in the Library
   C. Flash movie's file name

4. Fill in the blanks with mc_tommy or mc_head:
   You use a statement like this,

   `mc_tommy.mc_head.scaleX = 0.6;`

   when the movieclip instance _____ is nested inside _____, and you want to set the scaleX of _____ to 0.6.

5. You can create or edit ActionScript code in the Actions panel. How do you open the Actions panel?

Interactive Multimedia Authoring with Flash: ActionScript—Part 3

TABLE OF CONTENTS

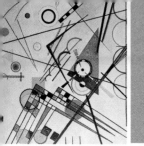
KEY CONCEPTS
- mouse and keyboard event handling in multimedia authoring
- frame event handling
- controlling objects' appearance and behaviors with Flash ActionScript

GENERAL LEARNING OBJECTIVES

At the end of this chapter, you should be able to demonstrate that you

- can program in ActionScript 3.0 to control object's appearance and behaviors.
- can create animation using ActionScript 3.0.
- can program in ActionScript 3.0 to let the user control an object's appearance and behaviors using the mouse and keyboard.
- have the confidence to read and modify existing code in ActionScript 3.0.
- have the confidence to further explore ActionScript and other programming languages on your own to build more complex interactive multimedia projects.

11.1 ADDING INTERACTIVITY

Multimedia projects are visually oriented and often highly interactive. In general, computer users interact with computer programs using a mouse and a keyboard. Thus, the most common types of interactivity in a multimedia project respond to mouse clicks, mouse movement, and key strokes initiated by the user. Actions such as animation and sound effects happen in response to the user's mouse activity and key strokes.

An *event* is something that happens while a program is running that interrupts the program's flow. Mouse clicks, mouse movements, and key strokes are the most common events that can be initiated by the user. These events can be used to signal that an animation or sound should be played, a different image should be shown, or a line of text should be displayed. Events like these make it possible for the user to provide input and feedback, exert some control over what happens, and become directly engaged in the activity onscreen. Hence, the key characteristic of programming in an interactive multimedia authoring environment is that it is event driven.

Event handling refers to specifying the actions in response to events. In this chapter, we will discuss event handling for mouse and keyboard events in ActionScript 3.0.

Before you start to write any code for event handling, you need to identify three elements.

- The event: How is it going to trigger the response? For example, it can be a mouse click.
- The event target: *Event target* is the object to which the event is going to happen. For example, it may be a button.

- The response: This is the action in response to the event. For example, it may be the playback of an animation with sound effects.

The main idea to add interactivity to your multimedia project is simply to associate responding actions with the event and the event target. To do so in ActionScript 3.0, you need to understand the concepts of event listeners and event handlers.

11.2 CONCEPTS OF EVENT LISTENERS AND EVENT HANDLERS

An *event listener* is an object that listens for events, such as mouse and keyboard events. An *event handler* refers to a function that will be executed when the event occurs.

A subscriber–publisher metaphor can be useful to explain how to program to deal with events and event listener in ActionScript 3.0. As you may know, many online stores let you subscribe to their newsletters. They email all the subscribers their newsletters whenever a newsletter is published. You will receive a copy of their newsletter if you are subscribed to their newsletters. In this metaphor, you are the listener. The event is the publication of the newsletter.

Let's stretch this subscription scenario a little in order to explain how to program with events in ActionScript 3.0. Suppose these online stores have various sales events: Summer sales, Christmas sales, Closeout sales, Back to School sales, and so forth. In addition, you can choose to track whether an individual product is on sale during the sales event. Up to this point, it should be quite clear that in this metaphor: (1) these sales events are analogous to the events—mouse and keyboard events; (2) you are a listener to those sales events; (3) the individual product you want to keep an eye on is the event target.

But what is the event handler in this metaphor? Well, what are you going to do when your desired product is on sale during these sales events? How you respond to this information is the event handler function. Suppose your response is to go buy it online. If we are using ActionScript event listener syntax to describe your subscription to the Christmas sales event newsletter to track if your favorite smartPhone is on sale, this is how we would say it:

```
smartPhone.addEventListener(ChristmasSalesEvent, goBuyItOnline);
```

addEventListener() is an ActionScript method. ChristmasSalesEvent is certainly not a valid event in ActionScript. Later, you will see the valid events available in ActionScript. For now, let's keep on interpreting the statement based on our sales event metaphor. addEventListener() is a method of *smartPhone*, and it associates the *goBuyItOnline* function with the *ChristmasSalesEvent*.

There are several points from this metaphor we want to make regarding writing event listener code in ActionScript.

- Each store has various sales events, but you can subscribe to listen to each event separately.

  Likewise, if you want to let the user click on a movieclip instance named mc_balloon, to play an animation of popping the balloon, you write it like this, assuming you have the event handler function named popIt() defined in the code:

```
mc_balloon.addEventListener(MouseEvent.MOUSE_UP, popIt);
```

Object: In Object-Oriented Programming (OOP), an object has properties and behaviors. The properties are variables or constants that represent the object's qualities or attributes. The behaviors are functions which define what the object can do.

In ActionScript, an event listener is an object. Event listener is not the only object used in ActionScript. You deal with objects all the time in writing code in ActionScript, but you may not notice it. Movieclip instances are objects, too. They have properties, such as position and size. They have functions that define what they can do—for example, gotoAndStop(). These properties and functions of movieclips will be discussed later in the chapter.

Object-oriented programming is beyond the scope of this introductory text. However, in learning ActionScript, it is inevitable to encounter terminology related to OOP.

You can associate another event with a different or same function. Suppose you want to play a sound when the user places the mouse cursor over the mc_balloon. You can add the following statement, assuming you have the event handler function named playASound() defined in the code:

```
mc_balloon.addEventListener(MouseEvent.MOUSE_OVER, playASound);
```

- A store may have Christmas sales event, but the sales may not apply to smartPhone. Similarly, in a Flash movie, the user may click on somewhere on the Stage. This triggers a mouse up event. However, if the mouse up does not occur on the event target, the specified event handler function will not be performed.

11.3 WRITING EVENT LISTENER CODE IN ActionScript 3.0

When you write event listener code, you need to write two things.

1. An event handler function: A function definition to specify the actions to be carried out in response to the event. Here is the general syntax for this function definition.

```
function handlerFunctionName(eventObject:EventType):void
{
    statement(s)
}
```

The elements in italics are placeholders that you will need to fill in for your case. This is the regular syntax for a function definition, except that it does not return a value and it requires a parameter of an event type.
- *eventObject* is a parameter. You can give any name as long as it is a valid parameter name. In the examples throughout this text, we will name it evt to stand for event. However, evt is not a syntactical requirement. Any valid parameter name will work.
- *EventType*: You will need to use the correct name available in ActionScript for the intended event's type. There are many different event types available in ActionScript. The mouse and keyboard event types are MouseEvent and KeyboardEvent, respectively.
2. Call the addEventListener() method: You need to use the addEventListener() method to associate the event target with the event handler function, so that when the event takes place, the function's actions are performed. Here is the general syntax:

```
eventTarget.addEventListener(EventType.EVENT_NAME, handlerFunctionName);
```

The usage of addEventListener() has been explained in the mc_balloon example.
- *eventTarget*: This is the object on which the event takes place.
- *EventType*: For mouse event, the EventType should be MouseEvent. For keyboard event, it should be KeyboardEvent.
- *EVENT_NAME*: There are different event names available for different event types. For example, MOUSE_UP is one of the event names for MouseEvent, and KEY_UP is one of the event names for KeyboardEvent. You will see a list of event names for *MouseEvent* and KeyboardEvent in the next section.
- *handlerFunctionName*: This is the name of the function that you have defined, in the first step, to respond to the event.

In summary, the basic structure of writing event listener code is:

```
eventTarget.addEventListener(EventType.EVENT_NAME, handlerFunctionName);

function handlerFunctionName(eventObject:EventType):void
{
        statement(s)
}
```

WRITE EVENT LISTENER CODE

Activity/Exercise
The objective of this activity is to practice the two-step process for writing event listener code.

Instructions
Part I—Preparing the file
1. Create a new Flash file (ActionScript 3.0).
2. Create a movieclip, put it on the Stage. Name this movieclip instance mc_balloon.
3. Create a new layer as the top layer. Name the layer "actions". The script will be placed in this top layer in Part II.

Part II—Write code
1. Select the first frame of the "actions" layer. Open the Actions panel (Window > Actions, or hit the F9 key).
2. Write the code as shown in Figure 11.1a. Note that we have
   (i) a function definition, and
   (ii) addEventListener() method.
   Also note that the function defined here is to handle a mouse up event. Thus, the event type used in the function's parameter and in the addEventListener() is MouseEvent.
3. Test your movie (Control > Test Movie, or hit Ctrl–Enter).

Now, if you click on the balloon, you will see a message "You have clicked on the balloon." displayed in the Output panel (Figure 11.1b).

Let's summarize what is going on here. The mc_balloon is the event target. By using addEventListener() like that with mc_balloon in the code, mc_balloon is set to respond to the mouse up event with the function clickBalloonHandler().

In this simple example, there is only one trace() statement in the clickBalloonHandler() function. It simply traces out a message "You have clicked on the balloon." The balloon is not programmed to do anything visually.

This is a very simple example. It is intended to give you a feel of how the event target, event type, event name, and handler function all work together in the code. Later in the chapter, you will see more examples and learn how to incorporate more complex and interesting interactivity by using this same basic structure.

Notice that in the discussion of this two-step process, the handler function definition is discussed before the addEventListener() step. However, in the code shown in the Activity/Exercise above, the addEventListener() statement goes before the handler function definition.

```
mc_balloon.addEventListener(MouseEvent.MOUSE_UP, clickBalloonHandler);
function clickBalloonHandler(evt:MouseEvent):void
{
        trace("You have clicked on the balloon.");
}
```

(a)

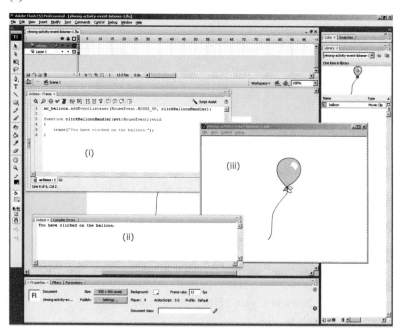

(b)

Figure 11.1 (a) Completed code for the Activity/Exercise (b) (i) The code in the Actions panel (ii) The message is displayed in the Output panel upon clicking on the balloon (iii)

> ⌐ **ActionScript Example: Event Listener** Flash file: The completed file for the Activity/Exercise on writing event listener code.

The order of these two in the code does not matter. It is the convention of this text to place all the function definitions at the end and the function calls at the top. Nevertheless, in terms of the thought process and planning, you do need to have the handler function, at least its name, before you can complete the addEventListener() statement, because it requires the handler function's name.

11.4 MOUSE EVENTS

The way a user uses a mouse to interact with a program is basically clicking or moving the mouse cursor. To interact with an object on screen with a mouse, the user can click on the object or move the mouse cursor over it.

Clicking actually involves two physical activities, each triggering a different mouse event: (1) mouse down: pressing the mouse button; and (2) mouse up: releasing the mouse button.

Recall the general syntax for the addEventListener() function:

eventTarget.addEventListener(*EventType.EVENT_NAME*, *handlerFunctionName*);

Table 11.1 lists the different mouse events available in ActionScript. It shows each *EventType.EVENT_NAME* (the name of the event to pass in the function addEventListerner()) in two forms—as an ActionScript constant and as a string.

TABLE 11.1	**Mouse Events in ActionScript 3.0**	
EventType.EVENT_NAME		**Description**
As Event Constant	**As String**	
MouseEvent.MOUSE_DOWN	"mouseDown"	when the mouse button is pressed down on the event target
MouseEvent.MOUSE_UP	"mouseUp"	when the mouse button is released on the event target Note: The object on which the mouse button is released can be different from the one on which the mouse button is pressed—this is different from CLICK (see below.)
MouseEvent.CLICK	"click"	when the mouse button is pressed *and* released on the same element
MouseEvent.DOUBLE_CLICK	"doubleClick"	when the user double-clicks on the event target
MouseEvent.MOUSE_MOVE	"mouseMove"	when the mouse cursor is being moved on the event target
MouseEvent.MOUSE_OUT	"mouseOut"	when the mouse cursor is moved off the event target
MouseEvent.MOUSE_OVER	"mouseOver"	when the mouse cursor is over the event target—does not require pressing the mouse button on it
MouseEvent.MOUSE_WHEEL	"mouseWheel"	when the mouse wheel is spun over the event target

The example code shown in Figure 11.1a passes in the event name using the constant, MouseEvent.MOUSE_UP.

```
mc_balloon.addEventListener(MouseEvent.MOUSE_UP, clickBalloonHandler);
function clickBalloonHandler(evt:MouseEvent):void
{
     trace("You have clicked on the balloon.");
}
```

The code can also be written using the string, "mouseUp", like this:

```
mc_balloon.addEventListener("mouseUp", clickBalloonHandler);
function clickBalloonHandler(evt:MouseEvent):void
{
      trace("You have clicked on the balloon.");
}
```

The first method using the ActionScript constant is the recommended method and the one this book is using. If you mistype the constant name, you will get an error message to point you to the typo when you test your movie. However, if you mistype the string, you will not get error messages; your event handler is simply not being called. This may cost you hours trying to figure out why it is not working.

11.5 KEYBOARD EVENTS

A common way for a user to interact with the computer via keyboard is by entering words in a text field on the screen, as when filling out a form. However, keyboard interaction does not only mean text input. This is especially true for interactive multimedia projects and games. For example, an object on the screen can be moved by pressing a key. In programming games, you often want to allow the arrow keys to be used to control the direction of an object's movement. You may also want to allow the use of the space bar, CTRL-key, or other keys on the keyboard to control certain properties and behaviors of an object.

Like the mouse click, hitting a key also involves two activities, each causes a separate key event: (1) key down: pressing the key down; and (2) key up: releasing the key. Table 11.2 lists the different keyboard events available in ActionScript.

TABLE 11.2	Keyboard Events in ActionScript 3.0	
EventType.EVENT_NAME		Description
Event Constant	String	
KeyboardEvent.KEY_DOWN	"keyDown"	when a key is pressed
KeyboardEvent.KEY_UP	"keyUp"	when a key is released

Figure 11.2 shows a simple example demonstrating a script to make a movieclip instance named mc_balloon to move five pixels to the left every time the user presses the LEFT arrow key and 5 pixels to the right when the RIGHT arrow key is pressed.

```
stage.addEventListener(KeyboardEvent.KEY_DOWN, keyDownHandler);

function keyDownHandler(evt:KeyboardEvent):void
{
   if (evt.keyCode == Keyboard.LEFT)
   {
      mc_balloon.x -= 5;
   }
   else if (evt.keyCode == Keyboard.RIGHT)
   {
      mc_balloon.x += 5;
   }
}
```

Figure 11.2 Example code

Key control is not limited to arrow keys. Each key on the keyboard has a key code—like an ID number—associated with it. For example, the key code for the LEFT arrow key is 37, RIGHT arrow key 39, UP arrow key 38, and DOWN arrow key 40. The key codes for letter "A" to "Z" are 65 to 90. The key codes for keys "0" to "9" are 48 to 57. These codes are ASCII codes, not specific to Flash ActionScript.

In fact, Key.LEFT is a predefined constant in ActionScript (recall the description of constants in the programming fundamentals section in Chapter 9). It is defined as 37, which is the key code for the LEFT arrow key. If you replace Key.LEFT with 37, the preceding code can be written as shown:

```
stage.addEventListener(KeyboardEvent.KEY_DOWN, keyDownHandler);

function keyDownHandler(evt:KeyboardEvent):void
{
   if (evt.keyCode == 37)
   {
      mc_balloon.x -= 5;
   }
   if (evt.keyCode == Keyboard.RIGHT)
   {
      mc_balloon.x += 5;
   }
}
```

The code can also be rewritten to use the 'a' and 'd' keys to replace the use of the LEFT and RIGHT arrow keys, respectively:

```
stage.addEventListener(KeyboardEvent.KEY_DOWN, keyDownHandler);

function keyDownHandler(evt:KeyboardEvent):void
{
   if (evt.keyCode == 65)      // the 'a' key
   {
      mc_balloon.x -= 5;
   }
   else if (evt.keyCode == 68)     //the 'd' key
   {
      mc_balloon.x += 5;
   }
}
```

> ⌨ **ActionScript Example: Keyboard Events**
> 1. Flash file: A movieclip instance moves left when the LEFT arrow key is pressed, moves right when the RIGHT arrow key is pressed, moves up when the UP arrow key is pressed, and moves down when the DOWN arrow key is pressed.
> 2. Flash file: Control an object using other keys besides the arrow keys.

11.6 FRAME EVENTS FOR ANIMATION

In addition to the mouse and keyboard events, there are frame events in ActionScript. Frame events are specific to frame-based authoring programs such as Flash. Unlike mouse and keyboard events, a frame event does not directly respond to user interaction. However, the enterFrame event is useful for creating scripted animation. The enterFrame event is triggered repeatedly at the frame rate of the movie.

Like writing code for mouse and keyboard events, you need to call the function addEventListener() when writing code for frame event. Recall the general syntax for the addEventListener() function:

eventTarget.addEventListener(*EventType*.EVENT_NAME, *handlerFunctionName*);

The type for the enterFrame event is: "enterFrame", or Event.ENTER_FRAME.

The event type is Event. The event target is stage.

If you, for example, specify a statement like this:

```
mc_balloon.x += 5;
```

in the frame event handler function, mc_balloon will be moving to the right five pixels at a time, at the frame rate.

Suppose there is a movieclip instance called mc_balloon on the Stage. The following code makes the movieclip instance mc_balloon move five pixels to the right and 10 pixels up, at the frame rate.

```
stage.addEventListener(Event.ENTER_FRAME, frameHandler);

function frameHandler(evt:Event):void
{
    mc_balloon.x += 5;
    mc_balloon.y -= 10;
}
```

> 🖱 **ActionScript Example: Event.ENTER_FRAME** A Flash file: Using Event.ENTER_FRAME in a scripted animation to move a square to the left.

ABOUT THE enterFrame Event

Flash movies update the screen according to the frame rate. This means that you will see all the changes specified in the frame event handler function at once, at the frame rate.

In the previous example, you will see mc_balloon move five pixels to the right and 10 pixels down all at once at the frame rate.

If the frameHandler function is like this,

```
function frameHandler(evt:Event):void
{
    mc_balloon.x += 5;
    mc_balloon.y -= 10;
    mc_balloon.x += 5;
    mc_balloon.y -= 10;
    mc_balloon.x += 5;
    mc_balloon.y -= 10;
}
```

you will see mc_balloon move 15 pixels to the right and 30 pixels up at a time, at the frame rate.

Most of the examples for this section are provided as complete Flash files, available at this book's Web site. If you have a copy of Flash CS3 or later, you will be able to open the example file, study how the Action-Script is constructed and where it is placed, and experiment by modifying the code.

11.7 CONTROLLING OBJECTS ON STAGE

Controlling objects using script is the fundamental and most common building block for interactive multimedia projects. The common types of tasks in controlling onscreen objects are:

- controlling and monitoring an object's:
  - position,
  - size, and
  - rotation.
- making objects disappear.
- changing the visual content of an object.
- making an object draggable.

Table 11.3 lists the ActionScript syntax that can be used for these tasks, along with brief descriptions, and example usages.

TABLE 11.3	A List of Commonly Used Properties of Movieclips and Buttons Available in ActionScript 3.0		
Category	**ActionScript 3.0**	**Description**	**Example**
position	x	*x*-coordinate, in pixels	mc_balloon.x = 300;
	y	*y*-coordinate, in pixels	mc_balloon.y = 300;
size	scaleX	horizontal dimension; 1.0 means 100%	mc_balloon.scaleX = 0.5; This halves the original width of mc_balloon.
	scaleY	vertical dimension; 1.0 means 100%	mc_balloon.scaleY = 3; This triples the original height of mc_balloon.
	width	horizontal dimension, in pixels	mc_balloon.width = 110; This sets the width of mc_balloon to 110 pixels.
	height	vertical dimension, in pixels	mc_balloon.height = 260; This sets the height of mc_balloon to 260 pixels.
orientation	rotation	rotation angle, in degrees, from the object's original orientation. Positive values represent clockwise; negative values represent counterclockwise	mc_balloon.rotation = 30; This rotates mc_balloon to 30° clockwise.
visibility	alpha	transparency is from is 0 to 1, 0 is fully transparent, and 1 is fully opaque. The object is still enabled, i.e., can be clickable, even when its alpha is set to 0.	mc_balloon.alpha = 0.5; This sets the transparency of mc_balloon to 50%.
	visible	true or false to specify whether or not the object is visible. When set to false, the object is disabled, i.e. it cannot be clicked.	mc_balloon.visible = false; This sets mc_balloon to be invisible. It also disables mc_balloon.

To help you see the underlying concept and the very basic structure of the code required for the task, each example used in the following subsections focuses only on a single task at a time. The resulting interactivity in one example itself may seem uninteresting. However, these techniques can be extended and combined to build a complex project.

11.7.1 Controlling and Monitoring an Object's Screen Position: x and y

There are at least two things you need to know in order to be able to program this task: (1) how the coordinate on the Stage is measured, and (2) the ActionScript syntax for getting or setting an object's position on the Stage. You have learned that the ActionScript coordinates for a movieclip instance's position are x and y (Table 11.3). Now let's look at the coordinates of the Stage (Figure 11.3).

The Stage dimension is measured in pixels. The position of each pixel can be referenced with an (*x*, *y*) coordinate. The coordinate (0, 0) refers to the pixel at the upper left corner of

You should note that there is always more than one way to get the same results. The code that the examples in this section are demonstrating represents only one possible way—one that the author feels is the most straightforward and clear for beginners in general to learn. The code may not be

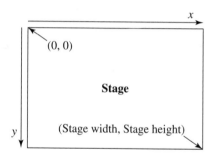

Figure 11.3 The stage coordinates in Flash

the most efficient or robust way that a proficient Action-Script programmer would choose. Learning to optimize codes is an important topic, but is beyond the scope of this introduction to ActionScript.

the Stage. The *x*-coordinate increases from left to right, and the *y*-coordinate increases from top to bottom. Hence, the coordinates for the lower right corner are (stage width, stage height). In ActionScript, they are `stage.stageWidth` and `stage.stageHeight`.

All the coordinates within the stage area are positive. The coordinates of an object can be negative. A negative *x*-coordinate means outside the left edge of the stage, and negative *y*-coordinate means outside the top edge of the stage.

The object to be controlled should be either a movieclip instance or a button instance. There are other types of objects you can control using script. This text will focus only on movieclips and buttons. Either one will need to have an instance name.

Suppose you want to move a movieclip instance named `mc_balloon` to (300, 100), the ActionScript code looks like this:

```
mc_balloon.x = 300;
mc_balloon.y = 100;
```

To move the balloon upon a mouse click, you will need to add the event handling code for a mouse click. Recall that you need to identify the event target, the type of event, and the actions in response to the event.

> 🖱 **ActionScript Example: Controlling and Monitoring an Object's Screen Position**
>
> 1. One Flash file: Clicking on a balloon movieclip instance to make it move to (300, 100).
> 2. Web page: Discussion for variations.

- Event target: It is `mc_balloon` for this example, because `mc_balloon` is the object to be clicked on.
- Type of event: It is a mouse event. For a mouse click, we can choose CLICK or MOUSE_UP. There are slight difference between CLICK and MOUSE_UP, which are described in Table 11.1. Let's choose MOUSE_UP here.
- The actions in response to the event: These would be the code to relocate the `mc_balloon`.

Now, we have identified these three elements. We are ready to write code. Recall that in writing event listener code, you need to (1) define an event handler function; (2) call `addEventListener()`. This is how the code looks like.

> 🖱 **Interactive X-Ray Scanner (Lab)**
>
> Let's revisit the x-ray mask example (Figure 11.4) from Chapter 8. The animation of the mask in this example is a tweened animation. Now, you can program to make the scanner bar follow your mouse. The code involves mouse move event listener, `mouseY` and the scanner bar's y property.

```
mc_balloon.addEventListener(MouseEvent.MOUSE_UP, clickBalloonHandler);

function clickBalloonHandler(evt:MouseEvent):void
{
    mc_balloon.x = 300;
    mc_balloon.y = 100;
}
```

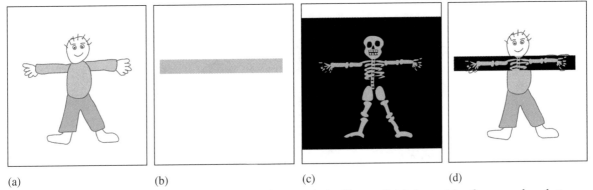

(a)   (b)   (c)   (d)

Figure 11.4 The movieclips used in the x-ray mask example in Chapter 8 (a) A graphic of a man, placed at the layer below the mask and maskee (b) A rectangular bar representing a scanner bar; it is the mask (c) The skeleton is the maskee, i.e., the object being masked

11.7.2 Making Objects Disappear: x, y, alpha and visible

All of the preceding situations deal with objects currently on screen. However, there are occasions when you want to make an object disappear, for example, a missile disappearing after hitting a target enemy. Here are two simple ways you can do so.

1. Move the movie clip to outside of the Stage—for example, to a large negative x- and/or y-coordinate. If the object will appear again soon on the Stage later and it is not constantly being animated off the Stage, this can be a good trick to make the object disappear.

2. Setting visibility property of a movieclip instance: visible controls the visibility of a movie clip instance. For example, the following codes set the movie clip called mc_balloon to be invisible.

```
mc_balloon.visible = false;
```

11.7.3 Changing the Visual Content of an Object

In an interactive multimedia program, the visual content of an object can often be changed in response to certain events. For example, a balloon pops when the user clicks on it. Another example: the user may change the hairstyle of a character by clicking on one of the hairstyle selections (Figure 11.5).

One simple way to accomplish this in Flash is to make use of the movieclip's timeline and ActionScript's predefined methods to control the playhead on the timeline. The underlying idea is that different visual content possibilities are placed on the movieclip's timeline, each frame containing one possible visual content. To display a particular content, you send the playhead to the frame that contains the content.

We are not using the timeline for animation, but for holding a series of possible visual content choices—for example, a different hairstyle on each frame.

For example, you can create a movieclip in which the first frame contains the balloon and the second frame contains the popped balloon. The first frame has a stop(); as the

Figure 11.5 The user can change the character's hairstyle by clicking on one of the hairstyles on the right

frame script to pause the playhead at the balloon image. When the user clicks on it, the playhead is sent to Frame 2 where the popped balloon is.

Suppose the balloon movieclip instance is named mc_balloon and is placed on the first frame of the main timeline; here is the ActionScript.

> 🖱 **ActionScript Example: Changing the Visual Content of an Object** One Flash file: Pop a balloon when you click on it.

```
mc_balloon.addEventListener(MouseEvent.MOUSE_UP, clickBalloonHandler);

function clickBalloonHandler(evt:MouseEvent):void
{
    mc_balloon.gotoAndStop(2);
}
```

gotoAndStop() is one of the ActionScript's predefined functions for controlling the movieclip playback. Other useful functions for controlling playback include stop(), play(), gotoAndPlay().

stop()

stop() pauses the playhead, i.e. an animation on the timeline stops playing.

Suppose you have a movieclip that contains two frames: Frame 1 shows a balloon and Frame 2 shows a popped balloon. If you simply place this movieclip on the Stage, this two-frame animation will play continuously.

Suppose you name this movieclip instance mc_balloon. You can pause the playback by placing the following code on the first keyframe on the main timeline:

```
mc_balloon.stop();
```

play()

If the animation on the timeline has been paused, you can start the playback again by using play(), for example,

```
mc_balloon.play();
```

gotoAndStop()

Calling gotoAndStop() sends the playhead to pause at the frame that is specified as an argument. In the following example, a value of 2 is passed. It will send the playhead in mc_balloon to Frame 2 and pause.

```
mc_balloon.gotoAndStop(2);
```

You can also pass in the name of the frame label. For example, if the frame label of Frame 2 of the balloon movieclip is "pop", then the code can also be written like this:

```
mc_balloon.gotoAndStop("pop");
```

To assign a frame label to a frame, the frame has to be a keyframe. Select the keyframe, and enter the name in the Property Inspector (Figure 11.6).

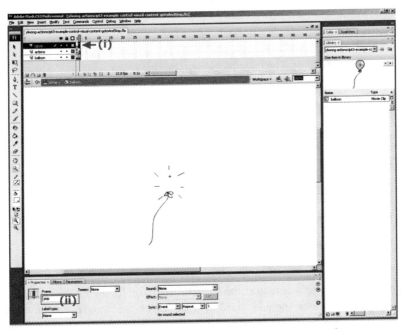

Figure 11.6 Giving a frame label to a frame: (i) select the keyframe, (ii) Enter the label in the Property Inspector

Using frame labels has advantages over frame numbers. If later the visual content in a frame gets moved to a different frame, you will not need to change your ActionScript code as long as you keep the same label with the frames. Using frame labels can also improve code readability because frame labels can be more descriptive than frame numbers.

gotoAndPlay()

gotoAndPlay() is very similar to gotoAndStop(). Like gotoAndStop(), calling gotoAndPlay() sends the playhead to the frame that is specified as an argument. However, it will then start playing from that frame instead of pausing. For example,

```
mc_balloon.gotoAndPlay(2);
```

or

```
mc_balloon.gotoAndPlay("pop");
```

> ⌐ **Hairstyle Customization (Lab)** The hairstyle on a character changes to the one on which the user clicks (Figure 11.5). This lab lets you practice programming: (1) for a mouse up event; (2) controlling the playhead using gotoAndStop() to change the visual content of a movieclip. Feel free to design your hairstyles and the character's head.

11.7.4 Making an Object Draggable: startDrag() and stopDrag()

The ActionScript method for making a movieclip instance draggable is:

```
startDrag()
```

To use startDrag(), you need to use the dot notation to specify which movieclip instance becomes draggable. Don't forget to define the trigger too, i.e., when the movieclip instance becomes draggable.

Suppose you have a movieclip instance named mc_racket that you want to be draggable when the user holds the mouse button on it. In this case, the trigger is pressing the mouse button (mouse down event). The code looks like this.

```
mc_racket.addEventListener(MouseEvent.MOUSE_UP, stopDragRacketHandler);
mc_racket.addEventListener(MouseEvent.MOUSE_DOWN, dragRacketHandler);

function dragRacketHandler(evt:MouseEvent):void
{
    mc_racket.startDrag();
}
function stopDragRacketHandler(evt:MouseEvent):void
{
    mc_racket.stopDrag();
}
```

ActionScript Example: Making an Object Draggable A Flash file: Click to drag a movieclip on the Stage.

Note that this script also includes the mouse up event to stop the dragging by calling stopDrag(), so that when the user releases the mouse button, the mc_racket will stop following the mouse. If you do not include stopDrag() code for the mouse up, then once the mc_racket is clicked, it will always follow the mouse even after the user has released the mouse button.

11.8 MONITORING THE MOUSE POSITION

Interactivity often involves interaction with an object on the Stage—for example, clicking on an object or placing the mouse cursor over an object. However, just the mouse position itself can be used to trigger different responses even there is not a particular object underneath the mouse cursor upon mouse click or mouse over. For example, you may want to

- place a tool tip at where the user clicks.
- let the user use the mouse to draw freehand lines.
- let the user use the mouse's position to control the direction of scrolling of a visual content, such as a big image or a long list of items.

For these situations, you will need to be able to track the mouse position. The ActionScript keywords for mouse position are mouseX and mouseY.

Suppose you have a movieclip instance called mc_balloon. To make mc_balloon move to the mouse cursor wherever the mouse clicks (more specifically, when mouse up), the code looks like this:

```
stage.addEventListener(MouseEvent.MOUSE_UP, clickBalloonHandler);

function clickBalloonHandler(evt:MouseEvent):void
{
     mc_balloon.x = mouseX;
     mc_balloon.y = mouseY;
}
```

> ⌐ **ActionScript Example: Tracking the Mouse Position**
> A Flash file: A balloon moves to where the user clicks on the Stage.

Note that the event target now is the Stage, stage, because we want to detect the mouse up anywhere on the Stage, not just on mc_balloon.

> ⌐ **A Ball-and-Paddle Game (Lab): Part 1 of 3**   You may know about a video game called Pong. In the game, on one side of the screen, there is a thin vertical rectangle representing a paddle. There is a small square block representing a ball. The player controls the vertical position of the paddle to hit the flying ball.
>
> What this lab is supposed to do:
> You can use the mouse to control the vertical location of a paddle (Figure 11.7). A ball, starting at a random vertical position, flies horizontally toward the paddle. If the paddle catches the ball, the ball bounces back.
>
> Main ideas and techniques to be applied in Part 1 of this lab:
>
> 1. Use mouseMove event.
> 2. Use the vertical location of the mouse (mouseY) to control the vertical position of the paddle.
> 3. Use of enterFrame event and the x property of the ball to animate the ball move across the screen.
>
> Note: Parts 2 and 3 of this lab can be found later in this chapter where additional concepts and knowledge in ActionScript syntax are introduced.

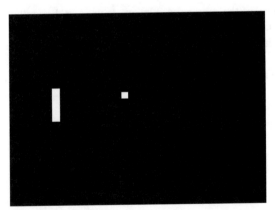

Figure 11.7 In this Ball-and-Paddle lab, the rectangular paddle on the left follows the vertical position of the mouse

11.9 DETECTING COLLISION BETWEEN TWO OBJECTS

Collision detection—i.e., detecting whether two objects overlap—is a common technique used for drag-and-drop activities and in games, especially the shoot-them-up games. The two methods in ActionScript for collision detection are: hitTestObject() and hitTestPoint().

Both methods will give a value of true or false. If overlap occurs, the method will return true, otherwise it will return false. These methods are used in combination with if statements.

11.9.1 hitTestObject()

The general syntax for hitTestObject() is as follows:

```
objectA.hitTestObject(objectB);
```

You use this to check whether two movieclip instances, *objectA* and *objectB*, overlap. For example, the following code checks whether the two movieclip instances, named mc_paddle and mc_ball, overlap. If they do, then the value of the variable named score will be incremented by one.

```
if (mc_paddle.hitTestObject(mc_ball))
{
    score += 1;
}
```

objectA and *objectB* are interchangeable. The following code works the same as the preceding one.

```
if (mc_ball.hitTestObject(mc_paddle))
{
    score += 1;
}
```

The bounding box of the movieclip instance is used in this collision test. A **bounding box** is the rectangular area that encloses an object (Figure 11.8).

It works well with rectangular objects, but not with nonrectangular objects. For example, the two circles shown in Figure 11.9 would be found to intersect based on their bounding boxes although their actual pixel contents do not overlap.

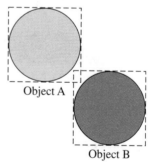

Object A

Object B

Figure 11.9 objectA. hitTestObject(objectB) would return true because their bounding boxes intersect

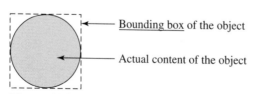

Bounding box of the object

Actual content of the object

Figure 11.8 Bounding box of an object vs. the object's actual content

11.9.2 `hitTestPoint()`

objectA.`hitTestPoint(`*x-coordinate, y-coordinate, trueOrFalse*`)`;

You can use this to check whether a point at (*x-coordinate, y-coordinate*) intersects with the movieclip instance, *objectA*. The third parameter takes a value of `true` or `false`. Here is how you determine which one you want to use.

- If set to `true`, the hit test will check against the *actual pixel content* of *objectA*.
- If set to `false`, the hit test will check against the *bounding box* of *objectA*.

Table 11.4. shows the collision test result in different scenarios. As shown in the last column, the third argument makes a difference in the collision test result when the point is outside of the object's actual pixel content but still within the object's bounding box.

> **A Ball-and-Paddle Game (Lab): Part 2 of 3** Building on Part 1 of this lab, you will apply the following new concepts and techniques.
> 1. Apply collision detection (`hitTestObject()`) to determine if the paddle hits the ball.
> 2. Use a variable to control the direction of the ball—toward the paddle or bounced away from the paddle.
>
> Note: Part 3 of this lab can be found later in this chapter where additional concepts and knowledge in ActionScript syntax are introduced.

TABLE 11.4	A Comparison of Collision Test Results in Different Scenarios	
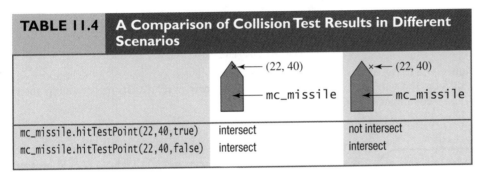		
`mc_missile.hitTestPoint(22,40,true)`	intersect	not intersect
`mc_missile.hitTestPoint(22,40,false)`	intersect	intersect

For example, the following code checks whether a point at the coordinate (22, 40) intersects with the actual pixel content of a movieclip instance named `mc_missile`. If it does, then the value of the variable named `score` will be incremented by one.

```
if (mc_missile.hitTestPoint(22,40,true))
{
        score += 1;
}
```

This example passes in numeric values for the point's *x*- and *y*-coordinates. However, you can also pass in an expression for a point's coordinates. Passing in the coordinates of a movieclip instance is a common way to perform collision detection. In doing so, you check the coordinates of the movieclip's registration point against another movieclip instance. Of course, do not forget the third parameter, setting whether you want to check against the actual pixel content or the movieclip instance's bounding box. To show you what this means, let's look at an example.

Suppose in a game, you have a squirrel jumping from tree to tree (Figure 11.10). You want to check whether the squirrel lands on a tree. The setup for this Flash file is like this:

- Trees: The trees are in one movieclip. Figure 11.10 shows its bounding box in dashed lines. Its instance name is `mc_tree`.
- Squirrel: The registration point of the squirrel is set at its foot (Figure 11.11). Its instance name is `mc_squirrel`.

Figure 11.10 In a platform game, checking whether the squirrel is landing on a tree[*] can be performed using `hitTestPoint()`

Coordinates of the
registration point of `mc_squirrel`
(`mc_squirrel.x`, `mc_squirrel.y`)

Figure 11.11 The registration point of the squirrel movieclip is placed at the bottom at its foot. The x and y properties of its instance `mc_squirrel` refer to its registration point's x- and y-coordinates of on the Stage.

> 🖱 **ActionScript Example: Detecting Collision of Objects**
> 1. A Flash file: If a missile hits a spaceship, the spaceship plays the explosion animation.
> 2. Web page: Discussion for variations.

To detect if the squirrel lands on a tree, we need to check the squirrel's coordinates against the actual pixel content of `mc_tree`. Thus, the third argument to pass in `hitTestPoint()` should be `true`. The first two arguments should be `mc_squirrel.x` and `mc_squirrel.y`.

The `if` statement using `hitTestPoint()` looks like this:

```
if (mc_tree.hitTestPoint(mc_squirrel.x, mc_squirrel.y,true))
{
    // stop falling down
}
```

Table 11.5 shows the collision detection results for different hit test strategies. For the scenario shown in Figure 11.10, `mc_tree.hitTestPoint(mc_squirrel.x, mc_squirrel.y,true)` gives the correct result regarding whether the squirrel has landed on a tree. The other two do not.

TABLE 11.5	The Collision Detection Results for Different Hit Test Strategies
Different Hit Test Strategies	**Collision Test Result**
`mc_tree.hitTestPoint(mc_squirrel.x, mc_squirrel.y,true)`	not intersect
`mc_tree.hitTestPoint(mc_squirrel.x, mc_squirrel.y,false)`	intersect
`mc_tree.hitTestObject(mc_squirrel)`	intersect

---

[*]Courtesy of Kevin Crace, a Wake Forest University student, who created these graphics in his platform game lab assignment.

🖱 **A Side-Scrolling Platform Game (Lab)** How the completed game works: You can control a "hero" to run forward or backward on a platform using LEFT or RIGHT arrow keys to scroll the "platform". There are "treasures", such as a spinning coin and a mysterious box. Mouse up on the stage makes the hero jump to collect the treasures. The treasure disappears when the hero touches it. Figure 11.12 shows examples of the completed lab with a variety of heroes, platforms, and treasures.

Main Ideas and Techniques:

1. Use key and mouse events.
2. Use an enterFrame event to animate the hero jumping.
3. Move the platform movieclip instances using the x property.
4. Apply collision detection (hitTestObject()) to determine if the hero is in contact with the treasure.
5. Apply collision detection (hitTestPoint()) to determine if the hero has landed on the platform.

(a)

(b)

(c)

Figure 11.12 Examples of the completed platform game lab (a) A traditional platform game: the hero, a humanoid character; the platform, rectangular ground; the treasures, coin and mystery box (b) A nontraditional platform game[†]: the hero, a squirrel; the platform, trees; the treasures, coin and mystery box. (c) Another nontraditional platform game[‡]: the hero, a fish; the platform, water; the treasures, coin and sand dollar.

[†]Courtesy of Kevin Crace, a Wake Forest University student.

[‡]Courtesy of Gretchen Edwards, a Wake Forest University student.

11.10 OTHER USEFUL FUNCTIONS AND CONSTRUCTS FOR INTERACTIVE MULTIMEDIA AUTHORING

There are common tasks in programming games, for examples, randomization, working with a list of items, and placing multiple movieclip instances on the stage. This section discusses some useful functions and commands that you can use to accomplish these tasks.

11.10.1 Randomize

Randomization is useful for adding nonlinearity and variations to an interactive project to provide unique experiences for users or in multiple playback sessions for the same user. Adding randomness to the *what* and *when* can make the experience a little unpredictable and add surprises.

Suppose when a user clicks on a box, something will come out of the box. It may be a little monotonious if the same object comes out every time or different objects come out in the same order every time—for example, always a bubble the first time you click on the box, and always a bird the second time you click.

Suppose there are two movieclip instances on the stage: one is named mc_hat and the other mc_magic. mc_magic contains an animation of a bubble floating up and an animation of a bird flying—sequenced on the time line one after the other. When the user clicks on the hat, mc_magic will play either the bubble or the bird sequence—randomly every time. Here is how the script may look:

```
mc_hat.addEventListener(MouseEvent.MOUSE_UP, magicHandler);

function magicHandler(evt:MouseEvent):void
{
        var r = Math.random();
        if (r < 0.5)
        {
                mc_magic.gotoAndPlay("bubble");
        }
        else
        {
                mc_magic.gotoAndPlay("bird");
        }
}
```

ActionScript Example: Math. random(): Magic Hat Example A Flash file of the magic hat example. Upon clicking on a hat, one of the two animations (floating bubbling and flying bird) will be selected randomly to play.

This script stores the random number in a variable r. If r is less than 0.5, mc_magic plays the bubble animation, otherwise it plays the bird animation. Why 0.5? Well, this example makes the chance of playing bubble and bird about 50–50. If you want to make the bubble have a higher chance than the bird to appear, then you will need to increase the value 0.5 in the condition. In addition, it is not necessary to use less than in the if-condition statement. Using r > = 0.5 instead of r < 0.5 should give the same result in this example.

In the Ball-and-Paddle game lab exercise, you can randomize the vertical position of the ball every time it is reset to start over, so that the ball will fly out from the right at a random position. You can also randomize its direction by randomizing its vertical or horizontal increment.

In addition to randomizing the *what*, timing is another element that can be randomized. For example, the timing of two birds starting to fly across the screen can be randomized to create a different combination of bird flying scenes every time the project is played.

In ActionScript, `Math.random()` generates a random number >= 0 and < 1. Although `Math.random()` can only give you a random number of between 0 and 1, you can use it in an expression to generate a number within any range. Here is the general idea of the formula:

`Math.random()` * **(max. of the range – min. of the range) + min. of the range**

Let's look at some examples:

- If you want to generate a random number between −10 and 30, then the expression is as shown:

  `Math.random() * (30 - (-10)) + (-10)`

  or

  `Math.random() * 40 - 10`

  Let's plug in some numbers to check if this expression will give a number within −10 and 30.

- If `Math.random()` generates a zero, then you will have:

  `0 * 40 - 10 = -10`

  Yes, this is the minimum end of the range from which you want to generate a random number.

- If `Math.random()` generates 0.9999 . . . , then you will have:

  `0.9999... * 40 - 10 = 29.9999...`

  This is the maximum end of the range.

- If you want to generate a random number between −11 and 11, then the expression as follows:

  `Math.random() * (11 - (-11)) + (-11)`

  or

  `Math.random() * 22 - 11`

? Self Test Exercise: Generate a Random Number within a Specified Range

Write expressions that can generate a random number from the ranges specified below.

1. > = −20 and < 20
2. > = 0 and < 20
3. > =10 and < 20
4. > = 1 and <6

Answers to Self Test Questions:

1. `Math.random() * 40 - 20`
2. `Math.random() * 20`
3. `Math.random() * 10 + 10`
4. `Math.random() * 5 + 1`

🖉 **A Ball-and-Paddle Game (Lab): Part 3 of 3** Building on Part 2 of this lab, you will apply the following concepts and techniques.

1. Use `Math.random()` to randomize the vertical position of the ball every time it is reset to start over on the right.
2. Construct expressions to make the ball move and bounce at an angle.

11.10.2 Array

You can use an ***array*** to store a list of items, for example, a repertoire of words that may be used in a hangman word game. Each item in an array is ***indexed***, i.e., numbered according to its order in the array. The index of the first item is 0, the second item is 1, and so forth. The index of the last item in an array is equal to the number of items in the array minus one.

Creating an Array

Like creating a variable, you need to use the keyword var to declare an array. The array name is followed by :Array. There are several ways to create an array. Here are two examples.

- Create an empty array and populate the array later.
  For example, to create an array called fruit:

  `var fruit:Array = new Array();`

- Populate the array when it is created.
  For example, to create an array called fruit that contains a list of text items: "apple", "orange", "grape", "pear":

  `var fruit:Array = new Array("apple", "orange", "grape", "pear");`

Note that in the first method, we show you how to create an empty array, but have not shown you how to populate the array after it is created. The following subsections show you how to add items to an array.

Regardless of how an array is originally created, you can still add or update items in the array.

Accessing an Item in an Array

To access an item in an array, you can refer to its index number by using []. For example, if you want to get the first item of this array fruit and store it in a variable named a, the statement looks like this:

`a = fruit[0];`

Adding Items to an Array

If you want to add more items to the end of the array after it is created, you can use push(). For example, the following code will add "peach" to the end of the array fruit.

```
fruit.push("peach");
```

The array fruit will become ["apple", "orange", "grape", "pear", "peach"].

You can also add an item by index. For example, the following gives the same result as the push example above.

```
fruit[4] = "peach";
```

Application of Arrays

Arrays are useful in storing data as a list of objects used in a project, for example, a list of treasures the player has collected in a game, or a list of words available in a word-guessing game.

The types of items that an array can store in ActionScript are not limited to text or numbers. You can also use arrays to store a list of movieclip instances. When used in combination with loop (which will be discussed in the following subsection), an array can be looped through to perform a set of instructions. For example, in the Star Catcher Game lab exercise (Figure 11.13) at the end of this chapter, the star movieclip instances are stored in an array. A set of instructions, such as rotating the star and checking collision detection with the wizard, is looped through every element in the array at the frame rate, so that each star movieclip instance is performing the rotation and checking if it hits the wizard.

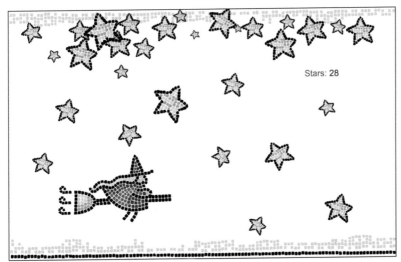

Figure 11.13 A screenshot the completed Star Catcher Game lab exercise, the stars are stored as movieclip instances in an array

11.10.3 Loop

Instructions that execute repeatedly are called *loops*. Loops let you repeat a block of statements while a specified condition is satisfied. There are five types of loops in ActionScript: for loop, for each...in loop, for...in loop, while loop, and do...while loop. Each type of loop behaves somewhat differently and is useful for different purposes. In many situations, any of these types can be used, but some types may require fewer codes than the others.

for loop is the most common type of loop. In this chapter, only the for loop is introduced and used in the examples that require loops.

In a for loop, a block of statements is looped a predefined number of times. The general syntax and explanation for a for loop is shown in Figure 11.14.

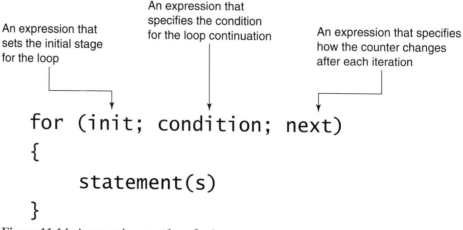

Figure 11.14 A general syntax for a for loop

An example for loop in ActionScript looks like this:

```
var i:int;
for (i = 1; i < 5; i++)
{
    sum = sum + i;
}
```

This code shows an example of a for loop. The curly braces ({}) are used to enclose the block of statements to be executed by the for statement.

The variable i in this example serves as a counter to control how many times the statements inside the loop is executed. The parentheses after the keyword for contain three parts:

- *init*: This specifies the start value of a counter.
  In this example, the loop starts with a counter of one, as specified in the first part, i = 1, in the parentheses.
- *condition*: This specifies the counter value that allows the continuation of the loop.
  In this example, this is i < 5, which specifies that the loop will continue as long as i is less than five.
- *next*: This defines how the counter changes after each iteration.
  In the example, this is i++, which means that the counter i increases by one after each iteration.

Thus, the for loop example will loop a total of four times, starting with i = 1 to i = 4. Table 11.6 explains this for loop iteration-by-iteration. As you see, when i become five, it breaks the condition of i < 5, and ends the loop. If the variable sum equals to zero before the loop, then at the end of the loop, the value of sum will equal (1 + 2 + 3 + 4), i.e., 10.

Iteration: Each execution of a loop is called an iteration.

TABLE 11.6	Tracing the Example for Loop Iteration-by-Iteration		
i Before This Iteration	**Is i < 5?**		**i at the End of This Iteration**
i = 1	yes	sum = sum + 1	i = 2
i = 2	yes	sum = sum + 2	i = 3
i = 3	yes	sum = sum + 3	i = 4
i = 4	yes	sum = sum + 4	i = 5
i = 5	no		

❓ Self Test Exercise: for Loop

How many times does each of the following loops execute?
1. for (i = 1; i <= 10; i++)
2. for (i = 0; i < 10; i++)
3. for (i = 10; i > 0; i--)
4. for (i = 0; i < 10; i = i + 2)
5. for (i = 0; i <= 10; i = i + 2)

Answers to Self Test Questions:
1. 10
2. 10
3. 10
4. 5
5. 6

This simple for loop example intends to show you how a for loop works. Using the for loop to calculate a sum is by no means an interesting application. for loop can be used in the visual environment, not just simple number crunching.

For example, in Flash, for loop can be used to automatically place a large amount of graphics on the Stage. To do so, you will also need to call other ActionScript functions in the loop to specify the graphic. The next section, *Generate Movieclip Instances Dynamically,* shows the ActionScript that you can use to generate multiple movieclip instances without having to manually place them on the Stage.

Use with Arrays

for loop is often used with arrays to perform a series of statements on each item in the array. The counter in the for loop in such cases serves as the index of the item in the array. Recall that the index of the first item in an array is 0. The following code performs a linear search on an array called fruit to see whether the word "grape" is in the array.

```
var fruit:Array = new Array ("apple", "orange", "grape", "pear");
```

```
var found:int = -1;
var i:int;
for (i = 0; i < fruit.length; i++)
{
        if (fruit[i] == "grape")
        {
                found = i;
                break;
        }
}
```

fruit.length refers to the number of items in the array, fruit. The example code loops from the first item (index 0) of the array fruit to see if the item is "grape". If "grape" is found, then the variable found is assigned with the value of i and the loop will be terminated (break). If the word "grape" is not in the array, then the value of found will remain −1.

LOOPS VS. ANIMATION "LOOPS"

The loops just discussed are different from *animation* loops.

Suppose you want to animate an object, say move 10 times to the right, five pixels each time. The loops just discussed are not the right tool. If you write a for loop to loop an object moving to the right five pixels for 10 times, all you will see is the very final result where the object has been moved 50 pixels to the right.

If you want to loop a scripted animation, use the enterFrame event or Timer.

If you want to loop a nonscripted animation—such as a tweened animation—that is sequenced on a timeline, you can simply add a gotoAndPlay() at the end frame of the animation sequence and specify the beginning frame number or label of the sequence inside the parentheses. For example, if a tweened animation starts at Frame 10, whose frame label is "walk", and ends at Frame 120, then you add a script at Frame 120. The frame script contains one statement:

```
gotoAndPlay("walk");
```

To learn how to use Timer, look up in Flash Help for more information.

Design time refers to the time when you are authoring your project in Flash.

11.10.4 Generate Movieclip Instances Dynamically

So far, in the examples shown, movieclip instances are manually placed on the Stage at design time. The manual placement of movieclip instances on the Stage has its limitations. For example,

- It will be a lot of work if you need many movieclip instances on the Stage, such as bullets for a shoot-them-up game and the stars in our Star Catcher Game lab exercise.
- The number of movieclip instances available at run time—when the movie plays—is limited by the number of the instances you place on the Stage at design time.

This section shows you how to use ActionScript to add movieclip instances on the Stage. You will need to first set the *Linkage* for the movieclip symbol that you want to be able to add to Stage using script. Assigning a Class name to the Linkage of a movieclip symbol lets you refer to the symbol by that name in the code, so that you can create new instances of that movieclip on the Stage using code.

There are two ways you can set the Linkage of movieclip symbols.

- **Method 1:** Set Linkage when you first create the movieclip symbol.
  1. In the Create New Symbol dialog box (Figure 11.15a), in the Linkage section, check the check box labeled "Export for ActionScript".

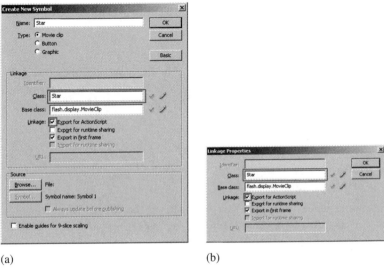

(a)   (b)

Figure 11.15 Two ways to set Linkage for a movieclip symbol (a) When the movieclip symbol is created (b) After the movieclip symbol is created

  2. Enter a name for the Class.
     - Note the name you give for the Class. It is what you will use in your script.
     - The Class name is not the name of the movieclip symbol. The Class name and the movieclip name are different things. You do not need to make the Class name and the movieclip name the same.
     - Keep the name one word, with no spaces.
     - It is a best practice to use an uppercase letter for the first letter although it is not a technical requirement.
  3. Check the check box "Export to first frame" if it is not checked yet.
  4. The Base class should have been filled in automatically for you after you check the check box Export for ActionScript. For the purposes of the exercises in this book, keep it as is and do not change it.

- **Method 2:** Set Linkage after the movieclip symbol has been created.
  1. In the Library panel, right-click on the movieclip symbol, and select Linkage. . .
  2. In the Linkage Properties dialog box (Figure 11.15b), check the check box labeled Export for ActionScript. Follow the steps 2–4 described in Method 1 above.

To write code to add the movieclip symbol on the Stage, you can follow the basic structure that follows:

```
var instanceName:ClassName = new ClassName();
addChild(instanceName);
```

The instance is created as a variable, as you can tell by the keyword var. The *instanceName* is the name you assign to the movieclip instance you want to create on the Stage. This is the movieclip instance name you would have entered in the Property Inspector if you were putting it on the Stage manually. The *ClassName* is the Class name you have given to the movieclip symbol as its Linkage properties (Figure 11.15). The addChild() statement lets you add the instance onto the Stage.

For example, suppose the Class name of a movieclip symbol is assigned as Star. The script to add this movieclip symbol on the Stage using script would look like this:

```
var mc_star:Star = new Star();
addChild(mc_star);
```

mc_star will be placed at the coordinates (0, 0) on the Stage, i.e., the upper left corner of Stage unless you specify its position. Recall that a movieclip instance's position is defined by its x and y properties. To place a star instance on the Stage at (100, 200) using script, the script would look like this:

```
var mc_star:Star = new Star();
addChild(mc_star);
mc_star.x = 100;
mc_star.y = 200;
```

This example places only one star instance on the Stage. To place multiple star instances, you can use a for loop and store the star instances in an array, like this:

```
var i:uint = 0;
var arrStar:Array = new Array();

      for (i = 0; i < 10; i++)
      {
            var mc_star:Star = new Star();
            arrStar.push(mc_star);
            addChild(arrStar[i]);
      }
```

The for loop generates 10 star instances and stores them in an array named arrStar. All the star instances are then referred in the code through the arrStar array and the index number. the 10 star instances can be referred to using arrStar[0], arrStar[1], . . . , arrStar[9].

⚓ **A Star Catcher Game (Lab)** In this lab exercise, stars are falling from top of the Stage and the player controls the wizard at the lower half of the screen to catch the stars (Figure 11.13). Of course, feel free to create your own falling object and catcher object graphics.

You will be able to practice many important programming concepts and ActionScript code writing you have learned in this and previous chapters. You will write code for: mouseMove event, frame event, controlling movieclip instance's properties, generating random numbers, for loop, arrays, variable declarations, assignment statements, if statements, function definitions, function calls, and collision detection. You will also be able to practice generating the star instances on the Stage dynamically by using Linkage and addChild(). This game is simple to play, but it is not trivial to program.

11.11 SUMMARY

In interactive multimedia projects, you often need to program to make the appearance and behaviors of objects respond to the user's interaction with the computer. The common ways of a user interacting with a computer program is through mouse clicks, mouse movement, and keystrokes.

Events, Event Listener, Event Handling: An event is something that happens while a program is running that interrupts the program's flow. Mouse clicks, mouse movements, and keystrokes are the most common events that can be initiated by the user. Event handling refers to specifying the actions in response to events. An event listener is an object that listens for events, such as mouse and keyboard events. An event handler is a function that will be executed when the event occurs.

The basic structure for writing event listener code is:

```
eventTarget.addEventListener(EventType.EVENT_NAME, handlerFunctionName);
function handlerFunctionName(eventObject:EventType): void
{
    statement(s)
}
```

An example code for a mouse up event:

```
mc_balloon.addEventListener(MouseEvent.MOUSE_UP, clickBalloonHandler);
function clickBalloonHandler(evt:MouseEvent):void
{
    mc_balloon.x += 5;
}
```

An example code for a keyboard event:

```
stage.addEventListener(KeyboardEvent.KEY_DOWN, keyDownHandler);
function keyDownHandler(evt:KeyboardEvent):void
{
    if (evt.keyCode == Keyboard.LEFT)
    {
        mc_balloon.x -= 5;
    }
    else if (evt.keyCode == Keyboard.RIGHT)
    {
        mc_balloon.x += 5;
    }
}
```

An example code for an enterFrame event:

```
stage.addEventListener(Event.ENTER_FRAME, frameHandler);
function frameHandler(evt:Event):void
{
    mc_balloon.x += 5;
}
```

The enterFrame event is useful for creating scripted animation.

The statements in the enterFrame event handler function are executed constantly at the frame rate.

Controlling Objects on Stage: The useful properties of movieclip instances that you can use to control them on the Stage include: x, y, scaleX, scaleY, width, height, rotation, alpha, visible.

Controlling movieclip playback can be used to change its visual content. The idea behind this is that the different visual content options of a movieclip are placed on the movieclip's timeline, each frame containing one possible visual content. To display a particular content, you send the playhead to the frame that contains the content. The commonly used methods for movieclip playback introduced in this chapter are: stop(), play(), gotoAndStop(), and gotoAndPlay().

Monitoring the Mouse Position: To track the mouse position, you can use mouseX and mouseY.

Detecting Collision Between Two Objects: The two methods in ActionScript for collision detection are: hitTestObject() and hitTestPoint().

Randomize: Math.random() generates a random number >=0 and < 1. It can be used to generate a random number within any range by constructing an expression with it.

Array: An array is used to store a list of items. Each item has an index number. The first item in the array has an index of 0. The index of the last item in an array is equal to the number of items in the array minus one.

The two ways to create an array introduced in this chapter are:

- Create an empty array and populate the array later.
  For example, to create an array called fruit:

  ```
  var fruit:Array = new Array();
  ```

- Populate the array when it is created.
  For example, to create an array called fruit that contains a list of text items: "apple", "orange", "grape", "pear":

  ```
  var fruit:Array = new Array("apple", "orange", "grape", "pear");
  ```

To access an item in an array, you can refer to its index number by using [], for example:

```
a = fruit[0];
```

You can add an item to the end of the array using push(), for example:

```
fruit.push("peach");
```

You can also add an item by index, for example:

```
fruit[4] = "peach";
```

Loop: Loops let you repeat a block of statements while a specified condition is satisfied. This chapter introduces the for loop. The general syntax for a for loop is:

```
for (init; condition; next)
{
    statement(s)
}
```

Generate Movieclip Instances Dynamically: Here are the basic steps to add movieclip instances on the Stage dynamically using script.

1. Set a Class name for your movieclip symbol's Linkage properties.
2. To write code adding the movieclip symbol to the Stage, you can follow this basic structure:

   ```
   var instanceName:ClassName = new ClassName();
   addChild(instanceName);
   ```

TERMS

LEARNING AIDS

The following learning aids can be found at the book's companion Web site.

ActionScript Example: Event Listener
Flash file: The completed file for the Activity/Exercise on writing event listener code.

ActionScript Example: Keyboard Events
1. Flash file: A movieclip instance moves left when the LEFT arrow key is pressed, moves right when the RIGHT arrow key is pressed, moves up when the UP arrow key is pressed, and moves down when the DOWN arrow key is pressed.
2. Flash file: Control an object using other keys besides the arrow keys.

ActionScript Example: Event.ENTER_FRAME
A Flash file: Using Event.ENTER_FRAME in a scripted animation to move a square to the left.

ActionScript Example: Controlling and Monitoring an Object's Screen Position
1. One Flash file: Clicking on a balloon movieclip instance to make it move to (300, 100).
2. Web page: Discussion for variations.

Interactive X-Ray Scanner (Lab)
Let's revisit the x-ray mask example (Figure 11.4) from Chapter 8. The animation of the mask in this example is a tweened animation. Now, you can program to make the scanner bar follow your mouse. The code involves mouse move event listener, mouseY and the scanner bar's y property.

ActionScript Example: Changing the Visual Content of an Object
One Flash file: Pop a balloon when you click on it.

Hairstyle Customization (Lab)
The hairstyle on a character changes to the one on which the user clicks (Figure 11.5). This lab lets you practice programming: (1) for a mouse up event; (2) controlling the playhead

using gotoAndStop() to change visual content of a movieclip. Feel free to design your hairstyles and the characters head.

⌐⊕ ActionScript Example: Making an Object Draggable
A Flash file: Click to drag a movieclip on the Stage.

⌐⊕ ActionScript Example: Tracking the Mouse Position
A Flash file: A balloon moves to where the user clicks on the Stage.

⌐⊕ A Ball-and-Paddle Game (Lab): Part 1 of 3
You may know about a video game called Pong. In the game, on one side of the screen, there is a thin vertical rectangle representing a paddle. There is a small square block representing a ball. The player controls the vertical position of the paddle to hit the flying ball.

What this lab is supposed to do:
You can use the mouse to control the vertical location of a paddle (Figure 11.7). A ball, starting at a random vertical position, flies horizontally toward the paddle. If the paddle catches the ball, the ball bounces back.

Main ideas and techniques to be applied in Part 1 of this lab:

1. Use mouseMove event.
2. Use the vertical location of the mouse (mouseY) to control the vertical position of the paddle.
3. Use of enterFrame event and the x property of the ball to animate the ball move across the screen.

⌐⊕ A Ball-and-Paddle Game (Lab): Part 2 of 3
Building on Part 1 of this lab, you will apply the following new concepts and techniques.

1. Apply collision detection (hitTestObject()) to determine if the paddle hits the ball.
2. Use a variable to control the direction of the ball—toward the paddle or bounced away from the paddle.

⌐⊕ ActionScript Example: Detecting Collision of Objects
1. A Flash file: If a missile hits a spaceship, the spaceship plays the explosion animation.
2. Web page: Discussion for variations.

⌐⊕ A Side-Scrolling Platform Game (Lab)
How the completed game works:
You can control a "hero" to run forward or backward on a platform using LEFT or RIGHT arrow keys to scroll the "platform". There are "treasures", such as a spinning coin and a mysterious box. Mouse up on the stage makes the hero jump to collect the treasures. The treasure disappears when the hero touches it. Figure 11.12 shows examples of the completed lab with a variety of heroes, platforms, and treasures.

Main Ideas and Techniques:

1. Use key and mouse events.
2. Use an enterFrame event to animate the hero jumping.
3. Move the platform movieclip instances using the x property.
4. Apply collision detection (hitTestObject()) to determine if the hero is in contact with the treasure.
5. Apply collision detection (hitTestPoint()) to determine if the hero has landed on the platform.

ActionScript Example: Math.random(): Magic Hat Example
A Flash file of the magic hat example. Upon clicking on a hat, one of the two animations (floating bubbling and flying bird) will be selected randomly to play.

A Ball-and-Paddle Game (Lab): Part 3 of 3
Building on Part 2 of this lab, you will apply the following concepts and techniques.

1. Use Math.random() to randomize the vertical position of the ball every time it is reset to start over on the right.
2. Construct expressions to make the ball move and bounce at an angle.

A Star Catcher Game (Lab)
In this lab exercise, stars are falling from top of the Stage and the player controls the wizard at the lower half of the screen to catch the stars (Figure 11.13). Of course, feel free to create your own falling object and catcher object graphics.

You will be able to practice many programming concepts and ActionScript code writing you have learned in this and previous chapters. You will write code for: mouseMove event, frame event, controlling movieclip instance's properties, generating random numbers, for loops, arrays, variable declarations, assignment statements, if statements, function definitions, function calls, and collision detection. You will also be able to practice generating the star instances on the Stage dynamically by using Linkage and addChild(). This game is simple to play, but it is not trivial to program.

REVIEW QUESTIONS

When applicable, please choose all correct answers.

1. The properties for a movieclip instance *x*- and *y*-coordinates are _____ and _____.

2. The property that you can use to specify the angle of rotation of a movieclip instance is _____.

3. The property that you can use to specify the transparency of a movieclip instance is _____.

4. The property that you can use to specify the visibility of a movieclip instance is _____. The value of this property can only be _____ or _____.

5. If you want to resize a movieclip instance relative to its original size—say 200%—you should use the properties _____.
   A. x and y
   B. scaleX and scaleY
   C. width and height

6. If you want to resize a movieclip instance to a specified pixel dimension—say 200 pixels—you should use the properties _____.
   A. x and y
   B. scaleX and scaleY
   C. width and height

7. The properties for the mouse position are _____.

    A. x and y
    B. xmouse and ymouse
    C. xMouse and yMouse
    D. mousex and mousey
    E. mouseX and mouseY

8. The correct keyword to make an instance draggable is _____.

    A. drag()
    B. dragStart()
    C. startDrag()
    D. beginDrag()

9. Which of the following methods can be used to perform collision detection?

    A. hitTest()
    B. hitTestObject()
    C. hitTestPoint()
    D. There is no predefined method in ActionScript to do collision detection.

10. Which of the following methods performs collision detection between two objects based on their bounding boxes?

    A. hitTest()
    B. hitTestObject()
    C. hitTestPoint()
    D. There is no predefined method in ActionScript to do collision detection.

11. Which of the following statements generates a random number $>= 2$ and < 10.

    A. Math.random()
    B. Math.random(10, 2)
    C. Math.random() * 10 + 2
    D. Math.random() * 8 + 2
    E. Math.random() * 2 + 8

12. fruit = ["apple", "orange", "grape", "peach"];
    fruit[0] is _____.

    A. "apple"
    B. "orange"
    C. "grape"
    D. "peach"
    E. None of the above. There is no fruit[0]. You will get an error trying to access fruit[0].

13. fruit = ["apple", "orange", "grape", "peach"];
    fruit[1] is _____.

    A. "apple"
    B. "orange"
    C. "grape"
    D. "peach"

14. `fruit = ["apple", "orange", "grape", "peach"];`
`fruit[4]` is _____.

A. "apple"
B. "orange"
C. "grape"
D. "peach"
E. None of the above. There is no `fruit[4]`. You will get an error trying to access `fruit[4]`.

15. How many times does each of the following loops execute? Assume that i is not changed in the loop body.

(i)   `for (i = -10; i <= 10; i++)`
(ii) `for (i = 10; i >= 0; i++)`
(iii) `for (i = -10; i <= 10; i = i + 3)`
(iv) `for (i = -10; i <= 10; i = i + 2)`

16. What will be displayed in the Output panel when the following code is executed? Feel free to try out the code in Flash.

```
var s:int = 1;
var n:int;
for (n = 1; n < 5; n++)
{
    s = s + n;
    trace(s);
}
```

17. Complete the code below. Suppose upon mouse up on a movieclip instance `mc_balloon`, it will move five pixels to the right.

```
mc_balloon._____ (_____._____,_____);

function clickBalloonHandler(evt:_____):void
{
    mc_balloon._____ += 5;
}
```

Index